Mavericks and Other Traditions in American Music

Mavericks and Other Traditions in American Music

MICHAEL BROYLES

YALE UNIVERSITY PRESS   New Haven & London

Copyright © 2004 by Yale University.
All rights reserved.

Designed by James J. Johnson and set in Electra types by The Composing Room of
Michigan, Inc.
Printed in the United States of America.

Library of Congress Cataloging-in-Publication Data

Broyles, Michael, 1939–
    Mavericks and other traditions in American music / Michael Broyles.
        p.   cm.
    ISBN 0-300-10045-0 (alk. paper)

    1. Composers—United States.   2. Music—United States—History and criticism.
I. Title.
ML390 .B862 2004
780'.973—dc22   2003021090

A catalogue record for this book is available from the British Library.

The paper in this book meets the guidelines for permanence and durability of the Committee
on Production Guidelines for Book Longevity of the Council on Library Resources.

10 9 8 7 6 5 4 3 2 1

In memory of
William Kingsley Broyles,
1905–1992

CONTENTS

ACKNOWLEDGMENTS

I am indebted to a number of people who were helpful in many different ways. First, thanks to historians James Mohr and Lewis Perry, who read parts of this book in somewhat different form. I would also like to thank a number of librarians and young scholars whose assistance was most valuable: John Brooks, Albert Franz, Steven Leinbach, Amanda Maple, Peter Reske, Kristina Shanton, Jason Stell, and Larry Wilt. My daughter, Tracy, an artist in another field, dance, has given me insights about differences and commonalities among the different arts. I have also learned much from my other daughter, Peggi Bloomquist. My appreciation also goes to the many people who contributed their ideas through discussion and comments when parts of this study were read as papers at several universities. Thanks to the anonymous reviewer for Yale University Press, who had many perceptive suggestions about how to improve the material, and also to some anonymous reviewers of journal submissions who not only provided useful feedback but confirmed my own opinion that this material lies far outside the bounds of musicological orthodoxy.

One person who read much of the manuscript and provided not only intellectual insight but much support, encouragement, and especially inspiration is my wife, Denise Von Glahn. Even she did not agree with some of what I said, but her contribution is more important. With Denise an old cliché has taken on new meaning for me: without her this book would not have been written.

CHAPTER 1

We, the Rebels

THIS BOOK IS ABOUT US. It is about who we are, or more precisely who we think we are. It is the story of fantasies and illusions as well as of some extraordinary individuals in American cultural history. It is about being marginalized and persisting. It is about dissonance, a dissonance between a collection of maverick artists and the world in which they lived. Above all, it is about what that dissonance tells us of that world.

Is there an us? Many still think there is; many are convinced there is not. Differences may matter, but the people introduced in this story, the eccentric individualist musicians, the fringe in an area itself fringe to American society, are united by those very forces against which they pushed. More generally the prevalence of some sort of atavistic, unconscious, or primal fascination with the character of the maverick in our culture points to a kind of us. It speaks of pressure points in American society, forces of conformance without which the very notion of maverick would be meaningless. "Us," here at its broadest, refers to a shared engrossment, prevalent in American culture, in outsiders, nonconformists, whatever their stripes. More specifically it refers to our own labeling of a group of composers, and why we relish that label.

Americans have reveled in the idea of the maverick, and along the way there have been many. Composers who lived unusual lives or flaunted norms, writing works their contemporaries found incomprehensible, even unplayable, have a long history in American music. The tradition goes back at least to the eighteenth century, to the first truly original American composer, William Billings. Yet to what extent are the mavericks a historical, cultural, or mythic creation of publicity, their own or others'; to what extent are they the result of a filtering process that occurs somewhere in our collective consciousness, by which we glorify, transform, and in some cases re-create our artists to fit our perceptions or our fantasies? Charles Ives, for instance, was one of America's great original voices. That he could by day be a businessman, a major innovator in the field of life insurance, and by night a composer who dreamed and created in splendid isolation, appeals immensely to the American psyche. Yet although Ives truly went his own way, was he really as far outside the musical mainstream as the popular imagination would have us believe?

Two centuries of mavericks suggests not an isolated phenomenon but a tradition. And, as the title suggests, this book is not about mavericks themselves; it is about *the maverick tradition.* It is about American society's longstanding fascination with the figure of the maverick, what that means about the place of music in American culture and what that tells us about American society. Along the way we will meet a lot of mavericks, most of whom are composers of art music, because in spite of what recent media images suggest, that is where the story of the American maverick tradition unfolds. But even though they are central to the story, they are not the story. The real story is how and why the figure of the maverick has assumed such a prominent place in the American consciousness. And although the focus is on art music, the very notion of art music itself is sufficiently slippery that the label need not be limiting or exclusionary.

To look at American society through the eyes of the mavericks takes us into a series of ever-broadening issues and questions, as they provide an entrée through which we can scan larger and larger vistas on the American cultural landscape. The first issues relate specifically to the figures themselves. Tracing the history of the maverick composer back 250 years demonstrates how deeply embedded this phenomenon is in American culture and how it evolved over time. Examining the place of the musician in American society helps us understand what made these composers who they were. And then there is the music: how did being a maverick affect the music composed, both individually and as contributing to an American musical tradition? Whether such a tradition actually exists is itself an important issue, raising the question of American exceptionalism.

More broadly, the presence of the maverick forces on us questions of American attitudes toward art. The very meaning of the word *maverick* suggests some dissonance between the musician so labeled and society. That dissonance allows an observer to get beyond platitudes and superficial notions to understand what attitudes about music really were. The friction that existed between these composers' artistic lives and society lays bare normally unspoken beliefs and prejudices. Here the principal issue is again not the mavericks themselves but why American society is so captivated by them. In that sense the mavericks are points of entry into one of the great debates in American history, the place of the arts in an open, fluid, and democratic society.

And finally, as important as these issues are, they pale beside a more fundamental matter: the nature of American culture. Is the United States an individualist or a communal society? This is both a political and a social question. Politically it involves two traditions, republicanism and liberalism (terms of political philosophy not to be confused with current usage as political labels), which in essence encompass questions of the common good and individual liberty. Socially it involves the place of tolerance, conformance, and conscience. Recent historians have demonstrated, I think conclusively, that in origins and traditions American culture is much more communal than many believe or would like to believe. The maverick musician tests this thesis. He or she stands outside. Where, how far, and how such a maverick is received speaks directly to the nature of American community.

The maverick tradition is thus at the center of possibly the strongest and most sacred myth of American society, that of rugged individualism. But the nature of the tradition itself raises questions about both the mavericks and the myth, whether they are exemplars of an American reality or a manifestation of our fascination with them.

To study the maverick tradition is to question the American myth, and to study the maverick composer allows one to get very close to the heart of the myth, principally because of the amorphous place of music in the American psyche. Music has long been the stepchild among the arts in America. It is the great tabula rasa of American culture, a ubiquitous but enigmatic presence, always there but little understood. To most Americans, music is a mystery, a force difficult to explain. Consequently, the music makers, especially the composers, are seen as distant, sometimes larger than life, as shamans, possessors of some mysterious talent whose secrets remain shadowy. These conjurers become what we want them to be: nationalists, experimentalists, rugged individualists, outsiders, men (usually) whose voice is unique. They are there because they persisted, and those who arrived on their own, the autodidacts, are especially esteemed.

Music's own marginalization in American culture can thus be turned to advantage. Why do the maverick composers interest us? Is it for their music? Often not, simply because most Americans, including many intellectuals well versed in other arts, find much art music an inexplicable enigma. More often the mavericks' music resonates for reasons that go far beyond the sound itself—that is, it often stands for something the listener finds, respects, maybe reveres, but probably does not discern. This process, often stated in disarmingly simple terms—I don't understand the music, but I know what I like—allows us to probe American cultural values as much as aesthetic ones. Precisely because of its very amorphous nature, music more often than not is a mirror reflecting the observer, and consequently a valuable means through which layers of attitudes, prejudices, and beliefs can be unearthed.

For many Americans, art music was suspect for other reasons. Economics, moral attitudes, and the political climate precluded the replication of European patterns of patronage in the eighteenth and nineteenth centuries, and Americans were wary of alternatives. At first even the notion of music as an art was virtually nonexistent. As this began to change, most middle-class Americans nevertheless continued to support and prefer music of the minstrel show, the military band, or the country fiddle, music that others were all too quick to characterize as vulgar and unworthy; later, such genres as opera and symphony elicited pockets of enthusiasm but were generally considered remote and exotic, unconnected with the American experience. That foreign musicians dominated art music only reinforced this perception. Foreigners could dominate precisely because music was so peripheral, at least to the majority. Political overtones also colored American attitudes. European patronage as well as some European practices were considered elitist and hierarchical, antithetical to the perceived democratic nature of American society. Americans inherited not only a general Anglo-Saxon aversion to music as opposed to the other arts, and an accompanying moral uneasiness with it that is traceable to the Puritans, but also a suspicion that it promoted political values contradictory to the nature of American society.

So the maverick tradition in music reflects a complex of attitudes, an ambivalent feeling about the arts in general and music in particular, and an uncertainty about American society itself. For many Americans the notion of culture was more important than the art itself.

Some looking for their favorite maverick will find him or her in this book. Some will not. William Billings, Anthony Heinrich, Charles Ives, Leo Ornstein, Carl Ruggles, Henry Cowell, Harry Partch, John Cage, La Monte Young, Steve Reich, Frank Zappa, and Meredith Monk are treated in some detail. They have been chosen for several reasons. They are individualists; they were in some way outside the norm, musically or personally (it is difficult in most cases to separate the two, for if their uniqueness does not show up in their music, that leaves serious questions about their artistic contributions). They are important artistically *or* historically — that is, either they have made lasting contributions to American music literature (I hesitate to use the word *canon* here because of its political overtones; I mean simply pieces that are still being played or recorded), or historians and critics have perceived them as seminal historical figures. Their presence raises fundamental issues in American music; principal themes or traditions cannot be understood apart from their contributions.

This book is not, however, a series of mini-biographies, although it contains some enthralling stories. The context in which each person maneuvered is often as important as the details of the individual's life and contributions. Composers appear as part of a broader narrative, not through some arbitrary choice or fishing expedition — in other words, not because I have cast a line for the biggest, oddest, weirdest mavericks I could catch.

Charles Seeger, for instance, who appears in Chapter 6, clearly made less of an overall impact on our musical culture than his contemporary Aaron Copland, and he contributed less to the musical canon than his wife, Ruth Crawford, who was one of the outstanding American composers of the 1920s. Seeger is here largely because he was a central figure in the New York avant-garde scene in the 1920s, a time critical to defining modern perceptions of the maverick musician. Secondarily his similar background to that of Carl Ruggles and Charles Ives allows exploration of a set of attitudes that go back three centuries and are fundamental to understanding how art music evolved during the twentieth century.

In addition to those listed above, many other composers appear, some prominently. After World War II several composers, such as Milton Babbitt, are vital in determining directions in new music. Although in my opinion Babbitt is not, in spite of himself, a maverick, he is discussed at some length, simply because that time cannot be understood without considering his ideas and contributions. Likewise, other composers who fit the image of the maverick extremely well and whose musical contributions are important, such as Lou Harrison or Conlon Nancarrow, are not treated at length because they did not reshape attitudes the way those selected did. They are not, however, ignored. To repeat a point, this book is about the tradition and what it tells us about the society from whence it came.

In that regard I have tried to step outside the musical world, especially the art-music world, as much as possible to understand what place music has in American culture at the beginning of the twenty-first century. This has been both difficult and rewarding. Difficult in that I have been involved with music, personally and professionally, all my life. My job places me in a music department at a large university. Most of my colleagues and friends are musicians. But I am also a historian, and in that sense I have an obligation both to the reader and to the world of historical endeavor to at least strive for a broader perspective. For those in music it is difficult to imagine that a patron of the arts would consider a William Schuman symphony atonal.[1] More important, it is easy for those in music to chuckle, as Schuman did, over the naïveté of a woman who so characterized it. Yet such misunderstanding, I believe, says as much about our musical culture as it does about the woman in Macon, Georgia, who made the assertion. We have to ask, is she possibly representative, and what does this conflation tell us about the musical world in which we live?

I do not want to suggest a reception history, although that figures significantly in this story. This book is about American society as it changed over two and a half centuries, as seen from the interaction between the American public and a specific group of musicians. It is about the elusive cultural space between composer and society summarized by the term *mavericks* itself. And it is very much about the label.

In tracing this history, several other themes or traditions surface: the continuing influence of Puritanism on American music; the role of nature, both physically, as topic and programmatic inspiration, and metaphorically, in opposition to notions of science and progress; the dilemma of art music in a democratic society; and the enduring belief in a uniquely American rhetorical voice. These topics formed leitmotivs that have, more than any other, shaped both composers' perceptions of what they do and the public's response to their efforts. Yet the maverick tradition is of special importance: it is in the maverick composer that all these other themes surface most clearly. The inability or in some cases conscious unwillingness of the mavericks to compromise has been precisely why their voices have remained clear, or at least why they were not overwhelmed by the predominant European culture. In many cases the principal themes are inherent in the notion of the maverick, in both specific composers' self-views and the public reaction.

The result is a story that unfolds in four parts, four time periods crucial to the creation of the modern concept of the maverick. Part 1 examines the long fallow time in American history when the place of music was so unclear to most Americans that there was little standard against which a maverick could be defined. Americans did not know what to make of musicians as artists, so all composers seemed a bit outside the norm. In this time, the Federal and antebellum eras, the place of music in American culture was anything but settled. Americans were not against music, but they had little sense about its potential as art. Yet at least two resolute individuals were willing enough to stake claims to being composers that their unique individualism deserves notice. William Billings and Anthony Heinrich especially tried in very different ways to bring the questions involved in being a composer into focus. Each had to be highly individualistic, or else neither would have even considered doing what he did. And although they themselves shared a vague similarity of aspiration and personality, their music was different as could be.

Part 2 describes the early twentieth century, when the idea of the maverick musician takes hold. It examines the forces both in the musical community and in American culture as a whole that account for the maverick's emergence. Part 2 breaks into two stages: a precursor time, roughly 1900–1922, in which the idea of an art music not only was set but ossified into a late romantic mold. Between 1900 and 1922 rumblings in all the arts began to surface, but musical activity continued relatively undisturbed. During that time two composers, Charles Ives and Leo Ornstein, one a native New Englander with deep American roots, the other a Russian émigré, each found a muse unlike any before him. One kept his work private, unknown to the musical world, while the other went to the front line, performing constantly. Although Ornstein created a stir, neither was able to shake the prevailing musical culture from its nineteenth-century roots. Yet their activity helped prepare for the revolution to come.

The idea of the maverick musician gestates in the second stage of Part 2. In the 1920s a number of composers, straining at the stultifying conservatism that prevailed, banded together to challenge the full spectrum of the musical establishment. At this point an irony becomes inescapable: only through communal self-organization were American experimental composers able to establish the image of the maverick, the staunch individualist, firmly and fixedly on American soil. As a consequence American musical culture underwent a geologic shift. Public perception of the artist changed dramatically, and the ultramoderns, as those composers responsible for this change were known, had much to do with that. The notion of the maverick became part of the public's expectation about the artist. This development, which is what Chapters 4–6 are all about, remains central to our cultural life today. It provided the contemporary model for the creative artist in all types of music. The rock artist, for instance, beginning in the 1960s, is essentially a continuation of the musician the ultramoderns defined in the 1920s. Because of the importance of this redefinition, which still very much affects present attitudes, I will look closely at the 1910s and 1920s.

Part 3 examines the decades immediately after World War II, when the full implications of the developments of the 1920s are realized, when America's fascination with the figure of the maverick comes full circle, to affect in significant ways the paths that American music took. Several compositional schools vied for the mantle of maverick, resulting in a second irony, groups of mavericks. It was a time when the classical world was split into factions, and the story of the maverick in the period after the war is the story of the conflicts between these factions. Musicians themselves embraced the qualities of the maverick in their own personas and self-perceptions. Spurred by new media, new patterns of patronage, and new societal attitudes, developments after 1945 completed the revolution begun in the 1920s, in ways those in the earlier time would not have anticipated. They also led to some unusual realignments in the musical world and some unusual expectations by composers and critics alike.

Part 4 attempts to both summarize and predict. Looking back over some of the composers discussed earlier, it considers more directly the fundamental question that the notion of maverick has raised: communalism versus individualism. Looking forward, it considers the implications of a trend that is just becoming apparent, the demise of the closed, independent, purely aural artwork. As a result the musical landscape at the end of the twentieth century was very different from what existed just fifty years earlier. Postwar American experimentalists began to define that landscape, and precisely because their eccentric individualism found such resonance with American society — because of the features that branded them mavericks — their influence on the direction American music took was great. In fact the American musical world is only beginning to perceive the significance of the new directions they pioneered. In the final chapter I consider just how different American music today is from only two decades ago and hazard a prediction about where it is heading.

In its most stripped down version, the complicated history of the maverick composer and public perception in the United States may be summarized as follows: First a composer was a maverick by default. Then it became a badge of honor to be one. Then it became lucrative. Finally it became a necessity.

Consistencies in the story appear in all four parts. The important themes of Puritanism, nature, and democracy surface in both of the earliest composers examined, William Billings and Anthony Heinrich. These topics do not go away in the twentieth century — one of my more remarkable discoveries in researching this book was the extent to which even Puritanism affected twentieth-century music — but they appear in different and surprising guises.

Even though the bulk of this book deals with the twentieth century, today's musical landscape cannot be viewed apart from the long legacy that created it. Earlier mavericks like Billings and Heinrich became important models for later critics and music historians who sought to integrate radical developments in the twentieth century into America's musical past. The maverick composer today, a figure revered in part because she or he *is* maverick, speaks both to and of an entire culture. In them we see us.

PART 1

Pioneers

To want to be a composer in eighteenth- and early-nineteenth-century America, one had to be a maverick simply because the idea itself was so alien.

A colonial or early Federal musician, invariably an émigré, was a journeyman, at best an artisan. He usually settled in a city and pieced together a variety of jobs: he would play in the occasional concerts that were offered, in the theater if one was active, and possibly in church. He would teach several instruments, organize singing schools, sometimes offer dancing classes, and often run a music store selling instruments, music, and generally other goods. He usually held jobs unrelated to music. What he did not do was compose.

Touring virtuosi were practically unknown, if only because travel was so difficult. A stage ride from Baltimore to Philadelphia, a distance of ninety miles, took three days. In the 1830s the railroad cut that to five hours, and only then did the age of the virtuoso begin.

The musical climate improved in the early nineteenth century, particularly with Americans' growing interest in instrumental music. New theaters provided employment for musicians, and in some denominations church music underwent significant reform. Yet to most Americans the *notion of music as art remained essentially unfathomable. This began to change in the 1830s, spurred by the arrival of foreign virtuosi and an aesthetic awakening to the uniqueness of the United States in the visual arts and literature. Any aspiring composer, however, still had monumental odds to overcome — what he did still made little sense to the vast majority of the population.*

Yet two composers flourished during this time: William Billings and Anthony Heinrich. Billings was a product of eighteenth-century Boston and the American Revolution. He was a strong supporter of the revolutionary cause, but in most other ways he was out of step with his time. Heinrich was a product of romanticism and shared a vision of America akin to that of the Hudson River school of painters. His conceptions were large, too large for the limited musical world he inhabited. Both composers were highly individualistic, indefatigable, and driven by a singular belief in the value of what they did. They had to be, as they pushed less against a conservative establishment or a hostile environment than against a vacuum.

CHAPTER 2

William Billings
Rebel with Many Causes

T HE BOSTON INTO WHICH William Billings was born in 1746 could
hardly have been less friendly to music. Music had little status, and
job opportunities for musicians ran from bleak to nonexistent. There
were of course no courts of the nobility to play for, and few churches could
afford the luxury of a professional musical appointment. In any case the strictures of Puritan doctrine, which limited music to unaccompanied psalm
singing, made the issue moot for the prevailing denominations. There were
no musical events on stage because in 1750 the General Court of Massachusetts outlawed theaters, a ban that lasted until 1792. The notion of music as art
was incomprehensible. Puritans saw music performed outside the church as
pure amusement or diversion, not to be taken seriously. In 1661 the Reverend
Leonard Hoar wrote a letter to his nephew Josiah Flynt, a student at Harvard:
"Musick I had almost forgot. I suspect you seek it both to soon and to much.
This be assured of that if you be not excellent at it its worth nothing at all.
And if you be excellent it will take up so much of your mind and time that
you will be worth little else: and when all that excellence is obtained your ac-
quest will prove little or nothing of real profit to you unless you intend to
take up the trade of fiddling."[1]

Hoar's irony is heavy here, for no one attending Harvard in seventeenth-
century Massachusetts would even countenance the trade of fiddling. Hoar
was speaking in a society that disdained frivolity and saw music only in those
terms.

Yet in this dismal environment America's first major composer ap-

peared. Billings was out of step with many facets of his world. He wanted
to be a composer, and his artistic drive knew no precedent in eighteenth-
century New England. He published biting satirical prose works that at times
embraced the macabre. He was doggedly eccentric throughout his life, and
almost consciously sustained the image of a bohemian rebel, in appearance
and conduct, some three-quarters of a century before Henri Murger's novel
Scènes de la vie de Bohème imprinted on the world the romantic notion of
the bohemian artist. All this was in still heavily Puritan Boston.

Billings was also a patriot. He fully supported the revolutionary side during the war for independence, and one piece of his, "Chester," a strong justification of the patriotic cause, became one of the compositions most frequently sung in eighteenth-century America. He composed in an idiom that
only a few years after his death was condemned for its naïveté and lack of scientific orientation, but his talent as a creator of popular, compelling melody
rivals Stephen Foster's.

How could someone like Billings arise in the climate in which he did? A
traditional musical education leading to a professional career was unthinkable. Not only was it all but unavailable, but for Billings, who did not come
from a wealthy family, lessons would have been financially out of the question. Billings apprenticed to become a tanner, a vocation he pursued for
much of his life. He found his solace and solution in nature, identifying with
the natural world to an extent that today seems almost incomprehensible. In
his preface to *The New-England Psalm-Singer*, Billings stated clearly, in italics: "*Nature is the Best Dictator.*" He continued: "It must be Nature, Nature
must lay the Foundation, Nature must inspire the Thought."[2]

Billings's view of nature as benign and a source of inspiration affected all
aspects of his creativity: his manner of composing, his prose writing, which was
extensive, and his activity as a literary editor. It lies at the very core of his work.
This affinity with nature is the key to understanding his vision of music and his
compositions. It also placed Billings in direct opposition to the prevailing Puritan view that nature was a hostile, savage wilderness to be reclaimed.

In spite of his unique vision, Billings did not retreat to compose alone, as
Charles Ives did many years later. Billings attempted later in his life to make
a living as a musician. He listed himself in the Boston directory as "Singing
Master," the only person in either the eighteenth or the nineteenth century
to do that. Almost all of his musical activities revolved around the singing
school, the predominant musical institution in eighteenth-century New England and the one musical activity explicitly condoned by the church. In that
sense Billings was in step with his world.

The singing school had arisen in the 1720s as the Puritan clergy's re-

William Billings, frontispiece to *The New-England Psalm-Singer*. The figure on the left may be Billings, and if so it is the only known portrait of him.

sponse to the chaotic state of church psalmody. During the service psalms were traditionally "lined out": an appointed leader would sing rapidly the next line or two of a psalm, followed by the entire congregation. Each member of the congregation, however, tended to go his or her own way, ornamenting and improvising, often with great gusto and little regard for tempo, ensemble, or even tune. There was no sense of group identity, but rather of many singers lost in worlds of their own making. The result, to critics, was sheer cacophony.

To Puritan clerics the issue was far worse than an affront to their sensibilities. As one of the few opportunities for individual emotional expression in an oppressive, conformist society, psalm singing threatened their control of the congregation. As one cleric observed, the emotional release that psalm singing provided could in a few seconds wipe out the entire effect of a sermon. And those sermons, often designed to terrify, lasted upward of three hours. Thus almost from the start, music, though an official part of the service, was subversive.

The Puritan clergy advocated musical literacy, to be learned in singing schools, on the grounds that tying the singer to a printed page would reassert group discipline. This did not work out as the clerics planned. They launched the singing school, but they could not control its content. Singing masters like Billings soon introduced a new style of music into the singing school that was lively, rudimentarily polyphonic, and immensely appealing, though not necessarily devotional. Imported from England, it quickly became popular. The Puritan clerics may have won the battle over sacred music in church with the establishment of the singing school, but with the new style they lost the war.

Billings began his musical career as the new style was arriving from England. We know virtually nothing of his early life, except that he was the fourth child of William and Elizabeth Billings. His parents had a pew at the New South Church in Boston, which suggests some status within the community. That it was a "back bench" indicates that they were not among the elite. Billings's father died when the son was fourteen, leaving his family one shilling. Probably around that time Billings began his apprenticeship as a tanner.[3]

When and how Billings obtained his musical knowledge is a mystery. It was probably through New South Church, for he seems to have become interested in music through John Barry, a tenor in the choir there and eleven years Billings's senior. In 1769 Barry and Billings joined to offer a singing school, the first concrete evidence of Billings's activity in music.[4]

In 1766 a young woman by the name of Clarissa wrote a letter to the *Boston Gazette*. Although she did not refer to Billings specifically, her letter does tell us much about music in the New South Church and about what a singing school was like. Serious and pious, possibly a cleric's daughter, she had just arrived in Boston to attend a boarding school. She visited New South Church expecting to hear "the jarring discords with which it [psalmody] is heavily dragged on" — that is, the old style of lining out — but was amazed to find singing "expressive of the truest devotion . . . fitted to elevate the languid soul." A "sublime entertainment," she called it. Whether Billings or Barry was behind this state of affairs we do not know, but almost certainly both were there. Clarissa then determined to attend a singing school. Another shock awaited her.[5]

The music was sacred, the text consisting of "the most solemn addresses to the Deity, in prayers, confessions, praises." But the company had clearly gathered for amusement, not worship, and the music was interrupted with jokes and interspersed with glasses of wine. The tone was lighthearted, anything but devotional. Clarissa was "dumb, shocked, greatly offended" by the conduct of the singers. The evening was "Blasphemy? Horrid trifling with the name of God?" The presence of a minister only confused Clarissa further, and she determined not to go again.

What Clarissa saw was not out of the ordinary. By the 1760s singing schools had become more social than religious. Attended mostly by young people, the singing school met nearly as often in a tavern as in a church. Drinking was common. And particularly if it met in a tavern, the tavern owner or someone else would frequently get out his fiddle and lead in a round of dancing when the singing lessons finished. In a society that provided few opportunities for young people to interact, particularly with members of the opposite sex, the singing school proved immensely attractive.

On July 12, 1764, an article appeared in the *Massachusetts Gazette and Boston News-Letter*, signed W. B. Was this Billings? Odds are that it was. In tone and content it is consistent with his later beliefs, although at the beginning the author indicates that he copied it from another source. The article asserts the superiority of vocal music over instrumental, both because it can move and inspire and because the voice is a gift of nature itself: "Nature has given to Man the first and finest of all Instruments in his own Frame."[6]

Billings's career is an affirmation of this belief; not only did he frequently equate his art with nature, but not a single instrumental work of his survives. Yet an exclusively vocal orientation may have occurred through economic necessity. Billings, eighteen years old at the time, was at best a junior tradesman, more likely still an apprentice. The article begins with a somewhat bitter comment that hints that he may not have been able to afford a musical instrument: "Having seen lately advertised a Variety of Musical Instruments, which would serve those whose Leisure & Purse can afford the Expense of procuring them: I tho't it a proper Time just to transcribe, and request you, the following."

Singing in New South Church, studying and thinking about music, conducting a singing school, while working as an apprentice and then a yeoman, Billings was following a typical path of a young man interested in music. His letter suggests a passion beyond the ordinary, and Clarissa's report suggests he was in a musical situation better than most. Nothing, however, prepares us for what happened next. In 1770, the year after Billings's first known singing school, one of the most dramatic events in the history of American music occurred. Billings published his first tunebook, *The New-England Psalm-Singer*. It was a bolt out of the blue.

Tunebooks for use in singing schools were relatively common, although most were imported from England. A handful had been printed in America. All were anthologies, however, collections the author assembled from many different sources. *The New-England Psalm-Singer* was unique. It was no compilation. Billings himself wrote virtually all of its 126 compositions. All the tunebooks published in America before 1770 together yield no more than a dozen or so tunes by Americans. With *The New-England Psalm-Singer*, Billings increased that number tenfold.[7]

Given the magnitude of the work, Billings must have labored on *The New-England Psalm-Singer* for some time prior to 1770. In the preface he admits that the work cost him considerable "Time and Pains." He had also waited eighteen months after its completion to publish it because of a paper shortage in New England. But even before its publication Billings was apparently gaining a local reputation for his compositions. According to the preface, he published the tunebook because friends pressed him to do so. At the very least the 1769 singing school must have used music from the *The New-England Psalm-Singer*. Given Billings's later reputation as a singer, his vocal abilities would certainly have been apparent by the time he was in his early twenties, and word of such would spread quickly in a compact town of fifteen thousand, as Boston was. *The New-England Psalm-Singer* hints at another activity. Billings may have been a member of the Tans'ur Singers, a group of Boston musicians in the early 1760s who sang from the British publication *The Royal Melody Compleat*, by William Tans'ur. Tans'ur's publication became the model for many later collections of psalmody, and in *The New-England Psalm-Singer* Billings himself borrowed heavily from Tans'ur's introduction.

According to Billings's introductory material he also had a second volume, consisting of more elaborate pieces such as anthems, fugues, and choruses, ready should there be sufficient interest to warrant it. In 1778 he stated that it had been just on the point of publication when the war broke out, further delaying it. He finally published it in 1781 as *The Psalm-Singer's Amusement*. In the introduction, Billings confirms that "this Work is a Part of the Book of Anthems, which I have so *long* promised." Many pieces were undoubtedly revised, but there is no reason to doubt Billings's statement that the collection had been composed by and large by 1770.[8]

Two volumes of original church music by the age of twenty-four! This may seem modest beside the output of his contemporary Mozart, but nothing Mozart did compares with the sheer boldness and originality of Billings's vision. The idea of publishing an entire tunebook of original compositions was unprecedented, even in England. It was unheard of in America. Musical composition in particular had no acknowledged place or status. And all the time Billings worked on this project, he had a full-time, physically demanding job outside of music.

Billings continued to publish tunebooks throughout his life. His next book, *The Singing Master's Assistant*, appeared in 1778 and ultimately proved his most successful. Following *The Singing Master's Assistant*, Billings published *Music in Miniature* in 1779, *The Psalm-Singer's Amusement* in 1781, *The Suffolk Harmony* in 1786, and *The Continental Harmony* in 1794. In addition, Billings published many individual and occasional pieces, mostly anthems.

Billings's reputation was at its peak during the 1780s. *The Singing Master's Assistant* went through four editions; for some people, Billings *was* New England sacred music. In an article in the *Columbian Magazine* of Philadelphia titled "An Account of Two Americans of Extraordinary Genius in Poetry and Music," Billings was compared favorably to Handel. In 1841, *The Musical Reporter* commented about this time, "No other music for many years was heard throughout New England." Billings's pieces appeared regularly in other compilers' tunebooks, far more often than those of any other composer. Artistically this was a compliment, but in practice it was no favor. In the absence of a general copyright law Billings realized nothing from these piratings. He had attempted to obtain a special copyright privilege for *The New-England Psalm-Singer*, but even though the legislature passed it after two efforts, Governor Thomas Hutchinson refused to approve it. In spite of this setback, however, Billings was successful enough to purchase a home on Newbury Street in 1780 for six thousand pounds, a substantial sum, although the price was in war-inflated currency.[9]

Billings succeeded because his tunes were immensely attractive. Most of his pieces are short strophic hymn tunes, set in four predominantly homophonic parts. Only a small percentage were fuging tunes. Fuging tunes consisted of an opening chordal section followed by a second section in free imitation, in effect like a round, although imitation is strict in a round. They became very popular in singing schools because they were lively and the fuging section allowed the different parts some frolicsome interaction.

Billings also wrote a large number of more substantial pieces, mostly anthems. These appeared both in tunebooks and as separate publications. Most were sacred, although many were written for specific public ceremonial occasions. They vary in length and content; some, such as "Jargon," are short and satirical, and others like "As the Hart" are extended dramatic settings approaching oratorio scope. A few of these anthems proved to be extremely popular.

Two of Billings's most popular compositions during his lifetime were the anthem "The Rose of Sharon" and the song "Chester." Because of their popularity they shed light not only on the composer's style but on the way his

Rose of Sharon

William Billings, "The Rose of Sharon," mm. 48–58

contemporaries perceived him. "The Rose of Sharon" is one of the few pieces for which there is eighteenth-century commentary. The *Columbian Magazine* said that it and "The Dying Christian" were "two of his masterpieces." The writer was particularly taken with three parts in "The Rose of Sharon": the concluding verse, on the text "For, lo! the winter is past, the rain is over and gone"; the opening, which he considered so appropriate to the text ("The gentle breezes of the opening spring cannot affect more deliciously, than the gentle melody by which the return of the genial season, is so finely expressed"); and the "beautiful passage," "He brought me to the banqueting-house & c.," which "expresses in the happiest manner the lively joy of the spouse of Christ."[10]

The anonymous writer of this article focused on what most listeners would consider the most striking moments in this anthem. After several passages of marchlike duple meter, Billings switches to a rolling, undulating triple division of the beat at "He brought me to the banqueting-house." This effectively creates an entirely different mood. Two measures into the new meter Billings underscores the next phrase of the text, "His banner over me was love," with syncopation, followed quickly by a return of the undulating triple rhythm, this time with a much fuller sound.

As important as his larger pieces are, however, Billings is remembered chiefly as a craftsman — a "carver," as he called himself, of attractive melodies. His most popular tune was undoubtedly "Chester," which appeared in *The New-England Psalm-Singer* and, slightly modified, in *The Singing Master's Assistant*. Other compilers may have reprinted other Billings compositions more frequently, but "Chester" was probably sung more and known better than any Billings piece.

Much of the appeal had to do with the text, which Billings may have written at least part of himself. In its final version it is a stirring call to the patriotic side in the Revolutionary War. The words themselves cannot explain its popularity, however. Besides capturing patriotic sentiment so well, the melody is one of his best. And outside of singing schools or occasional home performance with a tunebook, "Chester" was probably sung frequently, informally, tune alone.

The melody itself is typical Billings. Each of the first three phrases begins with the same rhythms and similar notes, but the notes change just enough to keep it from being predictable. The turns and the twists are what make Billings melodies interesting. This is particularly apparent in the second phrase, which goes down to low F. Compare that phrase with what it would be if it simply descended to a half cadence: C–C–C–B-flat–A–G–F–G. The last phrase has a similar profile. It could well have ended at measure 15, but its leap up to B-flat with another stepwise descent gives it a much better rounding off.

"Chester" violates a basic rule of melody: its climactic note appears not once but four times. Each time, however, it is in a different position within the phrase. Finally in the last phrase it is the opening note, and clearly the climactic note of the piece, both because of its structural position and its rhythmic placement in relation to the beginning of the first three phrases. Multiple reiteration of the climactic note is in general unusual, but in Billings's music it is common. In *The New-England Psalm-Singer*, for instance, it oc-

Chester

William Billings, "Chester," mm. 9–16

curs in 41 of the 126 pieces. The only other composer to do this frequently and effectively was Franz Schubert.[11]

In 1785, Daniel Read set Billings's text to a tune that he called "New England." That in itself suggests the popularity of Billings's piece. Read's setting is quite different, however. It is much closer to the tunebook tradition. It is a fuging tune, and the harmony, with frequent open sounds throughout, is more typical of the tunebooks. Read also used literal tone painting in some of the obvious places: on the word *shake* in the first phrase, the soprano trills or shakes; in the second phrase the tenor stresses "clanking" and "galling" with embellished figures. The greatest difference between the two settings, how-ever, is in the melodies. Even allowing for the contrapuntal nature of the sec-ond half of the piece, Read's melody just does not have the appeal that the original has. All the twists, turns, repetitions, calculated continuations, and use of climax make Billings's melody special.

The appeal of "Chester" also illustrates another aspect of its composer's historical position. If Billings is to be compared to any other major American composer, it should be Stephen Foster. They seem dissimilar because Billings wrote church music and Foster penned sentimental songs and mu-sic for minstrel shows. Each, however, wrote in the most popular idioms of his time. Both pioneered roles as composers. When Foster decided to try to make a living as a composer, even of popular songs, the idea was considered as unusual as Billings's decision some three-quarters of a century earlier. Nei-ther was financially successful in the long run, but both composers' works were very well known in their lifetimes. Most important, however, their styles are similar. Both wrote simple, strictly diatonic melodies that have a natural-ness and flow about them equaled by few of their peers.

Foster has fared much better in our world than Billings. His music is still familiar. That of Billings is known only to scholars and a few choral musicians. One reason for this is harmony. Foster's harmonies can be subtle, but they are simple. They consist mostly of the primary diatonic chords, with either an arpeggiated or oom-pah accompaniment. It is the same harmonic style of gospel, country, and much popular music, and it is still with us. Billings's har-mony is of an older folk idiom no longer found except where traditional mu-sic still flourishes. It was geared to choral singing and does not easily adapt as solo song or song with accompaniment, such as piano or guitar.

Billings and Foster wrote about different subjects. Religion and patrio-tism dominate Billings's music, which does not have the deeply personal quality that Foster's does. Foster was a dreamer. He wrote about love, gentle-ness, stillness, and death. His music speaks from the heart directly to the heart. Even in our modern, hard-edged age Foster's music maintains its ap-peal. Billings's concerns seem more remote, less direct and personal. The eighteenth century in general seems distant. As media and the popular press demonstrate, we are still fascinated by the Civil War, but the Revolutionary War interests us less. Billings seems from an age that strikes us as different, but not sufficiently different to seem exotic.

Billings's reputation suffered in the nineteenth century, however, for reasons other than remoteness. Reformers found his harmony woefully inad-equate according to scientific European standards. But even the most zeal-ous reformer respected Billings's melodies. Were it not for some parallel octaves and fifths and some unresolved dissonances, Billings's place in American music, and indeed the whole history of music in nineteenth-century America, might have been quite different.[12]

The writer for the *Columbian Magazine* was well aware of an important characteristic of Billings's music, its naturalness. He contrasts Billings with Martin Madan, a British composer of psalmody, whose works he considered more "laboured," and with the "Italian taste," which he did not define but by which he probably meant ornate elaborate melodies. He extols Billings's closeness to nature: "Nature, true genuine nature, pervades all his compositions. His melody is simple, noble, and pathetic." This anonymous writer early on recognized why the music Billings wrote stands out.

The very first composition in *The New-England Psalm-Singer*, "America," places his country in the bosom of nature. The song depicts America as a refuge of justice and democracy in a world of political persecution. The land is a wilderness chosen, "our calm retreat." Like other Billings pieces that refer to nature, nature or the wilderness itself is not the focus of the text; religious and patriotic thought interested Billings far more. When nature is present in his works, however, it is invariably benevolent. His own text to "Bridgewater," which he set a second time to the tune "Sunday" in *The Singing Master's Assistant*, refers to the singer's "rapture and surprise," "Where e're I turn my wondering eyes."[13]

Billings's attitude intersects with three widely contrasting views of nature held in the eighteenth and nineteenth centuries. His belief in a benign nature as comfort and solace presages early-nineteenth-century romanticism. His concept of nature as artistic inspiration and model parallels European Enlightenment thought. But even though he may have anticipated romanticism and emulated the Enlightenment, Billings lived in a Puritan culture, and his attitudes about nature clashed head on with mainstream Puritanism. In championing nature in his music in eighteenth-century Boston, Billings was much a maverick.

No social, religious, or intellectual movement in the history of the United States has had a stronger, more pervasive, and deeper impact on American culture than Puritanism. It affected the arts, including music, well into the twentieth century. It not only established an artistic hierarchy that prevailed through at least much of the nineteenth century, but it probably did more to shape attitudes toward the place and the value of both the arts and the artist in society than any other factor. Many of those attitudes continue, though masked, to this day.

Even though Puritanism as a theocracy had lost much of its original force by the 1760s, when Billings began to compose, Boston remained heavily under Puritan influence. His time was less than a generation removed from the Great Awakening, still close enough to remember vividly the controversy that surrounded the writer and Puritan preacher Jonathan Edwards, who was banished to a frontier parish because of a theological dispute. Puritan values and attitudes prevailed throughout New England. Billings published *The New-England Psalm-Singer* just as George Whitefield, the leading revivalist of the Great Awakening, died, and he found the event significant enough to include in his introduction a eulogistic poem about Whitefield, even though it had nothing to do with the music collection itself. And the entire singing school movement, although subverted into something more secular by teachers like Billings, was nevertheless thoroughly Puritan in design and purpose. It was begun by Puritan ministers to reform music in their churches.

To the Puritan, nature was not benign. The wilderness was a place of terror. It was essentially satanic, evil itself. John Bunyan's *Pilgrim's Progress*, the archetypal statement of the Puritan view of life, tells the story of Christian, the allegorical hero, who must endure a series of trials and hardships before he can reach the celestial city, the ultimate goal of each true Puritan believer. Not coincidentally much of the story is set in America, which is seen as a desert, harsh, hostile, and inhabited by savages and other creatures who make Christian's life miserable. The wilderness was basic to Puritan thought; it was the metaphorical terrain the believer had to traverse to reach the ultimate goal of a life beyond the present one.

Bunyan's vision was imaginary, but for the American Puritans, the wilderness, although not a desert, was all too real. It both imposed tangible hardship and, as darkness and unknown, elicited genuine fear. Where reality began and ended, however, was not always clear. Rhetoric blurred the lines, and the Puritan world was built on rhetoric. From the three-hour sermons to the many tracts and pamphlets that came off the early presses, rhetoric held the community together. Rhetoric alone, of all the arts, was valued.

In a world so commanded by rhetoric, in a world that believed in a literal personified devil, symbol and reality, metaphor and illusion became inexorably mixed. American Puritans, seeing the wilderness as a place to be conquered, linked three metaphors: the wilderness, the garden, and the hedge. The garden was the wilderness subdued. The hedge was the boundary that separated them, the barrier that held the wilderness in check. The Puritan mission in America was to create a garden out of the wilderness.

Billings, in contrast, saw much in nature that was good and benevolent, enough to use it as his inspiration. Nevertheless he also saw what the Puritans saw, the wildness. There, however, he turned the Puritan view on its head.

Billings associated fully with the wildness. He aligned with it so thoroughly that he himself became the outsider, the wild man whose values subvert prevailing standards.

Contemporaries described Billings as of medium stature, physically deformed, with one eye, a shrunken arm, and one leg shorter than the other. He was by all accounts unkempt, crude, vulgar, and totally neglectful of his appearance. His wife's father apparently opposed his marriage. He used snuff heavily and was neither polite nor subtle about it. Tanning itself involved noxious chemicals, and Billings could not have avoided having their residue on his person. Combined with his own physical irregularities, he must have seemed to many a grotesque sight. Although born with physical problems, the adult Billings seems to have gone out of his way to cultivate a wild-man image. One can easily see his attraction to the animals and the outsiders so loathsome to Puritan society.

With Billings the line between animal and human blurs. He had a deep-seated affinity with animals and a deep-seated cynicism about men. His choice of work is significant, tanning itself being in one sense the re-creation of the animal through the manipulation of the hide. This runs parallel to humans in primitive societies who donned animal skins to identify with the animals they needed to kill in order to survive. They found through those animals allegories and connections with the world about them. According to legend Billings actually recorded his first compositions with chalk on the hides of the animals in his tannery. This anecdote is likely apocryphal, but its very existence suggests that contemporaries sensed in him a deep and fundamental connection with this aspect of nature.

Billings left a substantial body of prose in addition to his many compositions. Much of it is found in the introductions to his various tunebooks, but he also published several pamphlets and edited the first issue of *Boston Magazine*, which includes some articles that he himself likely wrote. These writings are saturated with animal allegory, and in many cases the animals come across better than the humans. One *Boston Magazine* article, "On the Seduction of Young Women," contrasts men unfavorably with mountain wolves who "have their objects of prey separate from their own species." In a parenthetical aside Billings states flatly that man has less humanity than non-human creatures.[14]

The introduction to the *The Singing Master's Assistant* contains a two-part explanation-satire on his piece "Jargon," a satirical work of unrelenting dissonance. The first part, addressed to the "Goddess of Discord," describes war strategy for a battle between concord and discord. The second, shorter part discusses how to perform the piece and suggests appropriate effects.

These include a braying ass, a squealing hog, a cracking crow, a howling dog, and a squalling cat.

When Billings edited *Boston Magazine*, he chose as the lead story a description of Carl Linnaeus's animal taxonomy, "The Animal Kingdom of Linnaeus, reduced into Classes, Orders, Genera and Specie." The article, neither allegory nor satire, is a straightforward description of animal classification. It was placed first in the magazine and, too long for a single issue, conceived to be a continuing series. It leaves no doubt about his fascination with the animal world. Significantly, when the magazine was reconstituted with new editorship for the second issue, this article was dropped.

Billings's most extensive animal allegory is his prose story *The Fox Turned Preacher.*[15] A scathing satire on the hypocrisy of the clergy, it describes a fox who, noticing the difference between his own lean, struggling existence and the fat life of the clergy, decides to profess a conversion and become a preacher. He sends out an address to all the "Geese, Turkeys, Ducks, and Dung-hill Fowls throughout the whole Country of Fowldom," announcing his conversion and, through many scriptural allusions, promising to be a vegetarian. The land of Fowldom rejoiced, ignoring an ominous P.S.: "Please to meet me without delay, as my bowels yearn for you exceedingly."[16]

The service was set. After some initial prayers, a psalm was to be sung by the animals, which according to the writer would have exceeded the music of the British composers Thomas Augustine Arne and George Frederic Handel. It was cut off by the fox, on scriptural and moral grounds, allowing Billings to deliver a biting satire of the Puritan attitude toward music in church.[17] Then the fox delivers his sermon, and as he rambles on, the Country of Fowldom catches on to his real intentions, and creates such a stir that the farmer comes out and chases the fox away.

Like all allegory, Billings's animal stories and references are really satires about human folly. Frequently, however, he wrote directly about humans. Billings published many articles and stories about specific people, some real, some fictional, and in these stories he reveals much about himself. All the characters he chose were marginal, living either on the fringe of society or in some cases beyond. They were outside the usual rules and mores. And just as Billings identified with animals, he seemed to have identified or at least been fascinated with these reprobates.

Billings's most extended effort in that direction was with *The American Bloody Register*, published in 1784. The full title describes vividly what the publication was all about: *The American Bloody Register: containing A true and complete History of the Lives, Last Words, and Dying Confession of three of the most noted Criminals . . . Richard Barrick and John Sullivan, Highway*

Robbers. Together with the Dying Confession of Alexander *White, a Murderer and Pirate.*[18]

It was to be a series. The "Life and Dying Confession of Richard Barrick" was incomplete, "to be continued." And if there was any doubt about its sensationalistic quality, the self-advertisement following the title page dispelled that: "If encouragement is given to the Register, the other Numbers will contain . . . a select and judicious Collection of all the most remarkable Trials for Murder, Treason, Rape, Sodomy, High-way Robbery, Piracy, House-breaking, Perjury, Forgery, and other Crimes and Misdemeanors committed in England and America; from 1760 to 1784 inclusive. Also the Lives, last Words and Dying Conffssions [*sic*] of all the most noted Criminals that can be obtained."

This is tabloid journalism; the entire project, particularly the advertisement for future issues, is remarkably lurid when viewed in the context of a still tightly controlled Puritan society.

Yet precedence existed. Such descriptions were common in "execution sheets" popular as street literature in England at the time. A type of broadside, these were the equivalent of working-class newspapers and were sold as such. The "chaunters," or ballad singers, who hawked the broadsides often appeared with a pictorial board on a pole that contained gaudy or grisly illustrations of the subject being sold. As with tabloids today, sensational subject matter sold well, and balladeers were always on the lookout for it. Murders and executions, which were very much public spectacle, were especially popular.[19]

What was Billings's motive here? Was he unable to overcome his working-class mentality enough to see the inappropriateness of this as a respectable publication, or was this purposeful, a desire to shock, possibly even offend, done in anger over having been peremptorily removed from the editorship of *Boston Magazine*? Possibly it was done simply for profit. Whatever the reason, Billings was unafraid to pursue his own strange muse.

As if to justify the pamphlet, a gloss of morality overlays it. The different confessions are preceded by such biblical quotations as "The Wages of Sin is Death" and admonitions about the consequences of crime. The biblical quotations are set in large type surrounded by a thick black border, sometimes accompanied by crude graphics, such as a skull and crossbones. And preceding the final story, a sermon delivered by Timothy Hilliard just before the execution of three criminals is advertised as soon to be published. The last page contains a drawing of the criminals hanged, surrounded by a large crowd witnessing the event. All this contributes further to the sensational nature of the issue.

The American Bloody Register, last page

Yet in spite of the clumsy, possibly disingenuous efforts to provide a veneer of moral disapproval, there is an attempt to understand these renegades. They lived beyond the mores of society, but they still retain some sort of tenuous connection with society. A human quality is always present, although it is sometimes hard to find. More important, these portraits are real and recognizable. The thief, of course, was all too common in early Federal America, someone that upper- and middle-class Americans — the likely purchasers of the magazine — knew and feared, but really did not understand.

The fox in *The Fox Turned Preacher* could well have been in *The American Bloody Register.* The fox represents another type of criminal, the con man. He was probably even more familiar to most Americans, as the line between sharp business practice (or simply presenting oneself in the best light) and out-and-out deception was not always clear. Truth had its own aura of absoluteness in Puritan society, but truth, even to the theologians, could be disputed. The most radical aspect of Billings's story of the fox is that he took full aim at the clergymen themselves. In his portrayal of false conversion and corrupt clergy, Billings attacked directly and specifically the most powerful and respected institution in New England society.

All these characters, however, pale compared with Sawney Beane, by far the most extreme renegade in Billings's writings. His story, a legend that goes back to Elizabethan Scotland, appeared in *Boston Magazine*. It was graphic in its detail. Sawney Beane and a woman "as viciously inclined as himself" ran away to a cave, supporting themselves by robbery. They always murdered and then cannibalized the victim. Many people disappeared over a period of time, including all parties sent out to investigate the disappearances; judges began to execute so many innocent people, trying to end the atrocities, that innkeepers moved away and the area became generally depopulated. By this time Sawney Beane's family numbered forty-eight, including children and grandchildren. All the grandchildren were begotten by incest. The authorities finally found Beane's cave and took the entire clan to Edinburgh, where they were all executed.[20]

Sawney Beane differs from all the other marginal types that Billings presents, either directly or in allegory. With Sawney Beane we move into the realm of the macabre and the horrific. The thieves were either real, which attests to their fascination, or in the case of the fox real enough as fable to be recognizable. Each represented a type all too common in colonial America. Sawney Beane, however, is pure fantasy, too extreme to be associated with any ordinary criminal.

The Sawney Beane story returns to the Puritan view of the wilderness, depicting the world beyond the hedge as a savage place where the most horrid events occur. It so exaggerates the Puritan view, however, that it becomes a satire on it. The Sawney Beane story anticipates the Davy Crockett myth popular in the 1830s and 1840s. In many ways Sawney Beane is an early incarnation of Davy Crockett, at least the Davy Crockett of the *Almanachs*, a series of yearbooks that contained fanciful and outlandish stories of his exploits.

The Davy Crockett *Almanachs* present a man who goes into the wilderness, encounters and conquers the savage, represented by the Indian, but in doing so takes on the savage's character. The Davy Crockett stories provided the nineteenth century a metaphor for a fundamental issue: the tension between the civilized east and the savage west. To many in the east, the west represented the breakdown of civilization; it was an area of lawlessness in which all morality vanished. It was metaphorically the Puritan desert. The European inhabitants of the frontier lived constantly on the fringe of civilizations and, in the case of Crockett, went beyond it. An element of both fascination and horror pervades these stories. In less exaggerated ways the tension was constantly played out in American life: Andrew Jackson's presidential election in 1828 set off wild fears, and the press responded with vicious caricatures. Church music reformers feared greatly the unrestrained emotionalism of frontier hymnody. In the nineteenth century Billings's own reputation was tainted from this perception; once the reformers placed him outside the domain of correct, scientific church music, they began to label his style barbaric.

Yet in the "morality play of westward expansion" Davy Crockett was both hero and savage. Even though Crockett himself succumbs to the savagery of the wilderness, he stills wins; he beats the Indians, usually in hand-to-hand combat, and either kills or domesticates the wild animals he encounters. In rhetoric and metaphor the Crockett frontier was far removed from Puritan allegory, but the belief was the same: the wilderness, including its inhabitants, the native Americans, was the villain, and the pioneer who conquered it was the hero.[21]

A tradition of the wild man existed in Europe for centuries, far predating the New World savages described by early explorers. Both Sawney Beane and the Davy Crockett myth fit into that tradition. The wild man and cannibal is found in the earliest epics, for example Cyclops, and by the time of Herodotus had become historical. By the eighteenth century he was even enshrined in science, for Linnaeus listed five races of humankind: Europaeus, Asiaticus, Afer (African), Americanus (American Indian), and Ferus (wild). We know from the *Boston Magazine* that Billings was interested in the Linnaeus classifications. He may have gotten the idea of publishing the Sawney Beane legend from his *Boston Magazine* article on Linnaeus.

The Davy Crockett stories help explain Billings in another important dimension. Crockett, like Billings, identifies with the animals he encounters. That is the symbol of Crockett's coonskin cap. The animals in Billings are much less savage than those in the Crockett stories, ironically faring worst when, like the fox, they attempt to emulate humans. But the Crockett stories illustrate the thin line between animal and human; Crockett, as he becomes less civilized, becomes more like the animals around him.

Although this theme in its parallelism is less overt in Billings, I believe it is an important aspect of Billings's satire, and of his own sense of place in New England. Billings's fascination with animals and with humans outside the bounds of accepted conduct ultimately merge. In his prose writings and in the texts of some of his music, Billings all but becomes the animal. In spite of its immorality, it is the fox's voice that we hear; the fox's sermon, inter alia Billings, with its many unconventional points, dominates the story. The animal's chorus surpasses Arne and Handel, a thinly veiled self-wish. And as we noted Billings believed animals to be more human than humans.

Billings's view is diametrically in contrast to the Puritan view of the wilderness, which was populated by horrible beasts and creatures of terror. The wild man merges with them, and both assume a supernatural quality. In 1630 William Higginson reported the existence of "Serpents of strong colours and huge greatnesse." The Mathers described the wilderness as full of "wild boars," "Wild Beats, and Wilder Men," "dragons," and "Fiery flying serpents." Cotton Mather warned of wolves who would "not leave the Bones till morning," and in the same sentence he referred to "Droves of Devils." On hearing roaring in the woods, William Wood speculated that it must be "eyther Devills or Lyons." To the Puritan, wild animals, the wild man, and the devil himself were virtually interchangeable. All were evil itself. They formed and defined the wilderness.[22]

Sawney Beane proved too much for Boston. Shortly after the first issue appeared, *Boston Magazine* was reorganized and Billings was removed as editor. In a pointed rebuke to Billings, the second issue, in November 1783, was renumbered volume 1, number 1, and the new editorship specifically disavowed the previous issue.

As a tanner, Billings's social position never had been high, and he had failed in the one area of the arts that could have enhanced considerably his status in the community. No matter how successful or original he was with his tunebooks, a literary magazine in eighteenth-century Boston enjoyed a prestige that a music collection never could.

At precisely this point Billings became involved with *The American Bloody Register*. Apparently wishing to remain connected with literary publication, he turned to subject matter that, like himself, lay essentially beyond the pale. The criminals must have held a fascination to Billings, just as Sawney Beane did. Precisely what Billings saw in these real and fictional characters we will never know, but he almost certainly identified with some aspect of their lives.

Yet in spite of his odd, almost disgusting, personal demeanor, eccentricities, and disdain for many values and mores of society, Billings seems to have been accepted. Something obviously compensated. There was first his patriotism. "Chester" is only the most famous example of many pieces of his that express revolutionary sentiment. "Lamentation over Boston" grieves over the city's fate in 1775–76, when it was occupied by British forces. The piece gains force by paraphrasing Psalm 137, which allows Billings to equate his city to biblical suffering. This is one of his longer anthems, and the melody of the opening chordal section is particularly effective. In A minor, it winds continuously around the first five notes of the scale, creating both tension and a tone of poignancy and sorrow.

Practically all the people connected with Billings were patriots. Paul Revere, who engraved at least the frontispiece for *The New-England Psalm-Singer*, made patriotic engravings, including a widely circulated one of the Boston Massacre. Revere was a member of the Sons of Liberty, the revolutionary organization founded in 1765, and he played a leading role in the Boston Tea Party. Benjamin Edes and John Gill, the publishers of *The New-England Psalm-Singer*, also published the *Boston Gazette and Country Journal*, which was considered a leading journal of the patriots. They also strongly opposed the Stamp Act and the tea tax. Gillam Bass, one of the sellers of Billings's book, was a member of the Committees of Correspondence.[23]

Billings's most important patriot association was with Samuel Adams, one of the leaders of the revolution. Adams was a devoted Christian, having been converted in the Great Awakening in 1741, and he was also extremely fond of music. His cousin John, the second president, not known for any interest in music, commented that Samuel had "an exquisite ear for music and a charming voice, when he pleased to use it." Adams, like Billings in his youth, was a member of New South Church, and according to reports that Nathaniel Gould took from contemporaries, Adams often performed with Billings and a Dr. Pierce both in church and in concerts. It may well have been William Billings and Samuel Adams singing in New South Church that so impressed the young woman Clarissa who wrote to the newspaper in 1766.[24]

Particularly tantalizing is Gould's reference to "concerts." There is no record of Adams and Billings singing in any formal concerts in Boston or its environs. Adams reportedly used his musical abilities, however, to rally working-class support for the revolution. According to Judge Peter Oliver, one of his Tory opponents, "He had a good Voice, & was a Master in vocal Musick. This Genius he improved, by instituting singing Societies of Mechanicks, where he presided; & embraced such Opportunities to ye inculcating Sedition, 'till it had ripened into Rebellion." Given Billings's connection with Adams through New South Church and his own patriotic fervor, it would be natural for Adams to ask Billings to help with some of these societies, or at the very least to perform occasionally for such or similar assemblies. These were probably Gould's "concerts."[25]

Further reports from Billings's time suggest that Adams may have actually collaborated in the composition of "Chester." If Billings and Adams sang together to instigate rebellion, they would undoubtedly have sung "Chester." And between *The New-England Psalm-Singer* in 1770 and *The Singing Master's Assistant* in 1778, probably when much of that activity would have occurred, four new verses were added to "Chester." If Adams had a hand in the song, this is probably where it happened.

One glaring exception to Billings's patriot associates was Mather Byles. The grandson of Increase Mather, Byles was a Puritan minister, noted for his pompous manner and social preference for those of position and authority. During the Revolutionary War Byles was tried, placed under house arrest, and forced to resign his position as pastor of Hollis Street Church for his Tory sympathies. He and Billings seem to have inhabited different worlds.

Yet Byles and Billings had much in common. Byles himself was a maverick. Given his ancestry and intellect the ministry was virtually preordained for him. Byles, however, was more a poet, humorist, and satirist than a somber Puritan minister. His humor, consisting mainly of puns, was often biting, like Billings's. His problems during the revolution had more to do with his satirical tendencies than his politics, which posed no serious threat. William Tudor observed that he probably would not have been prosecuted for his political convictions had not his wit provoked considerable enmity, for Byles "sometimes exerted this talent where good nature would have refrained, and left a lasting sting by a transient jest." At the time of the trial John Eliot, a young man later to become a minister, wrote Jeremy Belknap: "All that could be proved was that he is a silly, impertinent, childish *person*; I should say inconstent, if his whole conduct did not manifest him to be one consistent lump of absurdity. . . . His general character has been so despicable that he seems to have no friends to pity him."[26]

Byles shared Billings's enthusiasm about music, although he did not attempt to compose. Byles's creativity turned to poetry, and he contributed several texts for *The New-England Psalm-Singer*. Byles wrote the text for the canon that appeared on the frontispiece, for "Hollis Street," which was probably named in honor of Byles, and for "America," the first piece in the book.[27] He also wrote a poem, a paean to music, which begins, "Down Steers the *Bass* with grave majestic Air." Billings included this in the introduction to *The New-England Psalm-Singer* and later adapted it for the piece "Modern Music" in *The Psalm-Singer's Amusement*.

In 1739 Byles published a sermon that must have sent shivers through the orthodox clergy. In it he called the Song of Songs the "finest poetical composure now extant in the world" and labeled it a "Pastoral Opera." He then extended the metaphor, referring to its dramatic nature, its action, dialogue, and character, even dividing it into three acts. This was at a time when opera was considered anathema to the Puritan clergy. Byles then picked up the pastoral theme, and like Billings and in sharp contrast to Puritan orthodoxy spoke positively of the wilderness. He concluded with a "Hymn for the Spring," which in tone though not poetic style anticipates Robert Frost:

> The painted Meads and fragrant Fields
> A sudden smile bestow,
> A golden Gleam each Valley yields,
> Where numerous Beauties blow.
>
> A Thousand gaudy Colours flush
> Each od'rous Mountain's Side:
> Lillies rise fair, and Roses blush
> And Tulips spread their Pride.
>
> Thus flourishes the wanton Year,
> In rich Profusion gay,
> Till Autumn bids the bloom retire,
> The Verdure fade away.
>
> Succeeding Cold withers the Woods,
> While heavy Winter reigns,
> In Fetters binds the frozen Floods,
> And Shivers o'er the Plains.[28]

It is no wonder that Billings was attracted to Byles. He had a biting satirical bent, held similar unorthodox views about nature, must have felt excluded in spite of a strong desire to belong, and was passionately devoted to music. The extent of their personal contacts is unknown, but Billings did join Byles's Hollis Street Church. If he was a member while Byles was still in the pulpit, Billings could not have escaped Byles's notice. From all accounts no one could be in the same room with Billings and not be aware of his voice. Since Byles's "New-England Hymn" appears nowhere other than in *The New-England Psalm-Singer*, it is likely that he wrote it specifically for Billings. That would suggest that their association dates from at least 1770.

Byles and Billings were determined to pursue their art regardless of consequences. This personal trait was probably necessary for any artist, no matter what the field, in eighteenth-century Boston. Yet this does not mean they did not care about reception. In spite of his eccentricity and apparent disdain

for convention, Billings wanted to belong and be recognized. In the preface
to *The Singing Master's Assistant* he tells us what he felt when *The New-England Psalm-Singer* was published:

> And truly a most masterly and inimitable Performance, I then thought it to
> be. Oh! how did my foolish heart throb and beat with tumultuous joy! With
> what impatience did I wait on the Book-Binder, while stitching the sheets
> and putting on the covers, with what ecstasy, did I snatch the yet unfinished
> Book out of his hands, and pressing it to my bosom, with rapturous delight;
> how lavish was I in encomiums on this infant production of my own numb
> skull? Welcome; thrice welcome, thou legitimate offspring of my brain, go
> forth my little Book, go forth and immortalize the name of your Author; . . .
> thou art my Reuben, my first born, the beginning of my strength, the excel-
> lency of my dignity, and the excellency of my power.

Few documents from the eighteenth century depict so vividly the inner
excitement of an artist about his work. But as Billings admits, the excitement
gradually gave way to an awareness that the book was not all he had hoped.
Between the publication of *The New-England Psalm-Singer* and *The Singing Master's Assistant*, Billings realized that he had much to learn: "But to
my great mortification I soon discovered that it was Reuben in the sequel,
and Reuben all over; for unstable as water, it did not excell. . . . I have discovered that many of the pieces in that Book were never worth my printing,
or your inspection." Billings did not give up, however. In *The Singing Master's Assistant* he republished, corrected, many of the tunes from *The New-
England Psalm-Singer*.

Billings was ahead of his time. He was a revolutionary, rebelling against
Puritan strictures that still entrapped many. He believed in nature, in freedom, in joy and personal expression. The excitement he described in the introduction to *Singing Master's Assistant* characterizes much of his music.
And Billings addressed topics frowned upon by Puritanism. He wrote at least
seven pieces that celebrate Christmas, at a time when the holiday was still
considered a pagan ceremony, entirely inappropriate for Calvinism. His
satire, both in music and in words, was biting and harsh. It was aimed at prevailing standards.

Yet even though Billings's work flaunted societal norms in many ways,
Bostonians seemed to have recognized and respected the artist in him.
William Bentley, a prominent liberal minister, was touched enough to write
a one-paragraph obituary in his diary when Billings died. Bentley described
him as someone who, in spite of physical handicaps, "spake & sung &
thought as a man above the common abilities." It was Billings the singer that
drew the most respect. Everyone remembered his voice, powerful, robust,

stentorian. It was that all-consuming voice that drew and held Bostonians. When John Eliot referred disparagingly and in horror to the first edition of *Boston Magazine,* which Billings edited, he referred to him as the psalm singer, not the psalm composer. At the same time Eliot admitted that, in reference to *The Singing Master's Assistant,* "we have one original genius among us.[29]

An idea of the power of Billings's voice is found in his own comments in *The New-England Psalm-Singer.* He wanted his choirs heavily weighted toward the bass. He recommended three basses for every singer on other parts, and for a group of forty, twenty basses, with the other parts divided among the remaining twenty. Interestingly, Mozart recommended a similar preponderance of bass for an orchestra. By his own admission Billings was after a deep, full sound that would "cause the floor to tremble," which he claims to have often achieved. Almost certainly he was referring to his own voice, and other accounts suggest that indeed he could make the floor tremble.

The Reverend John Pierce describes in his memoirs what it was like to stand next to Billings singing: "I have sung with him, agreeably to the fashion of the times, with all my might, without being conscious, that I enunciated a sound, so completely was my utterance drowned by his overpowering screams." Nathaniel Gould, who called Billings's voice "stentorian," added the following observation: "Every one who has ever heard Dr. Pierce sing, especially at Commencement dinners, at Cambridge, knows that his voice was not wanting in power."[30]

What a sight! That voice and those melodies coming out of this small, deformed, unkempt frame! And then the bizarre prose writing. No wonder Billings made a deep impression on Bostonians. No wonder many elite Bostonians, including Paul Revere, Samuel Adams, and Mather Byles, found themselves attracted to Billings in spite of every reason not to be.

Implicit in Bostonian reactions to Billings, music is tacitly recognized as an art, even though it was not consciously so. Its effect, both in church and as a patriotic weapon, was acknowledged. Most important, for the first time we see recognition that the artist is someone whose art overcomes his own person. For eighteenth-century Boston, in the case of Billings at least, art transcended life. In him appears one of the first incarnations of American fascination with the artist as an odd figure, eccentric, a maverick. It is difficult for us to realize what a radical notion that was at the time. Only later did writers, beginning with Tocqueville, find American society highly individualistic. The artist as bohemian oddity was not established for another half-century. In any event, in the minds of most, music was not art.

Billings was successful, however, only as long as his music was viable. By the 1790s, interest in his style of church music began to wane, as other kinds of music came to hold more excitement for Bostonians. Theater was finally allowed in Boston in 1792, and music was integral, even if the play was not musical. The orchestra often performed for an hour before curtain time, and passions about what the orchestra should play ran so high that fights between spectators and physical abuse of orchestral players were common. Some of the Congregational churches in Boston were acquiring organs, and with them came an entirely new style of church music. Billings, of course, was totally unequipped to preside in such situations. Finally, not unrelated to the appearance of organs, criticism began to mount of his own musical style. Although the complaints did not become a full chorus until the nineteenth century, charges began to surface that the musical style of Billings was old-fashioned and less "scientific." That is, his music was somewhat backwoods and no longer sophisticated.

As a result of these changes, Billings's fortunes declined rapidly in the 1790s. We do not know when the slide began, but the *Columbian Centinel* of December 8, 1790, advertised a benefit concert of sacred music for Billings, "whose distress is real, and whose merit in that science is generally acknowledged." He was forced to take a mortgage on his house in 1791. He could no longer afford to finance his publications. *The Continental Harmony* was published in 1794 only because a committee made up from several musical societies in Boston lobbied the publisher to bring it out. Billings had apparently given up tanning to pursue his musical career, and there is no way to estimate the number of singing schools he taught. Other than publication, they would have been his main source of income. By the 1790s, however, as Bostonian taste turned more to secular music, the singing school movement itself was on the wane.

Billings's wife died in 1795. Six of his nine children, ranging in age from three to eighteen, were still alive. Sometime in the 1790s he had to rent out his house, although he managed to keep ownership of it until his death. William Billings died on September 27, 1800, and was buried in an unmarked grave, possibly on the Boston Common.

Only many years later, in the 1830s, when the new style had been established and enough distance put between the practitioners of the new and the memory of the old, could Billings's music be revived. A Billings and Holden Society was formed in Boston in 1834, but it was clearly as an act of nostalgia. This was old-fashioned music that was preserved as a historical curiosity for the benefit of those few older singers who might remember it, and for the memory of younger ones who might be curious as to what it was.

CHAPTER 3

The Log Cabin Composer

IN 1822 LOWELL MASON, a banker in Savannah, Georgia, published his first collection of sacred music under the sponsorship of the Boston Handel and Haydn Society. Unlike the collection of William Billings, little of it was original. Most of the tunes were pilfered, but the sources were new. For his melodies Mason went to the European classics, to Mozart, Haydn, and Beethoven.

Mason was riding a wave of religious fervor that had been growing since 1801, and he did what he did with a purpose. In 1801 a group of evangelical leaders gathered in Cane Ridge, Kentucky, then on the fringes of the frontier, to conduct an extended service. Hundreds showed up, preaching continued nonstop for days, often with three or four preachers holding forth simultaneously. Members of the audience went into delirium, rolling on the ground, speaking in tongues. The air was electric, an outpouring of mass religious emotion unprecedented. One witness described more than five hundred people collapsed with "shrieks and shouts that rent the very heavens" and people whose bodies twitched "as if they must . . . fly asunder."[1]

Cane Ridge was the beginning of a mass movement that swept the American west. Barely organized, in scope and passion it was unlike anything that had been seen before, even in the Great Awakening. It also thoroughly frightened the eastern establishment. Here was a spontaneous outpouring whose emotional intensity threatened the decorum and the order of society. And a big part of it was music, a frenzied, natural, spontaneous mass singing. As the movement marched north and east, it threatened to overtake the whole country. By 1832 it even invaded solemn, Puritan Boston, when Charles G. Finney began a series of revivals.

The Presbyterian-Congregational church, upholder of dignity and restraint in mainstream Protestantism, needed to counter the threat of such unencumbered emotion. Lyman Beecher, the pastor of Bowdoin Street Church and spiritual leader of the Boston Congregational establishment, told Finney that if he came to Boston, "I'll meet you at the state line, and call out all the artillerymen, and fight every inch of the way to Boston, and then I'll fight you there."[2] In music the older style of psalmody would no longer work. Ever since the singing school it was suspect. A musical savior that would restore decorum and taste was desperately needed. With the Handel and Haydn Society collection that savior seemed to have arrived.

No one could have played the part better. Lowell Mason was truly religious. He was also upright, pompous, domineering, and deadly serious, sure of the rightness of his cause and his own ability to deliver. He was the answer to the unrestrained hymnody of the west. Unfortunately he was also the antidote to Billings and all that he stood for. Mason was to see that church music, and by extension American musical taste, adhered to a proper, "scientific" model. Mason meant, simply, that such music should imitate European classical practice. Beginning with Mason, notions of taste, propriety, and science trumped natural spontaneous melody, and banished such untutored rubes as William Billings to those segments of society that did not know better.

It was a dichotomy that later echoed through the rest of American musical history. Propriety, cloaked in the garb of science and progress, versus naturalness, tainted as untutored and backward: the city versus the country. It was not new with Mason. The reformer William Hastings had laid the foundation for the movement when he published his *Dissertation on Musical Taste* in 1822, and the entire process had been played out, on a smaller scale but with no less intensity, a century earlier, with the Great Awakening.

In his massive volume *A History of the American People*, Paul Johnson postulates the Great Awakening as a pivotal event in American history because it democratized the country. In the case of music it also set forth the basic tension that was to define music in America well into the twentieth century, the tension between a music that stressed restraint, order, and rationality against one that reveled in the untrammeled release of bacchic emotions. The case of the musical reforms that unfolded with the Great Awakening is ironic, for they worked precisely against the democratizing movement. Musical reform in the early eighteenth century was a tactic of the old guard, the Puritans who wanted to maintain control. It did not succeed, as Billings and the singing school subverted and then deflected it.

In the nineteenth century the same battles were fought, only the stakes were higher and the outcome was totally different. Mason and Hastings and their kind captured the high ground. Music from the start had been subversive, in their view, so music had to be controlled. In the nineteenth century the conservatives succeeded. They first defined church music, and building on that they defined classical music, and finally they defined high culture for America. From that point on the tension existed, and it only grew more severe as technology widened the gap between the high and the low.

The history of high culture in American music is the history of a counterrevolutionary movement. To carry the sacralization metaphor further, it is the musical counterreformation in America. In the 1960s the building of the great architectural monuments, such as Lincoln Center, was part of the same tendency. Sacralization in this case meant going back to religious roots, but not the religious roots of Americanism that Johnson talks about — rather the religious roots of the conservatives.

But while Mason and his followers triumphed, other voices could not be silenced entirely. By then the issue had shifted from sacred church music to secular instrumental music. Led by John S. Dwight, founder of the Harvard Musical Association and the most important musical journal in the nineteenth century, *Dwight's Journal of Music,* champion of abstract sacralized instrumental music, psalmody gave way to symphony. And coloring everything was the specter of romanticism. Romanticism redefined not only music but the very nature of art and the most fundamental images that the public had of the artist.[3]

By the late nineteenth century most American composers had reconciled romanticism and the sacralized image of music that Dwight propagated, but in the first half of the century one composer synthesized his own brand of romanticism, creating a life and a body of work that are unique in the history of American music. Anthony Philip Heinrich is America's nineteenth-century maverick, and his story unfolds on the backdrop of the many tensions surrounding art music in the nineteenth century, as Americans grasped to come to terms with the very nature of the medium.

Heinrich's story almost did not get told. In 1917 Oscar Sonneck, head of the Music Division of the Library of Congress, acquired the papers and manuscripts of Heinrich. What he found startled him. The collection was massive, containing scrapbooks of newspaper clippings, many published compositions, and manuscripts of large, grandiose works — some twelve hundred pages all together. Sonneck called it "out of the ordinary in every respect."[4]

Heinrich, the papers revealed, had been one of the most respected composers of antebellum America. He had written some 350 compositions. He was active in Philadelphia, Boston, and New York, and had been one of the principal founders of the New York Philharmonic Orchestra. He had been showered with benefit concerts, even grand festivals in his honor, and was known in London and Austria as well as the United States. One contemporary writer had called him "the Beethoven of America." After examining the collection, Sonneck judged Heinrich "easily the most commanding figure as a composer in America before 1860."

Yet that was not what startled Sonneck. Oscar Sonneck, holder of the most important position in musical scholarship in the United States at the time, universally recognized as the preeminent scholar of American music, had never even heard of Heinrich. He was not mentioned in any of the major histories of American music. His works were in no publishers' catalogues, and Sonneck could not recall ever having seen his name on a program. Heinrich had been lost to time.[5]

How could someone of Heinrich's stature so totally disappear to posterity? Making the question even more puzzling was Heinrich's own life and work. Both were far from ordinary. Indeed, both verged on the bizarre. Sonneck dubbed Heinrich "the oddest figure in American musical history." A maverick in every respect, Heinrich carved his career through sheer persistence and dogged resolution, a career that abounded in contradictions. This quality fascinated Sonneck.

In one sense Heinrich was typical of his age. In imitation of early European romantic composers, he wrote huge orchestral works that incorporated many programmatic themes important to antebellum America. He experimented with an expanding chromatic vocabulary. But Heinrich's vision was also his undoing. His compositions were too different and too bizarre; they exceeded the abilities of any orchestra in the country. Heinrich could not confine himself to the limitations of his time. After he was no longer there to press for the performance of these daunting works, no orchestra would touch them.

Heinrich proudly proclaimed himself an American composer well before Ralph Waldo Emerson's call to take up such a cause in literature. He sought to portray himself and his compositions as a product of the American imagination as well as the wilderness itself. Heinrich was, however, born and raised in Austria, and he did not even begin to compose until he was thirty-six years old. A merchant by profession, he came to the United States as a young man already established in his career. He had inherited from his foster father a prosperous international business, dealing in linen, thread, wine, and financial exchange. He worked hard to expand it and became one of the most prominent merchants in Bohemia. This took him throughout Europe and eventually to the United States. Heinrich's movements are not clear, but sometime before 1810 he married a young woman from Boston, and by 1810 he was in Philadelphia, directing the orchestra of the Southwark Theatre as an amateur without compensation. He had studied violin and piano as a child and had purchased a valuable Cremona violin in his earlier travels.[6]

Then disaster struck. The Napoleonic wars had seriously weakened the Austrian economy, and Heinrich's own business had been threatened. Rumors of financial speculation and dishonesty engulfed the European banking industry, and only through direct contact and a full accounting to all his merchants was Heinrich able to escape the storm. But his position was seriously weakened, and he brought a shipload of Bohemian glassware to America to recoup and open new markets. At first it seemed to work. In 1811, however, the Austrian government went bankrupt, and with that Heinrich was wiped out, totally.

We know nothing about the next two years, but by 1813 he had decided to return to Austria. After a long and difficult trip he and his wife arrived at his family home in Schönlinde. Soon a daughter, Antonia, was born. Heinrich's wife had been seriously weakened by such an arduous journey while pregnant and found herself in a harsh climate and a country whose customs and language were unfamiliar. She became desperately homesick and her health deteriorated alarmingly. They decided to return immediately to Boston, but they were forced to leave Antonia in Austria with a distant relative, probably because of her mother's health. Heinrich would not see his daughter for another twenty years.

The travel proved too much for Heinrich's wife, and she died shortly after returning to Boston. By 1814, Heinrich had lost his business and his wife, and his only child was a continent away. One more brief attempt to resume a business career, as the American agent for the Austrian export firm Theodore Loehley, proved abortive. Through no fault of Heinrich, Loehley's business failed, and Heinrich was again without resources or income. According to his own account he was at one time worth more than one million Austrian florins, which would make him a multimillionaire in today's U.S. dollars.[7] By 1814 he had nothing left.

Heinrich was in Philadelphia when Loehley went under, and to earn a living he returned to the Southwark Theatre orchestra, this time as a professional. From this point on Heinrich's life was governed by two passions, music and a burning desire to be reunited with his daughter. Neither proved easy, and for the next forty years he showed remarkable persistence and resilience in the face of enormous odds and setbacks.

Soon after joining the Southwark Theatre orchestra Heinrich was in-

vited to become musical director at the Theatre in Pittsburgh. Utterly destitute, he made the three-hundred-mile journey on foot; once there, he found,
in the words of a contemporary, "Such a theatre! the poorest apology for one
I had then ever seen." That mattered little, because it folded almost immediately after Heinrich arrived. Again out of a job, he decided not to return but
to continue west, to Lexington, Kentucky.[8]

The decision seems strange, particularly given Heinrich's desire to be reunited with his daughter, and the difficulty of inland transmountain travel.
Heinrich had no job offers, and travel to Lexington involved a four-hundred-
mile trip down the Ohio River, along the very edge of the frontier, and then
another sixty miles overland. But Lexington was the largest city west of the Alleghenies, and by 1817 it had become well known as the cultural center of the
west. It boasted the first higher educational institution in the west, Transylva-
nia University, and it had an active theatrical life. While in Pittsburgh, Heinrich had undoubtedly heard of Samuel Drake, who had brought his troupe
there in 1815 and found prospects so dismal that he left as soon as possible for
Lexington. Drake and his family were warmly received in Kentucky, and by
1817 he had established a theatrical empire featuring regular performances
in Lexington, Louisville, Frankfort, and Cincinnati. Spinoffs from his company went as far as Nashville and Fayatteville, Arkansas.[9]

Lexington provided a magnet and some vague possibilities, a chance to
shine in an environment without a lot of professional competition. Heinrich
had only just decided to turn professional, and he admitted later that he still
had much to learn. But he was also fascinated with the west. The grandeur of
nature, the enormous expanses of forest wilderness, and the many powerful
and unusual sights found in the western United States became principal
themes in his music. That was all to come later, however. At this time Heinrich was not a composer, and he left no record of these impressions. Later he
claimed he went to Lexington hoping that solitude in the wilderness would
soothe his grief. Motivation or romantic revision, it is difficult to know. But
his wanderlust was lifelong and insatiable, and the trek to Pittsburgh had
been both splendorous and arduous, the ascent over the Alleghenies through
dense foliage and virgin forests quite different from the more tamed landscape and settled roads of Europe and the eastern United States. The journey
to Lexington was if anything more spectacular; the upper portions of the
Ohio River, with its steep ascents on either side, had scenery rivaled only by
the Hudson.[10]

Once in Lexington, Heinrich wasted no time. He organized a benefit
concert that included a performance of Beethoven's First Symphony, "with
full band." This was only the second performance of a Beethoven symphony

in America. How he managed to pull it off in Lexington in 1817 is a mystery. Orchestral performances even in Boston, Philadelphia, and New York were plagued by a scarcity of personnel, particularly string players, and Beethoven symphonies, including the First, were considered difficult pieces at the time. Reviews from the early nineteenth century make it clear that the performance level was, by modern standards, abysmal, even in the most prestigious ensembles on the East Coast. In Lexington? How many true violinists, violists, cellists, and double bass players could be found? Were there any bassoons? No details are available, but Heinrich's proclamation of a "full band" suggests that he was able to assemble at least a passable array of forces for the performance. What the performance sounded like must be left to the imagination.[11]

Sometime between this inaugural concert and the spring of 1818 Heinrich became seriously ill with a high fever. This led to one of the defining events of his life. He retreated to a small log cabin near Bardstown to convalesce. In the isolated forest setting of Kentucky, Heinrich took up serious practice on the violin. This event later not only became a turning point but was quickly elevated to an antebellum conversion experience. In 1828 the London *Quarterly Musical Magazine and Review* described it: "His remittances failed, and he retired to the back settlements. During his solitary abidance in the wild, his eye one day lighted upon his violin which hung against the side of his hut, and which brought him back to the recollection of the advances he had formerly made in the art. He set to serious practice, and never having been taught the elements of harmony, he formed a theory of his own. His progress was sufficient to enable him to teach in some of the towns of America, from whence he at length came to England."[12]

The image is pure romanticism in its depiction of Heinrich, alone in his "solitary abidance in the wild," seeking to console himself, suddenly noticing his violin, and rekindling his fervor for the art. Of course Heinrich had abandoned his career as a merchant long before to take up music as a profession; he had walked to Pittsburgh from Philadelphia to assume a post as leader of a theater orchestra; he had arranged a concert as soon as he arrived in Lexington. But this is not just a story about Heinrich. It is about antebellum America. Rebirth occurs in the nurturing bosom of nature. The Arcadia of America becomes the prime inspiration of art. Billings, it seems, had it right all along.

In this case nature inspired Heinrich to do more than hone his skills on the violin. During those months in the cabin he also decided to become a composer. He had previous instruction in both violin and piano, but he knew that as a composer he was untutored. He himself claimed that he began to compose and develop a theory of harmony and composition only at this time. Heinrich also indicated that the original stimulus to compose came from the outside: "In the spring of 1818 J. R. Black, a young student of Bardstown, Kentucky, attracted by my well known seclusion in a retired log-house interrupted my studious application on the violin, by desiring me to adjust the following ode from Collins to music. I took pencil and instantaneously reciprocated with the present melody which in fact became the basis of all my after efforts. A. P. H."[13]

Heinrich threw himself into composition, and by early 1820 at the latest had completed the *The Dawning of Music in Kentucky*, a collection of songs, solo instrumental works for both piano and violin, and one remarkable piece for chamber ensemble, the "Yankee Doodleiad." All together, *Dawning* comprises 269 pages of often dense and complex music.

Later Heinrich made much of his stay in the log cabin, converting it with the skill of a twentieth-century spin doctor into an American legend. He never ceased to remind friends and public alike of the birth of his art in the Kentucky wilderness. Like Billings, his muse was nature, and Heinrich not only proclaimed this proudly but wrapped it in patriotic garb. Nature, the wilderness, the log cabin, made Heinrich an American composer. This was a time when few other Americans even ventured to compose, much less attempted to define an American school. In that regard Heinrich was at least seventy years ahead of his time.

Any later claims aside, Heinrich did not write the bulk of *Dawning* in the log cabin. In fact he spent only a small fraction of his time in Kentucky there. Accounts are not specific, but we know that Heinrich was in his log cabin by the spring of 1818 and was living as a guest on the estate of Judge John Speed near Louisville by January 5, 1819, where he remained for two years. His stay in the log cabin was likely confined to the warm months of 1818 and was almost certainly less than one year. It was essentially an idyllic summer.

The Dawning of Music in Kentucky was, like Billings's *New-England Psalm-Singer*, a bolt out of the blue, unexpected, unpredictable, and in content startling. With Heinrich, however, the locus had shifted from Puritan-revolutionary New England to the trans-Allegheny west. Nature remained a constant, but Heinrich's was a nature of romanticism, the nature of the Hudson River painters, the nature of grandeur. His music reflects these themes both in choice of subject matter and in style.

Heinrich wrote more than the *Dawning* while in Kentucky. In 1821 his melodrama *Child of the Mountain, or The Deserted Mother* was produced at the Walnut Street Theatre in Philadelphia. This was a major coup for Heinrich. Philadelphia was the largest city in the United States, and the Walnut Street was its most prestigious theater. It was essentially the same company that had been at the Chestnut Street Theatre, which had been destroyed by fire in 1820. Heinrich had theatrical connections in Philadelphia from his previous stay, and at least one actor, a Mr. Blissett, had been a member of both Drake's company in Lexington and the Chestnut Street Theatre. After the premiere of *Child of the Mountain*, Heinrich remained in Philadelphia to give a benefit concert, an elaborate event assisted by an ensemble that was about to become the Musical Fund Society Orchestra. Thirteen pieces by Heinrich, mostly songs, were performed at this concert.

Soon, though, the composer returned to Kentucky. Were the plays and the concert a success? Not enough to encourage Heinrich to settle in Philadelphia, but at the very least they strengthened and solidified his ties with the American stage in the early 1820s.

Within a year of returning to Kentucky, Heinrich's compositional efforts received a ringing endorsement from Boston in the form of a lengthy, laudatory review of *Dawning* in the *Euterpeiad*. The *Euterpeiad* was the first, and until the late 1830s the only, sustained musical journal devoted to serious criticism in America. It was founded in 1820 by John Rowe Parker, who had previously written a musical column in the *Boston Intelligencer and Musical Gazette*. Parker was a member of the wealthier merchant class and had a keen amateur interest in secular art music. It was relatively unusual for anyone in Boston to think of secular music in terms of art and progress as Parker did, and it was almost unheard of for a member of the merchant class to actively participate in music.

To Parker, Heinrich represented something not seen before in America. Stressing that *Dawning* is an "*American production*," he praised Heinrich for his "vigour of thought, variety of ideas, originality of conception, classical correctness, boldness and luxuriance of imagination." Parker's imagery is romantic: he refers to the "transformation" that Heinrich underwent in Kentucky and the composer's possession of "the key which unlocks to him the temple of science and enables him to explore with fearless security the mysterious labyrinth of harmony." Parker's accolade culminates in the pronouncement of Heinrich not only as a genius but as "*the Beethoven* of America."[14]

Parker also hinted that Heinrich had been active in New York, or at the very least that his music was known there, referring to a ballet, *La Belle Peruvienne*, for which Heinrich wrote at least some of the music but received no credit.

Heinrich in Boston

Spurred by Parker's words, Heinrich decided to leave Kentucky and try his fortune in Boston. Seldom was a musician so set up for success. Parker had further prepared the way with several follow-up articles in the *Euterpeiad*. Heinrich probably had additional connections through his theatrical activities in Kentucky, Philadelphia, and New York. His timing was ideal. The Philoharmonic Society of Boston, originally a group of amateurs who met privately to play orchestral works, had only recently become more professional and begun to present public concerts. Heinrich was offered its services for a benefit concert.

He arrived in 1823 as a conquering hero. The newspapers greeted his coming with pride and delight. The *Daily Advertiser* called him "the first regular or general *American* composer"; the log cabin in Kentucky had transformed even the nationality of this Austrian immigrant with a heavy German accent. The *Daily Advertiser* went further, however. It perceived that Heinrich was a man on the way up — "his fame is rising fast" — and equated attendance at his benefit concert with a demonstration of cultural superiority. "America will have good reason to be proud of him; while those who now patronize him, do best establish their foremost claim to taste, discernment, and liberality." The association of a certain type of music with taste may seem commonplace today, but in 1820 New England it was unusual.[15]

Heinrich himself knew how to exploit his own legend as the "log cabin composer." In a "card" published in a Boston newspaper, in a burst of modesty that reminded everyone of Parker's praise, Heinrich called himself "the humble Minstrel of the Western Wilds," speaking of his "adventurous muse which sprang in sequestered wildernesses, deep in the West." He soon followed *Dawning* with a shorter collection called *The Western Minstrel*.[16]

In spite of this unprecedented publicity campaign, Heinrich's concert was not a financial success; newspapers reported that receipts fell short of expenses. Yet his reception was better than what most musicians experienced at this time. Making a living in music was precarious in Federal America, and those who succeeded did so as much by versatility as persistence. They would move from one city to another until prospects appeared favorable, and then settle in to patch together whatever living was possible. For instrumental musicians this usually meant playing in a theater orchestra, something Heinrich did, teaching, possibly operating a music store or publishing business, and securing whatever odd musical jobs might come their way. Heinrich seems to have been unable or temperamentally unsuited to undertake such a career, the same way that Mozart could never have been content at the court of Salzburg. Possibly Heinrich's merchant days still haunted him.

After three years in Boston, Heinrich suddenly decided to return to Europe. The move appears precipitous and caught many by surprise, but Heinrich apparently had been laying preparations for some time. Beginning in 1823 and concluding in 1826 his third major publication, *The Sylviad*, appeared. It was a large collection comparable to *Dawning*; in fact, Heinrich called it a "sequel." If anything it was even more dense, virtuosic, and complex. Heinrich seems to have had a purpose for such a display, however. *The Sylviad* was dedicated to the Royal Academy of Music in London. As his own vision of a self-consciously learned style, he almost certainly intended it to be his entry into the European music world.

Like the *Dawning*, *The Sylviad* is a curious collection of disparate elements ranging from reels, cotillions, and songs to two highly virtuosic toccatas. There are unusual items, such as the "Barbecue Divertimento, Comprising the Ploughman's Grand March and the Negro's Banjo Quickstep." Predating Louis Gottschalk's piece "The Banjo" by thirty years, it is one of the first attempts by a European composer to capture the sounds of the banjo in print. It is also one of the few examples we have of the banjo style that predates the changes assumed to have occurred around midcentury.

Even Heinrich's less pretentious pieces are ornate and difficult. He dedicated a fancy cotillion to "Great Britain's Fair" — but this is no dilettante music designed to be played easily at home. Abounding in thirty-second notes, thirty-second-note triplets, rapid double thirds, and chromaticism, it would have been a challenge to most amateur pianists. The cotillion is followed by a Fantasy, "alla Pretense."

By far the most imposing piece technically was Heinrich's "Gran Toccata Cromatica," appropriately dedicated to "Dr. William Crotch, President of the Royal Academy of Music." The composer laid on the flattery with an aside, "chromatic ears are as rare as diamonds." The piece begins with much sound and fury, followed by an interlude, a set of variations on a simple 3/4 theme, and a *perpetuum mobile* "Finale o Fantasia Tripolata," based on sixteenth-note triplets. At one point in the first section Heinrich introduces 2048th-notes (nine beams).

When Heinrich ventures into counterpoint, his real lack of learning shows. Since the Middle Ages, handling of counterpoint was the test sine qua non for the composer. Mozart, Haydn, and Beethoven all worked hard to develop contrapuntal skills, which often came only after many hours of study and labor. With few models and no teacher, Heinrich's contrapuntal efforts

Anthony Philip Heinrich, "Great Britain's Fair"

are at best limited. His most extensive contrapuntal foray in *The Sylviad* occurs in a "Canone Funerale," which he possibly tries to excuse as "An American National Dirge." A basic four-note motive is over-repeated between two
voices with minimal offset, and when Heinrich finally reaches a cadence, he
botches that, avoiding parallel octaves, a compositional no-no, only by delay-

ing the resolution of one of the voices. The solution does not solve the problem.

The Sylviad is more than an attempted technical tour de force. It is also an extensive autobiographical statement, played out in the songs. This is most apparent in "The Log House," a song that became Heinrich's personal trademark. It was later performed frequently on his programs in both the United States and Europe, and Heinrich arranged it for orchestra and voice.

The piece begins, almost literally, with the cover. According to Richard Wolfe, it was the first song printed in America with a dated lithographic cover.[17] This cover depicts a log cabin with Heinrich seated, clearly identifiable, at the left, one of the few portraits we have of him. He is lost in his work, and manuscript papers are scattered about, each identified by title. To the right, looking around the corner on the porch of the cabin, is a black man, curious about what Heinrich is doing. Except that the composer is sitting

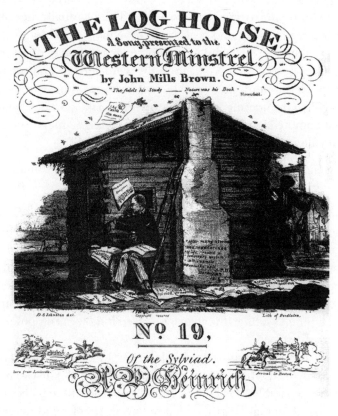

Anthony Philip Heinrich, "The Log House," lithographic cover

and writing rather than playing the violin, reference to his reported encounter with a Negro is clear.[18] John Mills is credited with the text, which he
presented to Heinrich, who is called the "Western Minstrel." Below the picture are two smaller drawings: one on the right titled "arrival in Boston"
shows Heinrich being welcomed there, and the one on the left, "departure
from Louisville," shows him on a winged horse, apparently fleeing a hostile
crowd. Did Heinrich have to leave suddenly under some sort of cloud? The
sources are silent on that.

The song itself, which Heinrich calls "A Sylvan Bravura," is a miniature
scene, a series of individual songs: "The Log House," "Il Malinconico," "Il
Entusiasta," and "Il Romantico." Heinrich makes it clear in both the musical
notation and with explicit directions that these are to be performed as a unit.
The song depicts a log cabin where the "endless wood sighs to the rushing
Cat'ract's flood," Heinrich's own arrival, "He came a wand'ring, wayward
Child; A Native flower, free and wild; With ardour fierce! With feelings
mild," and how music transformed him, "Tis Genius' boon, Then swept his
Minstrel Lyre and smil'd; For Fear had flown." This is virtually the entire text,
which is repeated, varied, and broken up throughout the different sections.

The vocal line is filled with bel canto ornamentation and text painting.
Running thirty-second notes appear on the word "flown" and ornamented
triadic leaps on the word "ardour." The melody drops almost two octaves on
the words "The thundering fall! The thundering fall!" On one point of extreme text compression, the music has an ascending C-major scale in half
notes, with alternating dynamics:

"mild,	fierce,	mild,	fierce,	mild,	fierce,	mild,"
p	*f*	*p*	*f*	*p*	*f*	*p*

Apart from these flights the vocal line is diatonic and relatively straightforward, with many sequences. The piano part varies immensely, from simple Alberti bass accompaniments to virtuosic cadenza passages to one or two
rudimentary attempts at polyphonic imitation. At times it follows the voice
closely, at other times interacts dramatically with it. The overall effect is of a
bravura operatic scene. In spite of the meager lyrics and the obviousness of
much of Heinrich's setting, the song has power. It shows a composer familiar
at least with the stage.

Yet was Heinrich writing true autobiography or further creating and
glossing his myth? It is hard to tell, and it may not matter. The two blend until they are inseparable. It is hard to come away from these pieces with any
opinion other than that Heinrich believed his own story, and never tired of
reminding the listener of it.

Heinrich in London with a Boston Interlude

Heinrich's stay in London began propitiously. He charmed one London reporter who described him as "truly entusiaste per la musica" and a "musician by nature" rather than by profession, "as music appears to be with him rather a natural instinct than an artificial requirement." This same reporter also characterized him as a man combining "great genius with the utmost simplicity of manner and character." Another London newspaper carried an article entitled "Remarkable Story of A. P. Heinrich," which related his experiences in Kentucky.[19]

None of that, however, could translate into performances. He dedicated several of his compositions to Mrs. Coutts, Duchess of St. Albans and a known patron of music, but they were returned without so much as a word of encouragement. Without patronage, Heinrich had little chance of success, as the writer of the "Remarkable Story of A. P. Heinrich" correctly observed.

Puzzled by a lack of public interest in his music, Heinrich turned to Sir Thomas Moore for an explanation. Moore was the author of *Irish Melodies*, a collection of folklike songs that had unprecedented success in both Great Britain and the United States. Moore examined a set of canzonets that Heinrich sent him and summarized the American composer's problem in one word: simplify. Moore told Heinrich that his compositions did not meet with much favor because the harmonies had too much science, "so far beyond the capacity or powers of execution of any of our ordinary amateurs of music." He then counseled Heinrich to "keep your science a little more in the background, and not let it interfere so much with the simplicity of your airs," and acknowledged that he was giving advice because "popularity is your object." The tone of Moore's letter suggests that Heinrich wrote to Moore expressing concern about his lack of popularity.[20]

Moore's criticism reinforces statements in the *Quarterly Musical Magazine and Review*, a London journal that reviewed a group of songs Heinrich had published in London. The anonymous reviewer refers to them as "most strange and wild," saying that at first he thought they were a joke, "satires upon the newest taste in vocal ornament." But the reviewer was won over: although they "frequently come upon the ear with a force that science may indeed disallow, but can hardly disapprove," the songs nevertheless "display extraordinary power and prove the author to be a genius."[21]

Both Moore's letter and this review contain striking parallels to the criticism that Johann Adolph Scheibe leveled on J. S. Bach a century earlier, that the composer suffered from too much science, that he was incapable of doing something simple, that he had a strong will and mind. There are notice-

able differences, however: Bach was criticized because he was too conservative, maintaining a style that had gone out of fashion. Heinrich was essentially untaught, and his style was his own; his music was strange and bizarre,
and "resembled nothing that we have ever seen before."[22]

Heinrich has not fared well with twentieth-century critics. John Tasker
Howard, disappointed because Heinrich, the first American composer to
create a large body of instrumental music, did not measure up, could hardly
contain his disdain: "The only thing missing is the genius. His friends hailed
him as the Beethoven of America, but the only similarity was that he may
have written as many notes." Yet should Heinrich be judged by the standards
of European art music? Is his music inferior, or is it different? Different indeed it is, but what is its frame of reference?[23]

From his earliest compositions through *The Sylviad,* Heinrich's music
was not a romanticized high art. It is not a music of the large-scale, abstract
structures of sonata form, or of fugue, of the common-practice, expanded,
tension-sustaining tonality of eighteenth- and nineteenth-century Europe. It
starts in a different place than Beethoven, Mozart, or Bach did. At its core
Heinrich's is a music from below — a music of fun, of simplicity, a music of
and for the people — that is made ornate by Heinrich's own febrile imagination. It is the music of the dance, the music of song, the music of the fiddle. It
is an expansion and elaboration on simple themes. A critic in 1853 nailed it:
"simple harmonies united to melodies highly florid."[24]

Heinrich's musical sources are twofold: first, popular or folk dance and
song. Music that demands embellishment, either in the tradition of improvisatory variation, as dance music does, or in the strophic tradition, whereby
in practice the performers add interest through often subtle changes in later
verses. Heinrich inherited both the style and the procedure — that is, both
the music and the elaborative approach. His second source was the stage:
Heinrich's is the music of the theater, but the early Federal American theater, a place of rowdiness, familiarity, and shirtsleeve passions. Much of early
Heinrich is the music of show, of the razzler-dazzler, the virtuoso reduced to
the most elemental tricks. The theater in which Heinrich lived and worked
would present Shakespeare one night and tightrope walkers, knife-throwers,
and fire-eaters the next. To Heinrich, this was art.

Antebellum theater was also a world of a purposeful, almost adolescent
self-consciousness, a world in which the figures on the stage were both close
and believable; in an America of village values, the stage was the village in
microcosm. A theatrical evening was an interplay, between the actors, perceived in part as characters in their roles and in part as entertainers whose
personalities, foibles, and faults were known, and an audience that was often

involved directly and overtly in the entertainment. The theater was boisterous, even riotous, with the separation between audience and performer often as blurred as the distinction between actor and part. In this context Heinrich's self-deprecating manner, his autobiographical compositions, and his offering to sing the most personal songs in spite of his own admitted shortcomings as a singer were comparable to a guest being invited to entertain host, family, and friends in a colloquy in which the rules were informal and the pleasure dependent on personal bonds established.

In such circumstances the standards of Mozart or Beethoven simply do not apply, and to criticize Heinrich's music on those grounds is to miss the point. But, and here is the catch, Heinrich *wanted* them to apply; he wanted to emulate high art, and therein lay his aesthetic undoing. In attempting to do so he created a dichotomy of his own making.

Like any composer, Heinrich in Kentucky was writing what he knew: dance forms, both German and American, and music for the stage, which included a smattering of opera. His instrumental pieces not only begin with these sources, but they form their principal limitation. Most of his instrumental works are extended variations, whether so titled or not. His choice of material provides little scope for harmonic expansion or development. A Mozart or a Beethoven could of course find such potential in the simplest of tunes, and imaginatively exploit what lay hidden. Heinrich had not that ability at the time, in part because he did not know what was possible. He wanted to write art music but had little experience of what others had done, at least at the level of compositional understanding. Consequently he drew on models not conducive to the creation of works of artistic scope and depth. His proclivity for harmonic complexity and melodic elaboration are extreme, but without the experience of models he was essentially out of control. Heinrich was thus forced to graft elaborate solutions onto material inconsistent with such attempts. His music suffers because there is a dichotomy between material and technique on one hand and intention on the other.

In London, Heinrich was once again reduced to earning a subsistence playing in the Drury Lane and Vauxhall Gardens orchestras. But he continued to compose, and in 1831 his music took another new direction. He composed *Pushmataha*, his first large orchestral work, and his first piece based programmatically on the American Indians. From this point on, Heinrich's major efforts would center on the orchestra, with nature and the American Indian as principal topics.[25] In the next four years Heinrich wrote for orchestra *Tower of Babel, or, The Languages Confounded*, *Complaint of Logan the Mingo Chief, the Last of His Race*, *Schiller*, "Grande Sinfonia Dramatica," *The Treaty of William Penn with the Indians*, *Concerto for Kent Bugle or Klap-*

penflügel, which may be the same piece as *Washington Centennial Overture*, *Fair Daughters of the Western World*, "Capriccio Leggiadro Scherzevole per Grand Orchestra," later renamed *The Mocking Bird to the Nightingale*, *The Indian War Council*, "Gran Concerto Bellico, A grand heroic divertissement for forty-one instrumental parts," *O Santa Maria*, "motetto concertante," *The Ornithological Combat of Kings, or The Condor of the Andes and the Eagle of the Cordilleras*, and *Gran Sinfonia Eroica Jäger's Adieu*, based on his earlier song.

These are all lengthy works, all but three of them over fifty pages in score, and several are more than a hundred pages. And for the rest of his life Heinrich continued to concentrate on orchestral compositions, even though there was no immediate reason for doing so. None were written on commission, although one, *Ornithological Combat*, was submitted for a competition, and most were never performed in Heinrich's lifetime.

With these efforts Heinrich's style seems to have matured. His later songs, for instance, do not have the same ornamental overabundance but are simpler and more direct. Heinrich still thought extravagantly, only now much of the extravagance focused on the sheer forces of the orchestra. He conceived music for gigantic orchestras, sometimes with thirty or forty separate instrumental parts, often with unusual, even bizarre instrumental combinations. *The War of the Elements and the Thunder of Niagara*, for instance, has thirty separate parts, including six for percussion, all of which play simultaneously.

What motivated Heinrich's turn to orchestral music and to Native Americans as subject matter? The two are not unrelated. London broadened Heinrich's musical horizons considerably. Historians have depicted London in the early nineteenth century as a musical nadir, a characterization that is quite misleading. England of this time produced few major composers, and musical activity in general was dominated by continental Europeans, either immigrants, such as Domenico Dragonetti, or frequent visitors like Felix Mendelssohn. But London was by far the largest city in Europe, its population exceeding one million. This compares with roughly 500,000 for Paris, 200,000 for New York, and 60,000 for Boston. And it had an extremely active concert life, certainly when compared with any other place Heinrich had been. In addition to opera, there were the Philharmonic Society Concerts as well as the Antient Concerts. Heinrich had little money to spend on concerts, and his work in the Drury Lane Theatre and Vauxhall Gardens occupied him most evenings, but even there the level of musicianship was certainly higher than in the United States. Drury Lane was under the musical direction of John Braham, one of the great nineteenth-century tenors.

It is hard to know how many concerts Heinrich attended, but apparently he was not entirely out of the loop. One of the major musical events in 1829 was Felix Mendelssohn's visit. He arrived in London on March 21, went to Scotland June 28, and returned to London on September 10. According to a letter Heinrich wrote many years later, he met Mendelssohn, dined with him, and actually had Mendelssohn visit his lodgings. Although there is no other confirmation of this event, something like it could very well have taken place, perhaps as a chance encounter. Both composers were native German speakers, and Heinrich could be quite engaging with his Baroque pomp and enthusiasm. There is no reason that he might not charm Mendelssohn, and no question Heinrich would try. From there Mendelssohn could have called on Heinrich or accompanied him to his lodgings.

Whatever actually took place, Heinrich throughout his life had a special fondness for Mendelssohn, and something did occur to change Heinrich's entire compositional direction. After 1829 the elaborate, effusive, overarticulated piano and violin pieces and songs disappeared. His music for voice and piano became much simpler, but more important Heinrich turned, with almost a monomaniacal passion, to large-scale programmatic, evocative orchestral music. At this time Mendelssohn had just been inspired to begin the *Hebrides Overture*, a pivotal work both for him and for his age. Called by Thomas Grey the "paradigmatic Mendelssohnian 'landscape' piece," it opened new dimensions to descriptive orchestral music for the entire nineteenth century. Mendelssohn may well have played some of it for Heinrich, spoken about what he was doing, and struck a chord, figuratively as well as literally. We know that Heinrich was highly responsive to the efforts of outstanding musicians — a visit by Nicolò Paganini to London in 1831 inspired him to write *Storio d'violin*, a work that takes violin virtuosity to heights of excess seldom achieved since. The final note is thirteen ledger lines above the staff, a note not even within the range of hearing of most humans.[26]

Simply put, whatever happened between Heinrich and Mendelssohn personally, Mendelssohn's visit to London seems to have been the impetus for Heinrich's sudden turn to orchestral programmatic music. But where did the Indians come from?

Heinrich's interest in the American Indian is as unanticipated as his style change. Dealing with Native Americans as subject matter was unprecedented in American or European music, and no other composer attempted to do so extensively until nearly the end of the nineteenth century. Once again Heinrich was at least half a century ahead of his time.

For many, Heinrich's Indians resided in the wilds of Kentucky, a view that surfaced in his lifetime: "Father Heinrich passed several years of his life

among the Indians that once inhabited Kentucky, and many of his compositions refer to these original companions. He is a species of musical Catlin,
painting his dusky friends on the music staff instead of the canvas, and composing laments, symphonies, dirges, and war-songs, on the most intensely Indian subjects. He would be the very one to set Hiawatha to music."[27]

Heinrich as a musical Catlin! A glib, flattering, and tempting portrait.
George Catlin, born in Philadelphia in 1796, was trained as a lawyer but decided to take up portrait painting. In 1824 he was in Washington when Pushmataha, a Choctaw chief, led a delegation of Indians to sign a treaty with the
federal government. He was so impressed with the Indians' quiet dignity and
their colorful ceremonial dress that he decided to dedicate himself to painting their world. He made several trips west, and in hundreds of paintings he
depicted a way of life that was soon to vanish, crushed under the Europeans'
imperatives of manifest destiny.

Heinrich, unfortunately, was no musical Catlin. He saw few Indians in
Kentucky; he admitted that "the yell of the war-whoop has become tacet"
there, and "the whistling of the tomahawk and other Furiosos of the ruthless
savage [has] ceased to vibrate." The "ruthless savage": his view at the time is
a manifest-destiny cliché, and his one musical piece that deals with the Indians before 1830, "The Sons of the Woods, an Indian Warsong," depicts Indian
warriors bent on revenge. Later, in Boston, London, and New York, he would
have had even fewer encounters with Indians.[28]

A number of books describing the American Indians appeared in the
nineteenth century, and Heinrich himself admitted that at least two of them
influenced him: John McIntosh, *The Origin of the North American Indians*,
and Maximilian, Prince of Wied, *Travels in the Interior of North America*,
1832–1834. For some scholars this settles the question: Heinrich's programs
came from these books.[29]

Yet this solution falls under its own chronology. Both books appeared in
1843, and Heinrich's interest in the American Indian not only began in 1831
but was intense throughout the 1830s. He may have learned from McIntosh
and Maximilian, but they were neither his inspiration nor his impetus.
Something else motivated him.

For Heinrich the source was close to home: it was the stage itself. Between 1820 and 1855, precisely the years that Heinrich not only was active as
a composer but was in the theater pits, plays portraying a sympathetic, sensitive, romantic Indian were common. The progenitor was Robert Rogers's
Ponteach: Or the Savages in America, written in 1766. It depicts a struggle between Ponteach, the epitome of Jean-Jacques Rousseau's noble savage, and
the European invaders, the emblem of corruption, who try to seduce her.

With nature on her side Ponteach triumphs. *Ponteach* was published in London but never produced.

The first play on an Indian theme to gain wide acceptance on the stage was James Nelson Barker's *The Indian Princess; or, La Belle Sauvage*, which first appeared at the Chestnut Street Theatre in Philadelphia on April 6, 1808. The play tells the story of Pocahontas and John Smith, setting Pocahontas in a romantic landscape reminiscent of the later Hudson River school of painters, and portraying her as so sensitive to nature as to be unwilling to kill even a bird. The play itself, particularly the climactic scene, in which Smith is prepared for execution, is a tour de force of romantic suspense. It was successful on both sides of the Atlantic, playing at the Drury Lane Theatre in London in 1820.

By the 1820s plays with Indian motifs were popular on the American stage, and between 1820 and the mid-1850s there were many. The most successful was John Augustus Stone's *Metamora: or The Last of the Wampanoags*, which opened at the Park Theatre in New York on December 15, 1829. Written for the actor Edwin Forrest, the play owed much of its success to his portrayal of Metamora. It was performed almost continuously for the next twenty-five years throughout the United States and spawned many further plays on the noble-savage theme.

How much did Heinrich know about these plays? He probably saw some himself, but regardless, in the world of Anglo-American theater, still a single world, news traveled fast. No question he would have heard of Forrest's success.

Heinrich did have direct involvement with one piece based on an American Indian theme, the ballet *La Belle Peruvienne*, for which he wrote some of the music. It appeared in New York on March 18, 1822. Under the direction of a Monsieur Labasse, it created a sensation, particularly because of Labasse's dancing. The *New York Evening Post* ran an unusually long review and description of the piece.[30] Essentially a variant of *La Belle Sauvage*, the story is the Pocahontas plot set in Peru; it involves a shipwrecked European, an Indian princess who falls in love with him, and two young Indian chiefs, one good, the other evil, who want the princess for themselves. At the climax of the story the princess saves the European, who has been condemned to death, using herself as a shield. All is well in the end.

There is no direct attribution of the music in either the playbill or the review. The reviewer assumes it was by "the best of modern composers, Mozart, Beethoven, and Rossini, if we are not mistaken," and observes that it "suits itself to the ear and the understanding of a mixt audience," meaning it was not too difficult or abstract. It was not uncommon for music to pass generally unnoticed or only vaguely acknowledged by theatrical reviewers, with few at the time competent to discuss it in any detail.

According to John Rowe Parker, Heinrich contributed much of the music. In addition to "other fragments" Parker specifically identifies the opening piece in the ballet as Heinrich's "March of Kinsky" in *Dawning*, the music that accompanies the princess administering aid to the shipwrecked stranger as the song "From Thee Eliza I Must Go," and the European's claims of innocence as from the "Ode to the Memory of Commodore Perry." Thus in a most direct way, Heinrich was introduced to the Indian motive of the American stage.

Yet even though Heinrich's Indians are fictional characters that inhabited the stage, and Heinrich himself had few encounters with real Native Americans, there are parallels between him and Catlin. Both were part of a trend in literature of depicting an idealized, romantic Indian. James Fenimore Cooper's Leatherstocking novels had an immense influence at the time. Even though Cooper did present the Indian's dark side, as in his portrait of Huron Hagua in *The Last of the Mohicans*, Cooper's Indians were romantic creatures of fiction. They portray a vision of the Indian derived from Rousseau, the noble savage.

Even Catlin's paintings romanticized his subject. His portraits of individual Indians are detailed, powerful, and direct, but he depicted them as innocents in a nature that was exotic and pure. Well aware of what was to befall them, he described "these unsophisticated people," "in the innocent simplicity of nature," who "from the towering cliffs of the Rocky Mountains, . . . will turn back his swollen eyes on the illimitable hunting-grounds from which he has fled, and there contemplate, like Caius Marius on the ruins of Carthage, their splendid desolation."

The Hudson River school of painters reinforced this vision. The Hudson River painters focused on nature as grand, majestic. When the Indian appeared he was part of the setting. Thomas Cole's *Landscape Scene from The Last of the Mohicans* shows the warriors in a circle on a flat promontory next to a cliff. The warriors, located at the center of the canvas, are nevertheless dwarfed and dominated by huge rocks, the side of a mountain, and a larger mountain in the distance. One rock in particular looms over them, balanced as if in air. The Indian could be there because he *is* nature. "Like the forests, the Indian exists in a state of nature, before he is cut down."[31]

Heinrich's portraits are equally romantic. Following the precedent of the stage Heinrich took real people and real events but presented an idealized stereotype, a Rousseauean innocent inhabiting the pristine forest. He made no attempt to incorporate actual Indian music into these pieces. He was

George Catlin, *The Cheyenne Brothers Starting on Their Fall Hunt* (National Gallery of Art, Washington, D.C., Paul Mellon Collection)

probably unaware of Native American music and would have had few resources on it available in London had he tried to find them.

But why did Heinrich turn to the Indian theme in 1830, and specifically in London? Except for *La Belle Sauvage* there is little evidence of Indian plays appearing on the London stage, but there was a strain of exoticism at the time, with such plays as Carl Maria von Weber's *Abu Hassan*, Esprit Auber's *The Maid of Cashmere*, Henry Rowley Bishop's *Englishmen in India* and *The Fall of Algiers*, Rodolphe Kreutzer's *Lodoïska*, and Gioachino Rossini's *The Turkish Lovers*. All these works played at Drury Lane in the 1820s. Heinrich seems to have given up the possibility for the moment of traveling to Austria to see his daughter, probably because his finances were too precarious. We know that he cared immensely for her and that he wrote her frequently but heard virtually nothing from her, because, as Heinrich learned later, her letters did not go through. So, having failed in London both financially and artistically, Heinrich by this time was contemplating a return to Boston, where prospects might be better and where his compositions might gain him success. He did go back to Boston in 1831.

Thomas Cole, *Landscape Scene from The Last of the Mohicans* (Fenimore Art Museum, Cooperstown, N.Y.; photograph by Richard Walker)

Heinrich sought a topic for the orchestral music he was planning. He had been exposed to a level of artistry he had not encountered in America, he was inspired by Mendelssohn, and he had seen the effectiveness of exoticism on the London stage. He sought an *American* topic, and what combined the elements better — romanticism, exoticism, nature, and America itself — than its native inhabitants in the idealized versions then being popularized. Large programmatic orchestral works modeled on Mendelssohn's and based on Indian topics provided Heinrich precisely what he sought.

That Heinrich chose for his first effort the same event that inspired Catlin, Pushmataha's journey to Washington, was no coincidence. The Choctaw chief's visit to the nation's capital and his sudden and tragic death there was one of the major news stories of the 1820s. Pushmataha died, probably of pneumonia, as leader of a delegation of Choctaws negotiating a treaty with the federal government. His funeral in particular generated news because of the elaborate, colorful ceremony with which it was conducted.

When Heinrich returned to Boston in 1831, two concerts were held in his honor, but neither contained his new orchestral music. Boston orchestras may not have been ready for it. By 1833 he was back in London, this time apparently determined to get to Bohemia. He remained in London for two years, continuing to compose grandiose orchestral works. In 1835 he submitted one such work, *The Ornithological Combat of Kings, or The Condor of the Andes and the Eagle of the Cordilleras* to a competition that the *Concerts Spiritual* of Vienna announced, "fifty pounds for the best new grand symphony for a full orchestra." Throughout his life Heinrich thought this his best piece. Soon after, he began his journey to the continent, hoping for a reunion with his daughter and the triumphal recognition of his status as a composer. He was disappointed on both counts. He did not win the prize, and when he finally arrived at the home of Joseph Hladeks, the relative who had cared for her, he learned that she had just sailed to America in search of him. After twenty years of waiting they again found themselves on opposite sides of the Atlantic Ocean.

Heinrich did remain in Europe long enough to hear a concert of his music sponsored by the Styrian Musik-Verein in Vienna on June 9, 1836. There he heard, probably for the first time, some of his new orchestral compositions. The featured work was the first movement of the *Combat of the Condor*, billed as "*Der Kampf des Condor, amerikanisch charakteritisches Tongemählde* von Anton Philipp Heinrich of Kentucky." Kentucky! Heinrich had not lost his promotional touch.

According to Heinrich's own account there were not enough orchestral forces, particularly strings, to perform it properly, but reviews were favorable, even laudatory. August Mandel not only praised the entire concert, he discussed Heinrich's relationship to nature: "Heinrich's muse is the daughter of Nature, but not of that Nature whose quiet, idyllic grace possesses us all unconsciously. He has sought out Nature in her workshop where she produces her mighty works, where great bridges of rock are thrown across streams; . . . where great lakes plunge with deafening roar to the depths below, and the tornado, with its crashing strength lays bare the impenetrable secrets of the primeval forests." Mandel further compared Heinrich to Gaspare Spontini and Giacomo Meyerbeer, opera composers noted for grand romantic effect, and referred to Heinrich's "orchestral scores as broad as the falls of Niagara."[32]

There is no record of Heinrich's piece *The War of the Elements and the Thunder of Niagara* appearing on the program, but Mandel's comment suggests that the composer showed him the score. Heinrich himself thought highly of it, although he probably never heard it performed in his lifetime. Other than the coda, which he titled "The Thunder of Niagara," there are no programmatic descriptions. But Heinrich likely had a detailed program in mind. John Hill Hewitt described Heinrich's later performance of a piece on the piano for President John Tyler, presumably his *Jubilee, A Grand National Song of Triumph*, a multisection work that seems not to have had a fixed form, and Heinrich's running commentary suggests that Niagara may have been in mind. He describes parts "representing the breaking up of the frozen river Niagara, the thaw of the ice, and the dash of the mass over the mighty falls." Peace and plenty were represented by soft strains of pastoral music, while the thunder of our naval war-dogs and the rattle of our army musketry told of our prowess on sea and land." President Tyler's response tells much about the disconnect between Heinrich and his time. About halfway through, Tyler went over to the piano, put his hand on Heinrich's shoulder, and said, "That may be all very fine, sir, but can't you play us a good old Virginia reel."[33]

Yet in many ways Heinrich is representative of his time. *The Thunder of Niagara* and many other Heinrich pieces portray the nature of the great cataract canvases of Thomas Cole and Frederick Edwin Church. It is a histrionic, narrative vision of nature, overwhelming in its power and grandeur. It stands in diametrical opposition to the more intimate, contemplative vision of nature that the transcendentalists and luminist painters, such as Martin Johnson Heade, soon promulgated. In those two conceptions we encounter, in Barbara Novak's phrase, "grand opera and the still small voice."[34] Heinrich's allegiance is clear. His life, real and invented, his work, orchestral and otherwise, is grand opera at its most extravagant and theatrical.

Heinrich not only identified with a grand American nature but, as an immigrant, he probably believed the principal myths about America. His genius was that he knew how to exploit those myths. His pride in being an American, his subject matter, Native Americans and nature itself, not only connected him to the American wilderness when the wilderness was being redefined but conjured the image of pathfinder, of pioneer, the solitary individual who conquers alone, the self-made man, reliant on only his own resources. Like Cooper, Heinrich understood the myths Americans wanted to believe and sought to supply them. This encompassed not only the pieces he wrote but the image of the composer himself. He understood that an "aw shucks" attitude of a backwoods country boy would play well to both American and European audiences. His public persona was the coonskin cap Benjamin Franklin calculatingly donned when he became ambassador to France. All this worked even though Heinrich was anything but a backwoods country boy. He was a member of the Austrian upper class, a wealthy merchant who had grown up studying the violin in Austria, and who had on his European travels as a young man bought a valuable Cremona violin. Precisely because he was such an outsider, however, he could appreciate fully the myths that Americans wanted, whether they were real or not.

And few were as adept and tireless in their promotion of these myths as Heinrich. In the twentieth century Heinrich would be a press agent's dream. Indefatigable, he sensed all these themes and self-promoted them with a thoroughness and constancy scarcely found until the twentieth century. He constantly reminded his listeners that he was a product of nature, of the wilderness, and of America.

New York: Triumph and Travail

The artist as loner, as individual, driven by a private muse, persisting unrecognized and unappreciated in a hostile world that neither cares nor understands: this is a romantic view, but it has had special resonance in America, where the historic lack of an economic infrastructure has pushed artists further to the societal margins. Heinrich was for many the American romantic artist par excellence. Always haunted by poverty, driven to create works that had little chance of success or even performance, Heinrich lived apparently only for his art. And then he was forgotten.

Heinrich indeed possessed a vision that was unique for his time, and he pursued it with singular passion, but he in no way worked in isolation. Outside of his composition, he maintained a career typical both in its direction and success. Most of his life he played in theater orchestras and taught. In his final years, mostly in New York City, he was at the very center of American musical culture, played a major role in several important developments, and was showered with honors such as few musicians before the Civil War were. In 1837 he returned to New York, finally had a reunion with his daughter, and except for another European trip in 1857 he remained there, very much involved in musical developments. None of his activities parlayed into financial success, however. America may have started to recognize its musical culture, but it was not ready to reward it.

Heinrich could not have returned to New York at a worse time. A severe depression hit in 1837 and theater attendance was down. Several theaters, including some Heinrich had contracts with, failed. In addition a series of fires in New York literally wiped out several others. Heinrich himself admitted that these were particularly difficult times for him. Recognition began to come, however. He was included in Gustav Schilling's *Encyclopädie der gesammten musikalischen Wissenschaften, oder universal Lexicon der Tonkunst* in 1836, probably because of his Bohemian background and his presence in Europe at the time. In 1839, F. J. Fétis's even better known *Biographie universelle des musiciens et bibliographie générale de la musique* included a sketch on him.

In 1842 a group of musicians decided to form a new organization, the Philharmonic Society of New York. This is the beginning of the New York Philharmonic Orchestra. At its organizational meeting Heinrich was chosen chairman, although when the society was finally formed Ureli Corelli Hill was chosen president and director of the society.

The most visible evidence of the recognition and respect accorded Heinrich were three festivals or benefits held in his honor, in 1842, 1846, and 1853. Benefit concerts were common in both Europe and America at this time, but these were unprecedented in their size and scope, and in the outpouring of support for Heinrich. The first, billed as a "Grand Musical Festival," took place on June 16, 1842. It opened with Heinrich's four-movement, programmatic *Grand Overture to the Pilgrim Fathers*, and contained several vocal works by him, including "The Log House." According to accounts, it featured nine vocal soloists, an orchestra of forty, and a chorus of sixty. The audience, numbering approximately one thousand, was enthusiastic, but the reviews were mixed, mainly because of problems with the orchestra.

Heinrich's greatest success occurred at the Broadway Tabernacle in 1846, at a benefit concert devoted exclusively to his music. Friends, including the transcendentalist writer Lydia Maria Child, who sent a lengthy article about Heinrich to the *New York Tribune*, plugged it heavily. The concert itself included Heinrich's *A Monumental Symphony*—"To the Spirit of Beethoven," and "The Washingtoniad, or the Deeds of a Hero," part of the *Oratorio of the Pilgrims*. For this concert the Tabernacle was nearly full, and the audience, estimated at fifteen hundred, went wild with enthusiasm, showering Heinrich with flowers to show their appreciation. One reviewer observed, "Such yelling, screaming, cheering, laughing and stamping; such showers of bouquets and wreaths, were never before seen or heard of on a similar occasion." According to another review a certain "lady-poetess, distinguished by her ultra-transcendental enthusiasm in musical matters," tossed a laurel wreath at Heinrich with such accuracy that it landed square on his head, "giving him the perfect appearance of a modern Apollo." Lest there be any doubt about the identity of this transcendentalist poet, a card dangled from the wreath bearing the initials L.M.C.[35]

This time the reviews were effusive, with one writer calling Heinrich's music "grand, glorious — sublime" and "undoubtedly ahead of the age," predicting that it "will be far more popular long after he is dead than now." Once again, however, Heinrich failed to realize a profit. Expenses ate up receipts and, if fifteen hundred people were there, the financial statement suggests that many did not purchase a ticket.[36]

Heinrich billed his 1853 concert as his "Grand Valedictory Concert." He had decided to make one last journey to Europe, which actually did not occur until 1857, when he was seventy-six years old. The 1853 concert was not entirely successful; two of his large orchestral works, *National Memories*, *Grand British Symphony* and *Tower of Babel*, were omitted, probably because the orchestra was not capable of playing them. Even though the orchestra reportedly had seventy of the best musicians in the city, critics referred to its ineffectiveness in the other pieces and the apparent great haste with which the program was put together.[37]

Yet the concert drew a large crowd of some fifteen hundred to two thousand. By this time Heinrich had become more than the log cabin composer he still called himself. He had become the epitome of the romantic artist. One writer promoting the concert visited Heinrich: "In a small attic, so high that the noise of the busy street scarcely penetrated the narrow window through which now beamed one bright stream of sunshine, sat an old man. . . . His eyes, full of tenderness and vivacity, were raised as in ecstasy, whilst his hands followed his inspirations on an old rickety piano. . . . He lives but for one idea, one hope, one ambition — to hear, before he dies, the full tide of harmony from the living sounds of an orchestra, manifesting orally those celestial harmonies which have been year after year teeming in his brain."[38] As incredible as it sounds, this probably describes Heinrich.

Heinrich's Eclipse

The total eclipse of Heinrich's reputation after his death is hard to imagine. The complexity of his orchestral compositions contributed much to that, but there were other reasons. Heinrich's promotion of his own Americanism, done with such thoroughness and imagination, may actually have been his own undoing. By the time of the Civil War, America's musical inferiority complex about being American was in full swing. The conflict that had played out between Billings and Mason happened all over again. When it came to art music, particularly orchestral music, America wanted European abstract music. It wanted music based on science, not nature. It wanted the vision defined by J. S. Dwight.

John S. Dwight was to Heinrich what Mason had been to Billings. He redefined American taste to prefer what was European, classical, abstract. Dwight's vision was all that Heinrich was not. Americans did not want a composer of nature, especially one writing about America's nature. They did not want large, loosely constructed programmatic pieces. They wanted to see the European classical symphonic tradition carried on. Tight musical logic trumped extravagant expression. That was the ground they chose for their composers. It was the terrain that the emerging New England school — John Knowles Paine, Arthur Foote, George Whitefield Chadwick, Amy Beach, and others — knew, understood, and cultivated. But this was ground inimical to Heinrich. He was temperamentally as well as technically incapable of tilling it. Heinrich's approach had to lay fallow for decades until another American, Charles Ives, as original and as pathbreaking as he was, took up the call once again.

PART 2

New Concepts and Forces in American Culture

With the aesthetic revolution of mid-nineteenth-century America, the notion of a pure, edifying music, typified by the larger abstract forms, had spread from coast to coast. A vital and buoyant concert circuit extended to almost every burg in the country, including such unlikely venues as Colorado mining towns. Orchestras, virtuosi, and even opera companies appeared all across the continent. And an elaborate support mechanism, ranging from individual patrons to concert societies, grew out of the wealth of the Gilded Age. Such music was supported as much for its perceived moral value as for the intrinsic pleasure it gave.

By 1900 the new patterns were in place, and the American musical landscape had become remarkably stable. Some new concerns had emerged: American composers became acutely aware of their national identity and sought in various ways an American voice. Not all composers concurred, but by the early twentieth century American composers, whether nationalist or not, had established an American presence.

A new wave of books, journals, articles, and newspaper

columns gave legitimacy and prestige to the new musical hierarchy. Music was linked to education: private study spread as the piano worked its way into almost every parlor; the battle for music in the public schools had been resoundingly won, and even higher education had finally recognized music as a legitimate branch of university study. Music as an Art, with a capital A, could stand alongside literature and painting as a monument to the human spirit.

Each part supported and at the same time limited the other. The academic connection both enhanced and ossified music. Most major composers of the late nineteenth century had academic appointments, and as a consequence the musical heritage on which they sought to build was constantly before them. Most important, as they educated American society to the canon, they were ever mindful that their efforts would be measured against that canon.

The system thus was quite circular. Composers, conductors, and touring virtuosi defined the canon and at the same time were trapped by it. Americans throughout the country had a thirst for art music, but woe unto the touring artist who strayed too far from accepted norms. The situation guaranteed a stable, smooth landscape.

CHAPTER 4

Precursors
Charles Ives and Leo Ornstein

W ITH THE ESTABLISHMENT of the musical canon in the Gilded Age, American music settled into a lengthy status quo, which continued well into the second decade of the twentieth century. Many of the late romantic composers, including George Chadwick, Amy Beach, and Horatio Parker, continued active, their styles little changed. A few younger composers, such as Charles Martin Loeffler and Charles Tomlinson Griffes, had some quietly new ideas, and a stronger sense of national pride was apparent in others. Otherwise an observer landing in the American musical world in 1914–15 could easily have thought he was still in the nineteenth century. A new composition premiering in 1915 likely could have just as well been written in 1885. To Americans modernism in music meant Richard Wagner, whose last opera, *Parsifal,* premiered in 1882, Claude Debussy, whose only opera, *Pelléas et Mélisande,* was composed mostly in the 1890s, and César Franck, who died in 1890. When Leo Ornstein traveled to Europe in 1910, his biographer Frederick Martens observed, he "heard modern music for the first time." As an example of modern music Martens explicitly cited Franck's Sonata for Violin and Piano, an unabashedly romantic piece written in 1886. Martens was writing in 1918.[1]

Rumors had reached the United States of a new radicalism in Europe, of such composers as Igor Stravinsky and Arnold Schoenberg, but what little of their music American audiences actually heard were their earlier and more conventional pieces. Writing in 1916 Carl Van Vechten acknowledged the dearth of modern music in New York, saying, "Heaven knows that there is little enough modern music played in New York." He then specified that the most recent Schoenberg works heard there were his symphonic poem *Pelleas und Melisande* (1903) and *Kammersymphonie* (1906), and for Stravinsky — except for "three slight pieces for string quartet (1914) — nothing later than *Petrushka* (1911). Béla Bartók at that time was completely unknown.[2]

Van Vechten was not entirely right in his assessment. By 1915 there were signs of unrest. Before 1915 two American composers, Charles Ives and Leo Ornstein, were writing music so unusual and so original that they seemed to have been dropped from another planet. Their backgrounds, career tracks, and historical reputations are completely different, but they arrived at musical positions that were remarkably similar, and they suffered comparable problems in the outside world's reactions to them. Neither seemed to have influenced the other. Ornstein had no chance to hear Ives, who kept his modernist compositions almost completely to himself until 1921. In 1915 Ornstein, a virtuoso pianist, began to present his own and other truly modern compositions to startled New York audiences, who nevertheless flocked to his concerts as if witnessing an act of sheer public madness. Did Ives hear Ornstein? He never mentioned it at the time, and later he denied it vigorously.[3]

Ives's denial appears disingenuous. Given Ornstein's high profile in New York from 1915, it would have been hard for Ives not to notice him. Yet by the time he would have come into contact with Ornstein's modernist pieces, Ives had completed much of his own work. Had Ives heard Ornstein, it probably had little effect on his own compositional direction.

Ives, whose modernism dates to at least 1902, earned a living completely outside music. Except for church organ positions he held as a young man, he never appeared in public as a concert artist. Yet Ornstein and Ives are similar in many ways: both were excellent pianists, both had shy, generous, nondissimulating personalities, and both came by their musical convictions, that is, their compositional styles, honestly and in their own singular way. Both wrote programmatic music in the broadest sense — that is, music that came from their own personal experience — both had extraordinary ears for sound combinations and used complex dissonant harmonies for their coloristic qualities, and both were more interested in creating a specific musical effect in a piece than following standard formal patterns.

The most important difference between Ives and Ornstein, however, is in their background, and here the difference is both geographic and ethnic. Ornstein, born near the Black Sea, was peripatetic, a product of several cultures — Russian, Jewish, and American. From an early age he was singularly focused on music as a career. He had more conventional training than Ives, study at the St. Petersburg Conservatory in Russia and the Institute of Musical Art, later to become the Juilliard School, in New York. His studies, as well as his professional career, it should be noted, were as a pianist, not a composer. Ives came from a respected, solid New England family, and although he spent most of his adult life in New York City he was never more than a short train ride from his birthplace. His musical training was less systematic, first from his father, an experimental, eclectic musician, then only as a sideline at Yale University. Ives eschewed a musical career and went into the insurance business. He not only made a fortune as a founding partner of one of the largest insurance agencies in the country, but his reputation as a creative, innovative thinker in the insurance field rivals his musical accomplishments. True to his roots, Ives remained the crusty Yankee throughout his life. He seemed to cultivate the role.

Leo Ornstein was born in 1893 in Kremenchug, a town on the Dnieper River in southwest Russia. His father was a Jewish cantor, and he spent the first years of his life under reasonably comfortable circumstances. His big break came when he was about ten: the famous pianist Josef Hoffman came to Kremenchug, heard him play, and recommended him to the St. Petersburg Conservatory, a world-renowned institution founded by Anton Rubinstein. Soon thereafter he was enrolled.[4]

It was both a difficult and an extremely heady experience for Ornstein. He quickly found himself popular in the salons of the Russian nobility, in some of the most opulent surroundings in the world. At the same time he had to earn his way, which he did partly by coaching opera singers. It must have been surprising for an established opera singer to encounter his coach for the first time and find an eleven-year-old boy who, small for his age, looked even younger. Shy, sensitive, and extremely homesick, Ornstein suffered from the emotional strain of his new life. The change had been sudden, and he was essentially cut off from his family. But there was also real terror. In the following year, 1905, revolt broke out in Russia, and Ornstein for the rest of his life remembered having to dodge Cossacks charging down the narrow street where he lived, ready to run down anyone in their way. He was personally witness to some of the bloodletting that occurred during the revolt, such as the slaughter on Admiralty Square.

When the revolt was suppressed things got ugly for Ornstein and his family. Counterterrorists, officially known as the Union of the Russian People, unofficially called "the black hundreds," began an assault on those elements of society deemed hostile to the czarist regime. High on the list were Jews.

The situation continued to worsen, and by 1906 Ornstein's family felt they had no choice but to emigrate to America.

Ornstein soon found himself in New York City. In three years, at an impressionable age, he had made two major cultural changes, from small-town Kremenchug to the capital of imperial Russia, and then, in Paul Rosenfeld's words, from "the pianist infant-prodigy of Petrograd society into the boy of a dense and livid slum."[5] Rosenfeld, who knew Ornstein personally, exaggerated. Ornstein's father, a highly respected cantor, had connections in New York, and he soon found a prestigious position as cantor of the Bialystoker Synagogue. Ornstein's life was more middle-class, but it was on the Lower East Side, an area notorious for its packed tenement houses and noisy streets. In any event lower-middle-class Jewish New York was a world apart from either St. Petersburg or Kremenchug, and the cultural shock was great. Ornstein, who left essentially an extended autobiography in tones in a large corpus of programmatic works, remained forever a man in two worlds.

By sheer persistence Ornstein continued his musical career. His extraordinary talent won him a scholarship to the Institute of Musical Art, where he became the pupil of Bertha Feiring Tapper. She was considered one of the better pedagogues in New York, and she recognized fully the extent of Ornstein's talent. She and her husband, a physician, took him under their wing, and she began to groom him for a career. They took him to their summer home in Blue Hill, Maine, which had the environment of a proto summer music festival. Franz Kneisel, the founder of the highly popular Kneisel quartet, came to play sonatas with Tapper; nearby, Horatio Parker, Ives's professor and mentor at Yale, had a cabin. Ornstein heard Parker play most of his opera *Mona* there, and he showed some of his compositions to Parker, who responded with praise and encouragement. Tapper also carefully prepared Ornstein for a debut recital, taking him first to Europe in 1910 to win the stamp of approval of the eminent piano pedagogue Theodor Leschetizky, who pronounced him ready for the public. Ornstein later called Tapper the most important influence of his life.

Leo Ornstein's concert career began in 1911. He debuted in New York on March 5, with a meaty program. He played Bach's Chromatic Fantasy and Fugue, Beethoven's *Appassionata Sonata*, pieces by Chopin and Schumann, and Anton Rubinstein's Concerto in D Minor. For the latter he was accompanied by the Volpe Symphony Orchestra. Both critics and fellow musicians were so impressed that the New York Philharmonic asked him to repeat the Rubinstein concerto with them a month later. This was not typical; the Philharmonic did not normally extend invitations to teenage performers after only a single public appearance. Before the March concert Ornstein's most public outing had been at the commencement exercises of the New York music school.

By 1913 Ornstein had made two recordings with Columbia Records. The recordings, of pieces by Chopin, Grieg, and Ede Poldini, reveal a pianist of sensitivity, prodigious technical ability, and artistic maturity.[6] And he began to develop a following. His first champion was A. W. Kramer. Writing in *Musical America* in 1911, Kramer depicted him as romantic artist, drooping his head and lost in thought at the piano, mystically communing with his instrument. No question that Ornstein had within his grasp a major career in the mold of Hoffman, Rubinstein, or Paderewski. Yet to Kramer, Ornstein was not the typical virtuoso. There was something different. Kramer vividly described the young man: "Of medium height, slender, or a wiry frame, one notices immediately his extremely nervous temperament. He speaks in quick, short sentences, and with a considerable degree of assertiveness. An alert eye which observes even the minutest detail, a countenance that is intelligent in its every line and feature — all these give outward sign of the possession of extraordinary abilities."[7]

To his surprise Kramer found Ornstein mature, philosophical, and immersed in literature almost as much as music. Kramer noted his voracious reading habits, his knowledge of Shakespeare, which he reread every year, his understanding of Burns, Browning, and Ibsen. Maybe Ornstein was too thoughtful, too nervous, too engrossed, too innocent. He was a young man with a divine spark, but Kramer seemed uncertain about where that would lead.

Kramer could not have predicted what did happen, but soon afterward something snapped. One day in 1912, according to Ornstein, he began to hear, inwardly, some strange new chords. He carried them around for a time, and then suddenly, without warning, *Danse Sauvage* appeared in his head, in its entirety. He brought the new composition to Mrs. Tapper, who first thought it was some kind of joke; after determining that he was serious, her next thought was that he had gone insane. There was nothing in Western literature like it. *Danse Sauvage* is a study in rhythm and in dissonance, sheer driving, demoniac, unrelenting and unresolved dissonance. It is all rhythm, at times percussive with flurries of ostinato-approaching-tremolo dissonances, at times irregular, with unusual and constantly changing meter. There is no harmonic relief, no triads or tonal guideposts; the final chord, marked *ffff*, covers nearly six octaves and contains the notes D-sharp–F-sharp–A-sharp–C–E, in the left hand, and B–C–F-sharp–G-sharp–A-sharp–B-sharp in the right, the B-sharp being the highest note on the piano.

Ornstein himself was ready to concur with Mrs. Tapper. Many years

Leo Ornstein in 1912, nineteen years old, about to startle the musical world

later, when asked about his piece, he described its genesis: "*Danse Sauvage* was written by a young person with no experience whatever with modern music. . . . I still wonder at the age of eighty, why should I have thought of that? A boy that had been sitting at the piano practicing the *Twelfth Rhapsody* to try to astonish the ladies with the speed and accuracy of the passages, and blind the audience with the terrific glissandos and what not. Why suddenly that thing came into my head — I'll be blessed if I know. And as a matter of fact, I really doubted my sanity at first. I simply said, what is that? It was so completely removed from any experience I had ever had."[8]

Ornstein composed *Danse Sauvage*, then, at least according to his own recollection, before Stravinsky's *Le Sacre du printemps* premiered, and certainly without knowledge of Ives's compositions. It is preceded by Bartók's *Allegro barbaro* and Schoenberg's Op. 11 and Op. 19 piano pieces. Ornstein asserted that he had never heard of Bartók or Schoenberg prior to a European trip that he took in 1913–14, and Deems Taylor observed that as late as 1922

Bartók's music was "virtually unobtainable in this country." But even had Ornstein heard *Allegro barbaro*, it would not explain *Danse Sauvage*. While *Allegro barbaro* suggests the same driving rhythms of *Danse Sauvage*, melodically and harmonically the two pieces are worlds apart. Bartók's harmonies are essentially modal spiked with strong dissonances; they remain tertiary, that is, they are still based on traditional chords of Western music. Ornstein's harmony consists of chromatic clusters, several adjacent notes packed tightly together. The patterns bear little relation to traditional practices. But they are not random, and they are not simply all the white notes or black notes between x and y.[9]

As for Schoenberg: Ornstein owed little to Schoenberg, as he himself stated. Both came to a harmonic style that was essentially dissonant, compared with traditional practice, but that is as far as the comparison goes. Ornstein's use of dissonance is quite different from Schoenberg's. Schoenberg's grew out of a linear polyphony driven by the increasing chromaticism of romanticism. Ornstein's is not polyphonic; it is color. And Schoenberg's music never had the driving, savage rhythmic quality of Ornstein's. In that regard Ornstein is closer to Stravinsky and Bartók.[10]

Ornstein could have heard Stravinsky on his European trip of 1910. If so, it would be the Stravinsky of *Firebird*, not *Le Sacre*. Whatever Ornstein had absorbed, his early pieces give the impression of something sui generis.

Soon after Ornstein's startling revelation, Tapper took him on another European trip. No longer the pupil being whisked to the continent for a final check-up with an old-world pedagogue, Ornstein acted the part of the mature artist, both absorbing Europe's culture, old and new, and presenting himself to European musicians and public, who were just as bewildered as American musicians had been. Arriving in Paris, Ornstein was sufficiently moved by Notre-Dame cathedral to write his *Two Impressions of Notre Dame*, tone poems in his new idiom that nevertheless show a much wider range of expression and flexibility than his earlier pieces had. They also suggest a reconciliation with the past, with their at times Debussy-like painting.

In Vienna Ornstein again met Leschetizky, this time to perform *Danse Sauvage* for him. One can only imagine what the formal, nineteenth-century Viennese, whose ideas of modern music embraced possibly Franck or Max Reger, thought of this radical Russian-American. Leschetizky simply observed that it must be difficult to put all those notes on paper. The diplomatic silence speaks reams. Nevertheless Leschetizky was cordial enough for Ornstein to dedicate his *Impressions of the Thames* to him. On returning to Paris, Ornstein played for the critic and champion of new music Michel-Dimitri Calvocoressi, who could not believe such pieces originated in New

York. Calvocoressi was sufficiently impressed to arrange a private performance for a number of Parisian musicians, and then to ask Ornstein to act as illustrator at the piano for a series of lectures he was giving on modern music. Ornstein had his own pieces included in the lecture along with works of Richard Strauss, Bartók, Zoltán Kodály, Cyril Scott, Schoenberg, and Stravinsky. This was probably the first time he encountered much of this music.

In Paris Ornstein also met a young English composer, Roger Quilter, who invited him to Oxford and then London, and who arranged introductions leading to his first public recital of modernist, or as they were called then, futurist compositions.

The London recital, held at Steinway Hall on March 27, 1914, created a sensation only slightly less intense than Stravinsky's *Le Sacre* had in Paris. Ornstein played a Ferruccio Busoni arrangement of three choral preludes by Bach, two numbers from Schoenberg's Op. 11, Schoenberg's *Six Little Pieces*, Op. 19, and several of his own works, including *Impressions of Notre Dame*, *Three Moods*, Sonata Op. 25, *Impressions of the Thames*, and *Danse Sauvage*. Critics were outraged and sought to outdo one another in their condemnation. One called Ornstein's Sonata Op. 25 "four separate spasms of mental anguish too great to be borne." Another observed, "We have never suffered from such insufferable hideousness, expressed in terms of so-called music," although he did allow that "the skill that could devise the cacophonous, unrhythmic, unmusical always, two-penny colored rubbish which Leo Ornstein drove with the Nasmyth-hammer action into the heads of the long-suffering audience on Friday was stupendous!" Another critic, possibly remembering a recent performance of Schoenberg's *Five Orchestral Pieces*, which had set London on its modernistic ear, dubbed Ornstein "the sum of Schoenberg and Scriabine squared."[11]

Audience reaction was mixed, but mostly negative. The London *Daily Mail* referred to a "wild outbreak at Steinway Hall." The *Daily Telegraph* reported that "the audience remained to the end, hypnotized as a rabbit by a snake." Other members of the audience, possibly feeling uneasy, responded with laughter. Ornstein did create enough stir, however, to persuade the music publisher Schott to issue several of his compositions in London and to be booked for a second recital, on April 7, which was to consist exclusively of his own music.[12]

For the second recital Ornstein played only his own compositions. The audience reacted similarly to the first recital. Most "treated it as a joke," and there was some hissing. But the critics had had time to think. The *Musical Standard* acknowledged that Ornstein was "one of the most remarkable

composers of the day," that his music had "that germ of realism and human-
ity which is indicative of genius on the part of its composer." Finally the reviewer admitted, "I went half inclined to blame; I stayed to praise."[13]

On returning to the United States, Ornstein and Tapper laid plans to
launch an international career. A forty-concert trip to Norway set for the fall
of 1914 had to be canceled, however, because of the outbreak of war. With the
abandonment of the Norwegian tour Ornstein's career became exclusively
American; he never left North America again as a performing artist.

By far the most significant event in Ornstein's American performing career was a series of four concerts that he gave at the Bandbox Theatre in New
York, in January and February of 1915. Consisting entirely of modern music,
they allowed Americans to hear for the first time radical pieces by Schoenberg, Maurice Ravel, and Aleksandr Skryabin, as well as a host of other "futurist" composers, including of course Ornstein himself. The concerts created a sensation. They mark the beginning of musical modernism in the
United States.

Critics were dumbfounded. Conservative critics responded with outrage, bewilderment, and sarcasm, but even they grudgingly admitted the
presence of a significant artist. James Huneker referred to Ornstein as "Leo
the Intrepid," but he had to confess, "I went, if not to mock, at least in a rather
skeptical mood; but I remained to applaud; a sad commentary on my critical
consistency." Other critics called his music "bewildering, upsetting . . . very
mad." But even the Montreal reporter who wrote this had to admit that, "still,
on reflection, there was likely method in it; . . . perhaps ——." Others took
pity on the piano: "He has no more mercy upon smug enjoyment than on the
instruments he flails with his mighty fist." He "has left the piano with its keys
'as bloodstained as a Melville melodrama.'" Waldo Frank reported "blood on
the keys" after an Ornstein performance.[14]

For the next five years Ornstein led the life of a successful concert artist.
He was in demand, and he toured extensively. Whatever audiences thought
of his modernist pieces, the works gave him notoriety, and as today's media-
conscious world knows, notoriety sells tickets. But it was hard on Ornstein
personally: he was both a respected performing musician and a novelty act.
As his concerts became filled with curiosity seekers, he became an object of
amusement and lampoon. An anonymous writer in the *New York Times* described one of his concerts: "Mr. Ornstein still retains the power to delight,
puzzle, and amuse his hearers. . . . As far as amusing goes, that is reserved for
the moments when he plays some of his own queer compositions — and a
particularly loud guffaw from some male voice in yesterday's audience simultaneous with his striking of the final note in a 'trick finish' of his 'A la Chi-

noise' was a faithful commentary on the emotions of about 90 per cent of the audience — excluding those who maintained a very grim expression on their faces or walked down the aisle and out to register their disapproval."[15]

In spite of the strain Ornstein continued to compose, and his compositional activity took another bizarre turn. He began to develop multiple creative personalities, with highly contrasting compositional styles. There was his first manner, his second manner, and then there was Vannin. His first manner consists of modernist, dissonant, often atonal, at times savage pieces, his second manner of lyrical, more tonal but still modern pieces. Vannin was a pseudonym under which Ornstein published a few simple, tonal, often diatonic works. It is hard to tell whether Vannin was practical, an attempt to hide authorship, or another compositional voice. The Vannin style is not the same as his second manner.

Later in life Ornstein had completely forgotten Vannin. A man 105 years old, as he was, can be forgiven such memory lapses. But even in relative old age Ornstein remembered and was puzzled by his two different styles. In speaking of the Cello Sonata, Op. 52, a romantic work that remained one of his favorite pieces throughout his life, Ornstein spoke of the white heat in which he often composed as well as his dichotomous creative life of the time: "As a rule when I write at all I write rapidly. The *Sonata* was written in less than a week under a compulsion that was not to be resisted. At the time when I was tumultuously involved in the primitivism of the *Wild Man's Dance*, the *Three Moods*, etc., its lyrical quality was utterly unaccountable. Why I should have heard this romantic piece at the same period is beyond my understanding, but the same contrast of exteriors has continued throughout my life."[16]

The Violin Sonata, Op. 31, is Ornstein's most uncompromising foray into modernism, as he himself admitted. It is chromatic, atonal, highly dissonant, and unrelenting. Ornstein himself acknowledged that he had pushed his dissonant style, which he termed "abstract music," "to the brink," and that with Op. 31, he reached the verge of absolute disorder: "I would say that Op. 31 had brought music just to the very edge. . . . I just simply drew back and said, 'beyond that lies complete chaos.'"[17]

Ornstein's first and second manners were not entirely contemporaneous, as his comment above suggests. After the chaos of the Violin Sonata, he decided to pull back, to turn from a more "experimental" to a more "expressive" style, as he described it.[18] After 1916 or 1917 there are few pieces in the out-and-out radical style of the mid-1910s.

By the early 1920s Ornstein the concert artist was burned out. The concert world was wearing on him, and his interest focused more and more on composition. In 1924 he took a position at the Philadelphia Academy of Music, then the Zeckwer-Hahn Philadelphia Musical Academy, and in 1934 he opened the Ornstein School of Music. He continued to compose, and he appeared in public occasionally through the early 1930s. Some of his most important pieces were composed during that time, most noticeably the Piano Quintette, which was written under a commission by Elizabeth Sprague Coolidge in 1927, and the Piano Concerto of 1925, commissioned by the Philadelphia Orchestra.[19]

Ornstein never abandoned composing, at least during his first hundred years. Even late in life he wrote big pieces. He wrote his Seventh Piano Sonata in 1988, when he was ninety-five years old. He followed this with the Eighth Sonata in 1990, when he was ninety-seven. His later music is mostly unknown, but that is a tale in itself. For our story it is Ornstein the pioneering futurist that is of interest.[20]

To the champions of musical modernism, Ornstein was a symbol. For several years he was an enfant terrible, and a better candidate could not have been chosen. His music was truly revolutionary, thoroughly disorienting, radical in the extreme — a complete break with tradition. Not even the most bored concertgoers could ignore *Danse Sauvage* or *Three Moods*. These works assaulted the audience directly, demanding and defying the listener to take sides. And Ornstein was out there, on the front line. His concertizing not only gave modernism an airing it could not have secured any other way but his formidable musicianship, constantly on display, dispelled any notion that he was some crank.

Yet, like Heinrich, Ornstein has been all but forgotten (although that may be changing). Mentioned only in passing in most histories, a mere handful of his pieces were available throughout the twentieth century, when almost every composer was covered extensively in CD catalogues. Ornstein had mostly retired by the time the new music organizations of the 1920s appeared. Too early and too independent, Ornstein had little desire to participate in the modernist movement by the time it caught hold in the United States.

Ornstein's disaffection from the modernist movement was not all one-way, however. Ornstein had been ultramodernism's poster boy, the one musical modernist before the public, and he had been championed by writers and critics sympathetic to modernism, such as in his biography by Martens and his inclusion as one of twenty important composers in a book by Paul Rosenfeld in 1920. Rosenfeld was emerging as the principal spokesman of musical modernism, and in his book, *Musical Portraits: Interpretations of Twenty Modern Composers*, he placed Ornstein alongside Berlioz, Stravinsky, and Schoenberg.[21] Yet when Ornstein reverted to a more expressive style, just at the time other composers were discovering the new, his modernist champions felt betrayed. They never forgave him for that. Ornstein still received major commissions in the 1920s, and he was included on the boards of new-music organizations, as his name still had cachet, but generally he was considered a defector, a traitor to the cause, and thus was shunned. Ornstein himself seemed little bothered by the publicity or lack of it. He listened to only his own voice, and he was forgotten.

Charles Ives is one of the pivotal figures in this story. He is a composer of the first rank, to some the most significant composer America has produced. He lived at a crucial time in American history, when forces that had defined the nation in the nineteenth century began to disintegrate under the pressures of the newly emerging modern age. He inherited the world of the nineteenth-century village and a musical culture dominated by a Euro-complex and an overwrought gentility. He moved to New York City, thought globally about politics and social issues, and wrote experimental, rebellious music that contrasted sharply with the prevailing romantic tone. His compositions herald modernism, although Ives himself was ambivalent about modernistic developments in the other arts. Nevertheless a direct lineage runs from Charles Ives to the avant-garde that appeared between the two world wars. Composers of the 1920s set the course for American art music for the rest of the century, and they personally and consciously looked back on Ives as a pioneer and an inspiration. To them, Ives became the father figure they were seeking.

By day Ives was a highly successful businessman, a major innovator in the field of life insurance. At night and on weekends he composed. He kept his artistic and business careers almost completely separate; some of his insurance colleagues were not even aware that he was a musician. After several chilly, even hostile receptions to his music, Ives turned away from attempts at public performance. Only around 1920, as his compositional career came to an end, did he seriously attempt to promote his music. That effort eventually paid off, resulting in a belated but enthusiastic recognition, bordering on reverence, from a younger generation of musicians.

Ives was pure New England. He was born on October 20, 1874, into one of the most established and prominent families in Danbury, Connecticut. The Ives family had been in Connecticut since 1638, its members being founders of both New Haven and later Danbury. Charles Ives's great-grandfather, Isaac Ives, a graduate of Yale and an attorney, came to Danbury in 1790 and soon married into one of the most successful families there. Ives could count members of the Connecticut House of Representatives among his ancestors, and his grandfather was treasurer of the Danbury and Norwalk

Railroad and a director of the Danbury Bank, the Danbury Gas Light Company, the Danbury Cemetery Association, and the Mechanics' Association, as well as the principal founder of the Savings Bank of Danbury, which originally operated out of the Iveses' home on Main Street.

Yet this prosperous, bourgeois New England family had its black sheep, specifically Charles Ives's father, George. George Ives showed enough musical talent as a youth, particularly on the trumpet, to be appointed, at age seventeen, the youngest bandleader of the Civil War. His musical activities had been encouraged by his father, who allowed him, when he was fifteen, to study music with Charles A. Foeppl in Westchester County, New York. George was the only Ives until that time to show any serious interest or talent in music.

So far so good. But when George returned to Danbury after the Civil War, he decided to make music his profession. Had such a possibility even occurred to his father when he sent George to New York? Probably not, but the question is moot, because the elder Ives had died during the Civil War. What the rest of the family thought of George's decision is not entirely clear, but almost certainly they did not view it favorably. Such a choice was unheard of among the New England elite at that time. In mid-nineteenth-century America, particularly in mercantile New England, music was not a respectable profession. Many American youths played musical instruments, and the trumpet, the lead instrument of the military band, was an acceptable choice in those gender-conscious, militaristic times. But for a grown man in Ives's class to abdicate his responsibility and pursue a career in music, that was different. No matter how good, professional musicians occupied a different niche on the social scale.

Even worse, George was a bandleader. A distinction between art music and other types emerged in mid-nineteenth-century America, and involvement in art music garnered at least some respectability. Band music, immensely popular, was not considered art music. Many years later Philip Sunderland, three years older than Charles Ives, remembered vividly life in Danbury where he had grown up. His comments speak for his generation: "They [the people of Danbury] didn't take George Ives very seriously. He was only the bandleader."[22]

Only the bandleader! That judgment was to haunt Charles Ives the rest of his life. Equally humiliating was George's failure as a breadwinner. Although considered the leading local band musician of Danbury, he could not earn enough to support a family and was forced to take various jobs in family businesses. Fortunately for George the Ives clan stuck together, although his position within the family must have been difficult for him. Late

Two photographs of George Ives, Charles Ives's father. The one on the left, with Ives in full bandmaster regalia, was taken in 1892. The one on the right is scarcely one year later, in the last year of George Ives's life. (Irving S. Gilmore Music Library, Yale University, MSS 14, Charles Ives Papers)

in life he had to work as a clerk, in the bank that his father had founded. Most galling, he was the assistant to Howard Ives, his own nephew, some seventeen years his junior. The last known photograph of George Ives shows a man, at age forty-nine, worn out and utterly defeated by life.

The Iveses' sense of responsibility to their own served Charles well, because through the help of an uncle, Lyman Brewster, he was able to attend Yale, the first Ives to do so since Isaac had graduated in 1785. The Yale years were critical to Ives. They provided him contacts crucial to his later business career as well as his own family life. He met his wife, Harmony Twitchell, through her brother, David, a classmate and friend of his at Yale. Yale also allowed Ives to try his wings in music. He did not go to Yale to study music, but once there he did take advantage of the musical curriculum that was offered. His contacts with Horatio Parker, a newly appointed professor of music, taught Ives much and broadened his musical horizons.

After graduating from college in 1898 Ives got a job in New York City at the Mutual of New York insurance company. Once again the family was there for him. He landed the job through two family members, Granville H.

White and Robert Grannis, who were officers in Mutual. Ives continued to pursue music, at the time in a relatively conventional way. He secured a position as organist at the Central Presbyterian Church and continued to compose church music. There were occasional odd passages in his music, but through 1903 it remained largely within the nineteenth-century tradition. Much of it was choral, and much of it was very good. Had Ives never veered into his radical modernism he would still be remembered as a fine and original composer. In 1903, while continuing to live a dual but relatively conventional life, Ives made his last major effort before 1921 to reach the public. He presented his cantata *The Celestial Country*, a major choral composition in the mold of Horatio Parker's most important work, *Hora Novissima*.

Celestial Country was a watershed for Ives, or at least it has been so considered: disappointed at the reviews in the newspaper, he soon thereafter resigned his organ position, never to hold a professional musical appointment again, stopped writing choral music, and retreated to compose in silence and isolation in a new and radical style.

Did it happen that way? How sudden was the break, and did *Celestial Country* precipitate it? Ives's radicalism, or as he probably would have preferred, his experimentalism, was always there. It is apparent in one of his earliest surviving compositions, *Variations on America*, composed when he was seventeen years old. Ives inserted interludes between variations to get from one key to another. Rather than modulating, however, he began playing in the new key in one hand while simultaneously continuing to play in the old key in the other. According to Ives his father would not let him play it publicly as it "made the boys laugh." And this was no isolated attempt. When at Yale, Ives had several run-ins with his mentor Horatio Parker over bold and unusual harmonic passages in his pieces.[23]

The Celestial Country itself was not badly received; comments were positive but not unabashedly enthusiastic. Yet it was apparently not what Ives hoped for. Maybe he knew what lay ahead, what was in his head, and what the response would be. Maybe he had no intention of going on publicly. His choice of an insurance career had been well determined before 1903; *The Celestial Country* did not set him on that course.[24]

Ives's own New England background and family situation undoubtedly had much to do with his career choice. He had something to prove to the Ives family as well as to himself. Ives was in some ways the chosen one, selected by the family to go to Yale. He developed a close relationship with Lyman Brewster, who, though not technically an Ives — he married Amelia Ives, George's sister — was by sheer dint of success, as a lawyer, civic leader, judge, and state senator, the prominent member of the family. And Ives, in spite of his immense talent and love of music, was uncomfortable with being too identified with this aspect of his life. "What do you play?" "Shortstop," he would often answer.

Dasher, Quigly—Ives's nicknames at Yale—captain of the Danbury "Alerts" baseball team, member of Wolfshead, a senior society at Yale, most of all Ives wanted to be a regular guy. He saw his father fail as breadwinner, he saw his father die just as he entered Yale; Ives had something to atone, to the family, to himself, and to the values of his culture.

Ives's first experience away from home, his attendance at Yale, was a continuation of both his family and New England tradition. His move to New York was typical of bright, young, ambitious New England men of his time. In fact it was so typical that his first ten years there were essentially a continuation of college life. Ives lived in a series of apartments that he and his roommates dubbed Poverty Flat; the personnel changed as members married or moved on in other ways, but the group always consisted of several young Yale graduates. It was like a rolling fraternity house, a re-creation of Yale undergraduate society, with all the attendant chaos, youthful spirit, and hijinks. Ives stayed in that environment longer than most. When he finally married Harmony Twitchell in 1907 and moved out, he was thirty-three years old, one of the house's oldest members.

Yet at Poverty Flat Ives endured several personal crises that ultimately had much to do with both his personal maturing and his musical evolution. The first came in 1904 when his uncle Lyman Brewster died. Brewster had been a surrogate father to Ives, helping make Yale possible and even collaborating with him on an opera based on a Revolutionary War theme. The opera never came to fruition.[25]

The next year Ives's company, Mutual of New York, was the focus of the United States Senate's Armstrong investigation into fraud in the insurance industry, and the Raymond Agency, the branch of Mutual where Ives worked, came under particular attack. While Ives himself was never implicated, he could feel the heat, and the possibility that his career would be tainted was for a time real. This occurred precisely when his relationship with Harmony had turned serious, and Ives had to face as a prospective father-in-law Reverend George Twitchell, the acknowledged moral and spiritual leader of Hartford, Connecticut.[26] In the midst of all of this, Ives suffered a serious health crisis in 1906. Its precise nature is not known, although later medical records indicate that it was not a heart attack, as some biographers have suggested.[27]

Whether coincidence or cause, a new, more mature modernist sound emerged from this crucible. In 1906, Ives composed *In the Cage*, from a *Set for Theatre Orchestra*, and *The Unanswered Question*. Both works evince a new seriousness and experimentalism not seen in his music before. *In the Cage* was based on an incident that occurred at the Central Park Zoo. Ives and his roommate Bart Yung watched a leopard pace back and forth across his cage, until finally Yung queried, "Is life anything like that?" Ives then wrote a tone poem on the idea, with a melody in the English horn, a series of meterless chords accompanying, and a repeating figure in the timpani, depicting the surrogate leopard. Ives later added words, reduced the orchestral part to the piano, and published it as a song in 114 *Songs*.

The Unanswered Question is one of the first of Ives's pieces that address "the perennial question of existence," a topic that engaged him throughout his compositional career, to culminate finally in the massive Fourth Symphony. The music of *The Unanswered Question* unfolds in three layers. The strings, which represent "the silence of the Druids, who know, see, and hear nothing," play throughout a slow, quiet, mostly traditional chordal pattern. The trumpet, which enters periodically with a questioning chromatic motive, poses the question. The winds, the "fighting answerers," in their desperation to provide a solution, become more strident, frantic, and dissonant as the piece proceeds. The music, which is "utterly unlike anything before Ives," retains its serious, unsettling tone throughout, with each layer musically independent of the others. Such layering became a fundamental hallmark of Ives's style.[28]

Neither piece was performed publicly until many years later. After 1903 Ives tried to interest musicians in his compositions, but these attempts generally came to naught. Efforts at musical dissemination aimed at musicians rather than the public were necessary, for either Ives had to interest other musicians in performing his works or he had to appear before the public himself, as Ornstein had done. The latter course was unthinkable for Ives. His insurance career itself would have at least limited that approach; in addition, Ives was temperamentally unfit for that role.

When Ives tried to interest musicians, mainly by playing his works for them on the piano, most episodes did not go well. In 1914, Franz Milcke, former concertmaster of the New York Philharmonic, visited Ives, at Harmony's invitation, to play through some of the violin sonatas. Milcke started, stumbled, started again, and finally gave up, exclaiming, "This is awful! It is not music, it makes no sense." Ives patiently tried to play through the offending page. Milcke then ran out of the room with his hands over his ears, exclaiming, "When you get awfully indigestible food in your stomach that distresses you, you can get rid of it, but I cannot get those horrible sounds out of my ears."[29]

Ives heard words like "horrible" and "awful" many times. Not all encounters, however, were that unpleasant. Gustav Mahler, at the time music director of the New York Philharmonic, showed interest in his Third Symphony, and Ives harbored some hope that it would be performed. Mahler's tenure in New York was ending, however, and he might have taken the symphony back to Europe; there are stories that Mahler performed it there, but this has never been confirmed.[30]

Ives found a more willing reception for his music from theater orchestras. These were small, often irregular ensembles of journeymen musicians who sat in the pits night after night at the many theaters in New York. They had to be ready to play whatever the situation demanded. They were open to new music, they could read well, and they were versatile. Ives himself had played occasionally in the Hyperion Theater and Polt's Theater orchestras while at Yale, and he was comfortable with the setting and the musicians. He also knew that theater musicians were always looking for a buck.

Ives must have presented quite a sight to them. This tall, thin, shy man would appear with a sheaf of manuscript paper under his arm and money in his wallet and ask them to play the most unusual music. And he talked their language. Ives got on well enough with them that they expressed interest in playing his music in public. Unfortunately, they also realized the implications of such an act for audiences hardly expecting what they would hear.[31]

In the meantime, Ives made money. Lots of it. From 1909, when the Ives and Myrick agency opened, to approximately 1922, Ives made roughly $1.8 million. In 2003 dollars this would be approximately $22 million. In 1913, the first year of the income tax, he reported an income of $10,000, the 2003 equivalent of $186,000. By 1921 his reported income had risen to $41,000. As the agency's most prosperous years were in the 1920s, one can assume that his income from 1921 until his retirement in 1929 was even greater.[32]

By 1920 Ives had created a substantial oeuvre: four symphonies, several other multi-movement orchestral works, sets for chamber orchestra, two string quartets, a string trio, five violin sonatas, three piano sonatas, many other piano pieces, and more than one hundred songs.[33] But there was still no interest in his music.

In 1921 Ives made his most sustained effort to reach the public. By this time he had suffered a serious illness, possibly a heart attack, in 1918, and signs of diabetes were beginning to appear. He had printed, at his own expense, a collection of his songs, 114 Songs, the Concord Sonata, and separately an explanatory volume, Essays Before a Sonata, that explicated his musical aesthetic, which included a substantial debt to transcendentalism. He sent several hundred copies, gratis, to musicians and critics throughout the country.

Charles Ives in 1913, in New York City, at the height of his business and compositional career (Irving S. Gilmore Music Library, Yale University, MSS 14, Charles
Ives Papers; photograph by Bill Joli)

At first, reaction ranged from polite thank-you's to bewilderment. Gradually, however, enthusiasm grew. From Pittsburgh he heard from T. Carl Whit-
mer, who called the *Concord Sonata* "fine, original and altogether interesting." Henry Bellamann wrote from South Carolina to say that he found the
sonata a "remarkable piece of work," and planned to add it to a lecture-recital
on modern music that he was giving. Bellamann soon wrote the first detailed
review of Ives's music to appear in print, for the arts magazine *Double Dealer*.
And from Chicago he heard from Clifton Joseph Furness, who had wasted no
time and presented a lecture-recital on the *Concord* even before writing to
Ives. In a 1926 article Furness called Ives a "musical Emerson."[34]

Yet Ives's career did not take off until the end of the 1920s. Ives needed the collective clout of the new modernists to find an audience, but once he got a hearing his talent was recognized. By then a new generation of composers had organized and established a strong foothold on the American musical landscape. Ives was never overtly active in their organizations, but he quietly supported their activities, principally by providing needed financial aid. He was a particularly strong supporter of Henry Cowell's New Music Society and did much to keep Cowell's journal *New Music Quarterly* alive. It is thus no coincidence that a major step in recognition came when Cowell published the second movement of Ives's Fourth Symphony in his journal.

By 1928 his works were appearing regularly at new-music concerts in New York, and in 1931 Nicolas Slonimsky premiered Ives's *Three Places in New England* with the Boston Chamber Orchestra that Slonimsky had established. With financial support from Ives, Slonimsky took the piece to Havana and Paris. These concerts and the response they elicited marked a significant turn in the establishment of Ives's reputation.

By then Ives had become a revered elder statesman among the avant-garde. His reputation grew steadily through the 1930s, but he had not become familiar to the general public. That changed when John Kirkpatrick premiered the entire *Concord Sonata* at Town Hall in New York. The crowd responded enthusiastically. More important, Lawrence Gilman, music critic for the *New York Herald-Tribune*, praised Ives and his sonata: "This sonata is exceptionally great music — it is, indeed, the greatest music composed by an American, and the most deeply and essentially American in impulse and implication. It is wide-ranging and capacious. It has passion, tenderness, humor, simplicity, homeliness. It has imaginative and spiritual vastness. It has wisdom and beauty and profundity, and a sense of the encompassing terror and splendor of human life and human destiny — a sense of those mysteries that are both human and divine."[35]

Eighteen years had elapsed since Ives had sent the *Concord Sonata* to musicians throughout the country. That bold move inaugurated a process that ultimately proved successful, the establishment of his name before the musical world. During the 1920s and '30s Ives had done much to further that process, meeting with, corresponding with, and befriending musicians who showed interest in his work. He had also been very generous with his wealth, supporting efforts not just for himself but for other composers. But Ives was a beneficiary as well as a catalyst. For just as he began his solitary journey toward public recognition a number of other musicians, who had similar radical ideas if not always Ives's sheer raw talent, began to assault what to them seemed an ossifying status quo. Their tactics differed dramatically from

Ives's, but their efforts created a new atmosphere, one in which Ives's music could thrive. The ultramoderns of the 1920s found a way to upend the musical world, with results that not only benefited Ives but altered permanently the American musical landscape.

Ives and Ornstein had pushed the system to the edge of chaos. They represent two early leaps from the plain that American music seemed to have settled on. In his discussion of rugged fitness landscapes, evolutionary biologist Stuart Kauffman distinguishes between short- and long-jump evolutionary change, and between more rugged and smoother landscapes. Long-jump evolutionary change occurs when an agent has no opportunity to evolve in place, and must consequently find new and distant terrain. From the fitness peak on which each stood — that is, the style each began with — Ives and Ornstein found that their art dictated a leap to another mountain range.

But American culture was not yet ready to move to the new mountain, so Ives and Ornstein found themselves alone, cut off from the other agents that compose a musical world. Ives persevered by freeing himself from the need for a support system. Ornstein, like Ives, became his own patron: Ornstein the concert artist supporting Ornstein the composer. The latter, however, fed back to the former, with Ornstein's compositions gaining him publicity and notoriety that had both good and bad effects. That two of the most important composers in the United States between 1900 and 1920 could not move American musical culture one iota suggests just how entrenched it was. Ives of course was not even heard, and Ornstein's music had only rare performances beyond his own concerts.

If American music was to take a new direction, more than the occasional work of an isolated artist who carved out a unique career was necessary. Composer and public might be in different places on the mountain but could not continue on an entirely different range. In 1922 that began to change.

CHAPTER 5

"Prologue to the Annual Tragedy"

C HANGE MAY BE INEVITABLE, but most humans crave stability, or, barring that, at least continuity. Historians try to oblige. As they sift through the shards of the past, they seek that continuity, usually by searching for connections with the present. An explanation of origins, sources, and causes can serve a mediative as well as an intellectual function.

Continuity and connections thus become part of our world, ubiquitous, fundamental to the modern mind-set. They span television programs as well as books; they are an assumed, inevitable element of our thought. But unfortunately reality does not always cooperate. Sometimes change comes suddenly and dramatically. New developments appear, completely unanticipated, often disrupting a stasis that had been in place for many years. These sharp edges of historical fracture can loom disturbing or threatening, upsetting the haven of temporal coherence. As such they provide a challenge many historians relish, to wrest them in, to reestablish a smoothness and connection with the past. Yet in such cases historical accuracy may best be served if the historian *admits* that suddenness rather than trying to explain it away.

The arrival of modernism to the American musical world is one such dramatic break with the past. Although certain individuals had struggled mightily to plant musical modernism on American soil, in virtually every case it withered and died almost immediately, leaving very little residue.[1] The climate was too hostile for its nourishment, and a stasis that had been in place since at least the 1880s remained. Yet a break was imminent, and it came so suddenly that its swiftness has escaped the notice of most historians.

When and how did this happen? *When*, 1922, a pivotal year in the history of American music, one of the major fault lines in the American musical landscape. Before 1922, the American musical world seemed frozen in the late nineteenth century, lost on its own plain. After 1922 the musical world could no longer ignore or dismiss the artistic revolution that was unfolding.

How? In 1922 musicians, helped by sympathizers in the other arts, began to mount what was ultimately a successful campaign to establish a new outpost on the slope of modernism. In essence the ultramoderns succeeded because they organized in a way no musicians had done before, and in so doing they altered fundamentally the relationship between artist and the public. This and the next chapter are about how a group of maverick ultramoderns radically transformed the American musical landscape.

The suddenness of this upheaval has gone unrecognized precisely because of the continuity bias that pervades the historical disciplines. Scholars have stressed earlier attempts by composers, both singularly and collectively, to promote new ideas as steps on the way to the ultramodern revolution of the 1920s. Such material provided sufficient explanation to obviate the need to focus on specific and individual years. Yet the utter failure of the modernists to significantly affect the American musical world undermines the argument for smooth evolutionary development. Only Ornstein made any sort of impact, and even he retreated, for a complex of singular, personal reasons. When one looks at the American musical landscape immediately prior to 1922 it becomes apparent just how bleak the horizon appeared to the modernist.[2]

American Music, Stuck on a Plain

To many observers in the years following World War I, Charles Ives and Leo Ornstein had brought the America musical world to the edge of chaos.[3] From 1913 Ornstein had perplexed and disquieted audiences with his futuristic works, which to many obliterated all rationality in the music universe. Then, as suddenly as he came, he disappeared. And just as Ornstein departed from public view, Ives emerged from his two-decade withdrawal from the professional music world, startling musicians across the country with his *Concord Sonata* and his huge collection of songs. Beginning in 1921, hundreds of musicians to their surprise found packages of printed music in their mail, sent gratis, compliments of Mr. Ives.

Ives and Ornstein were not alone in their musical intuitions. In Europe, Arnold Schoenberg, Igor Stravinsky, and Béla Bartók were moving in the same direction. And on the West Coast, Henry Cowell had begun to experiment with tone clusters in ways both similar to and different from what Ives and Ornstein did. None of those composers had reached the American public when Ives and Ornstein began their treks, however. Cowell became known only in the 1920s after he returned from Europe, and, except for those whose works Ornstein performed, few European modernists were heard in the United States before 1920. The infant recording industry was interested mainly in Italian tenors and a few well-known instrumentalists; commercial radio stations simply did not exist.

Ives and Ornstein were in one sense too individualistic. Each followed his own drummer, but neither tried to change the way Americans went about the business of presenting and hearing music. Throughout the 1910s Ornstein did remain on the front line, introducing audiences to modernistic music. But it was not enough. Americans might be fascinated with the maverick, but the disdain he elicited precluded his ability to effect change. The dynamic quality of American culture came from its open, flexible nature, which supported the fluid, self-directed formation and reformation of organizations and alliances, not from the quirky individual. If American music was to find a new direction, more than the occasional work of an isolated artist who carved out a unique career was necessary, particularly when forces of resistance were as strong as they were in the 1910s. In other words composer and public might be in different places on a single mountain but one or two composers alone could not successfully maintain a foothold on an entirely different range. When one of the most profound changes in American musical culture finally occurred in the 1920s, it was only because a group of headstrong, individualist, imaginative, creative mavericks could somehow align themselves, at least briefly, into a community.

While the Other Arts Embrace Modernism

The situation in music is all the more ironic when compared to the other arts. By the 1920s literature and the visual arts had fully embraced modernism, and Europeans looked to the United States for the future. In 1917 the Italian dadaist Francis Picabia wrote: "It is in America where something must happen. Paris is nothing but a remnant of what it once was. In Europe, countries and cities: there's nothing to speak of." Picabia wrote these lines in a letter to the American photographer Alfred Stieglitz, the man who had almost single-handedly defined American modernism.[4]

That modernism had been part of the New York art world since the beginning of the twentieth century was primarily because of Stieglitz. His contributions were twofold: without question among the great photographers of

Alfred Stieglitz, *Paula* (1889), a work that revolutionized American photography (Courtesy of the Photography Collections, University of Maryland, Baltimore County)

all time, Stieglitz was one of the first American artists to master an out-and-out modernist approach; his gallery "291," located at 291 Fifth Avenue, became the intellectual locus of modernism in the first decade of the twentieth century, with Stieglitz as its resident guru.

Stieglitz's journey into modernism began metaphorically with *Paula*, a photograph he made in 1889, when he was studying in Germany. This haunting photograph of an otherwise unknown German woman, quietly writing at her desk as she is bathed in bands of light coming through the shades, evokes a quiet romanticism. But Paula is no grandiose, melodramatic romantic subject. She is real, and the moment is touching in its intimacy and its very ordinariness. The photograph itself is a technical tour de force; no one before had been able to resolve the values of light and shade found in the Paula photograph.

Stieglitz returned to his native city, New York, in 1890, after nine years of study in Germany, and quickly mastered his modernist approach. While painters in Europe were starting to dissect their world into interlocking cubes, Stieglitz eschewed the painterly approach of most turn-of-the-century photographers and celebrated the new urban environment of New York with images that combined the realism of straight photography with a powerful sense of mood and composition. In Stieglitz's best work we see little nostalgia for the old but rather a celebration of the new, of industrial life with all its ugliness and harsh beauty.[5]

Stieglitz needed an outlet for his work, however, and he founded several. He organized a group called the Photo-Secession, a name borrowed from avant-garde or "secessionist" photographers in Austria who challenged the reigning realistic school of photography, and he established two magazines, *Camera Notes* and *Camera Work*, that further argued the case for modernism. His most important contribution was the gallery he established in New York, the Little Galleries of the Photo-Secession, better known as "291." It was much more than a vehicle for Stieglitz's own art. He mounted exhibitions in all media, and the gallery soon became a gathering place where artists and others interested in new art could discuss and debate the latest developments. The influence of the 291 gallery extended to Europe. Francis Picabia visited New York in 1913 and came away so impressed with Stieglitz's gallery that he modeled his new journal 391 on it. He wrote to Stieglitz: "You will receive a journal '391' that is a double of your journal '291.' . . . it's better than nothing, as here there is truly nothing, nothing, nothing."[6]

Gallery "291" lasted until 1917, but its heyday was from 1905 through 1912. The year 1913 brought the International Exhibition of Modern Art, which was held at the Sixty-ninth Regiment Armory in New York City and became known as the Armory Show. Probably the most important single event in American art, certainly the most significant event in the establishment of modernism in America, the Armory Show for the first time gave Americans a full sense of the new currents in Europe. It created a sensation. An estimated eighty-seven thousand people saw it in New York, and it made headlines in all the city's newspapers. After its New York run the show traveled to Boston and Chicago, where it met a similar reception. All together an estimated three hundred thousand people saw the exhibition.

The Armory Show was also the beginning of the end for the 291 gallery. In the political world of New York art, Stieglitz was essentially shut out of the show as a planner and participant, and he never quite regained the position he had. But by then it didn't matter; modernism was established in the United States, with the emergence of Arthur Dove, John Marin, Joseph Stella, Man Ray, Georgia O'Keeffe, and others. It got a big boost in 1915 when both Picabia and Marcel Duchamp, whose *Nude Descending a Staircase* had been the prime shocker of the Armory Show, immigrated to the United States. World War I had much to do with their decisions, but the success of the Armory Show contributed significantly.[7]

In literature modernist works had begun to appear even before the war. William Carlos Williams, a country doctor in Rutherford, New Jersey, published his first volume of poetry, *Poems*, in 1909. In New York and later Hartford, Connecticut, Wallace Stevens, an insurance executive whose life parallels Ives's in uncanny ways, was writing poetry derived from the symbolists of France. Beginning with his first published poem, "Carnet de Voyage" in *Trend* in 1914, Stevens's works appeared regularly in magazines over the next several years, culminating in his first book of poetry, *Harmonium*, in 1923. The *Egoist* in London published Marianne Moore's first poems in 1915. Six years later, when the Egoist Press issued a book of twenty-four of her poems, she was recognized internationally as a major modernist poet. Meanwhile, by 1909 Ezra Pound had settled in London, published his first books of poems, met William Butler Yeats and Ford Madox Ford, and joined the Second Poet's Club.

American literary modernism, a movement with poetry at its core, was promulgated in large measure through a series of small magazines founded in the 1910s and '20s: *Vanity Fair,* the *New Republic, Theater Arts Monthly,* the *Dial, Seven Arts,* the *American Mercury,* the *Saturday Review.* Many were political as well as literary. Some were primarily political, almost always leftist. The *Masses* was overtly socialist, using art, literature, and investigative journalism to attack the evils of capitalism. The *New Republic,* though more mainstream, was a journal of opinion rather than a journal of the arts, as James Oppenheim, the founder of *Seven Arts,* observed. Other magazines, including *Seven Arts* and the *Little Review,* did focus specifically on the arts. Yet even some of those that were not political nevertheless directly challenged conservative opinion. The *Little Review* defiantly published excerpts from James Joyce's *Ulysses,* an act that resulted in the publisher of the magazine being prosecuted for obscenity in New York in 1922.

Found guilty, he was fined fifty dollars and ordered not to publish any more from the book.

None of the magazines was more important to music or had a longer history than the *Dial*, which from the start blended political thought with literary pursuits and musical criticism. The original *Dial*, a vehicle for transcendentalism, was founded by Ralph Waldo Emerson and Margaret Fuller in 1840, with John S. Dwight as its music editor. Although the transcendental *Dial* survived only until 1844, in 1880 Francis F. Browne resurrected it in Chicago, and until his death in 1913 the new *Dial* published critical and political essays from many of the leading thinkers of the time.

The *Dial* continued uncertainly until 1916 when Martyn Johnson purchased it and made it into a voice of radical journalism. It never lost its literary orientation, however, and in 1919, through a complex series of insider moves, Scofield Thayer bought out Johnson's stake, moved it from Chicago to New York, and refocused it as a journal exclusively for literature and the arts. Beginning in 1920 the *Dial* played a major role in defining musical modernism.

But the Musical World Remained Aloof

Amazingly, the American musical world remained untouched by modernism into the 1920s, seemingly impervious to the tempest unleashed in the other arts. Both musicians and the public reacted to musical modernism as a thing apart, viewing it from the cocoon of a musical tradition handed down from the 1880s. Departures from the tradition were aberrations. When Ives tried to interest professional musicians in his compositions, or when Ornstein presented his new works to the public, the composers were looked upon as misguided eccentrics at best. At worst Ornstein was seen as some sort of circus sideshow, the price of a ticket allowing one to gawk and guffaw at a very public act of musical mayhem. A few connected Ornstein's explorations with those of the cubists and the primitivists, but the musical public in general continued to view him within the framework of a strictly musical world gone awry. To most, music was a one-of-a-kind art in America in the early twentieth century.

For those few interested in modernism, 1918–21 seemed a barren period in American music. A few foreign visitors attempted to interest the American musical public in new music. Busoni made his third appearance in 1915, having previously been there in 1903 and 1910. Ernest Bloch arrived in 1916 and decided to remain in the United States. Several of his pieces were programmed in 1916 and 1917, and through Paul Rosenfeld's influence Bloch was associated briefly with the *Seven Arts* magazine. Most notably, Sergey

Prokofiev appeared in 1918 and gave a number of concerts between then and 1922, playing several of his pieces, including the Second Piano Sonata, Op. 14, and *Visions Fugitive.*

Yet modernism seemed to make no headway. Stravinsky's *Rite of Spring* did not receive its New York preview until 1924, even though Sergey Diaghilev toured with the Ballets Russes in 1916. Diaghilev apparently concluded that the United States was not ready for the *Rite*, and he was probably correct. By 1920 Ornstein had begun to curtail his concert career and was already considering alternatives; he soon retreated to a teaching position in Philadelphia. He had also begun to compose more conservative, accessible music and play more traditional programs. Edgard Varèse was thoroughly rebuffed for attempting to do orchestrally in 1918 what Ornstein had done at the piano. Ives did not even try to reach an audience until 1921; and when he did he received little more than polite and puzzled thank-you's.

Some musicians who would later have key roles seemed oblivious to modernism prior to 1922. Onboard ship to Paris in 1921 Aaron Copland wrote home about three Frenchmen who instructed him in French and enjoyed immensely his linguistic faux pas. One of them in particular, "the painter, who is a man about 30," befriended Copland. The painter was Marcel Duchamp, and years later Copland admitted, "this meant nothing to me, despite the fact that in 1913, at the New York Armory Show, he had sent the art world into a tizzy with his *Nude Descending a Staircase.*" True, Copland was only thirteen at the time of the Armory Show, but as a teenager he regularly read literary journals such as the *Dial*, which were well attuned to various phases of modernism.[8]

Charles Ives seemed equally unaware of events in the other arts, or at least chose to ignore them. Recent research has softened the image that his earliest biographies presented of a man almost totally isolated from his surroundings. We now see him as very much a man of his time: Ives was quite familiar with the products of his European musical heritage and his contemporaries, and he was much in tune with social and political movements of his day. But no one has yet been able to establish a connection between Ives and nonmusical manifestations of modernism. Ives lived for many years in the heart of Greenwich Village, yet intellectually he was miles from the Stieglitz school, and there is no record of him even noticing the Armory Show. Given the press coverage, he must have known about it. Would he have gone to see it? Probably not. And did Ives read any of the new literary works? He and Harmony read a great deal, but what evidence there is suggests it was mostly nineteenth-century literature.[9] At best we are confronted with a stony silence from Ives.

Why did modernism and music seem to live in such different worlds in America? This situation contrasts strongly with Europe: in Germany music and literature had been closely tied since the nineteenth century; in France music derived much inspiration from painting; and in Austria Freudian thought profoundly influenced all the arts.

For Ives modernism was partly a moral issue. Many writers have seen him as the Victorian recalcitrant, morally disturbed by the shocking behavior of modernist artists and the positions they espoused. He could not even accept nudity in painting. Yet Ives was typical of his time in one respect: modernism was associated with Greenwich Village, and by the 1910s Greenwich Village was known as a hotbed of not only radical thought and artistic experimentation but disturbing (for the time) lifestyles, a place where free love, lesbianism, and homosexuality were condoned. Ives the typical New York businessman looked askance at such goings-on in the Village, as did many of his colleagues. Ives firmly believed in old-fashioned family values.[10]

Yet while the moral challenge to Victorian lifestyles that the new artists posed may have bothered Ives, it hardly accounts for the overall distance between music and the other arts. More important was the continuing strength of formalism. American musicians believed in universal principles long after art had called them into question. Leo Ornstein's pieces were blasted, not just because they sounded like cacophony to many listeners, but because they violated perceived universal rules of sound and form. In music system has always been important, and many considered its absence a critical flaw. Thus in 1914 Thomas Vincent Cator could write to *Musical America* that "Leo Ornstein uses no systematic harmonic construction; unless he is systematic in the use of none at all." Cator then went on to reharmonize the opening measures of Ornstein's first of *Two Impressions of Notre Dame* "according to the best principles of harmony with chords that are logically related to one another." Four years later Charles L. Buchanan, in a discussion of Ornstein, asserted that "music, as we of the Western world have understood it, is a disciplined sound, sound made captive by a kind of mathematical set of figures and indications." Ironically this is not only the same argument that was leveled against Charles Ives, but it is the same argument that serialists would use after World War II, when they sought to break with the past. It is an attempt to ground musical process in a formal tradition, or at least a formal system.[11]

The formalist conception of music undermined its importance in another way. Music in the late nineteenth century was considered to be in women's sphere, at a time when such gender separation was deeply embedded in the culture. Such a locus depended on the nineteenth-century notion that music was abstract and pure, part of the formalist assumption. Henry T. Finck confirmed that such attitudes marginalized the importance of music. In 1904 he addressed directly the question of the place of music in American life. He wished to "silence such *men*" who held the notion that music was merely a "plaything." (The emphasis is added here, but Finck's context stresses the point.) Yes, that was the problem, Finck observed: real men did not take music seriously. He then went on to suggest that music indeed was more than a plaything, citing three examples: music in the church, music for important social and ceremonial occasions, and music in the military. "The same man who sneers at music as a mere plaything would not want his daughter married without the atmosphere of solemnity and jubilation it gives the occasion, or bury a member of his family without the ongoing strains of a funeral dirge." Finck then appealed to the Gilded Age male where it counted the most, his family and his pocketbook: add up the cost of tens of thousands of organists every week, and then ask why would pastors spend so much money if they considered music "a mere plaything."[12]

Finck's argument helps explain Ives's own defensiveness, but it also underscores the distance between the place of music and the other arts in American culture. For instance, even though many novels were written by women at the turn of the century, there was no need to defend the work of William James or Henry Adams as being a "mere plaything." They may have needed defending, but for other reasons. Literature had a very different tradition in American culture.

Ives may be the exception, snorting, railing about music and its "sissy" role, although in all fairness most of his rhetoric came later, but Ives typified most musicians in one sense. They did not connect to the other arts around them; when it came to modernism they just didn't get it. And this condition lasted well into the 1920s. In this respect Ives was a typical musician, although possibly more extreme than many. He refused to acknowledge even new musical experiments. I find it inconceivable that Ives did not know of Leo Ornstein's Bandbox concerts of 1915, particularly given their coverage in major New York newspapers. Yet there is no mention of them in the Ives record, and in 1921 he wrote, "Ain't never heard nor seen any of the music — not even a god damn note — of Schoenberg — Scriabine — Or Ornstein."[13] Whether that is true or not, and it is likely not, is beside the point; the aesthetic distance remains.

The first to notice the insularity of the American musical world was Edgard Varèse, who had arrived in the United States in 1915. A bona fide musical radical, Varèse was independent, headstrong, and rebellious. Varèse took one look at the musical scene and was appalled. Where were the American modernists? He lamented both the timidity of composers and the conservativeness of musical organizations. He called them "Bourbons who learn nothing and forget nothing. They are mausoleums — mortuaries for musical reminiscences."[14]

Varèse attempted to stir interest in new music, but he met stiff resistance from both musicians and the public.[15] Like Ives and Ornstein, Varèse had leaped onto the slope of musical modernism, only to find himself cut off and isolated. Composers like Varèse and Ornstein were so distanced and removed they were unable to alter in any serious way the prevailing musical landscape.

The situation that so troubled Varèse persisted into the 1920s. The critic Paul Rosenfeld wrote a letter to his friend the novelist Sherwood Anderson that captured the mood of despair that hung over the New York scene. Although he surveys an arena much wider than music, his comments address the musical situation: "It seems to have been a miserable springtides for everyone. Poor [Ernest] Bloch in Cleveland has had a winter of physical ailment and the next thing to a nervous collapse. He looks as badly as I have ever seen him look. Ornstein I believe has done nothing at all. He worked for a month with the laborers on his place in the White Mountains and found that didn't satisfy him; now he talks of going into business. Stieglitz and [Georgia] O'Keeffe had a bad time of it, too, I think. . . . Everywhere there appears to be a sort of palsy. . . . I can readily comprehend that the general rottenness should have touched you, too. For it is a general rottenness in which we all are involved."[16] Six months later the mood had not improved. Rosenfeld again wrote to Anderson: "We are tired, aren't we? Everybody is dead tired."[17]

If any man had his pulse on the American music world in 1920 it was Paul Rosenfeld. From 1917 through the 1920s he was the most important voice for the musical avant-garde. Rosenfeld had grown up in New York, amid comfortable middle-class Jewish surroundings. After graduating from Yale in 1912, he studied journalism at Columbia, then went to Europe. While there he had an epiphany: expatriation, an idea he toyed with, was not for him; nor was it a solution for the arts in America. America must create its own art, unbeholden to European models.

Rosenfeld returned to the United States in 1916 with a mission and fell in with a group of young intellectuals and writers, including Van Wyck Brooks, Waldo Frank, and Ralph Bourne. He also met and was much influenced by Alfred Stieglitz. In fact Rosenfeld considered the hours spent at Stieglitz's 291 gallery one of the two most formative events of this time and came to look upon Stieglitz as a surrogate father. Although none of the modernists in these circles were professional musicians, music was ever on their minds, sometimes close to the center of their activities. As a young boy Stieglitz had dreamed of being a concert pianist, and Rosenfeld was the only nonperformer allowed to sit in on the evenings at Claire Raphael's house listening to an amateur string quartet that included Waldo Frank.[18]

The second defining experience for Rosenfeld was his friendship with Leo Ornstein, with whom he not only discussed music at length but also studied piano. The relationship began by chance, when Rosenfeld attended a private concert of Ornstein's at Claire Raphael's home. Rosenfeld identified immediately with Ornstein's futuristic works: here was the music of today. They reminded him of Stieglitz's photographs, except they were more violent: Ornstein's music recorded "not only the clangors, but all the violent forms of the city." To Rosenfeld, "Ornstein is a mirror held up to the world of the modern city."[19]

Rosenfeld wanted music to be about life and the contemporary world around him. His criticism of those composers who seemed to shun life was harsh. In April 1922 he reviewed a concert of the Music Guild, a group of young composers seeking to establish their styles. Rosenfeld was mostly disappointed with what he heard, pieces by Marion Bauer, Charles Haubile, Walter Kramer, and Deems Taylor, harmonies "out of the impressionistic period." *White Peacock,* by Charles Tomlinson Griffes, was "really The Afternoon of a Peacock, and by no means the first afternoon the peacock had had." Most of all Rosenfeld found these composers out of touch: their music was "of the sort given out by men who have very little contact with anything in the world save music, and who are unaware entirely of the fact. . . . They are fugitive from their own personalities. The world in which they breathe does not seep into their composition, and colour it. Like the audience's, their life remains somewhere within them, and never touches the earth."[20]

In 1920 Rosenfeld accepted a position as music critic for the *Dial,* where his regular column, "Musical Chronicle," had begun to appear in 1918. Before that he had published music and other criticism in the *New Republic* and *Seven Arts.* Later he became editor of the *Dial.*

By 1919 Rosenfeld had become, according to Copland, then still a teenager in Brooklyn, *the* person to read for the latest musical developments. Later, when Rosenfeld called Copland to compliment him on his *Passacaglia* and his piano piece *Cat and Mouse,* the first of the young composer's works heard in New York after his return from Europe, Copland commented, "I could not have been more surprised than if the President of the United States had called. To me, an okay from the critic of *The Dial* seemed better than approval from *The New York Times.*"[21]

Rosenfeld's musical descriptions were poetic and searing, yet powerful in their deadly accuracy. Typical is his description of Schoenberg: "Arnold Schoenberg of Vienna is the great troubling presence of modern music. His vast, sallow skull lowers over it like a sort of North Cape. For with him, with the famous cruel five orchestral and nine piano pieces, we seem to be entering the arctic zone of musical art. None of the old beacons, none of the old stars, can guide us longer in these frozen wastes. Strange, menacing forms surround us, and the light is bleak and chill and faint."[22]

This was written in 1920. It was signature Rosenfeld. As a critic Rosenfeld himself was a paradox — he used romantic weapons to write modernist criticism. The vivid metaphor, an intense, ornate prose, an excess of excess are Rosenfeld's. His rhetoric soars, his likes and dislikes are in the open, and he frequently aligns himself with the programmatic interpreters of the nineteenth century. He is the modernist and anti-modernist at once. He believes in something as nebulous as spirit in music, and he is staunchly anti-puritan, as the early moderns saw Puritanism. Yet he somehow managed to hang on to both edges of the chasm between criticism and poetry.

In the burgeoning world of musical modernism Rosenfeld was more than a music critic, however, as his relationship with Copland illustrates. From their first encounter Copland and Rosenfeld developed a warm friendship. Rosenfeld often invited Copland to his house for dinner, where the composer met a number of literary people, including Hart Crane, Lewis Mumford, Waldo Frank, E. E. Cummings, and Edmund Wilson. Copland described Rosenfeld as living "a bachelor life surrounded by the latest books." Rosenfeld also introduced Copland to Minna Lederman, and after the performance of the Organ Symphony Rosenfeld worked out a plan with Lederman to improve Copland's financial state. Copland was invited to play for several possible benefactors at Lederman's parents' house, but when that produced little, Rosenfeld, at Lederman's urging, went to Alma Wertheim, who eventually gave Copland a check for a thousand dollars. Later, after Copland had began to achieve a reputation and needed a place to work on his "Incidental Music for an Imaginary Drama," which eventually became *Music for the Theatre,* Rosenfeld pointed Copland in the direction of the MacDowell Arts Colony in Peterborough, New Hampshire.[23]

Copland was not the only musician to benefit from Rosenfeld's generous personality and concern for new music. His stature in the literary world gave him entrée into the homes of potential patrons, and Rosenfeld tapped into the New York world of individual patronage greatly to the benefit of music. He included musicians in his dinner parties, and when he heard of a new, talented composer, such as Roger Sessions, whom Ernest Bloch championed, Rosenfeld invited him to his house. Rosenfeld was always ready to come to the aid of someone he liked and respected, be it to cook a dinner or pay a hotel bill.

Rosenfeld was an ardent champion of new music, and in addition to his regular column in the *Dial* he published four books on American music between 1920 and 1930, *Musical Portraits, Musical Chronicle, Modern Tendencies in Music,* and *An Hour with American Music.* Rosenfeld also wrote four other books in the 1920s as well as articles on painters and writers, including John Marin, Marsden Hartley, Marcel Proust, Guillaume Apollinaire, James Joyce, Carl Sandburg, Van Wyck Brooks, Waldo Frank, Sherwood Anderson (with whom he was quite close), and E. E. Cummings.[24]

Friendships, however, never clouded Rosenfeld's judgment. In 1927 he wrote about Copland, "His gift is decidedly proficient but small, as yet so immature that it makes the impression not so much of something human, as of something coltlike: all legs, head, and frisking hide; cantering past on long uncertain stilts. . . . With all his grandiosity and *élan,* Copland has not yet found a largely symbolic and inclusive form for his gift; or achieved, symphony and concerto notwithstanding, an expression of prime importance." In a letter to Sherwood Anderson, Rosenfeld defended his integrity. The cause was an article highly critical of his friend Waldo Frank, a decision that caused Rosenfeld considerable agony and eventually a break with Frank. He wrote: "I can't have any subject on which I have to keep silent out of policy — that is dishonest and is unfair to myself as well as to others. I will not keep silent because a man is my friend, and if to-morrow I should feel myself cooking with some resentment against you or Van Wyck, I would go ahead, so help me God. Perhaps I ought not to have friends."[25]

Yet Rosenfeld's importance to American musical history goes beyond his efforts to help young musicians or even his writing, some of the most eloquent yet ornate prose in the history of music criticism. He was the principal link between music and avant-garde activity in the other arts. He was part of the inner circle of New York literati, and he was willing to bring music into that circle. Probably more than any other person Rosenfeld awakened the American musical world to literary and artistic modernism and the literary and artistic world to musical modernism. His efforts were both professional and personal. His constant stream of Baroque prose squarely in the middle of the most important literary journal of the twenties, the *Dial,* resolved definitively the problem of music's isolation. Rosenfeld was *the* music critic for the *Dial,* even though he also wrote voluminously on other topics.

Rosenfeld's literary style was much maligned and resented, a clear sign of success. When Gorham B. Munson launched a new literary magazine,

Succession, in 1922, the first issue included a diatribe against the *Dial*. Although not mentioning him by name, Munson leveled his heaviest artillery at Rosenfeld: "It [the *Dial*] features a wallowing ox of a stylist who retails each month acres of vague impressionistic excrement on music, painting, and books." This, of course, confirms that Rosenfeld was read. He simply could not be ignored, and consequently neither could his subjects.

Above all Rosenfeld was a champion of American music. In the modernist movement he saw America finally able to free itself from the yoke of European influence under which it had so long been burdened. This was an important part of how musicians and the public perceived their activities in the 1920s. This attitude is paradoxical because modernism was predominantly an international movement, a position stressed by some of the organizations that musicians formed at this time. But that fed back on itself, as the very international orientation of some of the organizations fomented resentment, splits, and the establishment of rival groups. The question of an American music did not go away in the 1920s; it was sometimes overshadowed by what seemed larger and more threatening issues, but nevertheless it remained an undercurrent, exerting a constant and sometimes powerful force.

In the summer of 1921 Rosenfeld, glumly anticipating the forthcoming musical season (1921–22), described just how mired in the past musical New York had become. The piece he wrote was called "Prologue to the Annual Tragedy":

> Without indulging in special thaumaturgical practices of any kind, without examining the entrails of any musical bird, you know exactly what is going to take place during the oncoming season. You know that what is going to happen is very much the same that happened last season; and that was next to nothing at all. There is no music to be had. . . . The profession of conductors will do heroic work as usual in preventing symphonies of any composers save Tschaikowsky and Brahms from being heard. . . . On the mouldering citadel of Wagner lies Bodansky like a thing of green bronze; he will conduct the 'Walküre' so inspiredly that she will sound an elder sister of 'Madama Butterfly.' As for the glorious company of the pianists, there's not a one of that exalted confraternity who won't be found playing the Chopin b-minor sonata and all its faithful attendants. If one of them does the Opus 111 of Beethoven, all will do the Opus 111 of Beethoven.[26]

By 1922 strains in the musical status quo in the United States had reached the breaking point. At that time Deems Taylor interviewed Fritz Reiner, newly appointed conductor of the Cincinnati Orchestra. Reiner, who came directly from Europe, mentioned a new generation of composers, Arnold Schoenberg, Béla Bartók, Igor Stravinsky, and Ildebrando Pizzetti.

(Pizzetti, mostly unknown today, created a considerable stir in 1915 with his opera *Fedra*.) Reiner went out of his way to stress that Strauss and Debussy were fine composers, but "their day is past, that is, as sources of inspiration for other men. We cannot go on building on their work."[27] America may or may not have wanted to hear Reiner's message, but his implication was clear: Americans were still a generation behind.

An article by Constantin von Sternberg that appeared in the *Musical Quarterly* in January 1921 unwittingly made clear just what Reiner meant. Entitled "Against Modernism," it is a vitriolic polemic blasting musical modernism and music critics who take modernism seriously. At one point von Sternberg contrasts modernistic composers with Palestrina, Monteverdi, Beethoven, Liszt, Wagner, and other historical figures who were considered radical in their time, always pointing out why the older composers are dramatically different from the modernists. But who are the composers von Sternberg criticizes? Throughout this ten-page diatribe he never once mentions a modernist composer's name! The only clue comes about two-thirds of the way through the article with a single reference to several pieces, "Eulenspiegel, Don Quioxte, Salome, Electra," followed by a diatribe against *Salome*: "The Bible dramatized! Ruth? Magdalene? Deborah? Not much! — *Salome!* Perverseness glorified. . . . Nice ethics, that! And why all this to-do? What for? Only and exclusively for the *laus dives plebeii* in terms of coin which the late Vespasian regarded as 'oderless.' Modernism — commercialism!"[28]

The four modernist pieces that von Sternberg specified were all by Richard Strauss, and they were written in 1895, 1897, 1905, and 1909, respectively. Thus in 1921, in possibly the most prestigious musical journal in the United States, Strauss was still considered the epitome of what was new and in von Sternberg's eyes bad about modern music.

A similar position regarding what was modern is found in the writing of W. J. Henderson, a conservative critic. In February 1921 he wrote in the *New York Herald* about "Obstinate Conductors [who] Play Music Progressives Do Not Like Hoping to Make Them Like It." To Henderson progressives were the enlightened public, those open-minded people on whom the future of the art depended. Yet Henderson had little sympathy for those conductors who tried to force modernist music on the progressives. Was he suggesting Varèse, Ives, Schoenberg, Bartók? No. In 1921 Henderson was referring specifically to Gustav Mahler and Aleksandr Skryabin, turn-of-the-century composers whose outputs were generated mostly between 1890 and 1910.[29]

Meanwhile forces beyond the control of modernist musicians or critics contributed to further destabilization of the American musical landscape. In particular a bifurcation between high and low culture, or classical and popular, grew into a major rift, with a concomitant loss of the middle ground. Some sort of split between high and low culture was of course nothing new. It had existed for centuries. Early understandings of the difference were as much political or place-bound as musical: music for the court as opposed to music for the countryside, music for the cathedral instead of the parish church. Music of high culture was often more complex, certainly grander, as it was designed to mirror and enhance the upper strata of the hierarchical society in which it was born. Music of low culture was often simpler, more spontaneous and less fixed, frequently dependent on oral tradition. But there was overlap; Mozart's final opera, *The Magic Flute*, as subtle, symbolic, and complex as any opera in the literature, was composed for a lower-class theater on the edge of Vienna, not the aristocrat-patronized houses that premiered most of his other works.

The idea of high and low culture was redefined in the nineteenth century, when high culture took on moral, idealistic trappings. Good music was good for you, and it was approached as a sacred object. Classical music became sacralized. To a writer like John S. Dwight the Adagio of a Beethoven symphony was as much a prayer as a hymn or psalm sung in church.

New electronic technology in the 1920s reordered cultural stratifications. The phonograph had existed since the late nineteenth century, but only after World War I did it become the mass medium that we know today. Similarly, radio broadcasting began only in the early 1920s, with the first commercial station originating in Pittsburgh in 1920. Radio and recordings had little direct effect on the work of the ultramoderns of the 1920s, but they intensified the split between high and low, with implications that affected all types of music making.

Emphasis on mass media took away the "genial middle ground" that Van Wyck Brooks spoke of in 1915. Much piano music of the nineteenth century existed somewhere in this middle area. Composers ranging from Edward MacDowell, for example, to many otherwise unknown today offered many small piano pieces to the public. How are they to be classified? MacDowell's "To a Wild Rose" was immensely popular, and it has since become a classic, in part because it was composed by MacDowell. Yet what about "Minuet Antique" by W. C. E. Seeboeck? Critics may not judge it as good a piece, but it nevertheless occupies much the same cultural ground as "To a Wild Rose," or "To a Waterlilly."

Nineteenth-century piano music was sometimes difficult to categorize partly because it was transmitted via the same mechanism, the printed page, as Beethoven's sonatas or Bach's fugues. With the increasing use of mass media in the 1920s, popular culture became more distinctive and easily identifiable. It became even more a commodity, a tendency that had begun with the development of Tin Pan Alley, but the new technology extended that tendency dramatically. It allowed what was then called low culture to reach millions of Americans in a way that hitherto had been impossible. Most important, it standardized such culture and in so doing created a truly mass medium.

Standardization occurred because the low was no longer dependent on local conditions. Musicians of all stripes had toured extensively in the nineteenth century, covering all areas of the country from the largest cities to the smallest towns. Yet in most communities the vast bulk of music experienced was local. For most Americans instrumental music was defined by small local ensembles, a dance band, a military band, or frequently just a handful of random instruments. More often than not availability determined instrumentation. For many dances a single fiddle sufficed. Local singers patched together entertainment from what Tin Pan Alley produced.

Tin Pan Alley and the minstrel show began the trend toward standardization, yet until approximately World War I the local filter remained. To Ives, the local stonemason John Bell bellowing off-key represented a sublime musical experience, but not all Americans idealized such singing the way Ives did. And one or two fiddles might suffice for the dance in the barn or "opera house," as local entertainment venues were often called, but the style and repertoire were defined by the tradition and the ability that the performers brought with them. And in most communities that meant the Anglo-Celtic tradition, with a smattering from the minstrel shows. Enjoying the products of Tin Pan Alley required either the ability to perform or an intermediary. That necessity defined the experience. Listening to a friend or relative sing "Wait Till the Sun Shines Nellie," even to join in, was quite different from listening to Al Jolson render "Mammy." For most Americans the latter became possible only in the twenties. With the spread of the phonograph, Jolson's nasal timbre became as much a part of shared culture as were the songs themselves.

But there was another even more important limiting factor, the printed page. For a piece to stick, to really enter the collective consciousness, sheet music was essential. After a period of time some songs did become sufficiently well known to be perpetuated orally, for example many of Stephen Foster's songs, or certain hymns like "Nearer My God to Thee." But even that occurred only after extensive written dissemination. Written transmission is problematic less because it limits reception to those capable of deciphering the code — they *can* play the music for others — than because it limits what can be transmitted. Most vernacular music contains much that simply cannot be put on paper. A performance style can never be fully duplicated. Many praised Henry Russell's performances in the early nineteenth century, but we can only infer and imagine their nature; we can actually hear Al Jolson, and we *know*.

The further removed from Western notational ability, the greater the limitation of stylistic transmission. Jazz developed at roughly the same time as ragtime, but ragtime became a rage around the turn of the century, while jazz spread widely only in the 1920s. That temporal divergence is due at least in part to technology: ragtime can be captured and reproduced fairly accurately in piano notation. Jazz cannot. One can only shudder at what some future generation of musicologists might think were they to try to resurrect the sound and feel of jazz only from transcription. Can anyone describe a blue note of a Louis Armstrong or Bessie Smith with such precision that someone who has never heard either could accurately conjure the sound?

After World War I jazz could enter the American collective consciousness in a way that earlier had not been possible. Technology created a distribution system geared perfectly to the low, the vernacular.[30] Consequently jazz, as a musical genre in its own right, and as a symbol of popular culture, became something that the ultramodern composer and critic had to encounter. Jazz elicited wide-ranging reactions. Some composers, such as Aaron Copland, sought to incorporate jazz into their works; others reacted vehemently against it. Still others, such as George Gershwin, sought to bridge the high-low gulf from below; using jazz-oriented popular language as his natural idiom, Gershwin attempted to expand it into a modernist style. Critics were equally divided about jazz. Gilbert Seldes, a supporter of vernacular culture in general, defended jazz in Paul Rosenfeld's own magazine, the *Dial*, whereas Rosenfeld saw no merit in it whatsoever. Rosenfeld's comments harbor both an unabashed elitism and an undisguised racism, and even Seldes succumbed to racial stereotyping when he tried to distinguish between white and Negro jazz.[31]

The bifurcation between high and low culture, however, meant that in the final analysis low culture could be ignored by the ultramoderns. It was not always, but the most radical ultramodernist could and often did. The ultramodern composer was thus freed not only from needing to incorporate popular idioms but from audience pressure to connect with other aspects of American musical life. Thus even such politically radical figures as Charles Seeger could disregard popular and folk music in the 1920s. In particular the ultramoderns were suspicious of new mechanisms of distribution. They ignored media such as radio almost entirely. Most were openly hostile to it.

Charles Ives, whose own work had earlier incorporated ragtime, hymns, folk songs, and popular tunes, was greatly troubled by what the new media spread. Ives probably spoke for many of his time and musical orientation when he railed against the popular arts, as much for what they portended regarding the interaction between producer and consumer as for what came out of the electronic media: "Is machinery, especially the combustion engine — & radio & photo movie-machines making America Saps! . . . Press a nice little button lie back in your easy chair and have it passed[?] the nice and regular standardized stuff to the mouth ears eyes and mind — as if what ever brain muscles are left haven't gone soft." Even a popular musician like John Philip Sousa could despair: "With the phonograph vocal exercises will be out of vogue! Then what of the national throat? Will it not weaken? What of the national chest? Will it not shrink?"[32]

Charles Seeger, Charles Ives, and John Philip Sousa may have had little in common, but each knew and sensed that technology was changing their musical world fundamentally, even though they were uncertain where it would lead. In one sense they may have feared the worst, and in another they sought the new. But no one in 1922 could have anticipated what would happen next.

CHAPTER 6

The Community of the Ultramoderns

Beginnings

FROM THE TIME of the earliest settlers, America has been shaped by the idea of community, a concept to be distinguished from society. People participate in a society out of self-interest, and only to the extent that the organization satisfies their needs or that they must. A society can be a golf club, a group of football fans, an entrepreneurial venture, or a governing body. Not all societies are voluntary: everyone lives in a state or nation and not everyone can choose which. Very few can opt out of society entirely.

A community is a closer-knit unit, in which individuals have an emotional commitment that often transcends self-interest or a limited range of activities. The most fundamental communal unit is the family, and from there the tribe. In that sense a strong nationalism fosters for its members a sense of community in regard to the state. Like societies, some are voluntary, some leave little choice for the participant. But communities can cohere for many reasons, such as religion, or even art. In many societal units, such as towns, an element of community exists, in some more than others.[1]

American communalism began with the New England town. Founded by like-minded individuals largely on the basis of religion, its will was absolute. Government in a New England town was by consensus, but consensus was expected, demanded. Dissent was not tolerated. Town and church mutually held sway over residents' lives; the two in fact were practically inseparable. But between individual and community, that is town, only community mattered. It was all-encompassing, and conformity was ruthlessly enforced, often by subtle social pressure, less often but no less effectively by the law itself.

The authority of the town resided in its own demographic stability and the lack of choices an individual had. Puritan thought portrayed the wilderness, specifically the American wilderness, as a fantastical desert, inhabited by equally fantastical but nevertheless deadly creatures. The town was a garden in that desert, separated from unknown but sinister forces by a metaphorical hedge. Other than organized efforts to found new communities, Puritan thought discouraged all but the most hearty or reckless from relocation. Thus the community could enforce its will and its conformity.

A pattern not entirely different developed in the South. There the emphasis was less on the town than on the plantation. Plantations mimicked the landed gentry of England, creating an agrarian society in which a few large landowners held disproportionate power. Plantations were relatively complete social units, and their hierarchy — affected in no small way by the institution of slavery — was rigid. Even those unconnected with the plantation, such as the many relatively poor, free whites, could not escape the influence of a plantation society. But unlike New England, both geography and the social system fostered more fluidity, and as a result expansion westward was relatively quick and easy, inhibited to a large extent only by the natural barrier of the Allegheny Mountains, which had been reached by the early eighteenth century. Yet for good or ill the plantation remained the fundamental communal unit of the South.

In the early years of New England settlement, Puritan doctrines were practical and probably necessary. To wander off or flee from the European community meant almost certain disaster. But as America became more mobile by the eighteenth century theocratic hierarchy began to break down, and the authority of the community eroded. With the opening of America geographically in the nineteenth century and the significant expansion of choices for the individual, the idea of community changed. Self-organizing social units in particular proliferated. From here on I will use the term self-organizing society to mean any social unit founded voluntarily and in which members maintain some voice and the right to withdraw. The term itself is neutral on the idea of community, although it often is a community.

Self-organizing societies ranged from small, local, sometimes temporary groupings, such as the wagon trains that plied westward, to larger communities that became complete and powerful entities unto themselves, such as the many utopian communes that arose. The growth of the idea of self-organization, and its effect on American communalism, is one of the defining characteristics of the nineteenth-century United States. This is especially true as the country was spreading to fill in the continent. In most cases towns arose from scratch, and even though many were little more than governing associations created out of the need for some sort of order in a barely civilized world, frequently the very necessity that engendered their rise fostered a sense of community.

Most founders of new towns or communities did not attempt to re-create a new or radical social organization, but rather essentially duplicated what they had left. Cincinnati, for instance, was founded in the early nineteenth century by New England Congregationalists, and until it experienced large-scale German immigration around midcentury it resembled many towns in Massachusetts.

Many other Americans moved into already settled places. Considerable migration occurred from rural to urban areas, and for many the city became a hostile, impersonal locus, filled with traps and pitfalls for the unsuspecting youth. Thus numerous advice books of the nineteenth century warned the young man (women were not expected to strike out on their own) of the dangers that awaited him in the cities. He was urged to join organizations, most specifically the church or a group like the YMCA, but in most cases emphasis was on selecting a community.

As mobility increased and as towns began to change fundamentally through growth, as they came to be seen as big impersonal cities, many Americans were left with a sense of rootlessness and began to look back nostalgically on an earlier time. This is most apparent in the northeast, where the New England revival of the second half of the nineteenth century attempted to re-create an old community that never existed. Artists, architects, and writers, including historians, looked back on earlier New England with a nostalgic glow that was as warm as it was fictional. They restored colonial buildings or built new ones in the style, they wrote about New England town government as the cradle of democracy. A turn to the past was also apparent in the South, where the effort was both intensified and complicated by the effects of the Civil War and Reconstruction. Changes in the way of life that many southern whites remembered were too radical, and the past too politically loaded, to allow a simple and peaceful retreat to an earlier time, however unreal, yet nostalgia remained a powerful, in some cases pervasive, factor. It is still seen today.

Well into the twentieth century, these two tensions — nostalgia for the past and communalism based on self-organization — affected the arts and particularly music in America. Ironically, they had their greatest impact on the most radical branch of musical activity. Charles Ives was driven by the nostalgia factor; many of his programmatic subjects involved remembrance of a nineteenth-century world that no longer existed. His memories were often located in the nineteenth-century village, but not a real one — rather one idealized fully in keeping with the New England revival around him. Ives chose to keep his memories personal, and to an extent private, although the latter choice was not entirely his own. He did attempt to place his music before the public, without success. These efforts were fairly meager, however, and never sustained. It was as important for Ives to keep his memories vivid as it was for him to avoid Danbury itself as an adult. Reality and memory often did not agree with Ives, and when they clashed, as they did when he attempted to visit Danbury later in his life, memory almost always won.[2]

The ultramodern composers of the 1920s had little use for nostalgia, and they took the other road, self-organization. Rather than go it alone, as Ives and Ornstein had done, they specifically recognized the need for collective action. Many years later Aaron Copland commented, "Contemporary music as an organized movement in the U.S.A. was born at the end of the First World War."[3]

Yet musicians forming organizations to promote new music or themselves was nothing new. Concert organizations had been active in Europe since at least the eighteenth century and, depending on the definition, much earlier. In London in the 1760s, for instance, Johann Christian Bach and Karl Friedrich Abel sponsored a series of performances, the Bach-Abel concerts. Most musical activity in the United States well into the nineteenth century was the result of similar organizations: the Handel and Haydn Society of Boston, the Musical Fund Society of Philadelphia, the St. Cecelia Society of Charleston, South Carolina. These were quite different in purpose and function from the societies of the 1920s, however. Earlier organizations filled a void; they were there to establish a concert world that would not have otherwise existed. They created a musical culture.

Later organizations, such as the Manuscript Society of New York, founded in 1889, or the New Music Society of America, founded in 1905, functioned essentially to augment the concert world as it already existed. They did little to change its direction, and their impact was slight. Most folded soon after they were formed. Others, such as the Wa-Wan Press, founded in 1901, had more specific purposes in mind. Arthur Farwell, who believed that an American musical identity could be based on the indigenous music of Native Americans, established it to promote the cause of American musical nationalism. In that sense it functioned closer to the societies of the 1920s. Its impact, however, was limited. For a variety of reasons American musical culture as a whole did not embrace the nationalistic solution of Farwell.

The new organizations of the 1920s differed in major ways from the older societies. They were international in outlook and usually in membership. They were fiercely dedicated to the cause of new music, frequently ideological, and often incestuous. Most important, however, as they became the principal vehicle for the presentation of new music, they created a relatively self-contained community. When the mainstream concert world turned its back on new music, these societies allowed ultramodern composers to turn their backs on the concert world — although they never stopped seeking a broader audience. But in their self-contained completeness, in encompassing much more than the composer, they were different. The ultramoderns began a tendency more typical of the later twentieth century: the creation of a distinct subculture within but not entirely at ease with the larger culture.

The idea for a new type of musical organization originally came from Edgard Varèse, a French immigrant who had arrived on U.S. soil in 1915. Varèse not only formed the first successful new-music organization, the International Composers' Guild, but became the predominant force behind the drive for acceptance of ultramodern music in the 1920s, either as leader or flash point against which others reacted. Temperamental, charismatic, volatile, and passionately devoted to the cause of new music, Varèse had been a rebel since his youth. Growing up he detested his father, Henri, who had a violent temper, something that Varèse inherited. Henri was also physically abusive and adamantly, forcefully opposed Varèse's interest in music. Varèse's loathing came to a head when he was seventeen. Three years earlier his mother had died, and his father had married a woman who was good to Varèse and his younger siblings. Finally, when Henri Varèse inevitably raised his hand to her, Edgard exploded. In a blind rage he came to her rescue and, turning the tables, beat Henri as Henri had beat him. Following that incident he never saw his father again.

Varèse immediately left Turin, Italy, where the family lived, for Paris. For several years he enjoyed a bohemian life of extreme poverty but exhilarating freedom. Finally able to pursue music, he gained admission to the Schola Cantorum, but enmity between him and his principal teacher, Vincent d'Indy, soon surfaced, and Varèse decided to leave after one year. He then secured a position as secretary to the sculptor Auguste Rodin, but once again the father-son drama played out. Rodin promised Varèse considerable help with introductions and connections, but personally he was as imperious as his massive sculptures. Apollinaire once commented, "Rodin resembles the eternal father" [Rodin ressemble au Père Eternel].[4] That was too much for Varèse, who found his pronouncements on music particularly offensive. After one expostulation, Varèse flew into a rage that ended with him calling Rodin "un con" [a shit]. Then and there Varèse's employment and mentorship ended.

Back in Paris, Varèse had been accepted into Charles-Marie Widor's composition class at the Paris Conservatoire, but to Varèse music as taught at the Conservatoire was too prescriptive, too limiting, and after two years he quit. This decision was not entirely his own, however. Many years later Varèse admitted that Gabriel Fauré, the administrator of the Conservatoire, after "a rather nasty exchange of unpleasantries, . . . kicked me out."[5]

Varèse went to Berlin, where he encountered a true radical modernism. The futurists, under the leadership of Luigi Russolo, had declared war on the current art world. In a manifesto, *The Art of Noise*, Russolo advocated, "We must break at all cost from this restrictive circle of pure sounds and conquer the infinite variety of noise-sounds," and "we get infinitely more pleasure imagining combinations of the sounds of trolleys, autos and other vehicles, and loud crowds, than listening once more, for instance, to the heroic or pastoral symphonies."[6]

The acknowledged leader of musical futurism in Berlin was Ferruccio Busoni, one of the great piano virtuosi in Europe. He also composed, wrote profusely on music (his most important work, *Entwurf einer neuen Ästhetik der Tonkunst*, appeared in 1907), and actively promoted concerts of younger composers. Varèse found in Busoni a mentor and supporter who understood him and whom he could respect and admire. Through Busoni at least one orchestral work of Varèse, *Bourgogne*, was performed.

Varèse returned to Paris in 1913. He planned to go back to Berlin, but the outbreak of the war changed that, and after six months in the French army, where he suffered double pneumonia, he found himself again a civilian, but unemployed. Because of the war career opportunities in Europe were bleak, and in December 1915, Varèse decided to test his fortune in the United States.

Varèse left France as a man with a mission. He came to America to "do good work for French music," and to "launch a big movement." He aspired for a career principally as a conductor. According to Varèse he was surrounded by reporters on arrival and became an instant celebrity.[7] Not, however, for his music, but because he supposedly had information about the political and military situation in France. Whatever may have fed into reporters' accounts of France, the New York newspapers are silent about Varèse the musician.

Edgard Varèse in 1916, soon after arriving in the United States (Photograph courtesy of *Musical America*)

Yet Varèse wasted no time. Within a month he had dined with Otto Kahn, one of the most important patrons and musical executives in New York, and established a connection with Cornelius Vanderbilt. On April 1, 1917, Varèse's big break came. He was asked to conduct a lavish performance of Hector Berlioz's *Requiem* at the Hippodrome Theater in New York. For this performance Varèse had at his disposal an enlarged New York Philharmonic Orchestra — 182 players all together — and a choir of 400 from Scranton, Pennsylvania. The event was sponsored by the Guggenheim, Pulitzer, and Vanderbilt families, along with Max Eastman, Thomas Edison, and Nikola Tesla, among others. Musicians of many stripes gave honorary support, including Amy Beach, Daniel Gregory Mason, Horatio Parker, Leopold Stokowski, Fritz Kreisler, and Ignacy Paderewski. The concert took place on the eve of the United States' entrance into World War I.

Kahn probably arranged the Berlioz performance. Varèse referred to "being with the biggest manager," and marveled that this single event would cost fourteen thousand dollars. It is hard to imagine who else could organize an event of this magnitude. Kahn not only had the clout, the resources, and the contacts, he was also one of the staunchest and most outspoken supporters of France and the Allied cause during this time. He had close contacts with the French community in New York and even transformed his own house, at 6 East Sixty-eighth Street, into a club for French soldiers and seamen. For Kahn's purposes, the arrival of this charismatic French musician was probably a godsend, and the concert itself could not have been more consistent with his other activities on behalf of France.

Support from so many patrons was an endorsement more for the Allied cause and a demonstration for France than for a relatively unknown musician. Unfortunately the same patriotism that put Varèse on the podium soon worked against him. The United States focused on the war effort and, if such were possible, became even less interested in radical activity in the arts. Soon after, Varèse commented: "The situation for artists is becoming as painful as in Europe. . . . As for creating new organizations, . . . all that will have to be abandoned. America, which must organize itself, is compelled to make a great financial effort."[8]

Varèse stated that in addition to the concert he was offered his own orchestra for the next season. This did not happen, and the war may not have been entirely to blame. Reviews of Varèse's concert were not good. While Paul Rosenfeld claimed Varèse possessed the "inspiration of genius," other critics were less generous: the *New York Tribune* spoke of a "rather rough performance," "far from inspired," and the *New York Times* called the performance "stodgy" and Varèse's conducting "not free from disappointing features."[9]

Varèse the conductor still had opportunities. He was invited to lead the Cincinnati Symphony Orchestra on March 17, 1918. The situation in Cincinnati was tense. The Cincinnati Symphony's regular conductor, Ernst Kunwald, a German, had been interned by the U.S. government, as had a number of other well-known German musicians. In a country where anti-German sentiment reached almost feverish proportions, Varèse faced an orchestra of predominantly German immigrants, in a city with a strong German heritage. And he was to play an all-French program. Nevertheless he succeeded. Reviews were promising, noting that Varèse, "the young Parisian orchestral leader," was, if anything, unconventional, and a tour with the Cincinnati Orchestra was planned.[10]

Suddenly, however, the tour was canceled. Why? Although the reasons are not entirely clear, Varèse probably brought it on himself. In Cincinnati he spent most of his time with German or German-descended musicians, including Kunwald's son, while ignoring those segments of society supportive of the orchestra. More seriously, however, he scandalized Cincinnati society with his open relationship with Louise Norton, then a divorcée who only later became his second wife. Although Varèse and Norton took separate rooms, they nevertheless stayed at the same hotel. That was too much for Mrs. Charles P. Taft, president of the Cincinnati Symphony board, sister-in-law of the former president of the United States, bulwark of Cincinnati society, and a staunch upholder of Victorian morality.

Varèse integrated into American culture only slowly, and in some ways he never did. As the above incident shows, he either did not or would not play the role expected of a musician. In his early years in the United States he was part of a tight-knit group of French expatriates. Most were artists—Albert Gleizes, Henri-Pierre Roch, Juliette Roch, Marcel Duchamp—and they supported one another and often dined together. Varèse lived in a French-owned hotel described by the American sculptor Jo Davidson as "a little corner of France" and by Louise Varèse as "Paris in New York." These connections helped Varèse, who knew little English when he came, survive. They also impeded his assimilation.[11]

Varèse was close to several European dadaists who came to the United States in 1915. In fact he briefly shared an apartment with Francis Picabia in 1916, and he contributed to Picabia's Dada magazine, 391 (a clear takeoff on Stieglitz's 291). He absorbed many Dada ideas, such as the incorporation of outside sounds, the "sounds of the street," his use of nonsense syllables for voice parts, his refusal to be called a musician. Varèse adamantly maintained, however, that he was not a dadaist. To him music was important and serious, something that kept life from being absurd. In later years he stated, in capital letters, I AM NOT A DADAIST. It should be noted, however, that Duchamp and Picabia both did the same later in their lives.[12]

In the spring of 1919 Varèse organized the New Symphony Orchestra with the support of "125 prominent women of New York." Its purpose was to introduce new music to the public. As Varèse explained to a group of journalists, "There is an urgent need for an organization that shall take what *has been* for granted and lay stress upon what *is*." The first two concerts consisted of Debussy's "Gigues" from *Images*, Alfredo Casella's *Notte di maggio*, Bartók's *Deux images*, and Gabriel Dupont's *Le Chant de la destinée*. The critics' reaction was so negative that the musicians, fearing a complete loss of audience, demanded a change in programming. Varèse refused to compromise, and two weeks later he resigned.[13]

Yet Varèse had even more grandiose plans. At the same time that he was organizing the New Symphony Orchestra he proposed a "League of Nations in Art." In a letter to the *New York Times* he offered a humanitarian vision of a world brought closer together through art:

In art, as well as in politics, we have been jarred out of our traditional isolation. And the result will be good. The contact, the emulation, the competition will spur us to greater accomplishment. . . .

Art is nearer to the people than it was before the war. The great struggle has shown up the sham of conventionalism. It has brought us face to face with the real. And it is this new human quality in expression, this appeal to men and women in all walks of life, which makes possible the League of Nations in Art.[14]

Exactly what Varèse had in mind is not clear. He was never a populist, and his projected league remained only a fantasy in his mind, although elements of it resurfaced in modified form two years later in the International Composers' Guild.

While Varèse was struggling to become a conductor and dreaming of a new world for new music, other musicians who played key roles in the modernist movement of the 1920s were gravitating to New York and seeking each other out. Bit by bit a musical community of highly individualist but likeminded souls was coalescing. By 1920 Carl Ruggles, Charles Seeger, and Henry Cowell had arrived in New York and discovered one another. Although other musicians, such as Dane Rudhyar, Aaron Copland, and Ruth Crawford, had a significant impact on the shape of new music, these three, along with Varèse, established the direction and the intellectual parameters that it took.

Carl Ruggles was the first to arrive in New York, in 1913, just as he was starting his compositional career. Born Charles Sprague Ruggles in East Marion, Massachusetts, in 1876, he was two years younger than Ives. Similarities went beyond age. Like Ives he could claim New England roots of several generations. His genealogy goes back to Staffordshire, England, in the thirteenth century, and his American forebear arrived in Roxbury, Massachusetts, in 1637. Many of his ancestors became prominent in New England military and political life. His great-grandfather, like Ives's grandfather, founded the local bank, the Fall River Savings Bank of Rochester, Massachusetts.

The fathers of both Ruggles and Ives were considered the black sheep of the family, but there the comparison ends. Ives's father lost respect because of his career choice — a professional musician was not a source of pride to upper-class nineteenth-century New England families. He apparently cared for his family and worked hard to provide, to the extent of taking outside work later in life that must have been demeaning to him. He was intellectually curious, creative, and inventive, and Ives idolized him. Ruggles's father, on the other hand, was weak, a ne'er-do-well who drank heavily, played the horses, squandered a considerable inheritance, and was completely dominated by his own ill-tempered, explosive father. Young Charles had no respect for him, and in 1905 he left, never to see his father again.

At that point Ruggles undertook to reinvent himself. He began to refer to himself as Carl, and he glossed the family legend considerably. He claimed that his grandfather, who was a riverboat captain on the Ohio, Illinois, and Mississippi rivers, had been a captain of one of the whaling boats that worked out of East Marion, a seaport town on Cape Cod. The difference between a riverboat and a whaling captain to Cape Cod society was comparable to that between playing in the National League or double-A ball. He maintained that he was Harvard educated as all men in the Ruggles family were. Neither claim is true. Ruggles had studied briefly with John Knowles Paine, but only privately, not as a student at Harvard. The Harvard myth gained credibility in 1917 when he stayed at the home of Dr. Frederick Bartlett, a distinguished pediatrician in New York who belonged to the Harvard Club. Bartlett arranged for Ruggles to use the Harvard Club, and he not only frequented it but used its stationery for much of his correspondence. Ruggles went so far as to deny, vehemently according to reports, that he even had any siblings. He had a sister, Mary, six years older, and a brother, Edward Milton, three years younger, neither of whom he got along with.[15]

By 1905 Ruggles was struggling to make a living from a variety of activities, most connected to music. For a time he wrote regular weekly music columns for the *Watertown Tribune* and the *Belmont Tribune*, played in theater orchestras, and occasionally taught violin. His interest in modern music surfaced, and in 1906 he teamed with Alfred Devoto to give a series of lectures on "Modern and Ultramodern Music," Ruggles lecturing and Devoto illustrating at the piano. With marriage to Charlotte Snell imminent, Ruggles needed a steadier income, and he found it in an out-of-the-way place, teaching violin at a school in Winona, Minnesota. That job soon folded, but Ruggles had the opportunity to found and conduct the Winona Symphony Orchestra. Studying with Christian Timmer, concertmaster of the St. Paul Symphony, he soon gained the acceptable technique that he originally lacked, and like Varèse might have made a career as a conductor. Like Varèse and Ornstein, however, composition intervened.

Visiting New York in the summer of 1912, Ruggles met Charles Henry Meltzer, who had translated a play by the German dramatist Gerhart Hauptmann, *Die versunkene Glocke* (The Sunken Bell). Meltzer thought the play an excellent candidate for an opera, and he had connections with management at the Metropolitan Opera. Somehow Ruggles, whose experience as a composer was virtually nil, convinced Meltzer that he was the musician to compose the opera.

At age thirty-six Ruggles became a composer in earnest. Thinking he could complete the opera in two years, he resigned as a conductor and moved to New York. Two years stretched into seven. Through concentrated work on the opera Ruggles's style evolved, from one of bland chromaticism to an intense, ultramodern idiom. But the opera never came to be.

While Ruggles was struggling with "The Bell," Henry Cowell, a native of California, arrived in New York, in 1916. Cowell was the first of a number of composers from the west whose background and training in music was at best irregular and who were shaped by the landscape of their birth. Later we will encounter Harry Partch, John Cage, La Monte Young, and Terry Riley, each of whom had unusual, even unique backgrounds, but who all bore the imprint of the Far West in their work and outlook.

Cowell's education, both musical and otherwise, was sketchy. Born in California, he started violin lessons at age five, but symptoms of chorea (a type of muscle paralysis) a year or so later ended his violin studies. Recurrent attacks continued until he was fourteen, when they finally abated. Meanwhile his parents had divorced and he moved from place to place with his mother, a semi-invalid, including five years in the midwest, where they stayed with various relatives.

Because of the chorea, poverty, and his migratory life, Cowell had little or no formal schooling beyond age six. His parents had both been involved in the literary scene in San Francisco, and he himself became an avid reader, frequently discussing social and philosophical issues with his mother. By 1910 they had returned to California and somehow managed to acquire a piano. Cowell took to it avidly but never had formal training. He absorbed music around him, which consisted of Celtic folk music from his family, the oriental sounds in the Bay area, and sounds of nature itself.

When Cowell was thirteen he became, purely by chance, a subject of Lewis M. Terman, who was developing IQ tests at Stanford University. In *The Intelligence of School Children* Terman discussed Cowell as one of "forty-one superior children." He provides a vivid description of Cowell as a most unusual adolescent: "As a boy of a dozen years (13 1/2), Henry's appearance was odd and interesting in the extreme. His speech was quaint, and rather drawled and stilted; his face was childish, but he looked at you with eyes that seemed utterly void of self-consciousness; his clothes were often ragged and always ill-fitting; his hair hid his ears and straggled down to his shoulder; his face and shoulders twitched occasionally with choreic spasms."[16] Terman noted two burning interests of Cowell's, botany (he supported his mother partly by collecting orchids) and music, and wondered whether Cowell would "become one of the famous musical composers of his day."

Cowell soon had an opportunity to study music. In 1913 he was brought to the attention of Charles Seeger, who was chair of the Department of Music at the University of California, Berkeley. Seeger recognized in him "the most self-sure autodidact I ever met." Seeger realized that "the best way to handle autodidacts was to let them didact," and while providing guidance in harmony and counterpoint he did not try to impose the traditional regime on Cowell, although he did impress upon him the need to approach musical issues, such as rhythm and harmony, systematically.[17]

Cowell later wrote prodigiously on music, publishing complex treatises on rhythm and harmony as well as many other articles and essays. All the while he maintained an active touring schedule as a pianist, composed prolifically, and worked heroically to support other composers and the cause of modern music. Years later Seeger said of Cowell, "A kind of catalytic agent among the disparate elements of American musical life, Cowell has worked more unselfishly for fellow musicians than any other person, to my knowledge, in the country during these last two decades."[18]

Following Cowell's mother's death in 1916, Seeger recommended that he study with Walter Damrosch at the Institute of Musical Art in New York. At the time Damrosch was fifty-six years old and had been a fixture in New York for four decades. He was conductor of the New York Symphony Society orchestra, and a supporter of Wagner and many values of the late nineteenth century. He had strong opinions, particularly about modern music: "To me most of their [the ultramoderns'] music seems to express only a sullen, dyspeptic hatred of things as they are. They leave us with no elevation of soul."[19] Not surprisingly Cowell did not get on well with Damrosch, and the lessons soon ended.

Cowell met Ruggles at Frederick Bartlett's home in New York, where Ruggles stayed in 1917.[20] By then Cowell had also met Leo Ornstein, and when he returned to California he was considered something of a protégé of Ornstein, although there is no mention in the Ornstein records of their interaction. Many years later Cowell acknowledged that he was seeking out modernist composers: "Looking back, it is hard to realize that at that time, after following every clue which might lead to a musician who liked 'modern' music, I found only two who shared my intense delight to explore free dissonance: Charles Seeger and Leo Ornstein. Carl Ruggles was to make a third."[21]

Missing from this list is of course Edgard Varèse. But at this time Cowell probably knew nothing of Varèse the composer. At best he may have heard of Varèse the conductor, but the cultural chasm that the Atlantic Ocean represented in the world of modern music in the 1910s renders it almost inconceivable that Cowell would know of Varèse's Berlin reputation. Varèse the composer flourished only after the International Composers' Guild provided him a platform for his works.[22]

Cowell stayed in New York only briefly, as the Selective Service had other plans for him. He played in an Army band in 1918 and 1919. Following that he concertized extensively, but it was only in 1924, after returning from considerable success performing in Europe, that he established his reputation in the United States.

In the meantime, Charles Seeger had left Berkeley, where his antiwar efforts had not endeared him to the administration. Seeger's own career had been checkered. He was born in Mexico and grew up shuffling between Mexico and New York City because of his father's business. When in the United States the Seegers had a home on Staten Island. Like Ives and Ruggles, his family had deep New England roots, with one branch going back to the *Mayflower*; his ancestors eventually settled in Northampton, Massachusetts. Seeger's father was a successful, prosperous New England merchant involved in a variety of enterprises. He was also an amateur musician and poet, but consistent with his culture he believed these activities were suitable only as an avocation.

Thus in spite of his geography Seeger grew up with nineteenth-century New England values. Seeger himself assessed his background: "The family's traditions have been guided since 1800 by doctors and businessmen, all New Englanders, extremely independent and with strong puritanical leanings."[23] Seeger's immediate family was Unitarian, although they were not churchgoers, and Charles was sent to a Unitarian boarding school. Yet the Puritan values of discipline, patriarchy, and communal responsibility were deeply ingrained in him.

Harvard was as foreordained for Seeger as Yale was for Ives. Like Ives, Seeger did not go to study music, but while there he took as many music courses as possible. And like Ives he had a relatively low opinion of the music curriculum he found. Seeger's first major crisis occurred after graduation, when he informed his father that he would not play the role of designated heir to the family business. Spurning his father's guarantee that spending ten years in the business would provide him sufficient income for the rest of his life, Seeger decided to go to Europe to study music. Finally the elder Seeger relented and agreed to support Charles for a year's stay in Europe, which he managed to extend to two and a half.

At this point Seeger dreamed of being a conductor. A year's apprenticeship as a conducting assistant to the Cologne Opera convinced him, however, of his musical limitations, and also of his deteriorating hearing, a difficulty he endured his entire life. Seeger's next turn was to composition. In-spired by a soprano he met in Paris, he set out "to write the first American opera of any stature." Like Ruggles's, Seeger's opera was never completed.[24]

Also like Ruggles marriage changed Seeger's plans. He returned to New York in 1911 to live a quasi-bohemian life teaching piano, accompanying, and composing. A set of songs written in the French style gained him some fame and notoriety as an avant-garde and a radical. More significant, however, was a musical partnership with the violinist Constance Edison that soon led to marriage and impending family responsibilities. Seeger was uncertain what to do, when on the recommendation of a Harvard faculty member, the University of California at Berkeley offered him a professorship in music. Seeger quickly decided to take it, and at twenty-six he became a full professor.

Arriving in Berkeley, Seeger discovered that the music program was in tatters. There were twenty-five students, no department, no building, no cur-riculum, and certainly no tradition. Seeger's own professorship was in the College of Agriculture.

The need to think through a curriculum was a catalyst for Seeger. He moved quickly, virtually putting one together from scratch. He began to con-sider how music, especially music history, was taught, the place of folk mu-sic, the integration of contemporary musical developments into the histori-cal mainstream, and how to teach old and new techniques, particularly counterpoint. The latter eventually led to his theories of dissonance counter-point, which had considerable influence in 1920s modernism.

Seeger also began to think about a new subject (at least new to the United States), "musicology," and in 1913 he wrote a paper, "Toward the Es-tablishment of the Study of Musicology in America." This marked the end of Seeger the composer and the beginning of Seeger the theorist. For Seeger had caught the "virus of musicology." Although he would continue to com-pose and to perform as a pianist, from then on theoretical and philosophical discourse about the nature of music assumed centrality in his intellectual ac-tivities, which he used to carve a unique place in the ultramodern world of New York in the 1920s.[25]

Seeger had other problems at Berkeley. In particular his pacifism about the war put him at odds with the Berkeley community, and by 1919 he was physically and emotionally exhausted. Seeger arrived in New York in 1919 to take a sabbatical break, but the rupture from Berkeley soon became perma-nent. Whether the decision not to return to California was Seeger's or the university's is not clear, but neither seemed displeased about the outcome.[26]

Once in New York, Cowell quickly introduced Seeger to Ruggles, bringing him to Ruggles's home in Grantwood sometime around 1920. By this time Ruggles had also become familiar with Ornstein's works. Given Ornstein's fame in the 1910s it would have been hard for Ruggles to miss him, and he did make an impression; in 1922 Ruggles claimed that Ornstein was "the first American composer who ever interested me," and he praised his "reckless audacity."[27]

Seeger taught briefly at the Institute of Musical Art, where he developed an entirely new curriculum on musicology, myths, and epics. He believed that studying the epic tales was important to understanding Wagner. Most important, Seeger developed his theoretical ideas, which were to have a major impact on several composers, particularly Cowell, Ruggles, and Ruth Crawford, who later became his wife. He published several essays, and at the end of the twenties he and Crawford put together a major treatise, "Tradition and Experiment in (The New) Music." The treatise was never published during Seeger's lifetime, however.[28]

Forming a Community

In 1921, Varèse, Carlos Salzedo, and Varèse's wife, Louise, founded the International Composers' Guild. There is little question that it was the brainchild of Varèse. Claire Raphael Reis was soon named executive secretary. There was a board of technical advisers, originally consisting of Varèse, who had the title of director, Alfredo Casella, Acario Cotapos, Carl Engel, A. Walter Kramer, Julius Mattfeld, Salzedo, Karol Szymanowski, and Emerson Whithorne. Mrs. Harry Payne Whitney (née Gertrude Vanderbilt) and Mrs. Christian Holmes provided most of the financial support. Whitney had, since 1919, provided Varèse with a personal stipend of two hundred dollars per month.

An attitude of hostile independence characterized the ICG from the beginning. Varèse and Salzedo issued an initial statement, published in *Musical America* on July 23, 1921, and distributed simultaneously as a leaflet, entitled, in large block letters, MANIFESTO. According to the Manifesto, the guild's purpose was "to centralize the works of the day, to group them in programs intelligently and organically constructed, and, with the distinguished help of singers and instrumentalists to present these works in such a way as to reveal their fundamental spirit." Varèse and Salzedo found much fault with the status quo: when current organizations premiered a new work, they surrounded it with older ones and, even worse, chose "the most timid and anemic of contemporary production, leaving absolutely unheard the composers who represent the true spirit of the time." They were defiant: "The present day composers refuse to die." They vowed to fight "for the right of each individual to secure 'fair and free presentation of his work.'"[29]

To meet these goals Varèse announced a series of three concerts for the 1922–23 season, at the Greenwich Village Theatre. The first was held February 19, 1922. On the program were works by Emerson Whithorne, Louis Gruenberg, Alfredo Casella, Gian Francesco Malipiero, Ildebrando Pizzetti, Arthur Honegger, and Eugene Goossens.[30] All were complex, modernist pieces; there was no fluff or bow to popular favorites in any ICG concert. To the surprise of everyone, the response was positive.

This concert was no fluke; basking in the success of the first year, Reis found a larger venue, Klaw Auditorium, for the second, and by 1924 the ICG was turning away concertgoers, which prompted a move in December 1924 to Aeolian Hall, one of the largest and most important concert venues in New York City.[31] In 1924 the *New York Herald-Tribune* critic Lawrence Gilman acknowledged, "It is no longer possible to doubt that there is a public — large, alert, inquisitive — for the significant new music of our time." By 1927, when Varèse suddenly and inexplicably dissolved the organization, the ICG was attracting overflow crowds of more than fifteen hundred at Aeolian Hall.[32] With these public efforts the ultramoderns began a new offensive, with considerable success; suddenly the American musical world seemed ready for ultramodernism.[33]

Varèse and the ICG did not effect the revolution single-handedly, however. Within a year of its founding, displeasure with the ICG forced a number of composers to form a second major new-music organization, the League of Composers, which spun off directly from the ICG in 1923. Six of the founders of the league had been members of the eight-person executive council of the ICG. The league's original announcement hinted at deep divisions within the avant-garde musical world. It cited "irreconcilable differences" with the International Composers' Guild and promised that the league would "endeavor to present programs of such disinterestedness, impartiality and significance as to place the sincerity of its purposes beyond question." Although the ICG had promised to be catholic in taste in the presentation of its programs, it was a creation of Varèse, and even his closest allies admitted that it was essentially a vehicle for him and the music he preferred.

The League of Composers declared an open-door policy. All types of new music, whether radical or conservative, or even "the safe middle road," would be considered, and in a direct slap at Varèse the five composers on the board stressed that they would not exploit their position. Finally, repeat performances were to be allowed. This had become a particularly bitter issue at the ICG, and controversy over Schoenberg's *Pierrot lunaire* was ostensibly the impetus to form the league. The ICG's American premiere of *Pierrot lunaire* had been so successful that many members wanted a second performance. On the premise that the purpose of the ICG was to promote new music, however, repeat performances had been banned from the start, and on that issue Varèse was adamant. His intransigence made it clear to many members of the board that the ICG was Varèse's organization, and his autocratic administrative manner unsettled many who believed in a more democratic process.

Seeking to be open to many styles, the League of Composers saw itself as a voice of moderation. In a ten-year retrospective of the league written in 1932, Minna Lederman distanced it from both nationalism and radicalism and confirmed the policy of openness: "The chief objective of the league at its formation in the Spring of 1923 was the production of modern music of all schools. This was felt to be the outstanding need of the time. Existing mediums were devoted to particular contemporary phases either radical or nationalistic, and largely to the performance of premieres. The league announced at the very start its purpose of presenting all tendencies in the modern field and of giving second hearings."[34]

To many the league differed from the ICG principally in its programming. Its middle-of-the-road stance disturbed more radical critics, such as Paul Rosenfeld, who blasted it as "a social function where the performance of music served the ambitions of mediocrities."[35] An examination of programs suggests that this charge is not entirely accurate. The league never shied away from the radical. Its concerts featured many European composers, the same ones who were found on ICG concerts: Schoenberg, Stravinsky, Bartók, Ravel, Prokofiev, Francis Poulenc, Arthur Honegger, Darius Milhaud. And it presented works by such American composers as Henry Cowell, Ruth Crawford, and George Antheil. Composers in the United States who were featured by the ICG, such as Carl Ruggles, Dane Rudhyar, or Varèse himself, did not appear on league programs while the guild existed, mainly because the rivalry between the two groups forced a composer to choose: appearing on a league concert doomed one's chances for an ICG slot and vice-versa. The principal difference between the two was that the league leavened its radical offerings with more accessible music, rather than providing a steady diet of "that which is intellectual and uncompromising."[36] To some this was a sell-out; to others, reality. And in the idealistic world of 1920s ultramodernism, compromise was not always taken favorably. The league lived up to its promise to include a variety of styles, although it drew the line at such composers as Howard Hanson and Amy Beach, who continued to write in a late romantic idiom.

There were many similarities between the two groups. Both sought to promote new music mainly through concert performances, and both organizations identified more with modernism as an international phenomenon than with a national orientation. Whether a piece was interesting modern music mattered more than whether it was European or American. Thus a relatively high percentage of pieces on both organizations' concerts were of European composers. Later, when the League of Composers founded a journal, it was mostly about European music. The first two years' issues contained articles on Les Six, Stravinsky, "Italy Today," "The Downfall of Strauss," Skryabin, various music festivals in Salzburg, Vienna, and Prague, the new music of Spain, Schoenberg's operas, Ravel and the New French School, Ralph Vaughan Williams and Gustav Holst, and "Magyar Explorers" (Bartók and Kodály).

The most important difference between the league and the ICG was how they were run. Varèse did not understand the self-organizing, communal aspect of American society. The ICG was autocratic; it was Varèse's organization, based on a European hierarchical model, and he could not adapt to a more democratic approach. Ultimately this proved a fatal flaw, although ironically there was enough European hierarchy in American classical music that it was not apparent for some time. Even as late as 1930 Henry Cowell spoke of the orchestral conductor as a "benevolent monarch" and reiterated that, even though he tries to be fair, "yet he is a monarch."[37]

The ICG was European in other ways: The music performed was that of high modernism, mostly from Europe, the governing board was composed predominantly of European immigrants, and the organization itself attempted to associate with European societies, the Internationale Komponisten-Gilde in Germany, the Corporazione delle Nuove Musiche in Italy, and the Composers Collective in Russia.[38] The tactics of the ICG were also European: form a society, issue a manifesto, attack the prevailing class, specifically the bourgeoisie, proclaim lofty and sweeping goals, stake out a clear ideological position. Some precedent existed in American modernism with Photo-Secession and the work of Stieglitz, but nothing like this had occurred in American music, and for good reason. The class tensions behind Varèse's feelings were not replicated in America.

The founding of the league out of disaffection with the ICG was in part a rejection of the European approach, even though the league's programs also had an international cast. The league reconciled ultramodernism with the nature of American society, a reconciliation the ICG could not effect.

Less rigid and more open to compromise, the league created an organizational model more able to survive within American culture. In both philosophy and governance, it was much more democratic than the ICG. This difference affected all aspects of the league, from programming, and hence its public face, to major innovations and experiments, such as the journal it later published.

This difference also precipitated a split between Varèse and Reis that was to have significant consequences for both organizations. Varèse had asked Reis to be the ICG's executive secretary soon after it was formed. He realized the organization needed someone with strong managerial skills, and Reis had demonstrated both that and a commitment to new music. An accomplished pianist, Reis had studied with Bertha Feiring Tapper, in the same studio as Leo Ornstein, and had been openly supportive of ultramodern music since she heard his first works in Tapper's studio. Like many others, she was stunned. For Reis it was pivotal, "really the beginning, the ear opening, if not the eye opener for me."[39] After Tapper's death Reis continued to support Ornstein, sponsoring a series of concerts at her home in 1916. Paul Rosenfeld, who attended, suggested afterward to Reis that the audience for those concerts might "form the nucleus" for a "modern music club." It did not, at least immediately, but the idea had been planted.

In spite of Reis's pianistic ability her family considered a concert career out of the question: "Playing for charity was my mother's idea of bringing up a musical daughter." She was not ready to defy her family on the concert stage, but she had too much energy and drive to limit her role to the background. When she married in 1915, she and her husband agreed that each could pursue "business" interests during the day, as long as they would leave the evenings for each other and family.[40]

Reis reorganized the ICG concerts, brought in new patrons, and did much to establish the guild's success. Yet Varèse felt threatened. She seemed to be taking over the organization, and he was disturbed by her ideas about democracy and the people. Claire Reis held a much more democratic view of the arts than Varèse, and a much more idealistic vision of what music could do. Out of a desire to bring music to those to whom it was otherwise unavailable, in 1912 she had founded a People's Musical League, an organization that presented an extensive series of concerts to newly arrived immigrants. Both in that endeavor and in her later work she sought to reach, in her own words, the "man on the street," someone with little education who was not familiar with classical music. She felt that he (her language was gender-specific) would be more receptive to new developments than someone trained in musical tradition. The latter person tended to be more hostile to new music because it broke with that tradition. Reis felt it necessary to look beyond the upper-middle-class patrons that constituted most audiences and turn to the less educated: "To 'the man on the street' we must look for the future encouragement of contemporary art."[41]

Reis also saw clearly the nature of self-organizing societies in American culture, and she hoped that Varèse would understand this important point: "I saw, however, the point had been reached where what was regarded as Varèse's domination of the Guild was not longer acceptable to some of his colleagues. I did think that because he was European and rather new as a leader among colleagues of equal artistic and intellectual stature, his attitude might stem from a misunderstanding of the democratic method expected of the chairman of an organization in this country." Varèse of course did not see the organization as Reis did. Even his wife admitted that he "was an autocrat in all musical matters" and referred to his rule as despotic. Carlos Salzedo, a co-founder of the society and a European himself, stated flatly, "This is Varèse's society; it must belong to him." Reis herself later referred to Varèse as a "dictator."[42]

When the issue of the repetition of Schoenberg's *Pierrot lunaire* came up, Reis attempted to call a meeting. Varèse maneuvered quickly and incorporated the society, giving himself as musical director sole powers of decision. He then wrote to Reis: "I most respectfully submit to you the inadvisability of doing anything further by you at the present time, until appropriate steps are taken by those authorized to take them, as specified in the Certificate of Incorporation."[43]

Reis, fully understanding what Varèse meant, countered, "What if we start a society of our own?" Varèse replied, "Go ahead, just so you stop interfering in mine." According to Louise Varèse, this was how the League of Composers was born. Other accounts vary only slightly. Reis states that the suggestion to form the league came from Louis Gruenberg, Lazare Saminsky, and Alma Morgenthau Wertheim, the three board members of the ICG who had walked out of the acrimonious meeting about the repetition of Schoenberg's work. In any event Reis was ready to join the league, which promised to be much closer to her own convictions.[44]

In addition to the way each organization was run, the type of music programmed, and attitudes toward the public, there were geocultural differences, which the composer Dane Rudhyar articulated. Rudhyar, born Daniel Chennevière in France, chose his adopted name to symbolize his new life on arriving in the United States in 1916. He was profoundly interested in spiritual issues and later became an important writer on theosophy. In the 1910s and '20s he developed theories of dissonance that were closely tied to ideas about spirituality and exerted a strong influence on several composers, particularly Carl Ruggles, Henry Cowell, and Ruth Crawford. In the ICG, Rudhyar saw himself, Varèse, and Salzedo, "three Frenchmen with very progressive and rather, at that time, unpromising ideas," aligned against "two fairly wealthy social ladies, Mrs. Reis and Mrs. Wertheim and with them were a couple of American composers."[45]

Beneath these disparate continental outlooks there were also hints of darker tensions, primarily ethnic. The league was predominantly a Jewish organization; the ICG was not. Throughout its tenure the ICG was run by Varèse and Carlos Salzedo, with Louise Varèse providing important support and Carl Ruggles serving as a sort of mascot or local character, someone very much part of the inner circle, until he and Varèse disagreed over the problems of programming one of Ruggles's pieces. The three board members of the ICG who urged Reis to form a new organization, Gruenberg, Saminsky, and Wertheim, were Jewish. The executive board of the league originally consisted of Arthur Bliss, Louis Gruenberg, Leo Ornstein, Lazare Saminsky, and Emerson Whithorne; later Aaron Copland played a significant role. Except for Bliss, whose membership was essentially honorary, and Whithorne, all were Jewish.

Although most of the new organization's founders were originally members of the ICG, a distinct anti-Semitism may have contributed to the decision to establish the League of Composers. Olivia Mattis thinks that is the principal reason. There is no question that Varèse and Ruggles were anti-Semitic, although Varèse was less open about it. Varèse at the least was insensitive. His comments on jazz, for instance, contain barely veiled anti-Semitism. He saw the use of jazz idioms by classical composers, particularly pupils of Nadia Boulanger, such as Copland, Gruenberg, and Marc Blitzstein, as well as by Tin Pan Alley composers like Irving Berlin and Jerome Kern, almost as a Jewish plot. "Jazz is not America," he wrote. "It's a Negro product, exploited by the Jews. All of its composers from here are Jews. Jazz does not represent America any more than slow waltzes represent Germany." This attitude contrasted with that of the league, which in its first year sponsored "A JAZZ symposium by the leader of a popular orchestra [Vincent Lopez], a critic [Gilbert Seldes], and a professor [Burlingame Hill of Harvard University]." In the thirties Varèse's attitudes became even more harsh: in 1934, piqued by what he considered irresponsible behavior by a Jewish colleague, Varèse commented in a letter to André Jolivet that possibly Hitler was right, and in 1937 he wrote at the bottom of a letter to the painter Will Shuster, "Heil to Hitler."[46]

No one was more bitterly anti-Semitic than Carl Ruggles. In 1933 he wrote to Henry Cowell: "I agree with Adolph [Weiss] and [Carlos] Salzedo that it is a great mistake to have that filthy bunch of Juilliard Jews in the Pan American. They are cheap, without dignity, and with little, or no talent. That [Arthur] *Berger* is impossible. They will double cross you Henry, I'm sure, in every possible way. My advice is to promptly kick them out, before it's too late. Carl." Ruggles was so constantly outspoken about his anti-Semitism that in 1948 Richard Franko Goldman refused to conduct a performance of *Angels* at a Times Hall concert by the National Association of American Composers and Conductors. Even when he was in his nineties, Marilyn Ziffran interviewed him for his biography and was forced to silence his anti-Semitic remarks by pointedly observing that she herself was Jewish.[47]

If Ruggles is to be believed, his sentiment was shared with Salzedo and Weiss, two other prominent members of the ICG. Yet the situation was not clear-cut. Salzedo was Jewish, and he remained not only a pillar of the ICG but a close friend of Varèse. Reis herself referred to Salzedo as Varèse's "best friend" and denied any anti-Semitism. And another prominent Jew, Paul Rosenfeld, also supported the ICG in preference to the league. He praised the guild as "a hatchery for musical bacilli, where in glass boxes new combinations and voices, aesthetics and world-feelings germinated," and, as we have seen, he dismissed the League of Composers for its "social function" and its "mediocrities."[48]

Rosenfeld and Salzedo were both ambivalent about their own Jewishness. Rosenfeld indirectly highlighted his own Jewish identity in his music criticism, in his observations on the Jewish qualities of such composers as Ornstein, Schoenberg, and Bloch. Yet in a letter to Sherwood Anderson, Rosenfeld admitted being bored with the Jewish question "in any formal race-theory way," and expressed skepticism at Anderson's observation that there were six thousand Jewish intellectuals in New Orleans, on the grounds that "there aren't that many altogether probably." Salzedo's father was Jewish, his mother of Jewish heritage from a family that had converted to Christianity several generations before. As an adult he purposely distanced himself from his family, identified himself as Basque, and disassociated from any religion. Much of his childhood was spent in France, where he studied at the Paris Conservatoire, and he married his first wife, Viola Gramm, in an Episcopal ceremony in New York City.[49]

The ICG lasted only until 1927, when Varèse suddenly disbanded it. It is not clear why. According to Varèse the ICG had accomplished its purpose; new music was accepted and programmed by established organizations. The public was now "enlightened or at least compliant," and the "exhilarating atmosphere of struggle" that prevailed in its early years was gone. There was no reason for it to continue. According to David Joel Metzer, Varèse was not in good health and may have tired of the day-to-day management of the organization, particularly the financial problems it faced, but then he almost immediately formed the Pan-American Association of Composers. Varèse's decision may have been influenced by his falling out with Ruggles over the commissioning of *The Sun-Treader* for an ICG concert. Ruggles wanted an instrumentation that Varèse did not think feasible, given budget and administrative limitations. In a letter to Ruggles, Varèse telegraphed his ultimate decision about the ICG: "Remember that I am considering seriously giving up any activities which will show a source of trouble — less of time and interference with my work. Yourself are aware with the fact that platonical business and clerical work are not very much in harmony with composition."[50]

The League of Composers proved the most durable and successful of the new-music groups in New York, surviving until 1953. Yet the most remarkable aspect of the two organizations was not their rivalry but their combined success. In 1921 it would have been unthinkable that within two years not one but two organizations devoted to radical modernist music could continuously draw capacity crowds.

I have stressed the activities of the ICG and the league, particularly in its first years, because these were the pioneering organizations for new music, and their impact was greatest. Several other new-music organizations also appeared in the 1920s: the Pan-American Association, the New Music Society of California, the Pro-Music Concerts, and the Yaddo Festival. In addition the New School for Social Research sponsored courses and lectures in modern music. The most important of the other new-music groups were the New Music Society and the Pan-American Association. The New Music Society was founded by Henry Cowell in 1925 in Los Angeles, and moved to San Francisco in 1926.

Cowell was the apostle of new music. He was not only its practitioner but its salesman, its chronicler, and with Varèse its most significant organizer. Varèse did much to organize the New York musical world, but he was limited by his own temperament and his European outlook. Cowell had no fetters. He had carved his own niche since childhood. He had ideas, talent, and unlimited enthusiasm. His own music was wild enough to attract attention. Its principal feature, the tone cluster, was simplicity itself, an idea that everyone from the man on the street to the critic at the city desk could understand. It was the ideal emblem of new music. To discuss the use of fists, arms, and elbows on the keyboard required no grasp of the arcana of musical notation. It defined Cowell to the American public with a clarity that no other musician achieved.

Henry Cowell, c. 1925, demonstrating his tone-cluster technique (Photograph courtesy of *Musical America*)

More important, Cowell had vision. He was naive, but in an engaging way. Seeing the need for ultramodern music to take root on the West Coast, he modeled the New Music Society after the ICG. Cowell was also shrewd. The nonresident advisory board consisted of the inner circle of the ICG plus Eugene Goossens, by then a successful conductor who made frequent appearances at the Hollywood Bowl. The resident board included his friend and fellow composer the mystic Dane Rudhyar, the English composer Arthur Bliss, then living in the United States and relatively well known to the American public, and Henry Eichheim, a local conductor sympathetic to new music. Cowell himself refused the Varèseian title of director in favor of the more modest "organizer."

Cowell also played a major role in the the Pan-American Association, essentially running it, although it was a creation of Varèse. Varèse had formed the Pan-American Association, with many of the same members as the ICG, soon after he disbanded the guild. It was, if not nationalistic, at least hemispheric; it stressed music of the Americas. As such it contrasted with the European orientation of the league as well as the ICG, and has since provided a convenient distinction to historians: the league as the coterie of the Boulangerie (those who had studied with Nadia Boulanger in Paris), and the Pan-American Association as the promoter of American music, that is music with less European influence. There is much truth but also considerable irony in this situation: many league composers did embrace neoclassicism and more conservative European trends, writing music more in the symphonic mainstream, while the Pan-American Association remained the laboratory for greater experimentation and a more radical outlook. But Copland, a leading figure in the league, strongly supported many Latin American composers, and Varèse, the founder of the Pan-American Association, remained the most European of the immigrant musicians of the early twentieth century.

As the case of Claire Reis demonstrates, critical to the survival of these organizations was patronage, and in the 1920s that meant private patronage. The ultramoderns in one sense were lucky; patronage itself was in a state of flux following World War I, and the radical contingent of American music benefited directly from the interests and the energy of a new generation.

In one sense traditional patterns prevailed. Most patronage still came from individuals, and overwhelmingly from women of wealthy families who had developed a keen interest in the arts. In the nineteenth century this group had created one of the most important institutions in musical America, the women's musical clubs. Nothing could be further from the truth than to dismiss these clubs as groups of dilettantes occupying their afternoons. Men in the music business, men who knew, called them the most powerful force in American music. Throughout the country, from small towns to the largest cities, women's clubs made the important decisions about the musical life of their communities and then acted on those decisions. More often than not, they contracted for visiting artists, arranged locations, sold the tickets, and guaranteed the events. Women's clubs founded orchestras, and many women, especially those with managerial skill and those of wealth, went on to become impresarios and independent patrons. Young affluent women growing up in the early twentieth century saw this as an important role model, and many were drawn to continue the tradition. The innate conservatism of such patronage, however, began to break down from other pressures.[51]

Society itself was changing. The 1920s was a time of excitement, triumph, and a sudden loosening of energy pent up from the realization that the old order, the nineteenth-century world that Ives missed so badly, was finally over. Victoria gave way to Greenwich Village. The war had delivered the coup de grâce to the Gilded Age, and the country sought the new, the modern, and in its experimentation embraced the most baffling paradoxes. The automobile, the radio, and the airplane opened up society in a way comparable to what the railroad did in the previous century. Jazz, glitter, excitement, exuberance, all existed within one of the boldest social experiments the republic ever tried, Prohibition.

In the nineteenth century women had been the moral guardians of the old order. Now they had the right to vote, and they no longer bore quite the burden of the family as they had in the nineteenth century. They reveled in a newfound freedom allowing them to do things in public their Victorian predecessors would not have condoned. For some that meant embracing the most radical of the arts in entirely new ways.

Many of these young women chose to continue the role of patron, yet even in that realm they were only partially their mothers' daughters. Coming of age in America after World War I, they not surprisingly gravitated toward younger and more avant-garde music and musicians. Varèse, a young Gallic volcano, had been able to attract patrons. He did not, however, recognize that by the 1920s younger women were conquering new territory and would no longer be satisfied with a passive role. As early as 1901 the Gibson Girl, symbol of the new woman, was challenging the Steel-engraving Lady, whose image appeared in so many nineteenth-century magazines. The steel-engraving image depicted a fragile domestic woman, often with knitting or crocheting, gazing dreamily out her window; the Gibson Girl, remembered mostly for her new look, also had new ideas. The *Atlantic Monthly* published this conversation:

> *Gibson Girl:* When a man approaches, we do not tremble and droop our eyelids or gaze adoringly while he lays down the law. We meet him on a ground of perfect fellowship and converse freely on any topic.
> *Steel-engraving Lady:* And does he like this method?
> *Gibson Girl:* Whether he *likes* it or not makes little difference. *He* is no longer the one whose pleasure is to be consulted. The question now is not, "What does man like?" but "What does woman prefer?"
>
> I can do everything my brothers do, and do it rather better. . . . My point of view is free from narrow influences, and quite outside of the home boundaries.[52]

The Gibson Girl is not to be equated with the flapper, although both were the product of the times. The flapper was the frivolous side of the newfound freedom, the Gibson Girl the more serious; she was the feminist.

In spite of all the changes, wealthy young women interested in the arts remained in a bind. The Gibson Girl proclaimed proudly, "We're up to date and snuff, and every one of us is self-supporting." For many upper-class women large family fortunes had both removed the problem of livelihood and rendered the notion of self-support moot. But as always wealth brought restrictions as well as opportunity. For a wealthy young woman with artistic inclinations, a professional career remained problematic, but the traditional path to artistic involvement, patronage, continued to beckon. Most wealthy daughters were not ready to abandon that road, but some would redefine it.

Many young women, originally gravitating toward the arts because of significant talent, staked out artistic territory of their own. Others, having already taken on organizational roles in social or charitable organizations, developed not only considerable leadership skills but also, as they pursued their own artistic aims, new ideas about the place of the arts in America.

Several wealthy women played critical roles in the ultramodern movement: Cecilia Bok, Alma Wertheim, Gertrude Vanderbilt Whitney, Blanche Walton, Claire Reis, and Minna Lederman. Cecilia Bok and Alma Wertheim were the most traditional in their approach, generously funding efforts by the ultramoderns but remaining mostly on the sidelines. Claire Reis and Minna Lederman involved themselves in ways their predecessors had not and, in so doing, did much to influence the direction of modernism.

Gertrude Vanderbilt Whitney was in a class by herself. As flamboyant and unconventional as she was wealthy, she became a sculptor of considerable talent. From birth she had stood at the very pinnacle of society in America. Being born a Vanderbilt placed her there; in 1896 she married into the Whitney family, a move that only enhanced her position. To most people her life seemed the American dream. She had unbounded wealth and social status. She and her husband, Harry Payne Whitney, made a strikingly handsome couple. By her mid-twenties they had two children as photogenic as they were. Yet the marriage was troubled. Her husband, an attorney by profession, was interested more in polo and race horses, of which he owned several champions. Later she would find out his interests included other women. Gertrude herself was restless.

In 1900, at twenty-five, Gertrude Vanderbilt Whitney turned to sculpture. Previously she had done some drawing and clay modeling, mostly dabbling. Now, however, she decided to dedicate herself seriously to large-scale sculpture. Being a Vanderbilt had advantages. Sculpturing requires a large studio and relatively expensive material, a serious obstacle for many young artists. For her, no problem. She set up studios in Newport, Rhode Island (at the Vanderbilt summer home, the Breakers), and in New York. Her name also gave her entrée to well-known artists and the opportunity to learn from them. Being a Vanderbilt, however, created problems. There were many social and family obligations, and she was not ready to abandon them. To what extent could she dedicate her time and energy to her art?

Gertrude Vanderbilt enjoyed considerable success. By 1904, however, she realized that while her talent may have been no more than average, her wealth and position were not. She began to seek situations in which "her advantages count," and turned seriously to patronage. She was one of the primary patrons of the Armory Show of 1913, and she was in the audience when Varèse presented the only concert of the New Symphony Orchestra in 1919. Later she not only became the principal patron of the ICG, but supported Varèse and Ruggles personally, possibly because both composers had close connections to the visual arts: Ruggles had been recommended to her by Rockwell Kent and was himself a serious painter, and Varèse was not only close to European dadaism but was a friend of Joseph Stella.[53]

As essential as patronage was, however, both in making an undertaking financially possible and in providing administrative skill, it did not ensure survival. Varèse's New Symphony Orchestra was well supported, but it did not endure as a vehicle for new music beyond the first concert.[54] Although both the times and a new type of patron in the 1920s paved the way for the acceptance of a radical modernism, more than that was needed. Musicians interested in the new had to not only combat the prejudices of the conservative establishment but sustain interest in what they were doing, if ultramodernism was to get beyond the initial interest of curiosity seekers, who populated many of the first concerts.[55]

The ICG succeeded in large measure because it not only found a way to work outside the musical mainstream, bypassing the forces of stability that were still powerful in 1922, but reinvented a musical culture at all levels. It was a radical break with the past. The League of Composers, in adopting a similar pattern with greater success because it was more attuned to American society, built on Varèse's efforts. The completeness of the ultramoderns' solution had far-reaching consequences. The ICG and the league precipitated a fundamental change in the relationship of composer and public. With the varied activities of the self-organizing societies of the 1920s the role of agents — that is, components within the system, be it individuals, formal organizations, or simply groups of people with a collective identity — underwent a radical reorientation.

In a modern situation musical activity occurs through several mediators between the composer and the public: performers, managers, critics, and patrons. Prior to the 1920s roles were well defined; a composer might also be a teacher and a performer, but the overlap seldom went beyond that, at least in a major way. The system was linear and one-way. This situation can be pictured by arranging all the participants along a straight line running from left to right: composer — performer — manager — critic — patron — public. Activity moved only in that one direction, left to right, particularly when the system was stable, as it was through 1922. With one huge exception, those to the right had little effect on those to the left. The exception is important, however: those to the right had the ultimate power, the power to break the chain. Feedback in such circumstances was simple; those agents to the left that did not satisfy those to the right did not survive. A composer who did not write the kind of music the public wanted did not get his music performed. A performer who did not please a critic jeopardized his career. Likewise a critic that was too out of tune with public taste soon found himself out of a job.

The ICG changed all that. From its founding the ICG squared off against the rest of the musical world as if it was the enemy. The guild stated in its second year that it "was organized primarily last season to liberate the composer from existing conditions, which generally hamper his work being presented at all or in an ideal manner." Those conditions were "the self-interest of managers, the tradition of most conductors and performers, and the prejudices of a public." In other words, all those agents to the right of the composer on the line drawn above. Varèse thus attacked directly the linear system as it existed, with its various agents and intermediaries that stood between creator and public. He contrasted the role of the composer with that of the poet, sculptor, and painter, seeing their difference in terms of the nature of their contact with the public: "The composer is the only one of the creators of today who is denied direct contact with the public."[56] He blamed this state on both the need for an interpreter, the performer, and the organizations that chose programs, concert management.

The ICG not only did away with the role of professional concert managers but distanced itself from the traditional performing venues as well. The ICG presented concerts in the Greenwich Village Theatre, and later, when Claire Reis left to become executive director of the League of Composers, she continued the practice, renting the Klaw Auditorium, another theater.[57]

As for the public, Varèse also had little hope for them, seeing them in European class terms: "There is little to be hoped from the bourgeoisie. The education of this class is almost entirely a matter of memory and at twenty-five they cease to learn and live the remainder of their lives within the limitations of at least a generation behind the times."[58]

A pivotal development in the readjustment of artists, mediators, and public occurred when the League of Composers formed the journal *Modern Music* in 1924. Unlike other musical journals, which were about performers, impresarios, or agencies, *Modern Music* was about composers. It was written mostly by composers, but it was not for composers. When it first began, its intended audience was not clear. During the first year it went under the title *The League of Composers' Review*. A year later, however, the board affirmed, by a narrow margin, that it was not to be a house organ and changed its name to *Modern Music*. At first its circulation was only a few hundred, but by 1946 it had grown to three thousand.[59]

With *Modern Music* the league signaled a new direction for modern musical societies, to instruct and educate the public. Concert presentation was not sufficient; audiences must be taught about new music. This emphasis of the society predates the same didactic thinking that informed much early music programming on radio. It was also part of a larger new pattern of how the musician and society would interact.

Yet while the general purpose of *Modern Music* was "to rouse the public to a live appreciation of the new in music," an immediate target was also the press. Minna Lederman, the journal's editor, saw the critics more than the public as the principal problem. According to her: "A more precise point of attack would have been the American press of that time [as opposed to American elites]. The mandarins of the New York and also of the Boston papers had an ambivalent attitude toward new music. The concerts of contemporary works which they attended were legitimate prey for the ridicule they felt was acceptable to their daily readers."[60]

With *Modern Music* lines between agents blurred further. Minna Lederman was one of several wealthy patrons associated with such organizations. According to all accounts her role was as decisive for the journal as Reis's was for the organization itself. Composers themselves wrote many articles, taking on the role of both educator and critic. Composers, editor, and board also worked to solicit material from abroad and elsewhere.

The work of these musicians and the journals they founded were modeled on the new literary magazines. Like the literary magazines, the founders had a mission, theirs to spread the word about modern music. But unlike the literary magazines, their discussion had to occur in a different idiom, verbal, from the one in which they created, music. Their primary purpose was to educate, to explain what the new music was all about. Significantly, at this time the principal theoretician of the movement, Charles Seeger, began serious consideration of precisely that issue, what he later called the "lingocentric predicament." The problem was thick enough that it occupied Seeger for more than fifty years and formed one of the cornerstones of his philosophical investigation.[61]

A further didactic effort characterized the 1920s, lectures about modern music. These occurred in many venues, from the occasional lecture like the series of three Ruggles gave to the Whitney Club, or those Seeger gave to the Society for Ethical Culture, to ongoing series at the New School for Social Research, where Copland, Cowell, and Seeger regularly appeared. Most of the venues were alternative ones, outside the mainstream musical culture of

the time. The League of Composers, from the very beginning, sponsored lec-
ture-recitals as well as the more formal concerts.[62]

In spite of differences in the way they were run, most of the new-music
organizations were similar in other ways. The statement of purpose of the
Pan-American Association, for instance, could have been written for the
League of Composers. Some, however, were strictly concert venues. The
Yaddo Festival and the Copland-Sessions concerts fit that category. Others,
while having the presentation of concerts as their principal activity, also
sponsored journals and engaged in further activities promoting new music.
Henry Cowell saw that more than a few premieres of new music was necessary. Such music needed to circulate in print, and at that time the big printing houses would not touch it. For that end Cowell, through the New Music
Society of California, launched the journal *New Music*, which published
complete scores of major ultramodern compositions.[63]

The new-music scene was in fact a relatively closed community. With
the exceptions of the ICG after its first year and the League of Composers,
neither of which welcomed members of the other group, the same names appear over and over on the concert programs, the membership lists, the officers' lists, and in particular on the lists of the executive boards. Minna Lederman observed that the number of composers writing what she considered
new music in the twenties was small, possibly no more than fifty.[64] Attitudes
of those on the inside furthered their sense of distance from the main culture. Many looked on the outside with disdain. As we have seen, Varèse pit-
ted the ICG against the rest of the world in its statement of purpose. Other
composers' comments display similar hostility. Ruggles was openly disdainful of the public. In fact modernists in several fields harbored sentiments bordering on fascism. Musicians were no different.[65]

Even when composers were not hostile to the public, and many were
not, they saw their work as something apart. Elliott Carter observed how un-
European *The Sun-Treader* by Ruggles was: only an American composer
would feel free to write a piece so "dangerously out of line with proven aesthetic standards," because they did not have to write for a ready-made audience. "In a way, American works have been private works."[66] In this sense
Ives is the paradigmatic American composer; his own isolation, whether
myth or reality, whether conscious choice or necessity, appealed immensely
to the American mind-set.

Beyond the smaller circle of composers was the only slightly larger circle
of composers, critics, and patrons. In the 1920s they formed a tightly knit
group. Critics lined up patrons for composers, as Rosenfeld did for Copland
and others, and patrons became editors, critics, and managers, as Lederman

and Reis did.[67] But the most telling overlap had to do with the composers themselves: many of them became critics and journalists. Most, such as Copland and Adolph Weiss, wrote for the specialty magazines like *Modern Music*.

Like many developments of the time, the idea itself was not new. Deems Taylor, the music critic for the *New York World*, was also a composer and a member of the American Music Guild. Daniel Gregory Mason regularly wrote about music. Arthur Farwell founded the Wa-Wan Press and for a time was chief music critic for *Musical America*. The difference between the 1920s and earlier times is the relationship between composer-critic and public. Ultramodern composers wrote for their own outlets and saw their purpose as didactic. Virgil Thomson, who became music critic for the *New York Herald-Tribune* in 1940, is the exception, and his acceptance within ultramodernism was iffy.[68] Radical composers viewed the mainstream press at best with skepticism, generally as hostile. Even Aaron Copland, model of tolerance and amiability, finally had it with critics. At the opening of a festival of chamber music at Yaddo in 1932, Copland led an attack on the press by contemporary composers. "Frankly, I consider newspaper criticism a menace," he said. "We would be much better off without it."[69]

Musical modernism in the 1920s formed a relatively complete subculture: composers founded their own organizations to promote their own music, they acted as their own impresarios, lining up performers, halls, and audiences, they avoided the standard concert venues; they found patrons sympathetic to their cause, they found a kindred voice in the new journals that were redefining American literature, they took those new journals as models and created their own propaganda machine; they became their own critics, by their sheer audacity they attracted a public. Varèse with the International Composers' Guild was not the only composer-impresario. Henry Cowell did the same with the New Music Society of California, and Copland and Sessions with the Copland-Sessions concerts and the Yaddo Festival. The loop was closed, bypassing the established impresarios and venues.

The Public

The public. Who was the public, how did they react, and what *was* their role? When Varèse and Ruggles drew the battle lines between a radical, highly principled artist and a leery, scornful bourgeois public, they established an image that stuck, one in which avant-garde composers for more than fifty years could take solace, sometimes even turn to their advantage, as we will see in Chapter 10.

The situation that the ultramodern composer faced in the 1920s was complex. Composer, critic, and general public all conspired to construct a social situation in which new music could not only exist but thrive. The relationship to the public also underscores differences between the league and the ICG. Not all ultramoderns were hostile to the public, and those who openly disdained the public were probably a minority. Nevertheless the nature of most modernist compositions almost guaranteed a tension between composer and consumer.

Audiences were a problem of ultramodernism from the very first concerts of Ornstein. Initial reaction to modernist music was often more bewilderment than hostility, but hostility soon followed. Ornstein had encountered both in his first London recitals. Hostility, however, was something the ultramoderns soon thrived on. To shock and outrage was much a part of the modernist movement in the visual arts, and its effectiveness was apparent at the Armory Show in 1913. The reception of Stravinsky's *Rite of Spring* in Paris had given not only new cachet to such reactions in the musical world but also a model to emulate. Later some American composers, such as George Antheil, tried too hard; Antheil probably wrote *Ballet mécanique* to provoke a riot à la Stravinsky's *Rite*. It was a complete failure when it premiered in New York in 1927, with audience and critics concluding that, beyond the desire to provoke, there was little substance. In any event by 1927 audiences were sufficiently inured to what seemed bizarre; they were more bored than shocked. Antheil's shortcomings may have been as much a misreading of the American public as a weakness in his piece.[70]

Part of the problem was the very politeness of the American public. In 1923, in the *New York Tribune*, F. D. Perkins considered the question, Does the purchase of a ticket give you the right to hiss? He acknowledged that American audiences are charitable; when they like something they applaud, when they don't they applaud, only less vigorously. Generally when they don't like something they keep it to themselves.[71]

Perkins observed that before 1922 audiences did not hiss. But three instances in the 1922–23 season raised his concern: faint hissing at a performance of Arthur Honegger's *Horace victorieux* at a Boston Symphony concert, mild hissing over a Philadelphia Orchestra performance of Schoenberg's *Kammersymphonie*, and a serious ruckus created by a performance of Varèse's *Hyperprism* at an ICG concert.

To Perkins by far the most serious instance of audience disapproval occurred at the ICG concert. Yet Perkins was more concerned with the aftermath of the response than the response itself. On this occasion the audience divided and responded vigorously both for and against the Varèse piece. In the midst of the uproar Carlos Salzedo jumped up and yelled to the audience, "This is serious!" Then it was announced that the piece would be repeated, and those that did not wish to hear it were invited to leave. This response prompted Perkins's inquiry into audience rights. How far can the audience go when it does not like what it hears?

The debate itself is curiously American. The critic as educator informs the public of the bounds and the ground rules of acceptable behavior. The public, still sufficiently uncertain about the concert world, looks to the critic for cues. Here the critic is also arbiter, a role well recognized, but in the case of the ultramoderns, the extent of his influence is unclear. Most established critics tried to be open-minded; some were downright hostile.

Some ultramodern composers almost took glee in the hostility of the conservative critics and the uproar that their compositions caused. In 1926 Varèse wrote to Ruggles about the premiere of his *Amériques*: "I have wanted to tell you about 'Amériques' What a work! and what excitement! Hisses and hated — liked and lauded. It is pleasant to the taste that N.Y.'s two worst critics disliked it most — [Richard] Aldrich and Olin Downes (too much) Olga [Samaroff], you have probably heard — "[72]

Hostility and anger at least show that the piece had an effect, if nothing more than to unsettle preconceived notions of music. More disturbing to the ultramoderns, and much more common among audiences, was a different reaction: laughter. According to one newspaper account it was laughter, not hissing, that provoked Salzedo's angry outburst at the ICG premiere of Varèse's *Hyperprism*: "Mr. Varèse's work . . . makes much use of the caesural pause and this appears to be its undoing, for in the intervals of silence the ribald ones in the audience began to hiss. There rose shouts and catcalls and various noises. In vain did Carlos Salzedo, who had just emitted an astounding sonata for piano from the harp, cry to the people that this was serious music. They did not care how serious it was. The more serious, the more they objected. But *some of them laughed* — the crackling of thorns under a kettledrum, of course — and that was what evoked Mr. Salzedo's declaration."[73]

The ultramoderns had encountered laughter since Ornstein's first concerts. One critic noted in 1916 that "a particularly loud guffaw from some male voice in yesterday's audience simultaneous with his striking of the final note in a 'trick finish' of his 'A la Chinoise' was a faithful commentary on the emotions of about 90 per cent of the audience — excluding those who maintained a very grim expression on their faces or walked down the aisle and out to register their disapproval." Other critics spoke of audiences "giggling," "tittering," frequently "guffawing," and "laughing out loud." Olin Downes described the pieces on one ICG concert: "Some of the compositions were merely ugly and fiendishly dull. But others were extremely funny. Like the dog-faced boy, the more serious they were meant to be the more they made everybody laugh."[74]

Such observations were common for new music concerts. But even private performances were not immune to such reactions. Waldo Frank reported that when Ornstein played to an invited audience at Bertha Feiring Tapper's house, "ladies laughed hysterically."[75]

Laughter of course is one way of covering bewilderment or embarrassment. With modernism came a perplexity about art; many laymen were sincerely puzzled about what the new art was about. Laughter became a common reaction to new music. It was particularly useful to an audience that was not sure of its responses to music in general, much less to music that at the very least challenged. Writing in the *Little Review*, Margaret Anderson articulated that point: "What is there in this [Ornstein's music] to cause hysterics? The fact that it sounds different from the music you have been hearing? But that would seem to be a reason for interest, not merely for mirth. This reaction belongs in the same plane with patriotism and duty: — you laugh at what is strange, you love what is familiar, you obey what has been tested: — the three ready-made emotions, with which you can escape most effectively from art and life."[76]

Audience attitudes were also aided and abetted by critics, who found it good press to lampoon ultramodern music. Reporting on Carl Ruggles's *Angels*, the critic for the *Musical Courier* observed, "It was apparent that the angels had had a serious falling-out and many in the audience tittered aloud, possibly over the picture they were trying to conjure up of what 'Men' must be like if this was a true portrayal of angels."[77]

Even sarcasm had its advantages. It brought in audiences, as Claire Reis admitted. Louise Varèse observed, "People who didn't like [contemporary music] became subscribers because it was such fun." And generally the ultramoderns wanted an audience. But much of the audience consisted of curiosity seekers. For some, concerts became sport. It was also novelty, which meant that once the novelty wore off, the crowds diminished. This happened in California, with Cowell's New Music concerts. Critics referred to "interesting, intimate audiences"—that is, other composers and performers interested in new music. In New York, however, audiences apparently remained large through much of the 1920s, but they evolved into a select, familiar gathering. Claire Reis acknowledged that audiences were split between the "musical intelligentsia" and "members of cafe society and other sensation seekers." Deems Taylor commented that the audience "was so well acquainted that it had to be inducted almost forcibly into its seats by a bevy of distracted ushers," and that it used the intermission "to go visiting up and down the aisles and engage in a series of free-for-all musical debates." And Lawrence Gilman described the concerts of the guild as "Old Home Week Gatherings."[78]

Not all ultramodern composers sought an audience. Reis stated that many of the composers she worked with did not care about the audience. To Varèse the audience was the bourgeoisie, and the bourgeoisie was hopeless. He wished to appeal to the "aristocratic intelligentsia," a phrase that could come only from a European. And when the ICG was considering a touring chamber orchestra Varèse expressed concern about the "long preparation" needed, "considering the stupidity of the provincial audiences." Ruggles, as a member of the inner leadership of the ICG, was even more hostile. After a good turnout he fulminated, "I would prefer to see only six people at our concerts! If you had a full house last Sunday it only goes to show you've descended to catering to the public." According to Reis this remark, made at a meeting of the ICG, created such an uproar that the meeting disintegrated.[79]

Yet not all organizations were openly hostile to the public, and not all ultramoderns held the same animosity. What bothered composers most was the attitude of the mediators, the concert managers and the critics who frequently harbored a deep prejudice against anything musically radical, and the curiosity seekers, who often came for sport, and who apparently made up a considerable portion of the audience. Yet in spite of the disdain articulated by Varèse, Ruggles, and others, even the ICG succeeded in consistently filling its hall and covering expenses. The curiosity seekers were important to the success of the ultramoderns, and the mediators were largely eliminated.

With the self-organizing societies of the 1920s the extent and the nature of the feedback changed, and the arrow of influence running from composer through mediators to the public became a closed reiterative circle with activity pivoting around the self-organizing societies. This occurred in large part because of the blurring of roles: Composers began to assume roles of managers, supporters, patrons, public, and even critics. Patrons began to assume mediator roles, such as editors; and the public itself was essentially thrown off the raft. This does not necessarily mean antagonism toward the public, but the opinion of the public became less important. It was no longer the driving force, the final arbiter about the direction American music was to take. When engaged, the public was expected to conform. It was to be educated, it was to embrace the ideals and standards of the ultramoderns themselves. That it often did not, that it often reacted to premieres with hostility and amusement, both reinforced the ultramoderns' sense of isolation and reinvigorated their determination to indoctrinate. The public was to follow *their* lead, not the conservative critics'.

One of the most important aspects of the developments of the 1920s is their suddenness and unexpectedness. Most of the events I have described occurred in a four-year time period, 1922–26. Ultramodernism itself continued into the 1930s, when the Great Depression and new social concerns then led composers into other directions, but by and large the important events had happened by 1926. There was certainly little on the horizon before 1922 to presage what did occur. Those four years are American music's "Cambrian Explosion."[80]

The ultramoderns succeeded because they were able to create not just societies but a community, one typical of the later twentieth century, when subcultures within the broader culture flourished. And it is precisely because of the completeness of the community they established they were able to reorder the role of agents on the American musical scene. The decision by Varèse and Reis was simple at first — bypass the New York concert establishment in the presentation of their concerts — but the result was far-reaching. They not only broke the conservative isolationism that had held art music in a time warp since the nineteenth century, but with the reorientation of agents' roles the public perception of the artist and the artist's place in society changed fundamentally. A new definition of the artist emerged. It may have been a stereotype in the public's mind, in some ways inconsistent with reality, but the image itself was important. It also may have been a throwback to bohemian romanticism, but in music it was largely because of the activities of the ultramoderns beginning in 1922 that the artist as maverick became the expected norm in American society. The musical world has not been the same since.

Epilogue: The Last Banquet

In 1929, Henry Cowell conceived a new project: a book about contemporary composers by contemporary composers. It came to fruition in 1933 with the publication of *American Composers on American Music: A Symposium*. Intended to be a prophetic volume, it was portentous, but hardly in the manner Cowell originally envisioned. It turned out to be retrospective, a final summary by those of 1920s ultramodernism that lived it. By the time it came out the era was over, although its impact would resonate throughout the twentieth century. Cowell's retrospective was 1920s modernism's last banquet, a final assemblage of those who had made the decade something unique, and an opportunity for old friends and not-so-good friends to reminisce and pay tribute to one another.[81]

Cowell, however, found the idea difficult to bring to reality. He spoke of cooperation "proving difficult or dilatory." He sought only those composers who had a proven ability with words, a skill not all composers shared. Many begged off; some did not want to speak about other composers but were willing to comment on the general situation, which became a third section of the book. Ultimately Cowell had to rely on articles that had been previously published (ten) or came from his own pen (eight, four new ones). Thus of the twenty chapters on composers only six were original contributions from someone other than Cowell.

Nevertheless Cowell's achievement as a portrayal of 1920s modernism is salutary. The portraits are sympathetic and at the same time enlightening. Many are snapshots of a composer's career and style in midpassage. Others summarize what a composer has done, little knowing that the subject's creativity had come to an end. The guest list itself is revealing, both for those he did invite and those he did not. Cowell did not restrict himself to only ultramodern composers. He invited some who were more conservative, such as Howard Hanson and his newly emerging Eastman School. In the introduction he divided composers into eight groups, and he spelled out his criteria: composers invited must be at least moderately well known, have a distinct point of view, and be articulate.[82]

While Cowell sought to be inclusive, his leanings were apparent: he favored "progressives" and an "indigenous point of view," avoiding those who followed European models too closely. Backsliders, such as Leo Ornstein, received no mercy. Cowell, apparently feeling the heat over his absence, explained: "His work is not treated in detail here because it has not influenced the general trend since 1920 at the latest, and because since about 1920 his style has become more and more conventional until it can no longer be considered original." Two of Ornstein's most important pieces had appeared in the 1920s, the Piano Concerto in 1925, and the *Quintette for Piano and Strings* in 1928, but he had been radical modernism's poster boy throughout the 1910s, and when he abandoned that style for one more expressive the ultramoderns reacted as a lover scorned. Not even Cowell, known for his accepting temperament, could forgive Ornstein.[83]

At this point it did not matter, for by the time that the book came out the era was over. Some composers, such as Ruth Crawford, Charles Seeger, and Aaron Copland, had turned to radical social causes and a people's music. Others, such as Cowell himself, had turned to different musics, particularly of the Orient. Still others, such as Charles Ives, Edgard Varèse, Dane Rudhyar, and Carl Ruggles, had for a variety of reasons all but gone silent. The ebullient 1920s had already given way to the harsher reality of the 1930s.

PART 3

After the War

After World War II we enter a period as unsettled and surreal as any in American musical history. The aftermath of the war, new connections between Europe and America, the breakdown of traditional patterns of patronage, and, not at all least, new technology inaugurated a revolution in musical thinking, a period of extreme experimentation in which composers of art music challenged not only all the accepted parameters of music but the very concept of the art itself. It was one of the most febrile and paradoxical times in American music. It was also one of the most consistent, for underlying what seemed to be the principal practitioners' totally disparate paths were basic beliefs about society and the individual that united in aesthetic rationale and intention artists as different in personality and technical detail as Milton Babbitt and John Cage, Charles Wuorinen and Philip Glass.

Following the Second World War the very idea of the maverick becomes problematic. Who are the mavericks? In the world of music the question became, Who isn't? As the fantasy of the artist as eccentric, as outsider, attuned to his own drum, became the expected norm for a concertgoing, now high-fidelity-listening public, as the Lone Ranger became firmly embedded in the American psyche and the Marl-

boro Man the most successful image in the history of adver-
tising, the question turned in on itself. If maverickdom is the
new de facto standard, then are mavericks mavericks?

This question necessitates a new approach. After World
War II the musical world divided into factions, in which rad-
ically differing points of view were fractiously argued. Tradi-
tion was denigrated as each faction sought to claim the
mantle of the new. Audiences as in the 1920s were often be-
wildered and uncertain. Yet the 1920s had left a legacy, that
of the artist apart, and thus aesthetic distance and bad be-
havior became cachet in itself. After the war flaunting norms
became a cottage industry. In such an atmosphere audiences
splintered and subcultures flourished. A few individuals un-
derstood the dynamics of the late-twentieth-century media,
and manipulated them for incredibly successful careers, al-
though in all fairness the most successful had talent as well
as media savvy. This section deals as much with a number of
different trends, each with its own set of mavericks, as with a
few individuals. Thus we come to the ultimate irony of the
maverick in American music, that of groups or schools of
mavericks.

CHAPTER 7

New Directions

The Serial Wars

ALTHOUGH MUSICAL ACTIVITY in the 1940s by no means came to a standstill, it was nevertheless eclipsed by the war effort, the most total mobilization of American society since at least the Civil War. Yet World War II and the events leading to it had a major effect on American composers. Before the war, American composers went to Europe to learn their craft. After World War II the transatlantic road became two-way. This had begun in the 1930s when many European musicians came to the United States because of events in Europe. Arnold Schoenberg and Béla Bartók were only two of the most well known. But after the war composers crisscrossed, doing, learning, interacting. In a sense the Western musical world became one. John Cage lived in Paris, had his pieces performed there, and by 1950 had a greater reputation in France than in America. He also developed a close friendship with Pierre Boulez, and promoted Boulez's works when he returned to the United States. The Darmstadt festivals in Germany of the 1950s and '60s, a concentrated summer gathering of new-music activity, featured the works of many American composers. Other American musicians returned from the war with a truly global perspective. Some had seen not only Europe but also the Far East.

The depression and the war disrupted patterns of patronage. Through the 1920s many patrons took on a more active role in supporting new music, but composers and composers' organizations continued as they had been, funded mainly by individual patrons. That changed in the 1930s. First the depression and the New Deal, then the economic effects of the war and the escalating tax structure not only reduced many fortunes, but caused those whose wealth survived to institutionalize. Foundations rather than individuals became the source of private money for the composer, and the most successful were those who knew how to play the grant game.

World War II technology had multiple effects on music. During the war a small machine, little noticed at the time, was invented in Germany. After the war Pierre Schaeffer in France began to realize the potential of this machine, the tape recorder, and soon other composers, led by a contingent of rebel Americans, followed suit. Within a few years the tape recorder had revolutionized all aspects of music making.

None of this was apparent in the immediate years after the war. Prewar modernism was all but moribund. Such pioneering institutions as the League of Composers had long become stuffy and old-fashioned. Some composers in the 1930s turned to neoclassicism; others, seeking a more accessible style and a wider audience, turned to American folk roots and nationalistic or at least geographical themes. Composers who came of age in the 1930s, like David Diamond, Samuel Barber, and Roy Harris, followed this path with considerable success. Others became political converts: Ruth Crawford, Marc Blitzstein, and Charles Seeger embraced radical political thought and music for the people. Even Aaron Copland joined that movement. But after the war neoclassicism and a folklike Americanism had waning appeal to younger composers. Like the late teens, the late '40s seemed a time bomb waiting to go off.

Around 1950, it happened. All hell, it seemed, broke loose. Serious composers, experimental in the 1920s, socially aware in the 1930s, and quieted by war in the 1940s, suddenly diverged in two totally different but equally radical paths. Some, extending ideas of Arnold Schoenberg and Anton Webern, sought total determination of every nuance of a piece through mathematical calculations; others, exploring various chance and indeterminate techniques, wanted to eliminate the will and emotion of the composer. But all seemed to be moving away from mainstream audiences, and for the second time in thirty years the American musical landscape changed drastically.

The Serialists Bid for Control

The first to emerge were the serialists. They adopted and extended Schoenberg's concept of the tone row to all musical parameters. The tone row was a set of pitches that formed the structural foundation for a piece. In its pure form it contained all twelve notes within the octave, and the resulting music was called twelve-tone, dodecaphonic, or serial, the series being the row. The

act of composition involved manipulating the row in often highly sophisticated ways. The result was music that was chromatic, atonal, dissonant, and
to many listeners unsettling. Postwar followers of Schoenberg applied serial
technique to rhythm, dynamics, and even timbre as well as pitch, often using
complex, advanced mathematical procedures. The movement toward total
serialism, as it was known, occurred on both sides of the Atlantic, but it was a
European who first captured the headlines.

Pierre Boulez was twenty years old when World War II ended. Like
many of his generation he emerged from the war wanting to turn his back on
the past and reinvent Western culture. For Boulez this desire was intense; he
was, in Olivier Messiaen's words, "in revolt against everything." The past was
the enemy, and he wanted to destroy, to obliterate utterly the entire Western
tradition: "It is not enough to deface the Mona Lisa because that does not kill
the Mona Lisa. All the art of the past must be destroyed." It was a life and
death struggle: "The dilemma of music is the dilemma of our civilization.
We have to fight the past to survive." Boulez's comments parallel those of Pi-
casso: "In art one must kill one's father."[1]

Boulez's first move was to adopt serialism. He had studied with René
Leibowitz, a disciple of Schoenberg, and had learned the twelve-tone system.
He also studied with Olivier Messiaen, an eclectic composer who sought to
order parts of music other than pitch into repeating patterns, creating an in-
cipient serialism. Messiaen in particular experimented with ways of organizing rhythm and dynamics, and in *Mode de valeurs et d'intensités*, a piano
etude, created three separate rows corresponding to different pitch levels on
the piano. Each row involved the serialization of pitch, rhythm, and dynamics. This piece, written in 1949, is sometimes considered the beginning of total serialism. Messiaen did not pursue this idea further, however. That was
left for Boulez.

Boulez was not content to break with just the tonal past. For all his revolutionary thought Boulez still saw Schoenberg as part of the Western tradition, which meant he had to be destroyed. In 1952 Boulez shocked the avant-
garde musical world with an article in *Score*, a radical magazine devoted to
new music, titled "Schoenberg Is Dead." To Boulez, Schoenberg failed because he was unable to let go of the past. He deserved reproach, "for this exploration of dodecaphony, pursued so determinedly in a direction as wrong
as any in the history of music." Schoenberg failed from lack of ambition: he
was "overtaken by his own innovations," his desire to cling to a traditional
thematic approach with the row, an approach that retained many vestiges of
romanticism. For that contradiction he was doomed to failure. And the further Schoenberg went the worse it got. Schoenberg's "American period," the

last seventeen years of his life when he lived in the United States, "shows utter disarray and the most wretched disorientation."[2]

Today it is difficult to imagine how inflammatory Boulez's statements
were. Serialism was the wave of the future for younger composers, and
Schoenberg, who had died just the previous year, was on his way to deification. Schoenbergian serialism was especially important to a number of
American composers, some of whom benefited from Schoenberg's resi-
dency in southern California. Boulez saw the way of the future in Anton Webern. Webern, a pupil of Schoenberg, wrote works as quiet as his own personality, works that exemplify the word *pointillistic*. Webern did not extend
Schoenberg's serialism as much as he put it in service of a very different style.
For both Schoenberg and his other famous pupil, Alban Berg, dodecaphony
had a late romantic, expressive angst, as the music often unfolded in waves
of sound. Schoenberg's serialism was linear — contrapuntal and broadly
melodic. Webern reduced serialism to isolated points of sound. In his pieces,
invariably quite short, instruments enter with one or two notes, then return
to silence as the row passes to other timbres. Boulez and a number of other
subsequent composers adopted an essentially speeded-up version of Webern
serialism, in which cascades of melodically isolated, individual sounds bom-
bard the listener. It is a style that, as we will see, is not limited to serialism.

Boulez had been distancing himself from Schoenberg's approach from
his very first major works in 1946. In his Sonatine for Flute and Piano and his
First Piano Sonata, Boulez adopted a serialism closer to Webern than
Schoenberg. Thematic elements can still be found, but they are only short,
fragmentary motives. He went even further in his Second Piano Sonata, in
which, according to Robert Morgan, "thematic content is almost completely
dissolved." Boulez consciously set out to eliminate traditional structure in
this piece: "I mean I tried to destroy the first-movement sonata form, to disintegrate the slow movement form by the use of a trope, and repetitive
scherzo form by the use of variation form, and finally, in the fourth movement, to demolish fugal and canonic form." Since sonata form is based on
tonal opposition (which is fundamentally inimical to serialism), fugal form is
based on a relatively strict contrapuntal ordering of voices, and variation
form is inherent often even in scherzi, it is not entirely clear to what extent
Boulez's statement is more than self-aggrandizing rhetoric. But he left no
question of his intentions: he wanted to attack and obliterate the Western
musical past.[3]

The irony in Boulez's comments lay in his subsequent career. Soon his
compositions were eclipsed by his conducting, which culminated in a seven-
year stint as music director of the New York Philharmonic Orchestra. There

are few positions in the twentieth-century musical world more wedded to tradition than that of conductor of a major symphony orchestra. Thanks to the virtual deification of Beethoven's nine symphonies in the nineteenth century and the romantics' love of rich, varied timbres and the grandiose statement, the symphony orchestra became the prime symbol of a sacralized high art. By the twentieth century this had coalesced into a tradition and a ritual, the establishment of a symphony becoming a community's principal rite of passage to the higher realms of culture. The status of the community often rested on its orchestra, and no one was more central to this mission than its conductor and music director (usually the same person). As the oldest major orchestra in the United States in the largest city in the country, the New York Philharmonic held a particularly crucial position, which was further enhanced by the opening of Lincoln Center in 1962. Lincoln Center, the Philharmonic's new home, was a mega-complex of performing spaces, the grand temple of high art, and soon the model for cities across the country.[4]

The arrival of Boulez on the American musical scene as a central player in the 1970s underscores not only the distance he had come in a brief time but the extent that the art music world had become international. Boulez had not even conducted a full orchestra before 1955, nor had he done anything significant before 1959, when he was asked to substitute for the ailing Han Rosbaud, first for a festival orchestra and later for the prestigious Concertgebouw Orchestra in Amsterdam. And Boulez's lack of experience as a conductor was exceeded only by his ignorance of the United States itself. When he was asked to speak at Middlebury College in 1950, he had to write to John Cage and ask, "Where is Vermont?"[5]

Boulez had not given up his crusade against tradition with the appointment to the New York Philharmonic. In spite of his anger and his idealism, Boulez was practical, and he saw this as an opportunity to advocate for new music, particularly for serial avant-gardism. The results were mixed. His tenure was stormy, and his lack of choreographic showmanship, as well as his cool approach to the classics and avowed promotion of the atonal school, met with an icy reception in many areas.[6]

In the meantime serialism was spreading. Schoenberg was not the only German émigré to advocate it in the United States. In Europe other composers, notably Karlheinz Stockhausen, were soon to take it up. Stockhausen, three years younger than Boulez, came to it only in 1951. Eventually Stockhausen would usurp Boulez as the leader of the European avant-garde, but he never had the general impact in the United States that Boulez did, possibly because he was never as closely associated with American institutions. Through his leadership at Darmstadt, a summer gathering of experi-

mental composers, however, he strongly influenced several American composers.

While international focus was on Boulez as the leader of the serialist
movement, a composer on this side of the Atlantic discovered total serialism
even earlier. Milton Babbitt had grown up with an interest in both music and
mathematics. After a brief stint at the University of Pennsylvania as a mathematics major he went to New York to pursue music. He discovered Arnold
Schoenberg's music, studied composition with Marion Bauer and later
Roger Sessions, and received a B.A. in music from New York University in
1935. In 1938 Sessions, then at Princeton, secured for Babbitt a position on
the Princeton University music faculty. During World War II Babbitt was engaged primarily in mathematics, working in mathematical research for the
Defense Department and, from 1943 to 1945, teaching mathematics at
Princeton. According to Babbitt, his work in Washington was so secret that to
this day he cannot reveal what he did.[7]

Yet Babbitt's musical interests were broad. Going back to his early days as
a clarinet player — he studied both violin and clarinet from a young age — he
had a strong interest in popular music. Even today his knowledge of popular
song of the late twenties and thirties is encyclopedic. After the war he decided to try his hand in the pop world, writing songs, film scores, and one
Broadway musical, *Fabulous Voyage*. The musical never reached production, and Babbitt abandoned popular music for serialism. He never turned
back. He rejoined the Princeton University music faculty and remained
there until his retirement, eventually becoming the Conant Professor of
Music.

While Babbitt was pursuing a popular-music career, he was thinking
about serialism. He worked out many of his ideas in a monograph, "The
Function of Set Structure in the Twelve-Tone System" (Andrew Mead calls
it a Ph.D. dissertation). Babbitt dates the monograph, never published as
such, to 1946, and in a series of compositions between 1948 and 1950 he applied serial techniques to all parameters. The titles of these pieces are as abstract, formal, and no-nonsense as the works themselves: *Three Compositions
for Piano* (1948), *Composition for Four Instruments* (1948), *Composition for
Twelve Instruments* (1948), and *Composition for Viola and Piano* (1950). If the
mantle for the first totally serial work is to be awarded, it should go to Milton
Babbitt.[8]

In these pieces Babbitt went far beyond Schoenberg, but unlike Boulez
he never repudiated Schoenberg or the past. His respect for Schoenberg is
great, but he feels that "Schoenberg has not realized totally the implications
of his own system." Babbitt not only set out to explore those implications, but

in so doing took a radically different approach to the row. To Schoenberg the row was thematic. The series of twelve notes with their various permutations played horizontally could form melodic units whose thematic nature helped define the composition. Babbitt specifically repudiated the row "as a thematic thing," but saw it as essentially structural. This fundamental reconceptualization was the key that allowed Babbitt to expand serialism to other dimensions. Rhythm, for instance: "We can structuralize rhythm as we cannot in tonality. The great achievement and the compensation for sacrificing tonality is rhythmic independence." Babbitt also saw dynamics in structural terms: "dynamics are an absolutely organic part of the piece," and hence open to serial manipulation.[9]

Total serialism as such did not last long. Even those composers most identified with it, Boulez and Babbitt, recognized the limitations of a predetermined approach. Later these and other composers assumed a modified serialism: use of many serial techniques leavened with a considerable element of free choice, and with a reinsertion of some element of expressiveness.

Babbitt, in particular, never veered from an all-encompassing serialism, but he never remained static either. His compositional choices were rationally determined, but they were not mechanistic. He explored more involved types of sets and hexachords (the rows on which serialism is built), new ways of ordering rhythm, and in particular the creation of music through electronic technology. He was one of the founders of the Columbia-Princeton electronic music center, which used an early RCA computer and synthesizer that was far ahead of any comparable machine. It was a room-sized device that used vacuum tubes, and all inputting was done on a typewriter keyboard—this was before the days of computer screens, mice, or disks, much less MIDI interfaces—but it allowed the composer control over the finished product such as had not been possible before. It was of such complexity that Babbitt was one of the few, possibly the only person, to master it.

Babbitt's treatment of rhythm in particular is distinctive and often the principal connection with audiences. Although his serial music seems miles from the popular idiom, critics have found in it a "spiky," "jazzy" quality, sometimes directly attributed to Babbitt's own popular-music background.[10] His piece *All Set*, the title a deliberate pun on the jazz set, has a wit and rhythmic verve seldom found in serial music. And in spite of all his intellectual rigor, Babbitt can also portray moods. Possibly his most well known piece, *Philomel*, invokes a haunting, disturbing, and ultimately transcendent atmosphere. It is written for live voice and electronic tape, which is mostly synthesized but also includes voice samples. In the story, taken from Ovid,

Philomel, who has been raped and whose tongue has been cut out, is transformed into a nightingale. Babbitt's piece centers on the moment of metamorphosis. The interweaving of the soprano voice with the dense atonal sound continuum, in which voice samples contrast starkly with very obviously electronic sounds, portrays with considerable power Philomel as she sheds her human body to become a nightingale.

Babbitt's music is dense and complex, but as an atonal serialist that is hardly unexpected or exceptional. Where Babbitt stands out is in his inventive exploration of the rational bases for his actions. His theories predate his music, many deriving from his 1946 monograph on set structure in serial music. Babbitt the composer and Babbitt the theorist blend into one, for his compositions themselves are driven by his theories. To Babbitt each note must be justified rationally, often many times over: "I never choose a note unless I know why it is there." And Babbitt is arguably the most important theorist of atonal music in the second half of the twentieth century. Many fundamental ideas in theory during that time may be traced to Babbitt: pitch class, sets, derived sets, weighed, aggregated sets, time points. Milton Babbitt is to serialism what the German theorist Heinrich Schenker is to tonal music.[11]

The Serial Wars of the Twentieth Century

Serialism clearly shook up the musical world after 1950, but just what was its impact? For years a dominant narrative has prevailed:

> Serialism, whose influence was at first slight, gradually grew until it dominated the new-music scene. Composers quaked in its wake, knowing they had to jump on the serial bandwagon or be lost in its dust. Audiences were confounded and reacted with the only means available: they stayed away. Composers, having lost touch with the public, purposely spurned it and retreated to academia, where they took over composition departments as well as granting agencies. Just when new technology for both the production and distribution of music promised hitherto unheard-of potential, American music entered a perilous period in which new works seemed stripped of all that audiences held dear, and audi-

ences were chided by composer, critic, and performer alike for
not wanting to endure what the serialists had to offer.

Did it happen that way? For at least a generation that narrative has been so reinforced by newspaper and magazine articles as well as standard histories of the time that such was assumed. In recent years, however, current and former serial composers and theorists have questioned this narrative in almost all details. They have presented an alternative narrative almost totally at odds with the dominant one. This vision presents an open-minded, kinder, gentler serialist, whose efforts were misunderstood and whose tolerance was overlooked:

> *The serialists were a distinct and even persecuted minority, a*
> *group whose musical explorations met with hostility and dis-*
> *dain. They never controlled anything, they were not favored*
> *for prizes or commissions. Yet even when in positions of au-*
> *thority (in academia, and on grant and prize panels), they*
> *made no effort to impose their own ideology on the composi-*
> *tional world in general. Long-suffering because of the nar-*
> *row-mindness of much of the musical world, they believed in*
> *what they did but recognized a multiplicity of approaches.*

I have purposely painted these two narratives in their extremes, but there is little exaggeration of views in these statements. The end of the twentieth century saw a second serial war, if you accept the dominant narrative, or possibly a first one, depending on how you interpret the alternative narrative. Even the alternative, however, lends itself to the idea of a second serial war, which is about the historical position of the serialists themselves. Which narrative is right? There is little intermediate ground. From the point of the view of the two narratives, it is primarily a matter of who is the aggressor and who is the victim. The second serial war is really the fight over the first serial war. It is essentially a fight to claim the mantle of maverick.

The second serial war began somewhere around 1970, almost as soon as the first ended. In 1973 Leonard Bernstein referred to the "great split" between the serialists and the traditionalists. For many the career of George Rochberg typified the intensity of feeling between the two factions. Rochberg was one of the more important serialists until the tragic death of his son in 1964. To Rochberg "death could only be overcome by life itself," and that meant "by practicing my art as a living thing (in my marrow bone), free of the posturing cant and foolishness abroad these days which want to seal art off from life." Rochberg then became not only an eclectic tonal composer but an outspoken anti-serial polemicist.[12]

When George Crumb appeared on the American musical scene in the 1970s, he seemed the composer many had been waiting for. In an age when complex, dissonant, cerebral works were everywhere, Crumb offered a dark, brooding romanticism and an unparalleled sensitivity to sound. He spoke of the power and expressiveness of music: "I believe that music surpasses even language in its power to mirror the innermost recesses of the human soul." His *Ancient Voices of Children* and *Black Angels* reached out to audiences of all ages and backgrounds, far transcending the typical new-music circle. His scores themselves were visual works of art, with staves often swirling in circles and spirals.

Yet the romantic backlash was part of the first serial war. By the 1990s it seemed that this chapter in the history of American music was over. In 1991 Donal Henahan wrote in the *New York Times*, "And so we bid farewell to atonality." Its demise had been claimed as early as the 1960s, with prominent critics claiming that "post-Webern serial music [has] so lately passed out of fashion," "orthodox serialism is out," and "the younger composers are no longer strict serialists." Open to dispute is just what these comments mean, whether reference was to strict serialism, Webern-style serialism, or simply the use of twelve-tone techniques, and to what extent serialism had met its demise. These questions, however, hinge on the state of serialism itself during the 1950s and '60s, which is what the second war is about: was there a demise for serialism to face?[13]

The second serial war erupted into full public view in the *New York Times* in 1997. By then serialists had been marginalized, young composers were interested in widely variegated approaches, and only a few (by then) older composers resolutely hung on to serialism. Anthony Tommasini could write on Milton Babbitt under the title "Finding More Life in a 'Dead' Musical Idiom." In a lengthy article titled "In Contemporary Music, A House Still Divided," K. Robert Schwarz summarized the two narratives, calling them "mutually exclusive scenarios," and then interviewed several of the principals. The two sides could not have been farther apart, as can be seen from the following quotations that appeared in Schwarz's article.

GEORGE ROCHBERG:
> Serialism's most publicly aggressive proponents, early and late, presented and still present it as the only true faith. As such, they have proclaimed an orthodox cultural church, with its hierarchy, gospels, beliefs,

and anathemas. After the end of World War II it very quickly captured and dominated American academic circles, which it monstrously and bluntly politicized.

MILTON BABBITT:

There's this notion that we somehow dominated the prestigious Ivy League schools, but we never dominated anything. This is propaganda. It was simply not the case. I was here at Princeton with Roger Sessions. Was there anybody then at Columbia or Yale or Harvard? The attitude was very anti-Serial.

CHARLES WUORINEN:

The story goes around that there was a period during which this terrible Serial music was supposed to be dominant, some composers were forced to do it when they really didn't want to, and then they revolted and produced lovely melodies in C major. This is all nonsense. When I was a young composer at Columbia, the reigning orthodoxy was, on one hand, a kind of Coplandesque Americana and, on the other hand, the symphonism of Howard Hanson and Roy Harris. That was true everywhere. And in my entire life I have never seen anybody make someone write any particular kind of music. It's not that a bunch of beady-eyed theoreticians are forcing innocent students to do terrible, nameless things. So the whole story is a big fake.

JOHN CORIGLIANO (who attended Columbia from 1955 to 1959, the same time as Charles Wuorinen):

By the time I got to Columbia, this [serial dominance] was already the case. It wasn't that I was prohibited from writing the way I felt. But the general mode of thought was certainly not in my direction.

NED ROREM:

We [tonal composers] were treated as if we didn't exist. I asked myself where I stood as a composer, am I doing something wrong? But I can't change horses in midstream, and I wouldn't even if I could.

WILLIAM MAYER:

To be a tonal composer in the '60s and '70s was a deeply dispiriting experience. One was shunned as the last teen-aged virgin.[14]

Who is right? In the most extensive investigation of that question to date Joseph Straus approached it sociologically. He examined statistically who held academic posts, who received grants and awards, who was published, and who was performed. His statistics are well researched, and his conclusion is inescapable: the serialists were only a small minority in all of those categories. Theirs was not the dominant compositional style in any category. His title mirrors his findings: "The Myth of Serial Tyranny."[15]

Why then is the myth so pervasive, why has it remained the dominant narrative, and given the evidence that Straus presents how did it even manage to get started? More important, why does it matter? Straus's investigation, which is very good, has two shortcomings: first, as Anne C. Shreffler pointed out, he asks the wrong question. Straus's categorizations make perfect sense from the point of view of music theory. They reside in distinctions, however, that only some musicians and even fewer audiences would make.[16] Second, Straus's statistics mask a more fundamental problem: they confound tyranny with democracy. Tyrants work by force and intimidation, not majorities. *If* there was a tyranny, then the statistics would neither confirm nor refute it. Finally, it needs to be stressed that in something as intangible as compositional style, intellectual domination may not be malicious; it may stem from nothing more than artistic conviction articulated convincingly.

Ultimately this seemingly arcane academic debate matters because there is deep irony here: the serialists had the impact they did not because they were out of touch, but just the opposite. Even though they did not win large audiences, even though they seemingly espoused a disdain for the public, they were in concept and purpose more attuned to their time than many of the more traditional composers, although, as we shall see, not in ways normally thought.

Straus divides composers into four categories: serial, atonal, tonal, and experimental. He does recognize that some composers may belong in more than one category, and incorporates that into his statistics. Yet for most musicians, and for almost all audiences, how much difference was there between a serial and an atonal piece? For the student who examines the work in detail the distinction can be great. But audiences and critics usually get only one crack at a piece, although a conscientious critic will often inform himself about it prior to the actual performance.

For audiences the differences were even more evanescent. The distinction between a serial and a freely atonal piece was by and large meaningless.[17] In some cases the public could not even tell an atonal from a chromatic, tonal piece, much less a serial one. Even some experimental music sounded at the least non-tonal. Listeners simply knew that modern music was dissonant, harsh, and lacking in lyrical melody. William Schuman often told the story of a concert in Macon, Georgia, after which he was approached by a member of the audience who told him she liked his piece even though she did not generally like atonal music. Schuman tried to explain that his work indeed was not atonal, but tonal, even though the harmony may be complex. Finally she interrupted his explanation with the comment, "That's very well, Mr. Schuman, but in Macon, Georgia, your piece is atonal."[18]

Other than a handful of mostly older composers who maintained an essentially romantic style or a 1930s folk-oriented idiom, or some of the more diatonic neoclassicists, composers of all stripes were so far beyond public comprehension that it mattered little in what style they wrote. In addition, public aversion was exacerbated by the continuing presence of the image created in the 1920s of a fanatical avant-garde aligned with critics sympathetic to the new. The public was made to feel that they *should* like new music. As Carlos Salzedo shouted to an unruly audience at an International Composers' Guild concert in 1923, "This is serious!" Similarly, in the 1950s and '6os when a new piece was announced, the principal reaction of the public was not anticipatory, not excited, not reveling in the new, not cautiously optimistic: it was one of dread, of conflict, between wanting absolutely nothing to do with it and feeling that they *should* support it. Contemporary music events took on all the moral tones of a Puritan church service, with critics and composers themselves conspiring to deliver ample sermons to the public.

No sermon has had more influence that Milton Babbitt's famous 1958 essay for *High Fidelity* magazine, "Who Cares If You Listen?" It has been reprinted several times, sometimes with that title, which was *not* Babbitt's, and sometimes with the title that he intended, "The Composer as Specialist." It has been quoted often in both popular and scholarly literature. It has dogged Babbitt for years; it is the one essay that the musical public knows, and any Babbitt interviewer almost certainly brings it up. But it is an important statement of the mind-set that characterized some aspects of postwar compositional circles.[19]

In the essay Babbitt set forth his vision of the place of the composer in modern society, of the nature of what the composer does and his relationship to the public. His statement from the beginning is overtly positivistic. He sees his role as "telling it like it is," as the 1960s saying went. In the opening paragraph he lays out the "indisputable facts" about the position of the composer in contemporary society, which are: he is mostly ignored except by other composers and musicians. Few would argue with that point. Babbitt then explains why: because new music itself has become so complex that the average concertgoing layman cannot be expected to understand it.[20]

Far from lamenting this situation, however, Babbitt finds it healthy; the problem lies in the composer's attempting to speak to the public and, worse, in critics' writings that reinforce the public's feeling that "music is music," and the composer should be speaking to them. To Babbitt the greatest danger to the development of music is for the composer to pander to the public. Instead, "The composer would do himself and his music an immediate and eventual service by total, resolute, and voluntary withdrawal from this public world to one of private performance and electronic media, with its very real possibility of complete elimination of the public and social aspects of musical composition. By doing so . . . the composer would be free to pursue a private life of professional achievement, as opposed to a public life of unprofessional compromise and exhibitionism."[21]

In all fairness, Babbitt's attitude toward the public is relatively evenhanded, especially compared with that of other modernists. Babbitt allows, with some sarcasm, that the public has its music, "music to eat by, to read by, to dance by, and to be impressed by." This music, however, is not what the contemporary composer writes, and Babbitt sees little hope that the public will ever be able to understand that music. This attitude is mild compared with Varèse, who saw the public as the bourgeoisie and hopeless, or Ruggles, who felt that reaching the public was a sign of failure. No composer, however, was quite as disdainful of the public as Charles Wuorinen, who, in reference to the average concert audience, said, "I care no more about them and their reactions than I do about the audience for juke boxes in bars. Indeed the latter are preferable because they really enjoy what they hear (I think), and in any case are not under the impression that their passive reception of 'music' qualifies them for literate judgement. Besides one can drink in bars."[22]

Babbitt is also clear about a solution: the university. The university should provide a home for the composer. In spite of much audience-bashing and alienation that has been read into Babbitt's article,[23] it is fundamentally a blueprint for the *creation* of a community. It is an act of association, not disassociation. It is Babbitt's vision of a subculture, and as it turns out a remarkably prescient one. It is the composer's own justification for joining. The community is the university, and Babbitt makes an eloquent plea for the composer's acceptance. He not only argues the responsibility of the university to support the composer but in depicting the composer as research scientist he justifies the alignment. To Babbitt the composer belongs in the university.

Alliance with higher education gave the composer a forum to expound his position to the public. The times made that forum important. The G.I. bill of the 1940s had sent millions to college. The Soviet Union then exploded its first atomic bomb on August 29, 1949. Eight years later the Soviets launched Sputnik, the first orbiting satellite ever. These events sent shock waves through American society. In 2001 the *New York Times* commented: "It's difficult to recapture the sense of paranoia and self-doubt that Sputnik created in the U.S." Desperately the American public turned to academia to help neutralize the threat. Millions of dollars were poured into academic research, enhancing further the prestige of the university. Such research was not limited to the hard sciences. It encompassed languages, linguistics, history, and the arts themselves. Congress saw in the arts another weapon to promote American values worldwide. A major debate occurred in Congress regarding the establishment of a national endowment in the arts and in humanities. That debate centered on the issue of cultural nationalism. In its examination of such issues, Congress did not, however, examine closely the position of the academic composer. Few if any members of Congress probably even knew who Schoenberg or Webern was, much less Boulez, Babbitt, Sessions, or Piston.[24]

The impending cold war, the threat of nuclear annihilation, and then the launching of Sputnik not only made the universities wealthy, but brought to science a prestige that it never before had. American superiority and indeed the survival of civilization itself seemed under threat, and the nation collectively turned to science to save it. Billions were poured into science programs at universities, and discipline after discipline aligned itself with science. The social sciences, aided by the proliferation of computers, sought to provide a quantifiable, scientific basis for the nature of society (sociology), the economic system (economics), and even the human mind (psychology). Departments of language and linguistics received massive funds from the National Defense Education Act. Babbitt knew that the more scientific that musical analysis and composition became, the easier its acceptance into the university would be. And given Babbitt's background in mathematics, no one was more capable of bridging that gap. The scientific orientation of his writings is apparent to all.[25]

In the nineteenth century music had been admitted into the university curriculum on the argument that it was analogous with literature. Now that science sat atop the pyramid of academic prestige, if musical composition could be seen as a scientific endeavor, and the composer's work as analogous to that of a research scientist, then the composer's place in the university would be secure. Although Babbitt did not specifically say the composer was a research scientist, he left the impression that what they did was not that different.

It worked, to the extent that the study of music in many of the most prestigious research universities in this country, such as Harvard, Yale, Princeton, the University of Chicago, and the University of California at Berkeley, concentrates on academic investigation, not hands-on performance. Yale University is an exception, but to this day the Yale Music Department (academic) is separate from the Yale School of Music (performance). And in these departments composition is part of academic investigation.

Throughout most of the 1950s and '60s the university was *the* patron for the composer. Few composers did not have an academic appointment, and those that did not either were already sufficiently established, such as Aaron Copland, or worked in special environments, such as writing for films in Hollywood. In 1987 Babbitt acknowledged the importance of the university in the American musical landscape: "The fact most American composers are university-trained and are university teachers is the most compelling evidence of the intellectual reorientation of music in this country."[26]

If the composer is admitted to academia as a scientist, this does not occur without strings, though none may be specified. It has strong implications for what the composer does, that is, what composition is all about. In making the argument for the composer as scientist Babbitt pressed academic composition into a mold that is not always consistent with what a composer seeks to do. This may be apparent to us today, when science itself is undergoing interrogation about its methods, goals, and values, but when it was as pervasive as it was in the 1950s and '60s, questioning the viability of a scientific approach was tantamount to questioning church dogma in twelfth-century Rome. Thus a compositional style that was (or appeared) rational, objective, and quantifiable, or at least rooted in complex mathematical manipulation, seemed more appropriate in a university setting than a more angst-ridden, personal emotional expressivity, or a pounding, primitive-sounding repetitive style.

Yet the serialists could never unseat the establishment, as Straus's statistics demonstrate. The old guard was too entrenched. Traditionalists prevailed at conservatories in particular, where the study of performance far eclipsed the study of composition. For the performer, reaching an audience was critical, which meant paying attention to the standard literature. Thus musical institutions that stressed the training of performers were more aligned with tradition. It is no coincidence that the presidents of Juilliard, Eastman, and the New England Conservatory were composers of a strongly tonal bent, William Schuman at Juilliard, Howard Hanson at Eastman, and Gunther Schuller at the New England Conservatory. Schuller did experiment with atonalism, but his principal efforts were toward blending classical, popular, and jazz idioms in an approach he called Third Stream. But even at universities tonal composers such as Walter Piston at Harvard and Paul Hindemith at Yale exerted enormous influence.

Yet regardless of the extent to which tonal composers controlled the machinery, the serialists managed to cast an immense shadow over the postwar American musical world. Earlier we saw recent examples of conflicting opinions about serialism, as gathered by K. Robert Schwarz. The witness list of composers who felt the negative effects of serialism's predominance is much longer, and now is the time to call them to the stand. In later years composer after composer stepped forward; many were associated with premier academic institutions, but even those who were not felt the pressure.

JOHN CORIGLIANO, as mentioned earlier, was at Columbia at the same time as Charles Wuorinen and had a very different perception from Wuorinen's:

> It wasn't that I was prohibited from writing the way I felt [tonal music]. But the general mode of thought was certainly not in my direction.[27]

BRUCE TRINKLEY, another composer at Columbia in the 1960s, says of Charles Wuorinen's teaching:

> If you showed him something that was not serial, he simply wasn't interested.[28] [This is consistent with Wuorinen's statement, "We were not interested in that kind of music [tonal]. It wasn't a question of scorning it." For an aspiring composer, however, the message was clear.][29]

MICHAEL BECKERMAN, a composition student in the 1960s and '70s and later a musicology student at Columbia, observed of the compositional scene in those years:

> Trying to write tonal music at a place like Columbia University in the 1960s and '70s was like being a dissident in Prague during the same period, with similar professional consequences.[30]

ANTHONY TOMMASINI, a composition student at Yale in the 1960s, later music critic for the *New York Times*:

> Nowadays, a revisionist campaign is under way arguing that the "great split" was hugely overstated. The 12-tone commando squad never commanded anything during the fractious, much maligned 1960s, the line goes. True, the squad was uninterested in composers writing tonal music, but it did not condemn them, and certainly never controlled them.
>
> Don't you believe it. I was there, studying music at Yale, and the Serialists ran the place, as well as other composition departments at major universities. They made the appointments, granted the tenure, recruited the composition students. Put in a good word for the operas of Britten over lunch, and you faced sneers from the composers. Try to suggest that Shostakovich was somebody worth bothering about, and eyes would roll. Aaron Copland? That producer of Americana corn pone? Be serious.[31]

JOHN ADAMS, who later established himself as a premier operatic composer, with some minimalist leanings, was a student at Harvard:

> I was interested in jazz and rock, and then I would go into the music department, which was like a mausoleum where we would sit and count tone-rows

in Webern. It was a dreadful time. But then we were all going back to our rooms and getting high and listening to Cecil Taylor and John Coltrane and the Rolling Stones. . . . Right from 1967 I knew I was leading a double life — and that it was dishonest.[32]

DAVID DEL TREDICI was a student of Roger Sessions at Princeton and Andrew Imbrie at the University of California at Berkeley in the 1970s and became a successful composer of tonal music, his most well known being the Alice series (*Final Alice . . .*):

> I certainly didn't sit down and decide to become a tonal composer. . . . I fought it all the way. I came of musical age in the 1960s when atonality, whether you happened to like it or not, was widely considered the only viable contemporary musical language. So I had a lot of conditioning to shed.
>   The situation gave me a kind of nervous breakdown. I thought, "My colleagues will think I'm nuts! I can't be so tonal in 1976. It's crazy. It's not legitimate."[33]

JACOB DRUCKMAN, composer of vocal and chamber music in the 1950s and '60s, later known for orchestral compositions in a neo-romantic style:

> Not being a serialist on the East Coast in the sixties was like not being a Catholic in Rome in the thirteenth century.[34]

ROBERT STARER, Austrian-born composer who studied in Israel and at Juilliard and has since resided in New York:

> The serialists were fascists, and with the appointment of Boulez to the post as conductor of the New York Philharmonic, we knew it was all over for composers of my style.[35]

NED ROREM, who writes in many genres, all tonal, but is particularly well known for his art-songs, on returning to the United States in 1958 after living for several years in Paris and Morocco:

> We were treated as if we didn't exist. I asked myself where I stood as a composer, am I doing something wrong? But I can't change horses in midstream and I wouldn't if I could.[36] [H. Wiley Hitchcock commented about Rorem: "Ned Rorem was pretty angry for a long time about the lack of reception he was getting in the halls of ivy."][37]

GEORGE ROCHBERG, quoted earlier, was a successful serialist until he turned toward a tonal style in the 1960s:

> Serialism's most publicly aggressive proponents, early and late, presented and still present it as the only true faith. As such, they have proclaimed an or-

thodox cultural church, with its hierarchy, gospels, beliefs, and anathemas. After the end of World War II it very quickly captured and dominated American academic circles, which it monstrously and bluntly politicized.[38]

WILLIAM MAYER, composer of a variety of works, including an opera, *Death in the Family*, and two oratorios:

> To be a tonal composer in the '60s and '70s was a deeply dispiriting experience. One was shunned as the last teen-aged virgin.[39]

NICHOLAS TAWA, a composer in the 1950s who gave up composition to become a musicologist:

> Fledgling composers of such inclination [traditional] were knocked down repeatedly as they took their first steps. I can personally testify to this, seeing several talented acquaintances leave off composing altogether and, later, hearing from others that they had done the same. My Second String Quartet won the Knight Chamber Music Prize in 1951, but was deleted from a Fromm-Foundation concert because insufficiently atonal. It took me a few years, but I, too, eventually ceased composing music.[40]

WAYNE ALPERN, now at the Mannes College of Music, composer and in the 1980s copyist for Steve Reich, referred to:

> a time when composition was dominated by Cage versus Stockhausen, et al., atonal chromaticism, relentless dissonance, irregular rhythms, disjunct lines, perpetual variation, and inaudible nonmotivic complexity (enforced by composition departments we called the "chromatic thought police" back in the '70s).[41]

In spite of the serialists' conviction, one should not draw from this testimony that they insisted that all composers write in their idiom. According to Bruce Trinkley, with the exception of Charles Wuorinen members of the composition faculty even at Columbia were receptive to different styles. Wuorinen himself was denied tenure precisely because his dogmatism alienated the rest of the faculty. Yet no matter what the statistics, it is hard to deny a prevailing mood in the 1950s, '60s, and '70s. Whether fact or fantasy, a sense that serialists somehow had spread a reign of terror pervaded the compositional world, and practically all young composers and many established ones felt almost helpless in the grips of a serial tyranny. Testimony is overwhelming that composers who did not wish to write serial music felt intimidated and thwarted in their careers, be it positions in academia, prizes, or performances. As a consequence almost every major composer who came of age from the late 1950s to the '70s felt compelled to at least attempt serialism, regardless of leanings and preferences. Composers associated with styles far from serialism, such as La Monte Young, Philip Glass, and even Frank Zappa, went through an early phase of writing serial music.

If serialists were only a relatively small minority, why was their influence so pervasive? If their control is only a myth, why were its effects so chilling? Most serialists did not attempt to use direct force, or abuse their positions, but they are not the innocent victims of a counter-cabal. They saw serialism as a cause, one in which they fervently believed, so much so that some, as we have seen, were either hostile or condescending to other types of music. And while the atonalists never took over the academy completely, in their zeal they portrayed their vision as the only true one. The result was to cast doubt over anyone who was not one of them. In their fanaticism they tainted the pool. Thus even though many other composers wrote music actually closer to what the public preferred, not only did those composers themselves have to bear a heavy psychological burden and harbor considerable self-doubt, but the atonalists, in their pronouncements, also cast doubt in the minds of the public.

The serialists felt that history was on their side, and like the revolutionaries they styled themselves they were impatient to bring on a new order. And yes, history was on their side, although not in the way most serialists understood. More than other composers the serialists were aware of changes in American culture and knew how to exploit the new dynamics of the postwar world.

Babbitt's argument for a symbiosis between science and musical composition put the atonal composer, whether serialist or not, in a position to capture the rhetorical high ground, and it was as much on the plain of rhetoric as in the concert hall that the first serial war unfolded. The serialists controlled the rhetorical stage when rhetoric meant more than it did at any time in the history of music (only John Cage as contrarian caught on to this). And the serialists fully took the offensive. Their comments were direct, biting, and unambiguous. They pressed serialism as the wave of the future. Those not jumping on the bandwagon would be left hopelessly behind. The young composer was put in a bind. Comply or be utterly old-fashioned. Pierre Boulez wrote: "Every musician who has not felt — we do not say understood, but indeed felt — the necessity of the serial language is USELESS." Charles Wuorinen dismissed tonal composers as "backward-looking": "While the tonal system in an atrophied or vestigial form, is still used today in popular and commercial music, and even occasionally in the works of backward-looking serious composers, it is no longer employed by serious composers of the mainstream. It has been replaced or succeeded by the 12-tone system."[42]

Either write music the public wanted or music that proved its worth, either write the music of the future or the music of the past. To this binary dialectic the traditionalists had no defense, other than to continue to compose, and to get their pieces performed. Yet for the younger composer following in the traditional style, and there were many, not even that was sufficient counter. For the problem lay with audiences.

The atonalists were aided and abetted in no small way by the place of music in the public. For the most part the public did not know *what* to make of music. They did not trust their own intuition, and in the classical music world of the 1950s and '60s, in which the notion of good music as good for you still predominated, they were ripe for propaganda. And the atonalists were very good at presenting their case. Their certainty, their scientific-oriented argument, could cast doubt in the minds of the most musically sophisticated composer. It is no wonder that it could do the same for a generally unsophisticated audience.

Thus the public may have received serialism at best with sullen silence, at worst with overt hostility, but they did not rush to champion the tonal composer. For with rare exceptions the traditional composer's pieces were not winning audiences either. A few established, celebrity composers, such as Aaron Copland, Samuel Barber, and Leonard Bernstein, certainly did better than the serialists, but younger composers generally did not. And even Copland eventually felt the serial siren song. The tonalists did not have the overwhelming weapon that an Elvis Presley or a Fats Domino did; they could not rally the public so totally that the establishment had to pay attention to them. Neither could they cry all the way to the bank. To most of the public, new music was new music, and this played into the serialists' hands.

At first there seemed to be two choices: either adopt serialism or return to the romantic past. But even as late as the 1950s romanticism was still close enough to make a young composer feel uncomfortable. The entrenchment of the thirties had wiped out the experimentalism of the twenties, and the neo-romantics of the thirties, such as Roy Harris, David Diamond, and Howard Hanson, were only a generation away. The neo-romanticism of the 1930s also had a nostalgic quality, in its evocation of a mythical west or a sylvan rural idealism. It was clearly not the wave of the new, which the younger, fervent, articulate generation sought.

But gradually other choices emerged, as established composers like Elliott Carter and Roger Sessions evolved a free atonality, and as serialism was applied less rigidly. This had much appeal. It was intellectually rigorous, and it did not smack of romanticism. It allowed a more personal, expressive

idiom. Not only to the public, however, but to many tonally oriented composers it and serialism were much the same, as the lady from Macon,
Georgia, reminded William Schuman.

For the postwar generation a sense of the new was particularly acute and
particularly important. Europe was recovering from the trauma of the previous ten years, and had seen much of the old blown away, literally. Germans
mostly were exhausted and in collective shock. Around them rubble lay
everywhere, the remnants of hundreds of years of culture. The French
probed their own role in the events of the war and pondered its philosophical
meaning. In America optimism seemed unbounded. The nation had won
the war, had put the depression behind, and had, at least briefly, a monopoly
on the most powerful weapon of all, the bomb. The Russian explosion of a
nuclear device in 1949 put something of a chill on that optimism, but in spite
of the threat of nuclear holocaust, it did little more than hang an ominous
cloud in the sky of economic expansion. Whether driven by the euphoria of
unlimited potential or the specter of a haunted past, emphasis was on the
new, an age in which science in particular could overcome the problems of
the world in ways hitherto unimaginable. Medical breakthroughs promised
unheard-of control of diseases, and the forces that created the bomb also
promised unlimited nuclear energy, with some experts predicting that the
energy it generated would be so common as to be cost-free. And new media,
the tape recorder, the LP, and more important, television, promised an
abundance of art and entertainment.

Thus when the serialists, atonalists, and experimentalists relentlessly
portrayed the more traditional composer as being of the past, as having had
his day, as being out of touch with the new, it hit home. The traditionalists
may have still occupied positions of authority and commanded resources,
but the age itself conspired with the emerging avant-garde to cast doubt and
uncertainty on the place of compositional traditionalism. And when the serialists managed to wrap themselves in the mantle of science, the ultimate authority of the time, the coup was virtually complete.

Yet there was another, bigger reason that the serialists' ideas resonated so
well with post–World War II America. For rather than going against the
grain, the serialists were ironically consistent with a broader mood that pervaded the culture of the time. In the end they shared a similar attitude with
the experimentalists, and even the minimalists, but decidedly not with the
traditionalists. The three very different directions that musical developments
took after the Second World War, serialism, aleatoric experimentalism, and
minimalism, were impelled by the same aesthetic, and together all these
groups put the traditional tonal composer in a position of discomfort and

doubt. The next three chapters explore this common thread and the matter of such strange bedfellows as Milton Babbitt, John Cage, and Steve Reich. The first of these three chapters focuses on the clear leader of the experimental school, John Cage, and the following one on Harry Partch and Frank Zappa, individualists who epitomize the idea of maverick. Only in Chapter 10, after also considering minimalism, can the story of the two serial wars finally be closed.

CHAPTER 8

Postwar Experimentalism
John Cage

H OW MANY PEOPLE in America or even the world know who John Cage is? Probably many. John Cage has become a familiar name, and only a slightly less familiar face. But how many people have actually heard music by John Cage? Probably few. John Cage exemplifies a trend of late-twentieth-century culture: the artist as icon has become separated from the art itself.

Such may not be happenstance. Cage himself had much to do with that. With his ideas, his life, and his music, he redefined much of how we see things. He also understood our times and particularly our media. He understood that the role of the musician in the late twentieth century, particularly the non-pop musician, is quite different from one hundred years ago, because music itself is perceived differently. And he understood not just the potential of specific media, but how media altered in subtle yet fundamental ways how our society and artists interact.

In that sense Cage was far ahead of his contemporaries. That his own status as a media celebrity undermines some of his positions about the desired role of the composer cannot be blamed on the media; Cage was more than a willing participant, and he knew what he was doing. Yet Cage would not have become who he was without vision. Cage indeed did have vision, and a deep understanding of how technology altered Western musical culture, but the surface Cage may not be the important Cage. Cage delivered a message, an important message, but as we will see what it was has not always been understood.

Even Cage's life is not easy to pin down. Stories about Cage are legion, many perpetuated by Cage himself, and it is sometimes difficult to determine their factual reliability. Cage does not help by giving many contradictory or at least inconsistent renderings of essentially the same set of events. This suggests no disingenuousness on Cage's part; when you answer as many questions as he did over so many years, memory is neither infallible nor static. Much of the main outline of Cage's life is clear, however, and when the *big*, carefully documented biography on Cage inevitably comes out, it's not going to change dramatically what we already know.

Cage rejected the basic premises of most Western music early, or in one sense had them rejected for him. Cage grew up in southern California, the son of an inventor, and his interest in composition led him first to Henry Cowell, and then to Arnold Schoenberg, who had arrived in the United States in 1934. Cage studied with Schoenberg for at least two years, although exact dates are not certain. But he did not impress Schoenberg with his musical talent. According to Cage, Schoenberg told him he had no ear for harmony, a point on which Cage agreed. Schoenberg told Cage that were he to continue in music he would run into a wall. Cage replied that he intended spending the rest of his life banging his head against that wall. Cage also realized that if he was to do anything as a composer, his music needed a basis other than harmony. Since Western musical structures for at least three hundred years, possibly longer, grew out of harmonic considerations, Cage was venturing into largely unknown terrain.[1]

Cage went so far as to deny that he was even a composer, calling himself an "inventor." This appellation came from Schoenberg, who in 1953 reportedly called Cage an "inventor of genius." Schoenberg did not intend his comment to be entirely complimentary. He made it clear that he was distinguishing inventor from composer, which, to Schoenberg, Cage was not. And Schoenberg was not the first to use the term *inventor* disparagingly. Earlier in the century Aaron Copland dismissed Henry Cowell as not a composer but a "mere inventor of sounds." But Cage wore the title proudly. He could draw on a line of twentieth-century composers who also abjured the title of composer. In 1912 Eric Satie wrote: "Everyone will tell you that I am not a musician. It's true. From the beginning of my career I classed myself among phonometrographers. My works are pure phonometry." And Edgard Varèse, who called his music "organized sound," said he was "not a musician, but a worker in rhythms, frequencies and intensities."[2]

As a way around the wall Schoenberg prophesied, Cage turned to composing for percussion, mostly unpitched. No problems of harmony there. In the mid-1930s he wrote a percussion quartet. Exactly when it was written and why — what prompted it — is not clear. According to James Pritchett he was inspired to do so by the abstract filmmaker Oskar Fischinger. Cage said: "He spoke to me about what he called the spirit inherent in materials and he claimed that a sound made from wood had a different spirit than one made from glass. The next day I began writing music which was to be played on percussion instruments."[3]

Yet according to David Revill, Cage was introduced to Fischinger by Galka Scheyer, an artist and art collector in Los Angeles, precisely because she saw the *Percussion Quartet* and recognized an affinity between Cage's and Fischinger's ideas.[4] This much is known: Cage and Fischinger did produce a film together, and Fischinger did influence Cage. The *Quartet* itself was for unspecified instruments, and Cage tried it on various objects, ranging from pots and pans to steel pipes to automobile brake drums. It was probably written before he met Fischinger. Cage's next effort, the *Trio*, is closer to Fischinger's views. It uses bass drums, tom-toms, various lengths of wood, and bamboo sticks, and has a more focused overall timbre, depending on finer gradations of similar material. Compared to *Quartet*, the *Trio* is simpler, subtler, and in some ways more spiritual.

Cage still needed steadier employment, and found it at the newly opened Cornish School in Seattle, which included a department of modern dance. He became accompanist and composer-in-residence. The move was decisive: it gave Cage the opportunity to work with dancers, it allowed him to explore the extraordinarily large collection of percussion instruments that the school owned, and, finally, it introduced Cage to Mercier (later known as Merce) Cunningham, a dancer with the school. By the mid-1940s, Cunningham had established his own company, and Cage had divorced his wife, Xenia, and entered into a lifelong artistic and personal partnership with Cunningham. Cunningham became as much an innovator and icon in dance as Cage did in music, and together they explored new ways dancers and musicians interact, or rather coexist. In a Cage-Cunningham collaboration, dance and music often occurred simultaneously yet completely independently. Each was in its own sphere, and in some cases Cunningham himself did not hear the music until the performance.

Cage remained in Seattle only briefly, but he began two other lines of experimentation there. The Cornish School had a radio station, which included two turntables and test recordings that consisted of a single steady pitch. This was well before the tape recorder and modern electronic synthesizers. Cage conceived a work that used the steady drone of a 78-rpm studio test recording. He varied the pitch by changing the speed of the turntables and created rhythm by lifting the needle off the record. The result was one of the world's first electronic compositions, a six-minute piece for turntables and percussion instruments. Of necessity performed live, it was beamed into an adjoining studio to accompany Jean Cocteau's *Marriage at the Eiffel Tower.* Cage called the piece *Imaginary Landscape.*

In 1940 Cage was asked to write music for Syllvia Fort, an African-American dancer. He discovered that the performance space had a small grand piano but no room for other instruments. Not wanting to write conventional piano music, he experimented with modifying the piano sound through the placement of various objects on the strings. Screws, nuts, bolts, plastic spoons, pencil erasers, all went into the piano. The result was a set of timbres that bore little relation to a conventional piano sound. Although Cage had tried this idea informally before, this piece began a decade-long exploration of what he called the "prepared piano." This line finally culminated in his *Sonatas and Interludes,* a set of twenty pieces, which many consider Cage's finest work before he began to allow chance to determine the course of a piece. Eric Salzman called *Sonatas and Interludes* Cage's "Well-Tampered Clavier."[5]

In 1942 Cage moved to Chicago. László Moholy-Nagy, a Hungarian painter and photographer active in the abstract art movement, invited him to teach a class in experimental music at the Chicago School of Design, which Moholy-Nagy had founded in 1937. They had met when both taught one summer at Mills College in California. The Moholy-Nagy connection typified one aspect of Cage's career: he was closer to, better supported by, and in more direct contact with dancers and visual artists than musicians.

In Chicago a series of percussion concerts that Cage arranged brought him local fame. The *Chicago Sun* referred to the percussion concerts as the "newest rage among the intelligentsia."[6] Reviews were at best mixed. Some critics decided it was good-natured fun and reacted accordingly. Pence James of the *Chicago Daily News* wrote: "It wasn't mountain music. It wasn't red hot jazz. Nor was it boogie-woogie or swing. So what was it?"

> Intellectuals, including several members of the University of Chicago faculty, were trying to figure out the answer today. Last night they went to a symphonic concert in Mandel Hall . . . but, somewhere along the middle of the program, there was an invasion by a daring young man named John Cage and his "musicians," who play beer bottles, flower pots, cowbells, automobile brake drums, dinner bells, thundersheets, and in the words of Mr. Cage, "anything we can get our hands on."

But the audience apparently had a good time: "At first, because of the serious mien of the performers (they were in formal dress) and the fearful novelty of the percussion orchestra, nobody smiled. Finally the audience began to enjoy itself, applauding enthusiastically, to be rewarded with a pleased-as-pie grin from Mr. Cage." And one member of the audience gave the ultimate compliment for 1942, "It's better than Benny Goodman."[7]

Other critics took a more dour view of the matter. Cecil Smith of the *Chicago Tribune* resigned himself to the inevitable: "Of the final artistic result, I can only say that we went thru all this once before in this [*sic*] 1920s, when George Antheil and Edgar Varese [*sic*] were at work, and I suppose we can go thru it again."[8]

In spite of the precedents of Antheil and Varèse, percussion concerts with a variety of objects, created and found, were very much a rarity in the 1940s. To most attendees and critics, beer bottles, flower pots, and brake drums were not the material of symphonic programs. But Cage was already articulating a broader purpose; he told James that the ensemble was not "an end in itself," but an attempt "to make all the field of audible sound available for music."[9]

In 1942 Cage and Xenia moved to New York, at the invitation of Max Ernst and Peggy Guggenheim. He soon fell out with Guggenheim over a concert venue, but by 1943 Cage had met many artists and dancers and had arranged a percussion concert at the Museum of Modern Art, sponsored by the League of Composers. The concert resulted in a two-page picture spread in *Life* magazine. *Life* characterized Cage as a "patient, humorous, 30-year old," and described his philosophy: "Cage believes that when people today get to understand and like his music, which is produced by banging one object with another, they will find new beauty in everyday modern life, which is full of noises made by objects banging against each other." This is a step forward from James's rendition, and although there is no Zen here, it represents Cage's basic belief about music, which he would carry all his life.

Except for brief stays elsewhere and much traveling, particularly as his fame increased in the 1950s and '60s, New York would be Cage's home the rest of his life. Awards from the National Academy of Arts and Letters and the Guggenheim Foundation allowed him to spend part of 1949 in Paris, where he became friends with Pierre Boulez. He also met Pierre Schaeffer, who had established an institute to explore the musical possibilities of a new invention, the tape recorder. Schaeffer was particularly interested in *musique concrète*, the use and manipulation of any sounds produced other than by musical instruments: street noises, mechanical sounds, voices speaking, anything the tape recorder could record. This struck an immediate affinity with Cage, consistent as it was with his advocacy of noise and sounds of the environment.

Sometime around 1950 Cage began to attend the lectures of Daisetz Teitaro Suzuki on Zen Buddhism at Columbia University. Suzuki, who was not a Buddhist monk, had married an American, lived on and off in the United States and Europe, and written dozens of books on Buddhism, some in Japanese, some in English. He seemed to have a special mission to explain Buddhism to the West, and following World War II he was invited to Columbia University.

Suzuki's classes were popular, especially with casual attendees like Cage. For Cage they were decisive. Cage became a disciple, devoted himself to Buddhism, and began to rethink his approach to musical composition. This led him to his most radical position, and the one for which he is most known, the abandonment of all personal expression by the composer for a music in which any and all sounds, in any or no pattern, with any or no connection, simply occur. From the early 1950s non-intention by the composer became paramount for Cage. Expression was to be excised as fully as possible, and sounds were, simply, to be themselves.

Cage began by letting chance operations determine the course of a piece. He used several techniques, including charts, the Chinese Book of Changes, I-Ching (which contained a number of hexagrams, whose selection was determined by flipping coins), following the imperfections on a piece of paper, and later, with the availability of computers, random number generators. Probably the most influential of these was the I-Ching, which Cage had originally seen in the early 1940s but became interested in only when a young student of his, Christian Wolff, brought him a copy in 1951.

Cage used chance techniques in the third movement of the *Concerto for Prepared Piano*, and more fully with *Music of Changes*. Both were written specifically for David Tudor, an extraordinary pianist who collaborated extensively with Cage over the next twenty years. For these works Cage consulted the I-Ching to create a set of charts, which contain the raw materials for the piece — pitch, rhythmic, or dynamic sources. The I-Ching also determined how the material from the charts would be selected. The result, however, is relatively traditional looking, although highly modernist sounding, music. The score is still written in conventional notation, which the performer is expected to follow closely.

Cage had not forgotten noise, however. In a step that reintroduced both noise and another level of randomness, Cage presented *Imaginary Landscape No. 4* in 1951. This is Cage's radio piece, and possibly, next to 4′ 33″, his most famous work. It consists of twelve radios on stage, each with two performers, one to manipulate the station selector knob and the other the volume control. Cage's score is detailed and specific, indicating precisely what each performer is to do when. Those directions, however, were determined by chance.

A second piece by Cage, *Water Music*, expanded even further his range of events. It is written for a pianist, who is asked to do a number of things beyond playing the piano, at least in any conventional manner. Cage had earlier asked the pianist to create sounds in ways other than by depressing the keys, something Henry Cowell had done, but with *Water Music*, the pianist is instructed to deal a deck of cards into the piano, blow a duck whistle, and at the climax of the work plunge the duck whistle into a glass of water while blowing it. The piece is essentially theatrical. It is also the first piece by Cage in which directions are given in clock rather than metrical time.[10]

By this time Cage had gathered around him a coterie of younger composers, Earle Brown, Christian Wolff, and Morton Feldman. All were interested in chance music, and Feldman and Brown in particular produced early landmarks in the genre. Brown pursued the idea of open form and graphic notation. His *Available Forms*, for orchestra, explored a number of musical units, which themselves leave unspecified some details such as exact rhythm or pitch. The order in which the units are played is determined by two conductors, who choose the units for their group during the course of the piece. Neither conductor knows ahead of time what the other will do. The effect is a sound sculpture, akin to an Alexander Calder mobile, which varies with each performance. Brown readily admitted that Calder's mobiles inspired this approach.

Brown went even further in leaving choice to the performer. In a series of compositions written in late 1952 he abandoned traditional notation in favor of graphic markings that only suggested patterns or gestures to the performer. His most radical piece, *December 1952*, consists of small horizontal and rectangular blocks scattered on the page, in a pattern that resembles a later computer punch card. Brown leaves no further directions for the performer.

Of Cage's followers only Morton Feldman achieved a reputation and influence close to his. Feldman met Cage at a concert and soon moved into the apartment building where Cage lived. It was a small artistic colony, also housing several other artists. Feldman, who had studied with Wallingford Riegger and Stefan Wolpe, had by then renounced serialism and begun to explore indeterminate pieces, graphic works similar to Brown's. His *Projection I* for solo cello, composed in 1950, consists of a grid of horizontal solid lines connected by dotted vertical lines, with squares and diamonds inter-

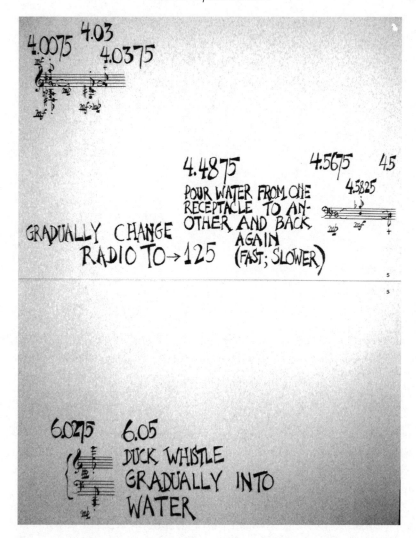

John Cage, page from *Water Music* (Copyright © 1952 by Henmar Press. Used by permission. All rights reserved.)

spersed. The squares represent notes, their horizontal placement pitch area, and their vertical placement time (the diamonds represent harmonics). The squares are so arranged to create a spacious quietude, with ample silences. This remained a Feldman characteristic, similar to much of Cage. As this piece indicates, Feldman always retained some musical specifics in his pieces, if only general indications of pitch, time, and timbre.

Earle Brown, *December 1952*, complete score (Copyright © 1961 [renewed] by Associated Music Publishers, Inc. [BMI] International copyright secured. All rights reserved. Reprinted by permission.)

In his later works Feldman returned to more traditional notation and became more precise about what he wanted, but some element of decision was still often left to the composer. His works became expansive, some lasting several hours. They nevertheless retained Feldman's quiet, static qualities; as such they evince the atmosphere of early minimalism.

Cage also began to experiment with electronic music in the early 1950s. Paul Williams, a young architect who had inherited wealth, established a "Project for Magnetic Tape," and Cage, Tudor, Brown, and Louis and Bebe Barron received a grant to explore music for tape recorder. The principal piece to come from this effort was Cage's *Williams Mix*, a mostly musique concrète work, in which Cage recorded a large number of sounds, classified them in various ways, ranging from their origins — "city sounds, country sounds, electronic sounds, manually-produced sounds (including music), wind-produced sounds (including songs), 'small' sounds requiring amplification" — to their acoustic properties, that is the nature of their frequency, timbre, amplitude. He then physically cut the sounds into small irregularly shaped fragments, to further vary the final sound, and spliced them together, using eight tracks. The 192-page score was a template of the cutout, similar to a dress pattern. It took Cage, helped by Brown, Feldman, and later another young student, Ben Johnston, over a year of steady work, ten to twelve hours per day, to cut and splice the tape. The result was a piece approximately four minutes long. Although the score was published, there is no record that anyone else has attempted to realize it.

Of all the Cage experiments in the fecund period from 1950 to 1952, 4′ 33″, the "silent piece," attracted the most attention and has remained the most well known. Cage himself, notorious for avoiding opinions or value judgments, made an exception for 4′ 33″: he called it his most important piece.[11] It was first performed at the Maverick Concert Hall in Woodstock, on August 29, 1952. David Tudor was the pianist. The concept is simple: the pianist sits at the piano, holding a stopwatch, for four minutes, thirty-three seconds, and makes no attempt to make any sounds. Cage determined the time of the piece by the I-Ching. He also divided it into three movements, specified in the score. Tudor demarcated the movements by closing and opening the piano lid.

Reaction was predictable. Earle Brown reported "a hell of a lot of uproar." And at the end of a lengthy discussion following the concert a local artist urged the audience to "stand up and drive these people out of town."[12] Almost forty years and hundreds if not thousands of performances later, 4′ 33″ still creates a titter in audiences, who are not sure whether to take it seriously. Cage left no doubt; he considered it a serious piece.

Cage's "silent piece" is many things. It is quintessential Zen on the concert stage. It is a meditation on the environment. It is a commentary on sound in a visual world. David Tudor described it simply and precisely: "It is one of the most intense listening experiences one can have. You really listen. You're hearing everything there is. Audience noises play a part in it. It is cathartic — four minutes and thirty-three seconds of meditation, in effect."[13]

Cage had been coming to 4′ 33″ for some time. In 1948 he described something akin to 4′ 33″, as a piece for Muzak, the company that packaged background music for businesses: "I have, for instance, several new desires . . . first, to compose a piece of uninterrupted silence and sell it to the Muzak Co. It will be 4 ½ minutes long — these being the standard lengths of 'canned' music, and its title will be 'Silent Prayer.' It will open with a single idea which I will attempt to make as seductive as the color and shape or fragrance of a flower. The ending will approach imperceptibility."[14]

At this time Cage still thought in terms of actually creating sound, not of environment as sounds, but even the dimensions are there. How far-fetched is it to find a continuity between this tongue-in-cheek reference to Muzak and 4' 33"? In this same article Cage also mentioned a second "absurd" idea he had, a piece for twelve radios. And later he confirmed that he had something like 4' 33" on his mind for about four years before he actually composed it.[15]

The work was never a fixed piece, even in Cage's mind. Before 4' 33" was published Cage gave handwritten copies to friends, and the timings of the movements differ from the original published score in *Source* magazine. The differences, admittedly, are slight, and may be nothing more than the way the score was reproduced. Cage originally wrote it in graphic notation, seven inches representing 56 seconds. But in 1960 he rethought the piece and decided that it was too constricting. He then simply wrote Tacet, Tacet, Tacet, and added the comment, "the work may be performed by any instrumentalist or combination of instrumentalists and last any length of time." Cage later suggested that 4' 33" could even mean 4 feet, 33 inches.[16]

4' 33" left Cage little room to maneuver. It was as if he had found the ideal means to make his point, and many of his later pieces indeed are glosses or variants on 4' 33". The most notable example of this is 0' 00", conceived in 1962. Cage subtitled it "4' 33" No. 2." In its original form, it contained only the barest instruction: "In a situation provided with maximum amplification (no feedback), perform a disciplined action." The situation is not entirely open-ended: Cage does require amplification, and he does qualify the type of action performed. The first performance, in Tokyo, consisted of Cage writing the sentence of instruction. Cage later added further qualifiers, allowing the performer to be interrupted, proscribing the performance of a musical composition, and instructing the performer not to repeat the same action in subsequent performances or to pay attention to the performing situation.

Yet it was difficult to take indeterminacy, the term Cage preferred for his later pieces that did not specify sounds and left open choice, beyond 4' 33", and many of Cage's later indeterminate pieces, such as *Fontana Mix* or *Variations II*, *III*, or *IV*, establish a set of rules or parameters in which choices are made. They are essentially variants of a board game: once the basic notion of the game is established, then how the pieces move can vary infinitely, but the basic concept of the game is understood. And each playing of the game differs from previous ones. Cage's imagination seemed to know no bounds in creating new indeterminate pieces, but conceptually they break little new ground beyond 4' 33". Cage's act of composition was to create the game. As he devised endless variants of the basic principles, where composition ended and performance began after 1952 was never clear.

Music Becomes Theater

But Cage had other new ideas in mind. These need to be put in a framework, however. If we look back at Cage's styles, we see a relatively steady trajectory between 1934 and 1950, as the composer explored first percussion music and then the prepared piano, which was essentially a subset of his percussion work. Consistent with his professed inability to hear any music before it was conceived, Cage almost from the start used various mathematical formulas to create his works. These were often quite sophisticated, and led to highly complex pieces that can be dazzling even when an audience is unaware of their mathematical formulation. They also began his interest in cultures of the Far East, as Cage absorbed ideas first from Indian rhythmic practices, then later from Zen and I-Ching. Cage also explored "noise" consciously and openly. This music owes much to Henry Cowell and Edgard Varèse, but Cage took it one step further, through his use of macro rhythmic structures. Cage's percussion pieces are analogous to fractals, mathematical algorithms in which large events are reproduced in smaller and smaller dimensions in a kind of self-recursion of the basic pattern.

The years from 1949 to 1952 are a transition period, during which Cage's interest in chance and in Zen intensified. Chance operations grew organically out of his percussion music, as matrices became increasingly important in his compositional process. Cage quickly discovered that the numbers on the matrix could just as easily be put there by chance operations, even though he was still composing structured percussion music. Then in a series of pieces he moved simultaneously from percussion to environmental noise and silence. He arrived there in 1952, with *Williams Mix* and 4′ 33″. And though 4′ 33″ is about silence, it is, as Cage often explained, equally about environmental noise.

The year 1952 is universally recognized as a turning point in Cage's work. In the conventional wisdom, noise, silence, chance, Zen, and the elimination of the ego had been achieved, and having "pledged his allegiance to non-intention from 4′ 33″ on," Cage had seriously challenged the very basis of what we understand music to be.[17] From then on he sought more and more imaginative ways to make us aware of the limitations of traditional Western thinking. Such an interpretation suggests a linear trajectory for the remainder of Cage's career, punctuated with many shifts of detail but nevertheless bearing a consistent overall vision.

I suggest an alternative reading: Beginning in 1952 Cage's style bifurcates. One line begins and ends with silence. This line, as a tendency for quiet, is apparent as early as 1932 — quiet not only as a sonic condition but as an absence of activity. In 1952 Henry Cowell described Cage's compositional orientation: "When I first met John Cage about 1932, he was writing strange little piano pieces with an unusual sense of the sound-interest created by odd tonal combinations. Then as now the music showed little desire to move about actively; it rather depended on very slight and subtle changes for its elaboration."[18] Cowell expanded on this idea: "The dynamics of silence, a relativity of silence as well as of sound, expressed by rests and extreme *pianissimo*, is a major concern in most of Cage's music." And: "Cage enjoys presenting longer and more complex silences in the course of his works. Sometimes he leads one toward absolute silence by increasingly greater degrees of softness until one can hardly tell whether one is really hearing anything or not."[19] These comments refer to *Imaginary Landscape No. 4*, the piece for twelve radios. In the premiere Cage indicated a dynamic level so low (Cage conducted) that the audience could not hear the radios. Cage's interest in lower dynamic levels and his inclusion of longer and longer silences lead clearly in the direction of 4' 33". The only question was how long before this tendency reached its apex. With 4' 33" Cage answered that question.

There are several recognizable features to Cage's music, quiet being only one, although probably the most important. In addition extremes of register are used, and motion (not synonymous with movement) is at a minimum, particularly in the late piano pieces. Cowell also observed that stillness might be a better substitute for silence and for quiet. That Cage was so fascinated with Thoreau and Buddhism is no coincidence. Both orient toward stillness.

Cage returned again and again to music of stillness. Some of it, such as his late time-bracket pieces, became formulaic. In these works, the performer is given a set of notes and a time frame within which these notes are to be played. The notes and the time frame are chosen by chance. Thus there are two levels of chance: those that determine the composition of the work and those that are left to the performer. Compositional choices, even though left to chance, are easily recognizable as Cage, however. Pitches tend to be widely separated and the notes are few. The result is an extremely wide musical space, most of which is empty, and a few widely separated, mostly soft notes, creating a sense of stasis and quiet. These pieces evoke a mood of meditation.

I have discussed silence at some length because so much has been made of it that it is easy to overlook its opposite. In contrast to his still pieces Cage can create the most ear-splitting din. Such pieces as *HPSCHD* or *Atlas Eclipticalis* come from a very different tradition, but one equally important to Cage. They also go back to a specific event that occurred in the pivotal year of 1952. At Black Mountain College, North Carolina, in the summer, Cage, together with Merce Cunningham, David Tudor, Robert Rauschenberg, and others, staged an event in which each was engaged in various simultaneous activity. Cage read a lecture from a stepladder; Cunningham danced; Tudor played the piano; Rauschenberg played an old wind-up phonograph, and his white paintings hung on the walls. The audience, which was carefully seated in "four isometric triangular sections," found paper cups on each seat. Left to ponder the meaning throughout the event, they discovered that at its end they were served coffee. The piece had no name; later it achieved notoriety as the granddaddy of the "happenings," popular, seemingly chaotic multimedia events that were staged in the 1960s. Cage used chance techniques to determine what would happen, but he made it clear that it was his creation: "I planned the thing. Without my deciding to do it, it wouldn't have happened." His stated purpose was nonintention, but performers were not entirely free to improvise. They were given time brackets, slots of time, say between minute four and minute eight, during which they could do what they chose to do.[20]

The event clarified a second, and ultimately more significant direction for Cage: toward theater. Cage articulated its importance clearly and frequently. Addressing the convention of the Music Teachers National Association in Chicago in 1958 on "Experimental Music," Cage stated: "Where do we go from here? Towards theatre." This address was reprinted in the brochure accompanying Cage's twenty-five-year retrospective concert in New York, and then again in his book of lectures and writings, *Silence*.[21]

Cage came to equate life with theater. His most specific discussion of this occurred in an interview with Richard Kostelanetz in 1966:

> *Would you consider this — now, here — a theatrical situation?*
> Certainly. There are things to hear and things to see, and that's what theater is.
> *If you were blind, would it be a theatrical situation for you?*
> I imagine so, because I would visualize from what I hear.
> *Therefore, the radio is not theatrical.*
> How are you going to separate it from the environment that it's in? That's really the way to get interested in recording — to include the environment. You'll find more and more in one of these situations that nobody closes his eyes as much as he used to.
> *Would you say, then, that all life is theater. That all theater is life?*
> It could be such, if we change our minds.
> *When did this occur to you?*

I don't know when I gave conscious expression to it. The year 1952 begins to
be very . . . If you look at my catalogue, you'll be amazed at the number of
things that happened in 1952. . . .
Is chess theater?
Well you have to ask yourself what is theater. I would answer that theater is
seeing and hearing.[22]

Cage clearly saw the Black Mountain College event as theater, as well as its
significance for what followed.

*Could you remember what was in your mind when you did that [the Black
Mountain piece]?*
It was the making of theater — to bring all these things together that people
could hear and see. . . .
Why didn't you develop anything in this area yourself?
I have been doing nothing else since.
So all your work since has been "theater" in your mind?
Surely.[23]

Theater lies at the heart of later Cage. Zen, silence, chance, and indeterminacy may garner headlines in connection with Cage, but as to the essential Cage, they are at the very least unsettlingly incomplete, a simulacrum
rather than a fully rounded image. Theater fills in the picture; it explains
many of the paradoxes about him, as well as many of the activities of his last
thirty years. It is ubiquitous. Later Cage did state that some of his pieces were
musical compositions, not works of theater. Other writers have followed that
line and sought to distinguish between Cage's musical and Cage's theater
pieces.[24] Such distinctions, however, are based on application of the Western notion of the *piece*, a slippery concept when dealing with Cage. Consequently these writers belie a fundamental inability to recognize the magnitude of Cage's own challenge to the established musical culture. That Cage
himself used this distinction, even though it seemingly undermined his own
philosophy, appears paradoxical. But the paradox paradoxically disappears
when the distinction itself is rejected.

If we begin with Cage's own premise, that life is theater, and take Cage
at his word, much then falls into place. If life and theater are synonymous,
and Cage's work is theater, we cannot consider Cage's work separate from his
life. And herein lies the rub: this is not a matter of influence or explanation;
the two collapse into a singularity. They cannot be separated. For at least the
last thirty years of his life we find John Cage playing the part of John Cage,
whether on the concert stage, in the dance pit, or on the lecture podium,
whether gathering mushrooms or cooking in his kitchen. Often his activities
are his compositions, such as *o′ oo″*, the first performance of which was Cage

writing out the score, on stage before the audience, or *Speech*, his piece for five radios, an expansion of *Imaginary Landscape No. 4*, in which Cage and four other people wander through the audience, including the lobby, carrying portable radios. Everyone by then recognized Cage, an element that cannot be overlooked, but only gradually did it occur to the audience that they were witnessing the piece.

Thus the essential *musical analytical* question becomes: Who is John Cage?

Who Is John Cage?

I am, by the way, not the first to ask that question. Eric Salzman framed it precisely in 1982.[25] Others have suggested it, although they may not have stated it as forthrightly.

Cage is first and foremost a performer. He is one of the great performance artists of the twentieth century. But consistent with his philosophy of life as theater, his performances were not limited to the concert hall. Cage not only understood the Shakespearean dictum that all the world's a stage, but he understood how new media of the late twentieth century expanded exponentially that concept's potential. Cage knew and understood Marshall McLuhan's message about the importance of media. Cage wanted to break boundaries, be they the concert hall, the definition of music, or life itself. Cage found music everywhere. Hence the silent piece and his lifelong fondness for it. Unlike most people, however, Cage was willing to carry his ideas wherever they might go.

The concept of life as theater was perfectly attuned to the role of celebrity in the late twentieth century. In the lingo of Madison Avenue, Cage knew how to work the media. Cage never stopped performing, whether on the concert stage, at the interview set, or in the lecture hall. Most striking is how little effort the performance took, for a Cage performance was Cage being Cage. Cage also understood thoroughly that in the late twentieth century performance, life as theater, and celebrity worked hand in glove, and that being John Cage was not a trivial or cynical aspect of what he did. The essential question is when did John Cage become JOHN CAGE?

Media, especially television, which McLuhan identified as a cool medium, created personality. Television allowed viewers to get to know their media figures, and it made possible celebrities who often had no other claim to fame than being media personalities. I do not mean to suggest that Cage is one of them: Cage indeed was a original thinker. He also had the informal infectious charm that a visual, intimate age demands. He realized the importance of the interview, and he gave many. In fact the interview is one of the principal means by which Cage communicated his ideas.

From his childhood Cage could open doors with his positive, infectious personality. Later he not only attracted scholars but charmed patrons, consumers, and colleagues as well. When he was twelve years old he conceived a weekly Boy Scout program for the radio. Radio in 1924 was still in its infancy. Public broadcasting itself had only begun four years previously, and the oldest station in Los Angeles was two years old.[26] According to Cage's own account he conceived it strictly on his own, did not even consult the Boy Scouts, managed to sell the idea to the second station he went to, and for two years conducted a two-hour program every Friday. The venture ended only when the Scout organization itself complained that he was not authorized to speak for it, and then took over the program, driving it into the ground in a year.[27]

Plausibility alone gives one pause about this story, the only source for which is Cage himself. On the other hand, Cage pulled off this sort of thing throughout his life. Similar stories continued until he had achieved an international reputation. At the height of the depression he managed to sell a series of lectures on modern art and painting to housewives by going door to door soliciting subscriptions. Cage told them that he knew little about either subject but would learn enough each week to lecture. In spite or possibly because of Cage's youth, naïveté, and sincerity, twenty to forty housewives were willing to put up $2.50 each for the series of ten lectures.[28]

Sheer chutzpah, enthusiasm, optimism, and directness served Cage well. When he decided to study with Schoenberg, he knocked on Schoenberg's door and stated his purpose, only to be told by Schoenberg that he could not afford his prices. Cage replied that he could not afford to pay anything. Schoenberg asked him if he was willing to devote his life to music, and Cage responded yes. Schoenberg took him on. A few years later Cage, needing a job, was recommended to Lou Harrison. Harrison had been offered a position as dance composer and accompanist for the Cornish School in Seattle but was not interested. Within an hour of their meeting Cage established enough rapport that Harrison recommended him for the position, one of Cage's first big breaks.[29]

In both cases Cage had at least some luck, but he also prepared the ground well. He had probably already attended one of Schoenberg's classes before he knocked on his door, and he had begun studying with Adolph Weiss, an assistant of Schoenberg, precisely to be ready himself for Schoenberg. In addition Schoenberg was known for taking on interested students who could not pay. Cage was not unique. Cage's visit to Harrison was paved by Henry Cowell, with whom Cage had studied earlier. Cowell was revered by the younger generation of composers, and a young man with an introduction from him was someone Harrison would not ignore. Cage's own interest in percussion, relatively unusual at this time, was also certain to pique Harrison's interest. Neither circumstance would have guaranteed, however, that Cage would walk away with a job recommendation, had not he been able to make the best of his visit.

Cage's most remarkable coup as a young man came in 1943 when he was asked to compose a nationally broadcast radio program from CBS. Cage had been to CBS Radio in Chicago to borrow electrical equipment and had met some of the local personnel. Building on that connection, he proposed to Davidson Taylor at CBS headquarters in New York that he create a special type of music for a radio play. It would use "urban noises," in radio parlance sound effects, but not as sound effects. Rather they would produce a musical continuity, a parallel script accompanying the play. The idea was radical, not the kind of suggestion to get the ear of a busy radio executive, especially coming from an untried source. Amazingly, Taylor did not throw this earnest young man out but bought the idea. He even asked Cage to recommend an author to write the play. Cage casually suggested Henry Miller, and thereupon found himself authorized to commission a play from Miller and to prepare a sound script for it.[30]

Miller did not work out and Cage contacted Kenneth Patchen, known through his *Journal of Albion Moonlight*. Patchen wrote *The City Wears a Slouch Hat*, and Cage discovered only four days before the performance that he had conceived a score well beyond what the studio engineers could execute. Needing to produce another score, quickly he reverted to percussion and electronics, and the program was broadcast in 1942. Resulting mail was mixed, falling curiously along geographical lines. They liked it in the midwest, but listeners on the East Coast were less enthusiastic. It did not generate enough response, however, for CBS to want to continue the experiment.

Cage's list of associates, contacts, and friends is impressive: Henry Cowell, Arnold Schoenberg, Lou Harrison, Pierre Boulez, David Tudor, Morton Feldman, Earle Brown, Christian Wolff, Karlheinz Stockhausen, John Lennon, Yoko Ono, John Steinbeck, Max Ernst, Peggy Guggenheim, Robert Rauschenberg, Jasper Johns, Marcel Duchamp. Association with other celebrities was important to Cage, and he was known as a name-dropper. At one point he commented: "I think I am actually an elitist. I always have been. I didn't study music with just anybody; I studied with Schoenberg. I didn't study Zen with just anybody; I studied with Suzuki. I've always gone, insofar as I could, to the president of the company."[31] From the start Cage knew and understood the importance of pedigree.

Cage could charm an audience much the same way he charmed individuals. He had a soothing, resonant, absolutely distinctive voice, coupled with a bright, upbeat disposition. His long face, with a distinctive hairline whether his hair was in a crew cut or over his ears, held eyes that simultaneously twinkled and bore in on the listener, while his mouth at any moment seemed about to break out in a wide grin. With a look of focused wonderment that alternated continually with his infectious, naive grin and an easy laugh, Cage gave the impression of total dedication and sincerity. He cultivated that image. In later years the grin and the laugh seemed to become part of the Cage repertoire, its appearance as predictable as the cadences at the end of sentences. For many who came to witness his performances, the most important part of the evening was Cage discussing what he was doing with the audience. That was what people left with. Somehow the weird sounds and the strange activity on stage seemed to make sense after Cage described them, even if his discussion was as unfathomable as the music. Somehow the piece, its presentation, and Cage's discussion created a single, mysteriously unified entity: Cage's persona, the strangeness of the music, and his charm together made the whole event less threatening and more fascinating. It also made a Cage evening one that not many would soon forget.

Cage could be equally unpredictable and challenging in an interview. Usually, however, he did it with such finesse, sincerity, and pleasantness that the interviewer went away with a warm feeling. Cage scholarship itself is heavy under the pressure of this. Cage told so many stories about himself so well, and so convincingly, that writing about Cage becomes a burden: it is hard not to believe something when it comes from the source itself, and even worse, few can say it better than Cage. If ever a composer wrote his own autobiography, Cage did. Only it did not appear in one book, but in many books and interviews, over many years. And typically it was for Cage always a work in progress.

As such Cage tells us what *he* wants us to know. Cage controlled an interview from beginning to end, with his charm, his ability to turn a topic in the direction he wished, and if all else failed, with sheer testiness, which was effective precisely because he was so charming. In 1955 Cage published a purported interview in his article "Experimental Music." In this article Cage argued strenuously for the renunciation of control by the musician. He envisioned an environmental music, and some of his well-known comments come from this article:

A sound does not view itself as thought, as ought, as needing another sound for its elucidation, as etc.; it has no time for any consideration — it is occupied with the performance of its characteristics;
Relevant action is theatrical (Music (imaginary separation of hearing from the other senses) does not exist), inclusive and intentionally purposeless [The entire passage is italicized in the original.][32]

The article contained questions from a hypothetical skeptical audience; the questions were likely a distillation of ones Cage had encountered in his many talks, and they contain the answers we may assume Cage would like to give, whether he did or not.

> QUESTION: *Then what is the purpose of this "experimental" music?*
> ANSWER: No purposes. Sounds.
> QUESTION: *Why bother, since, as you have pointed out, sounds are continually happening whether you produce them or not.*
> ANSWER: What did you say? I'm still —
> QUESTION: *I mean —* . . . *But is this music?*
> ANSWER: Ah! you like sounds after all when they are made up of vowels and consonants. You are slow-witted for you have never brought your mind to the location of urgency. Do you need me or someone else to hold you up? why don't you realize as I do that nothing is accomplished by writing, playing or listening to music? Otherwise, deaf as a door-nail, you will never be able to hear anything, even what's well within ear-shot.
> QUESTION: *But, seriously, if this is what music is, I could write it as well as you.*
> ANSWER: Have I ever said anything that would lead you to think I thought you were stupid?[33]

In reality Cage could be more blunt:

> QUESTION: *Are some pieces better than others* [referring to happenings]?
> ANSWER: Why do you waste your time and mine by trying to get value judgements?[34]

When he did not want to go where the interviewer was taking him, Cage would simply dismiss the line of inquiry: "That's not a very interesting question."[35]

Cage working an interview raises the broader question of ego and control. Cage insisted that the composer relinquish control, that he eliminate ego and allow sounds to be themselves. He faulted Varèse, who sought to broaden the sounds available for music: "Varese treats sounds as Varese." Cage's expressed intention was non-intention. The Renaissance ideal of individual expression and rational and logical continuity seems, with Cage, buried under the Zen concepts of selfless contemplation and objectivity. Cage believed strongly in Zen, but he never gave up the Western idea of the

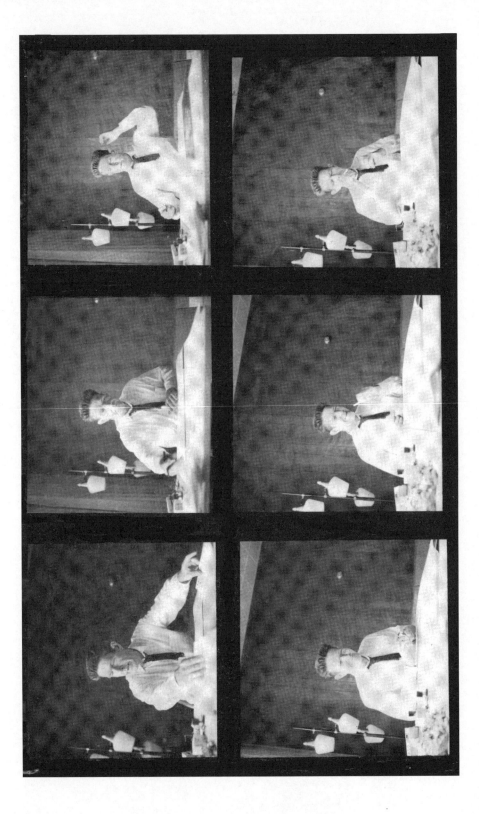

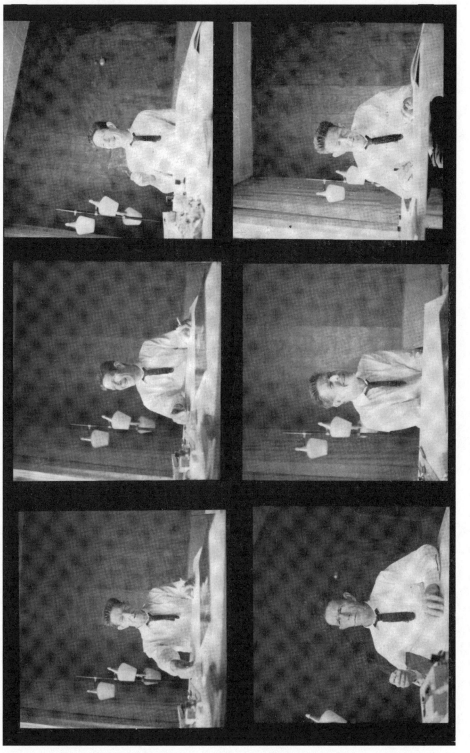

The many moods of John Cage, from the dust jacket of *Silence* (Photograph courtesy of Wesleyan University Press)

composer, his insistence on "inventor" notwithstanding. Yet the question "Does Cage control?" depends on a more fundamental question, "What does Cage compose?" For the answer to the latter also answers the former.

If music is assumed to be an autonomous art, as recent Western thought holds, Cage indeed relinquishes much control. His allowing the performer and the situation to determine many aspects of the sounds means that the very outcome of the composition *as a sonic event* is largely out of his hands. But Cage also realized that music was no longer a purely aural art — it was theater. That premise allowed him to retain considerable control. In many compositions Cage establishes theatrical situations, in which a drama, or at least a visual as well as an aural event, unfolds. Cage sets the wheels in motion and lets the game play itself out. But Cage establishes both the wheels and the rules of the game. Michael Nyman observed: "I've already noted that the performers, in order to produce the sounds that Cage wants, cannot renounce control, and when they did and behaved 'badly' then Cage was upset, perhaps justifiably so. Although Cage may not control — in the sense that Beethoven controls — precisely what and when a musician plays, he is controlling the social situation."[36]

Cage had a method and he had a style. His chance music, however produced, demanded great control of the performer. More than the sound it is the sound situation that Cage composes. Cage could be a stern taskmaster in the rehearsal room, demanding that his instructions be followed precisely and that the performer add absolutely nothing, in the way of gestures or expressions. David Tudor, totally deadpan as he pounded the underside of a piano or blew a duck whistle in water, epitomizes the Cage performance aesthetic.

In Cage's indeterminate pieces, the performer has more latitude, but Cage demanded that his instructions, however general, be followed, and in spite of his seeming indifference to results he could be furious when they were not. The spirit of what he was doing was important. Possibly the biggest performance disaster of Cage's career occurred when the New York Philharmonic programmed *Atlas Eclipticalis*. It was given three performances, and even though Leonard Bernstein himself conducted the concerts, members of the New York Philharmonic were not sympathetic to Cage's directions. Bernstein, it should be noted, was not actually on the podium. The piece, in eighty-four parts determined by astrological charts, called for musicians to improvise certain types of lines at certain times, and a mechanical device that indicated the time substituted for the traditional conductor. Members of the audience reacted vehemently and either left or vociferously attempted to disrupt the proceeding. By the third performance members of the orchestra laughed and talked among themselves, played whatever they wanted irrespective of directions, and hissed when Cage came on stage to take a bow. Critics were no less charitable: "If all of this sounds hideously obscure, it is. The music that emerges tortures the ear through its utter bedlam, dissonance, frantic scratches of tone, and absolute lunacy of organization."[37] Later Cage commented that the New York Philharmonic was "like a group of gangsters," and that its members "acted criminally." He also made known his displeasure to the president of the Philharmonic and the musicians' union.[38]

In several large event pieces of the 1960s — the circus pieces — Cage limited himself to the role of clockwinder. He set up the situation and let those involved determine the action. These were large-scale productions, spread out over considerable space. *Mewantemooseicday* had activities throughout the entire campus of the University of California, Davis, including concerts, lectures, and Cage's composition 33 1/3, in which he set up twelve LP record players with three hundred records, and let anyone wander in and play whatever they desired.

More often Cage in some way directly controlled the action. In *Musicircus* at the University of Illinois, an event held in the university's Stock Pavilion, Cage had several musicians perform simultaneously, along with enhancements, such as balloons, slide, and film. The result was predictable Cageian chaos. Cage's hand was ever present, however, as he worked the lighting console, a visual conductor guiding the audience. He also wired the console with contact microphones, so that each flip of the switch was amplified throughout the space.

In other large, theatrical pieces, such as *HPSCHD*, a multimedia event at the University of Illinois, or even *Atlas Eclipticalis*, Cage did more than set the wheels in motion. Both pieces involved large numbers of performers and a great variety of sound sources, which Cage specified within certain parameters. But the performances themselves were monitored by Cage. Sounds were fed to Cage, who sat at a large mixing board, deciding what should be brought out and what should be suppressed. What we hear is what Cage decides we should hear. From the listener's perspective, "the piece," that is, what reaches the listener, does so through the filter of John Cage.

JOHN CAGE

But let's get more specific about the question: *When* did John Cage become JOHN CAGE? When did he began to be taken seriously, recognized as someone who held special insights into the world of the late twentieth century? This question is only a variant of another, very close to the heart of what this

book is about: *Why* are we so *fascinated* with John Cage? And there is little
doubt that our culture is. With his lecture fees, his sold-out performances,
his media presence, Cage became one of the prime symbols in our time of
the avant-garde, off-beat artist. As I write I sit with an Amazon.com coffee
mug on my desk, sent to me I suppose because I once ordered books from
Amazon.com. On it are two quotations, one by John Cage, the other by
Henry David Thoreau. The pairing is insightful, as Cage himself often
turned to Thoreau and recognized fully his debt to the bard of Walden. Yet
the presence of Cage speaks even louder. In the age of media celebrity, what
could be a stronger statement about Cage, the epitome of the eccentric
avant-garde maverick, than his placement as an icon on a cyberbookstore
coffee mug?

Cage himself places the change in the mid-1950s. But even before that
he attracted plenty of attention. He became a celebrity beginning with his
percussion concerts in the early '40s, first in Chicago and then in New York.
His percussion music, his prepared piano, and then his expansion into other
unusual sounds in the early '50s held audiences in an almost charismatic fascination. And audiences understood what he was about. Writing in 1952
about the premiere of the *Concerto for Prepared Piano*, a piece that incorporates among other unusual devices a gong played underwater, Robert Bagar
in the *New York World-Telegram* acknowledged that the audience, "some
1,500 or more, seemed to thrill to this music." Other critics confirmed this:
according to the *New York Times*, the heartiest applause of the evening was
for the Cage piece, and according to the *New York Herald-Tribune* the audience not only rendered approval but wanted to hear more.[39]

Bagar himself understood Cage's message. Possibly he had heard, or almost certainly heard of, *4′ 33″*. Regarding Cage and silence he wrote, "And
to this reviewer some of the silences teemed with an import indefinable and
exotic. (Perhaps I was filling in the spaces between sounded imports, indefinable and exotic.)"[40] The statement itself is pure Cage.

If there is a single turning point in Cage's career, it would be the twenty-
five-year retrospective concert at Town Hall in New York, on May 15, 1958.
The concert included works arranged chronologically, beginning with *Six
Short Inventions for Seven Instruments* of 1934 and concluding with the premiere of the *Concert for Piano and Orchestra*. Percussion pieces, electronic
works, music of indeterminacy, and the prepared piano all made an appearance. Reviews were mixed. The audience was polarized. Earlier pieces were
well received, but the *Concert* created a storm comparable to the premiere of
Stravinsky's *Rite of Spring*.[41]

More important than the concert itself was the recording of it that

George Avakian issued. Avakian had arranged the concert. The recording consists of three LPs, the entire concert, including the applause and the protests that accompanied the works. It is more than a musical recording, however. As well as an aural documentation of the event, the package includes a detailed description of each piece along with a page of each score, photographs, and the complete text of some early Cage lectures. It is produced on rough sepia, newsprint-like LP-size paper, which itself gives an artistic patina to the endeavor. And Cage's scores frequently have a visual, artistic quality unto themselves, so much so that many have been exhibited in art galleries. The overall product was a well-rounded depiction of the Cage aesthetic, something that could reach far more listeners than his concerts. This appeared some years before *Silence.*[42]

Soon after the twenty-five-year retrospective, Cage went to the Darmstadt New Music Festival in Germany. From there he was invited to Milan by Luciano Berio. Cage's visit to Milan resulted in one of the most unusual episodes of his unusual career. He was chosen to be on a television quiz show, *Lascia o Raddoppia,* as an expert on mushrooms. If contestants could answer a series of questions on topics of their choice, they would be invited back. Each week the questions got more difficult and the money greater. A wrong answer and the contestant dropped out, keeping half his earnings. Cage answered some tough questions, survived five weeks, the maximum allowed, and came home with six thousand dollars, more money that he had received from his Guggenheim Fellowship. For Cage this was a lot of money at the time, but there was an added bonus: he was allowed to perform one of his pieces each week before the contest. He became an Italian celebrity, as week after week the audience watched this strange young American play very strange music with an odd collection of "instruments," all the while demonstrating an extraordinary knowledge of mushrooms. After he returned to New York he became one of the founding members of the New York Mycological Society.

Shortly after the retrospective recording appeared, several opportunities came John Cage's way. In 1960 he received his first appointment at a university, as a fellow at the Center for Advanced Studies at Wesleyan University. He also saw *Silence,* his first collection of essays, published in that year, and he was commissioned to write an orchestral piece by the Montreal Festivals Society. For that Cage composed *Atlas Eclipticalis,* a work that used star charts as the basis for chance operations. (This was the ill-fated piece that the New York Philharmonic later performed in 1964.) In 1962 Cage and David Tudor had a successful six-week tour of Japan.

By the late 1960s Cage's recognition was widespread. In 1967 he was

named composer-in-residence at the University of Cincinnati and an associate of the Center for Advanced Study at the University of Illinois. He was sub-
sequently appointed artist-in-residence at the University of California at
Davis, and in 1968 was elected to the National Academy of Arts and Letters.
In 1969 when *Stereo Review* did a pair of articles on the American avant-
garde, the two composers featured were Milton Babbitt and John Cage. By
then Cage could command a lecture fee of fifteen hundred dollars.

With the big lecture fees — and fifteen hundred was a big lecture fee in
1970 — Cage the individualist and anarchist was making money the same
way the serialists were, through the patronage of the university. But he could
at least support himself, and his lectures were theatrical events entirely consistent with his approach. More troubling are his recordings, where a rift between Cage's philosophy and his actions, noted earlier in relation to concerts, becomes a chasm.

Non-intention and the concept of *the piece* are fundamentally antithetical. Cage indeed knew that and addressed the point.[43] The Western system
of musical production and distribution is based, however, on *the piece*. The
concert venue, CDs, criticism itself, are all organized around it. Cage could
maintain his presence in the concert world because of the visual and theatrical dimension of the event. In a concert the visual element as well as the
sheer presence of his infectious personality allowed him to both use and attack the venue itself. It was high camp; and it was effective. Recordings
(whether LPs or CDs), however, reduced *the piece* to elemental sound. Except for opera, itself theater, and the protests of a few artists, who feared that
recordings would doom the concert tradition, that had been OK. To most the
concert remained an aural event, at least in theory, and *the piece* existed as a
self-contained collection of sounds. The concept of abstract, disembodied,
to-be-listened-to-only music had become so embedded in Western culture
that critics and teachers had trouble accepting even program music. They ra-
tionalized that good program music was good music, even without the program. (This point will be discussed further in Chapter 12.)

The moment John Cage put his post-1952 pieces on vinyl, he acceded to
the terms of the Western classical aesthetic. The absence of the visual element rendered impotent his strongest weapon to challenge Western musical
beliefs, for the nature of the medium transformed his dynamic events into
abstract, forever frozen monuments. It left him in many cases as an absurdity.
It is no coincidence that the most scathing denunciations of Cage's music
came from reviews of his recordings. In one review Oliver Daniel described
Cages *Variations II* (Columbia MS-7501) by saying: "[It] at times sounds like
a stylus being dragged over burnt toast. . . . It is all a sort of fun-and-games

affair in which anything goes for any number of players and any sound-producing means. . . . Freed from the conventional restraints of system, style, or the rational faculty, we are treated to what Cage describes as 'disorganization and a state of mind which in Zen is called no-mindedness.' It is another way of describing musical garbage, and twenty minutes and twenty seconds of protracted needle scratch is about as hallucinatory and attractive as scabies."[44]

With only the vinyl disc to hear, it is hard to disagree with Daniel's assessment. Even the recording of Cage's twenty-five-year retrospective concert fared badly. The anonymous reviewer for the American Record Guide called it "musical mumbo-jumbo that equates fetishism," and summarized Cage's compositional development: "exploratory-inventiveness has turned into shock, sensation the process of 'way out,' the axiom of '*delenda est Musica.*'" Locked into the notion that a recording was an aural document, the reviewer failed to realize that this LP came closer than most to an actual Cage event. The sounds with the expository and the visual material packaged with it form a single whole; it is a document of precisely what its title says: twenty-five years of John Cage.[45]

Such reviewers' comments indirectly raise a question frequently asked about Cage concerts: "Is it music?" Many early writers said, no. This question surfaced as early as 1943, when the *New York Times* reviewer of Cage's percussion concert at the Museum of Modern Art simply put the word *music* in quotation marks. More typical was Heinrich Stroebel's comment in an address at a modern music festival at Donaueschingen in 1954. Stroebel described Cage's pieces as experimental, and stated flatly that he does "not have the purpose of producing something that one could call music." As late as 1961 Cage was still seen as outside the bounds of music: John S. Weissman, writing in *Musical Quarterly* about *Atlas Eclipticalis*, said, "I am reluctant to call this haphazard assemblage of physical sounds music at all, however I might be prepared to stretch the *rapport* of the word."[46]

Part of the problem lay less with the definition of music than with the notion of art. Oliver Daniel recognized the game-like quality of Cage's music, but found that insufficient: "It may be a game 'in progress,' but when all is said and done, art is not a game." Even one of the most perceptive of the Cage critics succumbed to the traditional notion of art and the artwork. Richard Kostelanetz expressed his opinion of *Williams Mix*: "I personally take it to be the principal neglected masterpiece of Cage's musical oeuvre."[47]

It seems curiously contradictory to the Cage aesthetic to hear the word *masterpiece* used to describe a Cage work, especially one created by chance.

This comment, however, represents the problem of dealing with Cage: Do we do it on our terms or on his? And in each instance what are those terms? This is not a problem unique to Cage. It has bedeviled the arts throughout the twentieth century, and has been particularly prevalent in music, where cultural, technological, and aesthetic factors have demanded a rethinking of the medium itself, in regard to its materials and their manipulation, in regard to its function, whether in a focused situation such as a concert or in connection with other arts (including film), and in regard to its method of delivery, whether direct or through some form of electronics.

Historians have pushed Cage in the direction of the Western tradition by viewing his chance music as a reaction to serialism: total control followed by no control.[48] It is far from honest, however, to categorize chance music as a response to serialism. In some ways it *is* an antithesis of the entire prevailing Western musical aesthetic, which in large measure had been distilled into serialism — as abstract, autonomous, highly structured. Chronology if no other reason gives pause to reducing chance music to a reaction against serialism, for John Cage moved into it almost simultaneously with Boulez's and Babbitt's serial experiments. In fact for a brief time Boulez and Cage were relatively close, as both seemed to pursue similar aims, the use of mathematical methods to determine musical elements. Only when Boulez realized that Cage arrived at his numbers completely differently, through chance rather than planned formulas, did he break with Cage. But during that time Cage led a revolt against traditional musical standards easily as radical and far-reaching as any that the serialists attempted.

Cage's revolt was not isolated, however. Indeterminacy, an avoidance of personal expression, and a desire to challenge boundaries characterize much music since World War II. Cage succeeded because he was one of the few composers in the immediate postwar years to go beyond revolution and understand the implications of a major shift in the very meaning of music that was under way. This shift, toward a new type of artistic fusion, I believe marks the "end of the Renaissance" and is possibly the most important musical development of the twentieth century. Cage not only challenged old thought and practices but intuited what must take their place. Curiously the musico-intelligentsia community, while having inclinations about the presence of this paradigm shift, has not addressed its full implications.

CHAPTER 9

The Maverick Core

"*Harry Partch: A Biography* reads like a great mystery," says David Harrington, first violinist of the Kronos Quartet, on the dust jacket of the book by Bob Gilmore. "How did one of America's truly visionary composers, instrument builders, and rough-hewn individualists survive and persevere through horror at a young age, homelessness in the prime of his life, and nearly constant rejection and alienation by our culture?" Harrington's comment reads like the American myth: "rough-hewn individualist," the "horror at a young age," homelessness, rejection, alienation, and finally the vision. An outsider who turned his back on Western music, to develop in toto his own unique musical culture.

First came the theory—around age thirty Harry Partch expounded, in a dense theoretical treatise, a singular musical language, with its own complex pitch relationships and tunings. Then, he put theory into practice. This necessitated the creation, from scratch, of a large group of instruments on which to play his music, as he found Western instruments totally inadequate. Partch developed a new role for the voice, a new relationship between speech and song that owed little to Arnold Schoenberg's *sprechstimme*. He created a body of music that in effect rejected hundreds of years of the Western tradition, and that looked to Japanese and ancient Greek drama as source and inspiration.

Partch was an original, a genius—without doubt. Jacques Barzun called Partch's music "the most original and powerful contribution to dramatic music on this continent."[1] But what else was he? Was he, according to the myth,

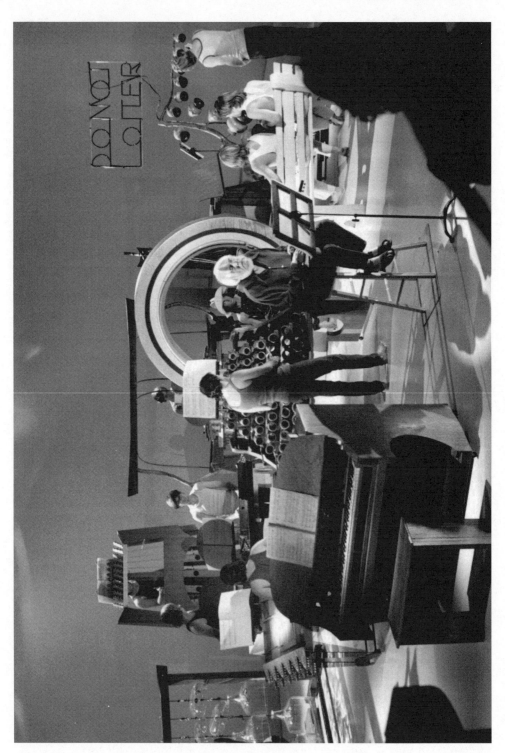

Harry Partch, with some of his musical instruments (Photograph © Betty Freeman/Lebrecht Music)

the perpetual alien, the outsider, the homeless bum for whom there was no place? Did he cultivate and exaggerate that image, turning it to his own uses? Was he shunned, almost totally, by twentieth-century American musical culture? Was he, as has also been claimed, the true son of the southwest, an autodidact shaped by a vast, melancholy, and lonely desert? Where is the real Harry Partch?

Partch may be elusive, but he is not untrackable. Tantalizing gaps exist in his biography, times when we don't know for sure where he was, but Partch in general left ample evidence, not only about what he did, but about what he thought. Partch could be difficult, sometimes contradictory, but he was open, even outspoken about his beliefs and preferences. And he was aware. His knowledge of Western cultural history was immense, and in razor-edge prose as well as in song he was a keen, if often caustic, observer of his own time.[2]

Bob Gilmore, author of the "great mystery" Harrington pointed to, offers many answers about Partch. In his book we encounter many Partches, and we also encounter many puzzles and more mysteries. For Partch himself often succeeded in covering his tracks. Or, at the very least, he sometimes left few tracks to follow. Gilmore's portrait is penetrating and thorough, but the real Harry Partch remains elusive.

And Partch has inspired prose. As much as any composer in American history, Partch has become his own story. For those that know him he has settled somewhere into our collective conscious, a shadowy figure, a necessary part of the American individualist myth who haunts like no other musician of the twentieth century.[3]

The Partch myth has taken on several guises: There is Partch the theorist and composer known and written about precisely for his tuning system, the composer who inspired the entire just intonation movement. There is Partch the Orientalist, the man who turned his back on the West and retreated to his parents' adopted roots, Asia. There is Partch the dramatist, the creator of a twentieth-century *gesamtkunstwerk*, a total theatrical experience, with roots in ancient Greece and at its heart his music, including his own unique instruments. And there is Partch the defiant, the man who rejected, in one grand epiphany in New Orleans, the entirety of modern Western musical culture, only to start over and to remain ever aloof from Western institutions.

In one very tangible sense Partch belongs to the desert, or at least the west. He grew up in a small railroad town, Benson, Arizona, which according to Partch had three hundred people and eleven saloons. Partch may have exaggerated, but only in specifics, not in character. The town itself was surrounded by a forbidding but spectacular desert, and it existed solely as a junction, originally for the stagecoach and later for the railroad. Catering to rail-road workers, with its saloons and other sources of pleasure, it was anything but a cultural oasis. And for Partch it was a lonely time. He mostly enter-tained himself, but thanks to the Sears and Montgomery Ward catalogues musical instruments came into the home. According to his own accounts Partch mastered several, but he took to the piano in particular, and by the time he was in high school he was composing and playing in movie houses.[4]

By then the family had also moved, at first to Phoenix and then to Albu-querque. The venues got larger, but these were all cities of the desert, still ex-uding a frontier atmosphere. For Partch, however, there was another major cultural influence, Asia. His parents had been missionaries in China and had returned shortly before Partch was born for several reasons: his father, Virgil, had begun to question and then reject Christian dogma, and their lives were in serious danger because of the Boxer Rebellion in China. Partch remembered all his life his mother singing Chinese lullabies and his father speaking Mandarin to Chinese visitors. He once commented that there were more books in Chinese than in English in his house. Partch himself never learned Chinese, and he never studied Asian music, but he never forgot those early sounds either.

By 1920 his father had died, and Partch moved with his mother to Los Angeles and enrolled at the University of Southern California, as a piano ma-jor. That he was accepted into the studio of Oleg Steeb, at that time one of the stars of the faculty, suggests a considerable talent and facility. But Partch was rebellious and impatient. He soon left USC, ostensibly because he tired of learning how to resolve a dominant-seventh chord. Years later that event symbolized his own rejection of Western musical thought: "I think I spent about three months on the dominant seventh chord, and I thought: Well, this is the end. I'll never touch this sort of nonsense again. . . . I decided one time to observe every damned rule, every one, and write something totally outrageous, which I did; and it was put up on the blackboard and ridiculed, because it wasn't music. . . . Of course I knew it wasn't! Oh, it was an absurd experience. I didn't want to learn. I think I knew more about the resolutions of the dominant seventh chords than he [the teacher] did."[5]

This rebelliousness led to another myth, Partch's New Orleans epiphany. For this we have only his own account. From 1920 to 1930 Partch led a nomadic life. He worked at times as a proofreader for newspapers, as a piano teacher, as a fruit picker for the California harvest, and as an appren-tice seaman on an oil tanker. He was also composing and educating himself, thanks to the public library, in acoustics and the physics of tuning and tem-perament. His compositional plans were ambitious, if not idealistic. By 1930 he had written a piano concerto, a symphonic poem, and a string quartet. Partch himself destroyed them in one grand gesture, so we will never know how good they were. In any event, given Partch's isolation from the musical establishment, the chances for performance of any of these works was nil. But he had some success in another idiom. Under the name Paul Pirate, he wrote popular songs, and had at least one, *My Heart Keeps Beating Time*, published, with words altered by Larry Yoell, better known then as Ted Lewis.[6]

Partch had arrived in New Orleans in 1930, for reasons that are not entirely clear. He found work as a proofreader at a newspaper and continued his acoustical experiments. For that he took an old cello fingerboard and had an instrument maker graft it onto a viola. The result was a viola with an extended neck. The extra length allowed him to indicate precisely various frequency ratios, which was the beginning of his expansion of pitches beyond the twelve notes per octave that had characterized centuries of Western music. This instrument, originally called the monophone, soon thereafter the adapted viola, was Partch's point of no return. With it he realized a pitch spectrum that seemed immensely richer than what Western culture provided. At this point he took all his previous manuscripts, the concerto, the symphonic poem, the string quartet, and others, and burned them one evening in an iron stove in his room. He called it "a kind of adolescent auto-da-fé" and "a confession, to myself, that in pursuing the respectable, the widely accepted, I had not been faithful."[7]

Did it happen that way? Probably. Some details may be off — the experience may or may not have occurred in New Orleans or in 1930, although there is no reason to doubt either — but it was the kind of dramatic gesture typical of Partch. And the future bears him out, for from that moment Partch never turned back. From then on he singularly pursued a vision that had no precedence in Western music. The full range of the vision emerged only slowly, and never stopped evolving, but Partch remained remarkably consistent to it throughout his life.

Partch's vision immediately took two parallel paths. He continued his theoretical explorations of pitch resources, evolving various scales ranging from twenty-nine to fifty-five notes. He ultimately settled on forty-three. Working primarily with pitch ratios, his work was complex and well informed — as an acoustician, Partch was no dilettante. His experiments also led to his first recognition. A colleague on the *New Orleans Times-Picayune*, where Partch was a proofreader, wrote an article about the experiments titled "Student Devises 29-Degree Octave Theory of Music." It featured a large picture of Partch playing his "monophone."[8]

The article unfortunately perpetuated one of the most persistent myths about Partch, one that he tried all his life to shed — that his work was essentially about many-note scales. Almost every article on Partch, almost every review, referred to his forty-three-tone scale. When he saw the title of Irving Sablosky's article in the *New York Times* in 1957, "Forty-three to the Octave," Partch was, in his own words, "appalled and revolted." Partch is considered the father of the just intonation movement, but he himself described this aspect as incidental, claiming "that precious 43 is the one-half truth of the one-fourth factor." Another time he said, "I am concerned with just intonation only incidentally, microtones only incidentally." Partch saw his theoretical work as necessary, a way to escape the twelve-note-per-octave straitjacket of Western music, but it was a means, not an end; his true work was composition, and the scale was only a vehicle to realize his expressive intentions. What mattered were the expressive results.[9]

Partch's search for new pitch materials was a result of his more important decision, to abandon abstract music and base his work on the spoken word. This was, as Partch himself acknowledged, an emotional decision. It opened up for him a second path: vocal compositions that exploit the pitch subtleties made available by the expanded scale. To this end he wrote his first major composition in the new style, the *Seventeen Lyrics of Li Po*, for voice and adapted viola.

Li Po was an eighth-century Chinese lyric poet, and Partch set his poems in a vocal style closer to speech than song, although the voice would occasionally launch more pitch-sustained passages. Partch referred to this style as both monophony and tone declamation. The viola acted as more than accompaniment; it provided dramatic counterpoint, at times an instrumental commentary or dialogue, to the intoning voice. The overall effect is close to the eighteenth- and nineteenth-century idea of melodrama, although because of the expanded pitch resources the sound and expressive potential are quite different.

By 1931 Partch had returned to San Francisco and, through a connection with Henry Cowell and his New Music Society, begun to collaborate with soprano Rudolphine Radil in a series of private and public concert-demonstrations of his new system. He aroused considerable interest in the press, with comments that ranged from enthusiasm to caution. An unnamed reviewer for the *Oakland Tribune* called the effect "eerie, exotic, and unmodern"; Redfern Mason, a prominent critic with the *San Francisco Examiner*, found in his sounds "a new and singular beauty." Paul S. Nathan, writing in the *Oakland Post-Enquirer*, called the music "interesting always, hypnotic in its power and capable of expressing great subtlety." To R.D.S. of the *Oakland*

Tribune, however, monophony offered "little of musical value," and Alexander Fried of the *San Francisco Chronicle*, while admitting that "it may very well have possibilities as a distinctive means of musical expression," felt that tone declamation "does not threaten to put conventional music out of business," and was "not even superior to standard poetic recitation."[10]

Partch's ideas did not catch on with the new-music coterie around Henry Cowell, and Cowell himself seems to have been less than enthusiastic about them. In exploring his expanded scale, Partch had taken a completely different tack from many avant-garde experimentalists, from Ives to Bartók and Boulez, who experimented with quarter-tones. Partch had long since rejected the quarter-tone approach, feeling that, as a division of the twelve-tone Western system, it kept one complicit in that system.[11] More critical, however, was Partch's attitude toward dissonance. Dissonance had been a central issue, indeed the hallmark, of avant-garde composers of the early twentieth century, whether as the foundation of a new harmonic system, as Seeger and Ruggles advocated, or as a manifestation of tone clusters, as Cowell and others had demonstrated. The emancipation of dissonance had become emblematic of breaking the restraints of the romantic style. In Partch's monophony, dissonance had no part. His was a system of consonance based on overtones. There was nothing against which to push, and Partch seemed out of step with what other composers were doing.

With few prospects in San Francisco, Partch moved to Los Angeles and generated considerable initial interest there, but again he seems to have quickly exhausted his possibilities. By this time he had conceived the idea of setting the W. B. Yeats poem *Oedipus Rex* to music, and toward that end he went all out to secure a grant from the new Guggenheim Foundation. He even moved to New York to establish contact with East Coast composers and others who might help him. He impressed, drew strong support from, and befriended Howard Hanson, Douglas Moore, and Otto Luening, and while the Guggenheim Foundation was unwilling to risk funding such a radical and unknown composer, officials there were impressed, and recommended him to the Carnegie Corporation, which did give him a grant.

In 1934 Partch sailed to London, to work at the British Museum, to interview Yeats, and to record the tone inflection of British actors. The year was a success, and Partch returned triumphantly to New York with Yeats's blessing, a theoretical treatise that explained his ideas, a new instrument, a forty-three-tone organ he called Ptolemy, and ideas for pieces.

Partch also returned to the worst depression the United States had encountered, to a "jobless America," and with that harsh reality his years of wandering began.[12] From 1935 to 1943 Partch lived off and on as a hobo, sometimes finding occasional work, sometimes living on charity, but never able to keep steady employment. The depression was not entirely to blame. In 1936 he was hired as a proofreader for the Works Progress Administration in Phoenix, but after nine months he had a blowup with his boss and decided to hit the road again.

Partch disappeared for two years, from 1937 to 1939, and to this day his whereabouts during that time are mostly unknown. His early wandering is less mysterious, because he kept a journal, which recounts in vivid detail life in the hobo camps of the west. Years later the journal was published as *Bitter Music*. In it Partch also recorded the tones and inflections of the talk around him, sometimes setting it to a complex, chromatic accompaniment. Possibly because he did not have his instruments, which were in storage, possibly because he had in mind a vocal-piano performance of these works, Partch fell back on conventional notation. But in the chromatic wandering of the voices and the accompaniments we can still sense him straining at the limitations Western notation forced on his thinking.

By 1940 Partch had settled back in California, found some work, and resumed composition and experimentation with instruments. By this time he was interested in constructing various instruments based on his acoustic ideas. Soon an adapted guitar and kithara took shape. And he began to tap his hitchhiker experience, writing *Barstow, Eight Hitchhikers' Inscriptions*, a setting of hitchhiker graffiti he had recorded in his years of wandering.

Partch, however, was restless, and through a chance encounter he received an invitation to visit Chicago.[13] The trip turned out to be important. He was able to quickly make contact with the new-music scene in Chicago and have *Barstow* and some of the *Li Po* settings performed, in a concert that also featured an "Improvisation by the Class in Sound Experiments," conducted by the composer, John Cage. Partch found Cage "charming, albeit shallow," and his music "precious and vapid." These remarks, it turned out, were some of the most complimentary things he would have to say about Cage.[14]

Partch continued to work on his instruments. He wedded Ptolemy to a harmonium to create a more easily playable instrument, the chromelodeon. And he made his first recordings, of *Barstow, Two Psalms*, and six of the *Lyrics of Li Po*.

The most far-reaching consequence of the trip to Chicago, however, was the trip itself. Unable to afford regular fare, Partch traveled as he had in the 1930s, hitchhiking, hopping freights, getting rides any way that he could. He kept a journal while traveling, noting "fragments of conversations, remarks, writings on the sides of boxcars, signs in havens for derelicts, hitchhikers' inscriptions, names of stations, thoughts." These became the raw material out of which he later fashioned *U.S. Highball.*[15]

U.S. Highball is scored for a "subjective" and an "objective" voice, and a collection of instruments. The subjective voice is the protagonist, a.k.a. Partch himself, and the objective voice is actually several voices, fragmentary comments by hobos that Partch encountered. They are the voices of his journal. The objective voice is intended to be sung by the instrumentalists, portending Partch's later practice of melding the instruments and the players into the essence of the drama. The trip itself is recounted as the subjective voice intones the various stages of the trip, in a choruslike motive:

> Lea — ving —— Californ-i-a
> Lea — ving —— Reno
> Lea — ving —— Winnemucca, Nevaducca
> etc.

This is a double-play on a typical train trip, in which the conductor goes through the cars intoning the various places as the train arrives. Hobos on a freight are not offered such a convenience, and the intonation, as Partch makes clear, is in the protagonist's own mind, which accounts for the odd enunciation. And the protagonist celebrates leaving, not arriving in each place, a point, as Partch explains, any hobo would understand.[16]

Partch originally conceived the piece for voice and adapted guitar, but before it was finished he realized it needed more instrumentation. In the first completed version he used the adapted guitar, chromelodeon, kithara, and double canon. In later arrangements Partch added more instruments but changed the character of the piece little. The instruments are critical to the piece, for much of the drama resides in them. They create the sense of movement, tension, excitement, and exhilaration accompanying the journey. Exploiting fully Partch's pitch resources, they create an ambience with little reference to the Western tonal heritage, freeing them to enter into the drama. *U.S. Highball* is one of Partch's most effective weddings of voice and instrumental sound; while presaging his later efforts, it differs in one respect. The instrumental depiction is so vivid as to create an entire drama aurally; only later did he integrate fully a visual dimension.

U.S. Highball was turning point for Partch. He called it "the most creative piece of work that I have done." With it Partch's sense of theater emerged, and he realized he was now ready to do something operatic. The piece inaugurated the second and most important phase of his compositional life: from *U.S. Highball* on, Partch's major compositional efforts would be theatrical, and his primary artistic goal would be to revive the Greek notion of drama, the re-creation of a total artwork that integrated music, drama, movement, and visual effect.[17]

U.S. Highball also coincided with a change in Partch's fortunes. In 1942 he moved to Chappaqua, New York, where he was invited to stay at the home of Donald Flanders and family. There he worked on new compositions and another Guggenheim application. He also began to receive invitations to lecture and demonstrate his music: at Bennington College, the Eastman School of Music, and Columbia University. The year 1943 found him in Ithaca, New York, where he had taken a bookkeeping job, and where he completed *U.S. Highball.* There he also received word that he had been awarded a Guggenheim Fellowship.

Partch commented that the Guggenheim marked the end of his own great depression.[18] He immediately began a series of ambitious plans to get his music heard, in Boston, at the New England Conservatory, and in New York, at a concert sponsored by the League of Composers, by then an established, venerable organization dedicated to new music.

The League of Composers concert occurred on April 22, 1944, at Carnegie Hall. Partch performed on the chromelodeon and the adapted guitar and sang. Soprano Ethel Luening also sang. The response was hesitant, as most critics knew not what to make of the piece. Paul Bowles complained about Partch's voice and manner of losing himself in the adapted guitar when he sang; H. in *Musical America* related it to Schoenberg's sprechstimme and observed that Luening had "used her fine voice to better effect than on this occasion"; an anonymous reviewer for *Musical Courier* said that the "multifarious queer noises that she [Luening] put forth" were "marvelous." Many critics, possibly relieved to have something tangible to discuss, focused on Partch's use of a forty-three-tone scale, although some admitted that most listeners probably could not hear it.[19]

Some musicians as well as critics simply found Partch's music either lightweight or dilettantish. Many looked back nostalgically at the halcyon days of the League of Composers in the 1920s and lamented that by the 1940s its offerings, and by extension modern music itself, had become dull and predictable. Partch's music was different, no doubt, but it didn't seem to have the heaviness and density of the true twentieth-century avant-garde. And critics were torn: even when moved they were reluctant to admit any profundity to the style. Lou Harrison found the music "negligible," but had to admit, about *San Francisco,* "Mr. Partch has woven a spell of about the foggiest and dampest music I have ever heard. I got homesick." Paul Bowles was a bit more positive, but acknowledged that Partch's music was moving "only in so far as it cursed, groaned, released sounds of pain."[20]

Audience reactions recalled those of the 1920s. Henry Brandt, who participated in the concert, categorized the audience, which included numerous musicians, as "annoyed, irritated, perhaps envious, a little hostile." The *Musical Courier* reported that the concert "stirred wonder and frequent laughter but made scant emotional appeal." Regarding the *Y.D. Fantasy*, Henry Simon reported that "the audience guffawed so that it was repeated." R.L. of the *New York Times* tried to cover all bases: "the season's most 'sophisticated' concert, or the most boring or the funniest, according to the point of view."[21]

The New York music scene was in a state of uncertainty. Otto Luening commented that "art for art's sake was temporarily moribund." Big-time composers, such as Copland and Harris, were producing a mainstream Americana. Copland himself had *Rodeo* and *Billy the Kid* behind him and later that year premiered *Appalachian Spring*. Copland was also the only member of the League of Composers' auditioning committee to oppose the presentation of *U.S. Highball* when Partch auditioned it. When the International Society of Contemporary Music presented a major festival in 1941, the music, of the avant-garde in both Europe and the Americas, seemed to critics old, tired, and out of sync with the 1940s. Olin Downes in particular blasted it as "lacking any degree of freshness, originality and creativity," and presenting nothing but "hollowness and barrenness." John Cage had created some interest with his percussion music in 1943, aided significantly by a spread in *Life* magazine, but his concert was only an isolated phenomenon.[22]

Thus when someone as original and unusual as Harry Partch came along it both raised expectations and bewildered listeners. An article by John Lardner in the *New Yorker*, written at the urging of Douglas Moore, captures the puzzlement Partch engendered. After hearing Partch intone some of *Barstow* and *U.S. Highball*, Lardner acknowledged that, in attempting to imitate conversation, he "made a pretty good stab at it." Beyond that, and particularly in regard to Partch's musical materials, that is, the forty-three tones, Lardner admitted that he understood it only "dimly," but that most people would feel that the twelve notes to the octave and the intervals it produces are close enough. But not for Partch; Partch wants more. Here the musical discussion breaks off and elides into politics, religion, and possibly metaphysics: "He feels, also, that the tempered scale is a form of regimentation, and he has long been opposed as to regimentation. This is evidenced by the fact that he has drifted restlessly from one occupation to another: schoolteacher, fruitpicker, apprentice seaman, writer, and proofreader, as well as indigent transient and composer. 'My father was a Presbyterian minister who turned agnostic,' he told us. 'Maybe that had something to do with it.'"[23] On that comment Lardner ends. This was probably as close as he could come to understanding what Harry Partch was all about.

With his Guggenheim, Partch moved to Madison, Wisconsin, to oversee the publication of his book *Genesis of a Music* by the University of Wisconsin Press. This was the first of several university connections Partch would have, at the University of Wisconsin, the University of Illinois, and the University of California. All were troubled, and in each a similar pattern developed: Partch was never accepted, particularly by the music faculty, although he fared better at some places than others, and his own conduct and deep-seated dislike of academia did little to endear him to the universities. Composers resented what he did, and music departments in which he was involved found him essentially persona non grata. His experiences in these universities did much to strengthen his image as an outlaw musician.

Partch became involved with the University of Wisconsin through the recommendation of pianist Gunnar Johansen, then artist-in-residence. Johansen had become familiar with Partch's music in New York through Douglas Moore. In its scientific bent Partch's proposed project, the completion of *Genesis of a Music* (then called *Patterns of Music*), appealed to the University Research Committee, which awarded him a grant. His Guggenheim gave him academic prestige while providing funds that took most of the strain off the university budget. Partch gave several lecture-demonstration concerts in Madison, which drew huge crowds but met with skepticism and even hostility from the music faculty. It should be noted that the concerts were sponsored by the Graduate School Research Committee, not the Music Department.

Partch's music created quite a stir in Madison, and opinion was polarized. One local critic called it "music of vigor and sensitivity, of inherent worth," and another observed that those in the capacity audience "were rewarded with the kind of evening about which they can talk about for days, if they can find words to describe it." A student wrote in, "I definitely did not like the 25th century jam session."[24]

Partch gave vent to his feelings and frustrations about the reception he got from musicians with three essays that he wrote in Madison, "G-String Formality," "Musicians as 'Artists,'" and "Showhorses in the Concert Ring." Only the latter was published, by *Circle*, a journal in Berkeley, California, in 1948. The first in particular, "G-String Formality," is sarcastic and vitriolic, a measure of Partch's bitterness toward musical academia. In it he took aim at the "rules" that constrict the composer:

And our schools are doing a bang-up job of preventing any changes in music. No investigation — it's not in the rules. No curiosity — it's not in the rules . . .

O, you took that individualism stuff that you learned in school seriously? O, no! You didn't! One must preserve a healthy cynicism about creativity — that's one of the rules too.[25]

Partch is particularly vitriolic about the reverence for Bach that characterized academia. He proposed several degrees, beginning with B.B., Bachelor of Bach, and M.F., Mistress of the Fugue (open only to female candidates), progressing through D.B., Doctor of Bach, and D.B.D., Doctor of Bachic Divinity, "which would require the candidate to undergo twelve solid years (one for each scale degree) of incarceration in a labyrinth lined with Bach biographies, each shelf dedicated to one minute of the master's life." And the final degree was the B.V.D., Bach Verus Dominus, which would require the candidate to "rewrite the entire *B-minor Mass* under massive doses of sodium pentathol [*sic*]." Later Partch refers to Bach's "*B-minor Mess* — excuse me — *Mass*."[26]

Although this ranting never saw print, given Partch's outspoken nature and his opportunity to give three public lectures on "Expanding the Musical Consciousness," which included one called "Verities Apart from the Swing Band and J. S. Bach," it is hardly surprising that Partch's relationship with members of the music faculty were at best cool. Resentment of the crowds that Partch drew and his success outside of music did not help. By 1946 Partch's Guggenheim had run out and the graduate committee recommended that he be given an academic appointment. The actual decision, however, was the music faculty's, which voted forty to one against, Johansen being the only yea.

Partch returned to California, in part thanks again to Gunnar Johansen, who provided a place for him on his ranch in Gualala. Partch remained at various places in California for ten years, some of the most productive of his life. He continued to expand his array of instruments and wrote a number of compositions, the most important being *King Oedipus*, which was produced at Mills College in 1952. It was performed to sold-out houses and considerable press and critical acclaim in the Bay area. It was also an important step for Partch, his first major piece that incorporated his new ideas about theater. His collaborator, Arch Lauterer, was in complete accord with Partch, recognizing the importance not only of the visual dimension but of the visual presence of Partch's instruments on stage. The piece was a theatrical tour de force, although not all reviewers were comfortable with Partch's intoned musical style.

The performance was disappointing to Partch in one way, however. He had hoped that this would lead to some sort of appointment at Mills College, but none was forthcoming. A university connection had to wait another four years, until he got an offer from the University of Illinois.

In the meantime Partch supported himself with recordings. In 1953 he moved his studio to an old shipyard in Sausalito, at Gate 5. Through the help of friends he established the Gate 5 recording studio, devoted to the production of LPs of his work. Partch handled all the details, including distribution of the records by direct sales. For several years this was his main source of income.

While Partch was at Johansen's ranch a young man, Ben Johnston, arrived. An aspiring composer interested in intonation, he had discovered Partch through *Genesis* and wished to study with him. Johnston and his wife, Betty, stayed with Partch for about two years, in spite of primitive conditions and Partch's original curmudgeonly incordiality. Later Johnston would take a position at the University of Illinois, and mainly through his efforts Partch received a commission to write a work for the university's 1957 Festival of the Contemporary Arts.

Thus began a pattern that would be repeated again. Things started well. The music faculty was cordial and open to him, in spite of some typical Partch outspokenness and gruffness. Then came the production of *The Bewitched*. It was both an outstanding success and a colossal failure. Partch later called it the greatest disappointment of his career.

Partch proposed *The Bewitched*, a dance satire that was finding no takers in California, for the Contemporary Arts Festival. *The Bewitched* far exceeded in length and performance demands what the festival had in mind, but Partch persisted, and the planners agreed.

Compared with other late Partch pieces *The Bewitched* is abstract, but only in the sense of having no actual spoken or sung words. It began as a vocal piece but in the end consisted of ten scenes with no dialogue, although even here Partch had a dialogue in mind, which he wrote into the piece's elaborate script. The script itself is one of the most detailed that Partch ever produced.

Three entities make up *The Bewitched*: the witch, the Chorus, and the Bewitched. The instrumentalists are the Chorus, considered the Witch's instrument, and the dancers are the Bewitched. They are ordinary and realistic people: undergrads, a pathological liar, teenagers, a basketball team, two detectives, members of a courtroom.

The Witch, the embodiment of ancient wisdom, is in essence Partch himself. "She belongs to the ancient, pre-Christian school. She is an omniscient soul, all-perspective, with that wonderful power to make other people see also. . . . The Witch is a different Greek oracle." The argument of the piece holds that "we are all bewitched," that is, unaware, and the goal of the Witch is to unwitch, that is to lead the bewitched to a new state of perception. Partch called the scenes "stories of release, . . . from prejudice, from individual limitations, even from the accident of physical form . . . each one [story] is a theatrical unfolding of nakedness, a psychological strip tease, or — a diametric reversal."[27]

The Bewitched was not only an important step for Partch, it was one of his purest statements of corporeality and the state in which humans find themselves. "Corporeality" was Partch's term for his belief in the oneness of mind and body. It was his revolution stripped to its essence, and he worked on it as a man obsessed. He later called *The Bewitched* "the most unconscious music I've ever written. One day later I had only a vague notion of what I'd written the day before."[28]

Partch had delegated the choice of choreographer to Ben Johnston, and after some investigation Johnston chose Alvin Nikolais, a young, controversial avant-garde choreographer at the Henry Street Playhouse in New York. It could not have been a worse choice. Nikolais was more well known than Partch, which gave him distinct leverage when the two inevitably clashed, but more important, Nikolais had developed a distinct style. His vision was modernist and abstract. It was everything Partch was not. It was if anything a choreographer's attempt to deny a dancer corporeality. Nikolais had sought to create abstract shapes and forms on stage by putting the dancers into large bags, efforts that had been branded by critics as dehumanizing. Regarding *The Bewitched*, Nikolais disregarded Partch's detailed script, to the extent of eliminating the characters of the drama, and presenting his own concept of "the fundamental idea of the total piece." Partch saw his corporeality disappear behind a set of abstract undulating shapes on stage. And by this point he knew that even his music lacked the power to override the impression formed by the visual dimension.[29]

To Partch's vehement protests, Nikolais offered to withdraw. Partch was trapped. He wanted to see the piece presented, and he and his ensemble had spent months preparing. It went ahead, as Nikolais wanted, much to Partch's chagrin.[30]

Adding to Partch's discomfort, *The Bewitched* was an outstanding critical and popular success. Predictably the critics aligned with the Nikolais orientation. Nikolais was in this collaboration the traditionalist, presenting what was then avant-garde mainstream, an aesthetic that the modernist critics themselves embraced. Any attempt on Partch's part was thus doomed: a revolution whose full scope could not even be determined. Nikolais was, in public acceptance, justified.

Judged as an artistic product in itself, *The Bewitched* was a success. To Partch, however, its essence, what he himself was all about, had been overthrown and sacrificed. It was not what Partch envisioned, and he felt that the piece was *his* vision. And he had called up this particular piece from deep inside himself. It was the culmination of twenty-five years of work, sacrifice, and searching. It is no wonder that he felt deeply betrayed. As a consequence Partch came across as a bitter, difficult person, unable to compromise or to delegate artistic responsibility where it belonged.

After the critical success of *The Bewitched*, Partch was approached with the possibility of a twelve-year research appointment at the University of Illinois. To the surprise of many he turned it down, partly because he hated Urbana, and partly because he recalled his time in Madison, where, "in three years I hardly wrote one page of music. I could see 12 years of sterility ahead of me. . . . I'll be god-damned if what time I am around is going to be sterile." Partch's attitude did not endear him to the University of Illinois musical community.[31]

Yet two years later, after some success in New York and elsewhere with *The Bewitched* and *Windsong*, one of the films Partch did with the filmmaker Madeline Tourtolet, he returned to Urbana and was offered a one-year grant from the University of Illinois Graduate School to prepare a new theatrical piece. The result was *Revelation in the Courthouse Park*. Its success garnered him another commission, and another year of salary and stability.

These efforts were strictly ad hoc, however, and while Partch had the support of the dean of the College of Fine and Applied Arts, the Illini Student Union Board, and several members of the music faculty, he still had no regular academic appointment, and none was to come from the School of Music. Partch himself suggested that the School of Music was adamantly opposed to his affiliation. And it is not clear that Partch would have wanted to stay in Urbana, although he had no other prospects. In 1963 he left Urbana for good and headed back to California, uncertain of his future and even of a place to live.[32]

A similar set of events unfolded at the University of California, San Diego, in the 1960s and early '70s. By this time Danlee Mitchell, a student Partch had met in Urbana, had been hired to teach percussion at UCSD. Mitchell and Partch got along well from the start, and in spite of Mitchell's youth, Partch respected him both as a friend and musician. Mitchell was often called upon to lead rehearsals and conduct the instrumental ensembles in Partch's pieces. Mitchell helped Partch locate in southern California and, aided further by a recommendation from Peter Yates, Partch was offered an honorary position of Regents Professor at UCSD and an opportunity to teach a seminar on his own theories.

Partch later acknowledged that the seminar was psychologically debilitating to him and a total failure for the students. He made his anti-institutional stance clear from the start — he opposed credits, degrees, and honors, and in the end he blamed the students. "It is not the teacher's fault that his class failed," he said. "Due to the general apathy of the students discussion of the ideas advanced never took place." Partch himself was often difficult. One student described a class session with him: "We were all terrified. Harry came in drunk and absolutely furious, and denounced the Music Department . . . and the whole state of American music, for about forty-five minutes, and [let fly with] invective, just pouring forth. And then sort of politely burped and excused himself and walked out the door. And we were just dumbfounded."[33] Partch resolved never to teach another course.

Partch's relationship with UCSD had been rocky from the start. A new institution at the time, it was just forming an arts and humanities area, and Partch had been invited to give a talk on his work, an opportunity for institution and individual to assess each other. Following the talk a cocktail party was planned. Partch, fearful of such social occasions, got drunk before the party and ended up offending several university people. And when talk of an appointment did arise, Partch would not accept the university's position that if he were to have an assistant it must be an enrolled graduate student.

By the time events at UCSD transpired Partch was nearly seventy years old. Years of frustration, an inability to find permanent housing, having to maintain five tons of musical instruments, health problems, and the lessening of energy endemic with age, all had taken their toll. It is remarkable that Harry Partch somehow managed to build and then keep together his remarkable instruments over forty years, given his unrooted nomadic lifestyle. At one point he made a list of the fifteen major moves he had made in the previous sixteen years. The sheer physical energy involved in storing the instruments, moving them, setting them up, let alone the stress of finding places to keep them, often when he was virtually destitute, the worry about them when they were stored and unavailable, as well as the strain this put on his creativity, were an immense burden for anyone to carry. The dedication, the drive, and ultimately the mental cost of this is extraordinary.

With Partch there is no dramatic turning point, no sudden collapse, but a steady wearing down, as he aged and as the energy to keep up the struggle diminished. One reads a weariness in his later comments, "I am doubtful that the instruments will come out of storage while I am alive. . . . I am too tired to care about [them]."[34]

But with the weariness also came a bitterness. The struggle throughout his life was great, and what victories occurred seldom met Partch's exacting expectations. There was little in which he could take solace. What drove him also destroyed him.

There is a marginal quality about Partch: always on the edge, never quite allowing himself to enter fully, and when on the inside he was restless. It is a place that he seems to have chosen. He earnestly sought support, grants, academic positions, and he received many, a Carnegie Foundation grant, two Guggenheims, university appointments that with the right moves Partch could have converted to something permanent. In addition there were many commissions and much help from private patrons. But Partch himself frequently seemed to work against his own best interest, and he lost many opportunities through his own doing. For Partch compromise seemed impossible. He may have recognized that he needed to stay apart, a misfit, for his art to flourish.

Partch's muse was so unusual that one has to wonder whether there could have been a place for him in any Western culture. Where patronage is more fully developed, where institutions were in place, could there be a Harry Partch? Could Partch have compromised enough to stay within a more established and vigorous patronage system? If so, would he have gone in the direction that he did? Or did it take a society that is a free and open and, equally important, nonsupportive, to nourish Partch's talents?

Such contrafactual questions defy conclusive answers, but some perspective on Partch's position may be gained if we place it alongside John Cage's. As two composers at odds with Western society and tradition, Partch and Cage beg comparison. Both were from the western United States, both had considerable although irregular musical training, both aspired to be pianists, both went to large California universities but dropped out after one year, both evolved toward composition for percussion instruments, and both developed unusual, original philosophies that called into question the entire nature and direction of several centuries of Western music. In fact each rejected, completely, the prevailing Western aesthetic of musical composition. Yet it is hard to imagine two more different approaches to musical composition than those of Cage and Partch. In philosophy, belief, and practical results they stand in total opposition.

For all his radicalism Cage was part of the general artistic temper of the postwar West, toward depersonalization. In fact Cage may be seen as the end point of that movement, the logical continuation of the desire to rid art of personal expression. In that sense Cage succeeded not because he was such a maverick but because he wasn't. Cage, like Boulez, Babbitt, Brecht, and Reich, was much attuned to his time, and his historical stature is in large measure because he was the only composer willing to realize fully the implications of what depersonalization meant.

Partch is the direct, unmitigated heir to the Western idea of personal expression. Cage's inspiration, governing ideas, and compositional orientation came from Asia, and Cage himself became a Buddhist. Partch, in spite of his early exposure to Chinese culture, never associated with the Orient. Partch said over and over: I am a Western composer. He commented that he never studied Eastern music, and that Asians themselves did not find his music Eastern. They were as baffled by it as Occidentals. Of all composers, Partch identified with an emotional, personally expressive style.[35]

Whereas Cage sought to bring the East into the West, Partch embodied the West. He is the dynamic sensualist of Wagnerian opera, the tragic hero of Greek drama, the intrepid explorer of Renaissance Europe, the lone individualist of frontier America. He is the myth of the West, of America, of two thousand years of European history. He wants the listener to feel, to be moved, to reach either the ecstasy of a Dionysian rite or the anguish of an Aeschylean tragedy.

Partch's legacy is not, however, romanticism, but an older, deeper cultural strain in the West. At a time when intellectual, cerebral, or just plain weirdly experimental music prevailed, Partch pointed a way toward a Bacchic sound-world that was not dependent on the nineteenth century. He was systematic, developing a theory that was not an outgrowth of the chromaticism of romanticism. Partch sought a personal expression whose roots were in ancient Greece, something he recognized and championed. It had flowered in Renaissance Italy, in the dynamism and sensuality of painting and sculpture and in the Italian madrigal, but then became muddled in the Baroque era and was finally compromised by the abstract forms that arose in the eighteenth century. Partch's most vitriolic broadsides were leveled against J. S. Bach.[36]

More than any artist since the eighteenth century Partch rejected, clearly and emphatically, the romantic notion of an abstract, one-of-a-kind musical product. In doing so he rejected not only the entire harmonic system of the past three centuries, including the atonal forays of the Schoenberg school, but the very notion of the piece as an entity unto itself. He could begin in ways that bypassed the classical/romantic heritage entirely. Finding a solution took many years of both theoretical and practical experimentation, and many years outside the mainstream, but only his rejection of the past allowed him to formulate and pursue the vision he did with such persistence and vigor.

Partch not only attacked abstract music, which to him negated the body, but showed a way out — a type of music that was neither abstract nor derivative. Partch's music is not anti-intellectual; it is not a-intellectual; it rests on an entirely different principle, embodied by Partch's term: corporeality.

Partch spoke of corporeality throughout his life, and like life itself, the term evolved. But neither its core meaning nor its importance ever changed dramatically. Early on Partch identified corporeal music with individual vocal music, "a music that is vital to a time and place, a here and now." Corporeal meant monophonic, vocal music that followed closely the inflected speaking voice. He cited epic chant, but stressed that corporeal music includes virtually all the ancient cultures, Chinese, Greek, Arabian, Indian, "in all of which music was physically allied with poetry or the dance." Corporeal music is "tactile."[37]

Monophony meant more than vocal texture, however. In his harmonic theories, which were essentially just intonation, he derived all his pitch materials from a single tone, all intervals being ratios related to the overtones of that one tone. That tone is not the same as a tonal tonic, but a unity, expressed with the ratio 1:1, a starting point from which all others are derived. As Partch explained, "Monophony may be regarded as an organization (of pitches) deducible from the sounding of one tone."[38] For Partch that tone was G.

Corporeal music, as inflected vocal chant, was associated with ritual and theater. A theatrical focus in Partch's music became more common as the monophonic prescription loosened, with the addition of many instruments engendering a special type of polyphony. Partch maintained the idea of monophony, however, the term becoming symbolic, the "one voice" standing for the composer's own. Yet even in his earliest monophonic pieces instruments had independent parts, undermining the notion of one single line.

To Partch corporeal music was common to many cultures, particularly primitive ones, but uncommon to recent Western, post-Renaissance culture. In that sense it was diametrically opposed to the Western concert experience, which presented an abstract, disembodied music to a passive audience. Ritual by nature demanded participation.[39]

Partch's disdain of the recent Western musical tradition may have begun with his desire to escape the limitations of twelve tones per octave, but from the start it had to do with the oneness that he saw between music and speech, and his refusal to put music in the background. He had learned about that firsthand, in the movie houses of the southwest, and he had firmly rejected any further involvement in that direction. Partch stressed again and again that the dramatic and the musical were to him inseparable.

Partch's music was his entire being, his mind and body. As such Cage's and Partch's approach to composition could not have been further apart. Partch found the idea of non-intention unfathomable, and rather than seeing Cage as a fellow maverick he saw in him all the hollowness that Cage himself thought he was exposing. On their first encounter in 1942, he had described Cage's music, at that time fully composed percussion pieces, as "shallow." Later the words about Cage's music became more harsh: "precious," "vapid," and "hokum." Partch found Cage's theories essentially empty, comparable to opening a door only to find a void there, and he saw Cage getting by on personality and showmanship. To Partch, who was more interested in results than metaphysical theories, Cage was all theory with results that always came out the same, "static."[40]

Partch harbored a personal resentment toward Cage. It may have been a product of Cage's success, or it may have resulted from what Partch saw as a "patronizing attitude" toward him. It may have been that Cage was uninterested in intonation. And it may have been that Cage did not understand what Partch was about. Thus when Cage tried to equate Partch with the number 43, that was too much for Partch.

In 1966 Partch wrote to Cage, who had requested a manuscript.[41] He sent him "Verse 12 — Spoils of War — Pity! Pity! The WhiteLeghorn Cockerel." He also sent him a short credo:

> I believe in many things; in an intonation as *just* as I am capable of making it, in musical instruments *on stage*, dynamic in form, visually exciting. I believe in dramatic lighting replete with gel, to enhance them; in musicians who are *total* constituents of the moment, irreplaceable, who may sing, shout, whistle, stamp their feet; in players who are in costume, perhaps halfnaked, or with fantastic headpieces, but certainly in some visual form that will remove them from the limbo of the pedestrian.

Cage, who was putting together a collection of scores for *Score* magazine, then edited Partch's statement to forty-three words, which prompted an angry response from Partch: "I tried not to be difficult. But when you insist on a statement from me that is exactly 43 words you are being difficult. I would really like to forget the whole thing." Partch did admit, however, that Cage's edited version was "probably better than my original statement." Cage's read:

> I believe in an intonation as *just* as I am capable of making it, in musical instruments *on stage*, . . . visually exciting. . . . dramatic lighting, . . . ;

... musicians ... *total* constituents of the moment, ... ; ... perhaps half
naked, ... in some visual form that will remove them from ... pedestrian.
[Cage's punctuation]

But the number 43 was more than Partch could take: "Again however, if you
dare to mention that number 43 you are deliberately misrepresenting me. It
is the one-half truth of the one-fourth factor. And I shall *curse* you. You have
been cursed before, but never by me, and if you are cursed by me there will
be a difference." To which Cage responded: "For Heaven's sake, please don't
curse me! I'd never recover. I promise, of course, not to mention numbers
again. But please let me know whether my excerpting and editing was acceptable to you, that is, whether we may use that statement. I haven't the
slightest intention of doing anything against your wishes." Cage did eventually set Partch's edited version for *Score*, and he did it with Cage graphics: it
was typeset using I-Ching operations giving the text a variety of fonts. The visual effect of the fonts dominated over both the message of Partch and the
forty-three-word count. We do not know how Partch responded to that.

The tension between Cage and Partch was not just personal, however.
Their concepts of music were so different that there was virtually no common ground. We have few comments from Cage about Partch, but he could
not have been in sync with a composer so committed to personal expression.
As for Partch, an aleatory approach was anathema: "This is not idea, it is the
absence of idea." And, "I chanced to attend a chance concert once, and it
was the dullest thing I ever experienced, next to a Cecil B. DeMille Spectacular."[42]

And personal expression was central not only to Parch's music but to his
notion of what art should be. It is difficult to imagine Cage embracing such a
concept as corporeality. In the 1950s–60s world of art music, however, it is
equally difficult to imagine the classical music mainstream embracing it.
Who here represents establishment values?

When society seemed to be splintering between generations, when
young people were captivated by the arrival of the Age of Aquarius, when values, even trust seemed to be on the line, Partch, by this time in his sixties, was
embraced by these same young people. Often the rebellious and disenfran-
chised gravitated toward Partch, and to many he became something of a folk
hero — partly because of his own sheer eccentricity, also because of his total
dedication to his art, and not least because of the art itself. *Crossover* is an inappropriate term to describe Partch's music, in part because it fits neither the
art-music nor the popular-music world. His music is at one level sui generis,
although as Partch himself stressed, it had deep roots in Western culture.

One composer of the 1960s did look at the chasm that existed between the classical and popular-musical worlds and attempt, consciously and zealously, to cross from one to the other. Frank Zappa was as unclassifiable as Harry Partch, although his trajectory could not have been more different. Anchored almost totally in the popular-music world, where weirdness had become a commodity in itself, Zappa stood out even there as a maverick. He exploited his own weirdness with an understanding of public relations as shrewd as Partch's was lacking. He quickly became a cult figure, but he disdained the role even as he consciously sought to maintain it. He looked out over the cultural divide and wanted to belong on the other side. He almost succeeded.

Regardless of who Zappa was, Zappa has become an icon. If Harry Partch is the maverick core at its purest, Frank Zappa is it at its most widely visible. The name Zappa has acquired a meaning, like the corporate names Xerox or Kleenex. It stands for a fringe, do-it-my-way, let's-satirize-and-be-gross-and-cool cynicism about the world and society. Zappa conjures images of youthful rebellion, of irony so heavy its weight can bury, and of freedom from restrictive mores of society. Zappa is seen as pure, quintessential, undistilled maverick — a maverick within the field of mavericks. And it is no coincidence. Zappa actively pursued that image, fully aware of what he was doing. Were there a maverick statue, Zappa's ungainly frame and hook nose would be at the top.

Aiding and abetting Zappa's iconic status is his sheer proteanness. Who is Zappa the musician? Is he some kind of genius, able to shift from the rock scene into the symphonic world? Is he one of popular music's great guitar virtuosi? Is he one of the world's great con artists? Is it all a fake, part of the game that Zappa was always playing on us? No question Zappa was serious about his serious music. But is the talent really there, or have we all been bamboozled by a monstrous ego and an above-average intelligence?

Except for William Billings, all the composers discussed thus far were trained in the classical tradition, albeit some tenuously, no matter how far they ultimately strayed from it. Even Partch and Cage were aspiring classical pianists at one time. Cowell is the purest autodidact of twentieth-century American composers. Yet Cowell did learn to play the piano, did study violin some, and when his talents were recognized as a youth, did study with Charles Seeger.

Zappa had no such classical background. He grew up on the other side of the musical world, in the vernacular tradition, although in high school he discovered and became fanatic about some twentieth-century classical music, particularly Varèse and Stravinsky, and for a while serialism. His under-

Franz Zappa with Pierre Boulez (Photograph © Betty Freeman/Lebrecht Music)

standing of their music at the time, however, was at best limited, at worst skewed, but these experiences later resurfaced to become major musical influences.

Although he was born in Baltimore, Zappa is, like Partch, Cage, and Cowell, a product of the West Coast. His family moved to Monterey, California, when he was ten, and this was followed by moves to San Diego and Lancaster. His musical training began at age twelve, when he was given rudimentary instruction on the drum. For several years he played drums in school and in various bands, particularly a rhythm and blues band, the Blackouts. The Blackouts were one of the few integrated bands in southern California at the time. Sometime in high school Zappa also began to learn to play the guitar, having appropriated his younger brother's instrument.

Zappa considered his most formative experience his discovery of the music of Edgard Varèse. Various legends have developed around it, some demonstrably false. Zappa is said to have become interested in Varèse when he was mentioned in a *Look* magazine article about the record store owner Sam Goody.[43] *Look* magazine on November 7, 1950, had a photograph of

Varèse, which may have been what attracted Zappa. But Sam Goody is not mentioned, for Samuel Gutowitz did not even open his record store until 1951. And there were no other features on Sam Goody in *Look* magazine in the 1950s. Zappa's description of discovering Varèse's album, however, is probably accurate: "[In a record store] I noticed a strange-looking black-and-white album cover with a guy on it who had frizzy gray hair and looked like a mad scientist. I thought it was great that a mad scientist had made a record, so I picked it up."[44]

Zappa wore the record out and attempted unsuccessfully to call Varèse, who happened to be out of the country at the time. Next Zappa discovered a recording of Stravinsky's *Rite of Spring,* and shortly after that Webern. Varèse and Stravinsky factor frequently in his later musical activities, ranging from pieces like "Igor's Boogie" to his befriending Nicolas Slonimsky and persuading him to re-record *Ionisation.* Slonimsky had premiered the piece at Carnegie Hall on March 6, 1933. Other classical influences on Zappa were Ives and Conlon Nancarrow.

In an interview in 1972 Zappa claimed that he started writing total serial music in high school. How far the tentacles of academic serialism reached! If Zappa's account is to be believed, they somehow found their way to Grossmont High School outside San Diego, California. Zappa had discovered Varèse; now he discovered serialism and determined that was the music he was going to write. In his own mind Zappa considered serialism his compositional birthplace. In the same interview, with Martin Perlich, he elaborated.

Perlich: Where are you going, Frank?
Zappa: I'm going wherever I can, y'know.
Perlich: Going out into jazz and into Webern and all those places?
Zappa: I started off in Webern. I'm trying to get back. (laughs)
Perlich: Working your way home?
Zappa: Yeah, working my way back from Vienna.[45]

From Vienna to southern California, from Webern to rhythm and blues.

There is one reason to believe this story: serialism was mathematical, and it was visual. Notation to Zappa was more a visual than an aural event. Zappa originally came to notation where Cage had left off. As a youth he showed exceptional talent in art, more so than in music. In high school one of his abstract paintings, *Family Room,* won a statewide art competition sponsored jointly by the California Federation of Women's Clubs and the Hallmark Greeting Card Company, and as a result Zappa represented California at the national level. At an Antelope Valley Fair his entries received first, second, and third prizes. Locally around Lancaster a real demand developed for his abstract paintings, and several attempts were made to mount exhibitions of his work.[46]

Zappa first approached classical notation as an art object. He composed only classical music until he was twenty years old and admitted that it was because he "liked the way it looked on paper." He saw himself creating a picture, not a sound. He elaborated further, "I was always interested in graphics, and I spent most of my creative time in my early days in school drawing pictures. I got a Speedball pen and a jar of Higgins India ink and some music paper and, shit, I could draw those [music scores]." He was fascinated and a little in awe that he could show his compositions to a musician and that "music would come out."[47]

Zappa realized there was little chance his classical music would be performed, and his own comments suggest that, compared to most serious and seriously trained composers, he really didn't know what he was doing. He also needed to earn a living, and he had zero interest in academia. Besides, he had another passion, rhythm and blues, and was developing his skills on a quintessential R&B instrument, the electric guitar.

So Zappa went into popular music, and like many young musicians for several years eked out a living, playing in various venues in southern California. He held other jobs, including designing greeting cards for Nile Running Greeting Cards and composing music for some decidedly unsuccessful grade B movies. Zappa even appeared on the Steve Allen show performing his Concerto for Bicycle in a duet with Allen.

In 1960 Zappa became acquainted with Paul Buff, who had built the Pal Recording studio in Cucamonga, California. Zappa began to experiment in the studio and turned out several recordings with Buff and various other musicians. Eventually Buff left to pursue other activities and, in 1964, Zappa essentially inherited the studio, which he renamed Studio Z. It was in Studio Z that Zappa was busted for producing an allegedly pornographic audiotape, which a police officer in a sting operation had requested.[48] The bust has become so legendary that it crowds out the more important lesson Zappa learned in the studio, that production technology was an inherent part of the creative process in music of the late twentieth century. Early on, well before the Beatles began to retreat to their studio to produce their late albums, Zappa recognized the importance of production, and later, when he acquired a Synclavier and established an elaborate studio in his home, this became the locus of his musical activity, easily squeezing out his work with his band. I believe Zappa's experience in Studio Z was the defining event in his musical life.

By now the classical-popular divide is so full of holes that it is of little use, particularly when describing music of the late twentieth century, and I hope not to extend the debate. But there is one aspect of it that is particularly relevant to understanding Zappa: the role of notation (less whether music is notated or not than to what use notation is put). This question is at heart a reflection of twentieth-century technology. Before the twentieth century music could be preserved (as opposed to simply being passed on as an oral tradition) only by notation. Recording technology changed all that. Zappa grew up in a world not only where the product was the recording, but where the compositional process involved the manipulation of recording technology. Zappa realized the implications of this change.

By the 1950s Partch, Cage, and a few others were on to this same issue, but they treated it differently. Partch never left the world of notation; he simply had to devise ways of overcoming the limits of the Western system. Cage exploited the visual effects of notation, creating pieces that were as much works of art as music.

Beyond Zappa's purely visual youthful experiments, notation, it seemed, never had the visual-aural connection to him that it did to classically trained composers. Thus when Zappa later approached classical composition, notation was a necessity, but it was not a central focus of his creativity. That remained elsewhere: improvisation on his guitar and electronic manipulation in the studio. Throughout Zappa's career the recording studio was his principal creative venue, whether it was mixing recorded sound, often improvised, or direct creation on the Synclavier, toward which he gravitated as technology caught up with his leanings. In that sense he *is* like Varèse, who waited decades for electronic sounds, and the freedom and potential they would unleash.

By the mid-1960s Zappa had put together the original Mothers of Invention, and in 1966 their first album, *Freak Out!* appeared. The title was chosen carefully, to celebrate the freak lifestyle of Los Angeles. Freak culture was L.A.'s answer to the San Francisco hippies. It was alternative, it was anti-establishment, but compared to the hippies it was wilder, more Bacchanalian, and even more bizarre. Ideals of love and flower power had no place in the freak world, which was grasping, self-centered, totally abandoned, live for the moment. *Freak Out!* was remarkable for several reasons: it was the first rock double album, antedating the Beatles' White Album by two years; it gave Zappa an image that he would assiduously cultivate the rest of his life, even though his own personal world evolved into something much more conservative; it was musically daring, and it integrated sight and sound, with a striking visual collage cover that Zappa designed.

Freak Out! set the tone for all of Zappa's later popular-music releases: the lyrics are satirical, cynical, sometimes obscene, and frequently offensive. The music was more sophisticated, more eclectic than that of other rock groups, something critics recognized immediately. In 1966 Robert Shelton observed that the Mothers were the first popular group to "successfully amalgamate rock'n'roll with the serious music of Stravinsky and others," and "compared to the Mothers of Invention, such earlier big-beat groups as The Beatles and The Rolling Stones emerge as Boy Scouts with electric guitars." Shelton referred to Zappa as the "Father (or Dada) of the Mothers of Invention."[49] Two years later Barret Hansen went even further, calling Zappa "the supreme genius of American music today," and then waxed eloquently: "Zappa's ingenuity in conception of form, in innovation of recording techniques, and in the integration of vastly different types of music, beggars all competitors. His rhythms and harmonies are truly sublime, and his lyrics contain the most brilliant satire in the whole pop world."[50] Zappa saw all of his music as one piece. When an interviewer for *Rolling Stone* asked him, "How do you look back on the albums you've made?" he answered: "It's all one album. All the material in the albums is organically related and if I had all the master tapes and I could take a razor blade and cut them apart and put it together again in a different order it still would make of piece of music you can listen to."[51]

Album covers, carefully designed by Zappa, became part of the production, combining synergistically to enhance what was on the LPs. Even more impressive on *Freak Out!* were the liner notes. Anticipating later cultural developments, Zappa integrated a lot of textual information into a striking visual format. His list of influences, itself worthy of extended analysis, contains names ranging from Muddy Waters and members of his band to Henry David Thoreau and Lawrence Ferlinghetti to Charles Ives, Roger Sessions, and Leo Ornstein. Where Zappa would have heard the name Leo Ornstein, much less any of his music, in 1966 is a puzzle.

Zappa's later album covers became works of art and satire. *Burnt Weeny Sandwich* is an ominous collage of disturbing, mechanistic images, including a bloody hand, a painted doll face with billiard balls for eyes, some odd electro-mechanical machinery, including coils, gears, and wires, against a riveted metallic background. *We're Only in It for the Money* extended the spoof on the Beatles to the jacket design, with the Mothers posing in drag in a photomontage that is a direct takeoff on the Beatles' *Sgt. Pepper* cover.

Zappa fully understood what 1960s rock was all about: youthful rebellion centering on the outrageous. Challenge established society, but first get its attention. Shock and disgust was one way, sheer volume was another. Zappa understood both. He was hired as a consultant for Unicord, Inc., a subsidiary of Gulf and Western that made amplifiers for guitars, among other things. Zappa pulled no punches. On the eve of a major electronics show in Chicago he told the CEO: "You're going to be showing the smallest, beautiful tone amplifiers in the show. . . . You're going to have to *eat* your beautiful tone amplifiers, because you won't sell them because kids don't want beautiful tone amplifiers. They want big, *giant* amplifiers." Zappa then elaborated to the reporter covering this scene: "Kids want sound. . . . You go to one of their concerts. You want to find out what your daughter is up to. So you go, and you walk in, and you say, 'That damn amp is so loud I can't make out the words.' The kids love that, because they already know the words, *and they know you don't.* The amplifier is their weapon of destruction." Zappa advised Mr. Mersky that his new amplifiers should be named "Weapons of Destruction," "or maybe, just Death."[52]

Zappa could of course shock and disgust, more so than most. It became part of his public persona as well as his music, and it got his albums banned from most radio stations and many record stores, while gaining him an underground cult status. His records were obscene by most standards, and coming at a time not far removed from Doris Day and the Kingston Trio, when rhythm and blues songs, a passion of Zappa's, were regularly cleaned up before they were covered by white singers, when any allusion to sexual acts was strictly taboo, Zappa's appeal and dangerousness were apparent. And on stage Zappa and his band would enhance the music's outrageousness with antics that were, if anything, even more outlandish. One time they invited a member of the audience to come on stage and whip a girl named Della. After some coaxing an old road manager of the Mothers came up, and according to Lowell George, a member of Zappa's band, the entire event got out of hand, with the band itself huddling together as the road manager went on a rampage, flailing anyone on stage with his belt.[53]

Zappa also recognized clearly the difference between an audio recording and a live concert performance, even though he tried to blur the distinction later with releases of his live performances (the *You Can't Do That on Stage Anymore* series). His concerts were not attempted simulacrums of his recordings, but rather theatrical additions to his (audio) pieces, in which the music was frequently the backdrop for stage antics. Zappa referred to his concerts as "Dada stagecraft." In spite of Zappa's professed seriousness of purpose as a composer, as a performer he and his band were doing a stage performance, the music being essentially the takeoff point. Sometimes the music was mere background, chosen for its incongruity, as when Ian Underwood would play Mozart's Sonata in B-flat, K. 570, while the other Mothers would perform a caricature of a ballet.[54] This piece was titled "Mozart Ballet, Piano Sonata in B flat."

Zappa's stage antics and provocative lyrics gained an audience, but they come nowhere near explaining the Zappa phenomenon. Within the obscenity and the ritualistic chaos that characterized a Zappa concert was a biting satire that was sophisticated and all-embracing. It was not subtle, at least on the surface, but there were layers that not every acid-head would have understood, or even needed to understand. Zappa was forthright about his intentions: "I am trying to use the weapons of a disoriented and unhappy society against itself. The Mothers of Invention are designed to come in the back door and kill you while you're sleeping." Even his musical pronouncements had the same edge. What would the average fifteen-year-old make of Zappa's suggestion that every pop music fan buy the Vanguard recording of Varèse's *Amériques:* "It blows my mind. It's my favorite top-40 record."[55]

As Zappa's career progressed he whittled his activity more and more to what he *wanted* to do. In that sense his career has pattern and consistence, which is sometimes obscured because there were at least three Zappas operating most of the time. One was the rock Zappa, the entertainer who was willing to go further than his colleagues in challenging the mores and the limits of what society would allow, the Zappa who aimed his music and his concerts at the adolescent rebellion that had exploded around him. This is the Zappa most people know; it is the public Zappa, cultivated by himself and guaranteed to garner the most media attention. There was also the angry Zappa, the social critic and cynic, who saw Western culture as shallow and hypocritical, morally decadent in its treatment of its members while professing narrow and bigoted standards, a society whose values were askew. This is the Zappa whose anti-censorship stand brought him before a Senate subcommittee, and who talked about running for president near the end of his life. This second Zappa is almost as well known as the first. With similar wellsprings, the second Zappa overlaps the first. Zappa was without question angry, bitter, and cynical. He himself said: "How can you live in the twentieth century and not be cynical. If you are not cynical, then you probably suffer some sort of brain damage."[56] And he cultivated those feelings personally, in his songs, in his concerts, and in his interviews.

Different is a third Zappa, Zappa the musician. Zappa would be only a small footnote to a turbulent and perplexing time were it not for his absolute and total dedication to his music. Even when the early Mothers toured Zappa focused on the musical results with an obsession that was unusual in the rock music of the time. He was cynical about much, but not about the musical results. He drove his band, he hired and fired, he insisted on standards few popular musicians could attain. He even subordinated sex to his music, something few twenty-something rock musicians were willing to do. Zappa is known for his relative abstinence with both drugs and sex. At the same time he would encourage other members of the band to have sex, *if it would improve their playing.* "Musicians tend to generate better 'texture' when they get 'The Blow Job.' Yes I want them to find that elusive cross between a waitress and an industrial vacuum cleaner."[57] Zappa's own work schedule attests to his dedication. Eighteen-hour days were common, particularly after he obtained a Synclavier and when he had his own studio set up.[58]

Zappa may have limited himself with his decision to work in the popular-music idiom, but he spent much of his life trying to escape those limitations. Much of his later career consists of his attempts to break out of the box that his involvement in the popular-musical world had put him in. The late sixties saw the clash of two musical cultures, whose sounds seemed as far apart as the generations that supported them. Much has been made of the Zubin Mehta–Frank Zappa collaboration that occurred at the Pauley Pavilion at UCLA on May 15, 1970. Zubin Mehta was at the time the musical director of the Los Angeles Philharmonic Orchestra. The evening was ostensibly an attempt to bridge the worlds of symphonic and rock music. It turned out to be mainly Zappa's show, but it was more than a clash of two musical worlds. It was a clash between music and theater, and as such it symbolized profound changes in Western musical culture.

Putting aside the probable cause of this event as a marketing ploy, a way for the symphony to tap into a much larger and younger rock audience, the symphonic contingent, including the audience and probably Mehta also, saw it as an attempt to bridge two disparate styles of music. To Mehta it was an exercise in musical exploration. Zappa saw it as theater. Beyond the music, he had members of the orchestra engaged in theatrical activities no symphonic composer (John Cage excepted) would consider: members of the orchestra burped and grunted, threw confetti, and "at one point the bass horn player stood up with his horn, twirled it around like a drunken elephant, and sat down." At another point the orchestra itself walked among the audience while continuing to play. During the encore, a performance of "King Kong," clarinetist Michelle Zurkovski "had a stuffed toy giraffe inserted up her dress" (the giraffe was a Zappa leitmotif; early Mothers' concerts featured a giraffe that squirted whipped cream over the audience), and the cellist Kurt Reher "established himself as a master freak." Exactly what Reher did is not recorded.[59]

David Felton, who reported the event for *Rolling Stone*, saw it, and the symphonic world itself, from the point of view of rock culture: "To those listeners [the young audience], the *theater* of symphonic music is so inartistic and irrelevant that it amounts to a political separation. The music, with its stiff-backed black ties and opening night fur pieces, has never been of the people but of the rich. Its theater has been drained of life, frozen and encased for the possessive pleasure of the museum-minded."[60]

Felton speaks for his generation in that he sees the symphony and implicitly music itself as theater. The difference is crucial. No classical-music critic in 1970 would describe the symphony as such. Embedded in this distinction is the clash of the aural versus the visual, and no matter how conservative youths of the '60s and '70s later became — Jerry Rubin after all ended up selling insurance — the visual, in this sense translated as the theatrical, continued to predominate. Distancing the symphony from rock was the very absence of theater in the symphonic world, which maintained the tradition of a purely aural art. Later Zappa tried to join that symphonic tradition.

Underscoring the difference between the two cultures was the way music was created, and consequently the nature of how it was received. Symphonic music depended on the score, and hence the composer, who elaborated the piece in detail before the event. The symphonic musician, including the conductor, was expected to respect and realize what the composer had created. Interpretation was essentially an exploration in the limits of musical notation. Symphonic music is highly composer-centric, for to the symphonic audience, what mattered most was the individual composer. Much rock music was based on group improvisation. While a song might be an original product of a rock group, the performance of it was essentially its composition. And while there are many examples of individual composers or teams within the rock idiom, such as Brian Wilson or John Lennon and Paul McCartney, and while many rock groups created their own pieces, the audience identified with the group, not the composer behind the group. The group sold tickets; rock music was performer-centric.

Zappa's work with the early Mothers lay somewhere between these two extremes. Much of what they did was based on group improvisation, but with one important difference. In this improvisation Zappa controlled everything. He had to teach some band members their parts by rote, as they could not read music, and on the stage Zappa would hand signal what he wanted them to play as the music unfolded. A piece was, to put it mildly, not completely worked out. It could vary depending on the hall, the response of the audience, and Zappa's own mood. But Zappa determined what happened. He saw his job as that of a puppeteer: "Well, let's say I know that Motorhead does a certain thing at a certain time and I gesture to another player that he has complete freedom to play whatever he wants. I just have to point to him and he'll play whatever comes into his head right then. I can get a pretty good idea what's going to happen, see. So I can play the personalities off against each other to make different flavors of madness. . . . Some of it has to do with the way the audience is behaving and a lot of it has to do with how you feel that day."[61]

It was, like much rock, a communal event, with Zappa the interpreter of the community, as well as manipulator. It was communal on two levels, band and audience as one community, and band itself as another. It was controlled and it was uncontrolled. It *was* improvisation, and Zappa's signals would often be only general indications of how he wanted a member to play. It was an extension of many jazz or rock ensembles, where a subtle sign from the leader, a glance, a nod of the head, said, take a solo. Zappa's signals were more involved, and his control existed through his assigning parts and his knowledge of what might happen when a certain signal was given. It depended, as Zappa stated, on his knowing his ensemble and being able to predict what would occur. It was, almost, group improvisation. Zappa still pulled the strings.

Zappa's methods also depended on the creativity of the group, and here things got rocky. To some members of the band, Zappa was not a creator but an appropriator, someone who stole ideas from several sources as his own. Those sources could be classical, Stravinsky and Varèse in particular, or popular, especially Don Van Vliet (Captain Beefheart), a longtime close friend of Zappa. Even worse to some band members, Zappa stole from them. Art Tripp, a percussionist in the band, once complained: "I'd say, 'Hey listen to this' and he'd mumble something like, 'Yeah, that's good' but there was never any acceptance, but later it would come out and all my ideas were used." Zappa's response was straightforward: "This guy plays in my group. I pay him $250 a week, sure I can borrow anything from him." He summed up his creative philosophy by saying, "Good artists adapt, great artists steal."[62]

Is this a problem with Zappa or with the genre? Without question the genre itself, based on group improvisation, is a major factor. Rock has long been distinguished from classical music because of its communal nature. Composer as individual creator and composer as appropriator blend into one, not only in Zappa but in the idiom itself. Keith Emerson quoted classics constantly; later composers such as Beck became masters of sampling, now a widely accepted technique. Other popular-music genres did the same. Jimmie Rodgers, Roy Acuff, and Johnny Cash mined and presented folk materials as their own. And who contributed what in Duke Ellington's band remains an issue of contention. But in rock in particular, the role of individual creator, prevalent in Western music since the eighteenth century, comes under its most serious and sustained attack. In a genre where individuality is an obsession, where the performers' appearance, behavior, and lifestyle push weirdness to the extreme, music making returns to a communal, improvisational activity. This is true even if the improvisation is, like wrestling, carefully choreographed.

As much as any other musician of the late twentieth century, Zappa applied fully the modernist concept of juxtaposition.[63] It is so striking in Zappa because the postwar years gave him such technology to work with. With the development of the electric guitar and massive amplifiers, rock music established an identity and a culture that was markedly different from what classical, or even jazz, players were doing. The acoustic-electronic divide for a time seemed unbridgeable. Electronic sounds had emerged in the classical idiom, but they were the province mostly of highly cerebral mathematics professors, or experimentalists who had taken the twentieth-century notion of free verse to a new level, with isolated sounds and noises, both musique concrète and electronic bleeps, spliced together freely so as to destroy any sense of musical time as traditionally defined. But whether electronically generated or the sounds of the street, a distinctive aural environment was created, characterized by its own unworldly unpredictability.

Then just as Zappa was experimenting, technological developments brought the worlds of electronic and popular music closer together, with the invention of the Moog synthesizer and the Synclavier. The Moog especially became a standard part of the rock sound and paraphernalia.

But no one in the rock idiom had quite the musical vision of Zappa, and no one in the classical idiom was ready to incorporate rock music as a natural part of their compositional language, as Bartók had done with Eastern European folk music, or Gershwin with jazz and Tin Pan Alley. Serious composers were if anything leery about the pounding, driving, relentless beat of rock, although the minimalists were fast catching on. They came at it from their own direction, however, and began to develop their own unique vocabulary and processes. Zappa maintained a constant eclecticism. He could mystify the listener with an atonal piano opening that resembled Bartók, Debussy, and Thelonious Monk rolled into one, then just as the idiom was beginning to soak in, blot it out with a pounding drum right out of heavy rock. This is what happened in *Burnt Weeny Sandwich*, released in 1970.

Zappa came into his own on *Burnt Weeny Sandwich*. The core of the album is "Little House I Used to Live In," eighteen minutes forty-two seconds long, one of the most intricate pieces to appear on a popular LP in the 1960s and '70s. But it is not a rock piece. It incorporates at least four different idioms, classical, rock, jazz, and electronic. Holding it together is the piano, which begins with an introduction consisting of augmented chords a half-step apart. The chords mostly slide up and down chromatically by half-steps, but not in tandem. Zappa himself described this passage: "The theme of the piece is the first three notes and the material derived from the superposition of augmented chords. The origins of that material are a piano exercise dated approximately 1962, and the rest of the piece consists of extrapolations of that material, influenced by the environments of a number of Holiday Inns across the country."[64]

After this Ivesian, or Bartókian, virtuoso cadenza passage, the drums suddenly enter and we are back at the Holiday Inn. The band riffs, but these are tightly controlled riffs, complex rhythmically, and carefully structured. The piano moves from a more rock-oriented style to pure jazz. Then after a slow interlude, the drums pick up the pace, moving from an earlier allegro to a full prestissimo. At times even the Saturday morning cartoons make an entrance (at approximately sixteen minutes into the work).

Zappa originally intended the piece to have more of a chamber music sound. In earlier sketches, "Little House" called for an instrumentation of piano, flute, two oboes, two clarinets, two bassoons, two French horns, tuba, and four violins. Most prominently, drums and guitars were added for the recording. After all, it *was* part of a Mothers concert.[65]

The 1971 Fillmore East recording of "Little House" stands in striking contrast to this one. It is much shorter. Gone is the piano introduction. The piece consists of rapid-fire juxtaposition between musical styles. It also contains considerable vocal music, but no words, until the very end, where the group announces, "mudshark." Which segues directly into the next piece, "The Mud Shark."[66]

The piece itself, particularly in the vocals, has the sound of parody. It is typical Zappa vocal style. The inflections are not subtle; they shout: this is not serious, this is parody. Nothing unusual about Zappa here, except the parody is his own music. The original "Little House" was one of the most ambitious pieces on his early albums. But this is a concert performance; in keeping with Zappa's aesthetic, it serves a different purpose, possibly the most ambitious. As one listens to the chorus at the end of "Mud Shark," it is apparent that *something* is occurring on stage. The focus is no longer just on the music.

Zappa later became completely enamoured with the Synclavier and channeled much of his creative efforts through it. But did machine replace people? In one sense no, because the early Mothers was in essence Zappa's music-making machine. He saw his employees this way: "I'm the boss of these guys. I run the show." One of his performers, Pamela Zarubica, known as Suzy Creamcheese, commented on later Zappa, who all but abandoned touring to spend his time at home with his Synclavier: "Yes, he's finally crawled himself into a hole and buried himself there with his tape recorders. See, I don't think Frank ever really communicated really well with people unless he's speaking to a bunch of people. I don't think he communicates well with people because he communicates better with machines." Gary Kellgren, recording engineer who worked with Zappa for months editing *Lumpy Gravy*, described him as "an android, a machine."[67]

Zappa later tried not only to be taken seriously by the classical-music world but to work within its traditions and methods. Some music and a lot of disasters resulted. Deals were struck with symphony orchestras, the Vienna Philharmonic, the Residentie Orchestra of the Netherlands, two orchestras in Poland, the Syracuse Symphony, but each time they fell through for a variety of reasons, invariably economic. Finally Zappa, having already spent several hundred thousand dollars in expenses, decided to rent the London Symphony Orchestra for a recording. The results were not entirely successful, partly because conditions were not ideal: the room was not good, creating major technological challenges, and the players were unaccustomed to both the music and the way Zappa worked. But the music itself was not fully compatible with the idiom. Critics noted that the high energy characteristic of Zappa's style did not quite make it through the orchestra. Zappa himself saw the problem and compared the symphony orchestra itself to a dinosaur: "The head is real tiny and the body is real big and by the time the thought goes from there to here, the tail has already rotted off."[68]

Part of the problem lay in Zappa's unfamiliarity with the medium. Working with one-hundred-plus musicians, and twelve to twenty separate parts, demands at least a rudimentary level of contrapuntal activity, as the different parts need to play off against one another. Zappa's music for small ensembles does that, partly because of the improvisatory aspect that was the very nature of the idiom, partly because such interactions were natural to Zappa's ear. Zappa's symphonic music can be busy, at times even Ivesian, but it does not exploit the structural interlocking that characterizes such an ensemble. As a result, it often sounds flat.

Shortly after the LSO experience Zappa became acquainted with Pierre Boulez. He visited Boulez's laboratory at the Institut de Recherche et de Coordination Acoustique/Musique, better known as IRCAM, originally to examine Giuseppe di Giugno's 4X digital signal processor. He impressed Boulez enough that Boulez decided to record three of Zappa's pieces with his Ensemble InterContemporain. Only one piece, "The Perfect Stranger," was new. The album that resulted, *The Perfect Stranger*, Zappa's first CD release, included three live pieces by Ensemble InterContemporain and four pieces that Zappa created on the Synclavier, a digital sound computer that he had acquired in 1982.[69] At the time it was an expensive, state-of-the-art tool for creating music synthetically. To Zappa it was a godsend, an opportunity to create precisely what he wanted, and for the last ten years of his life his creative work revolved around the Synclavier.

Zappa's Synclavier pieces on *The Perfect Stranger* have a shimmering percussive quality, far removed from the rock idiom. They are complex rhythmically, owing something to Conlon Nancarrow, whom Zappa admired. They are also not far removed stylistically from the Ensemble InterContemporain pieces, particularly "The Perfect Stranger." In fact, the stylistic differences between "The Perfect Stranger" and the two earlier pieces, "Naval Aviation in Art?" composed in 1975 and "Dupree's Paradise," composed in 1974, show how far Zappa had traveled in ten years.

Each of the seemingly abstract instrumental works is accompanied by a typically satirical, absurdist program written by Zappa. The entire program of "The Perfect Stranger," the longest piece on the album, reads:

> A door-to-door salesman, accompanied by his faithful gypsy-mutant industrial vacuum cleaner (as per the interior illustration on the "CHUNGA'S REVENGE" album cover), cavorts licentiously with a slovenly housewife.
>
> We hear the door bell, the housewife's eyebrows going up and down as she spies the nozzle through the ruffled curtain, the sound of the little bag of "demonstration dirt" being sprinkled on the rug, and assorted bombastic interjections representing the spiritual qualities of chrome, rubber, electricity, and household tidiness. The entire transaction is being viewed from a safe distance by Patricia, the dog in the high chair.

Classical doors opened after *The Perfect Stranger*. The Chamber Symphony of San Francisco, the Berkeley Symphony Orchestra, the Kronos Quartet, the Aspen Wind Quintet, the Birmingham Contemporary Music Group, the Composers Ensemble of London, Ensemble Modern, and the Juilliard Ensemble performed Zappa's pieces. He was invited to give lectures or keynote addresses at the Music Media Exhibition in Amsterdam, before the American Society of University Composers, at a New Music Seminar in New York City, and at UCLA with Pierre Boulez.

Until the very end Zappa was active in both the classical and the popular fields. He no longer toured, but reworked earlier touring material in his studio, and continued to produce pieces on the Synclavier. Zappa may have been cynical about the popular world, but not about his music, and when he appeared on stage in the last ten years of his life, his band performed mostly instrumental pieces, with extended guitar solos by both Zappa and a young virtuoso, Steve Vai.

Like Partch, Zappa cannot easily be classified. Unlike Partch, who maintained a rock-solid vision throughout his life, Zappa's vision was as diffuse as his many images. Zappa first conquered a world that he professed to despise, becoming a cult icon for those in it. His own disdain for the world he inhabited only enhanced his maverick image, as did his cynicism about the world in general. Appearing at a time when the very fabric of society seemed to be coming apart, Zappa represented America's worst nightmare. As such the public loved him. He was the popular-music version of radical chic, laying bare what the public wanted, and much of what it didn't. He originally spoke to the disaffected, but as irony became the dominant mode of expressive discourse in American culture, he seemed to resonate, albeit often with fear and loathing, with everyone. Zappa was that icon you love to hate.

Nowhere were the Zappa contradictions more apparent than in the classical-music world. Knocking, indeed pounding, on the door of the classical establishment at a time when that world seemed sundered from within and tottering from without, Zappa the classical iconoclast in some ways seemed a godsend. The Zappa-Mehta 1970 venture may have been a failure, but Zappa's own persistence and dedication ultimately paid off. Zappa was always a slow starter — he was well into his rock career before he really mastered the guitar — and by the time he had acquired sufficient technical facility to be taken seriously, he was everyone's idea of the maverick. Just by being Zappa he could sell tickets. Boulez may have originally championed him for such very reasons, but ultimately Zappa did bring a refreshing vitality and verve to the classical world with his later compositions. He proved, if nothing else, that as a cultural force he could not be dismissed.

CHAPTER 10

Minimalism and Strange Bedfellows

WHILE Cage and the academic serialists were pursuing their apparently contradictory aesthetics on the East Coast, another compositional wave was forming on the edge of the Pacific. Early swells appeared in the Bay area of California, particularly at the University of California, Berkeley. Stirrings began with a student who, like many young composers, was writing serial music, only La Monte Young's time frame was different. In 1958 he composed his *Trio for Strings*, a work that in pitch content fit the prevailing academic mold: it was serial, and it was dissonant. It was also static. The three instruments, violin, viola, and cello, sustain the opening three-note cluster, C-sharp, D, and E-flat, for four and one-half minutes. Silence ensues for thirty seconds before the next notes, a double-stop on the violin of F-sharp and B, enter. While these notes sound, the viola and cello enter and drop out on their own pitches, F and B-flat on the cello and E and A on the viola. The violin's double-stop is held for nearly five minutes, followed by over a minute of silence. The entire piece proceeds in this manner, with the dynamic level remaining mostly in the multiple *piano* level. The piece was so radical that Young's teacher, Seymour Shifrin, arranged for a private performance on the assumption that Young couldn't possibly have heard what he had written.

Young knew what he was doing. Sustained tones were his bread and butter. No composer in the history of Western music has so consistently exploited the use of long, sustained notes. Young traces this interest to his early childhood on a desolate plain in Bern, Idaho. A tiny log cabin,

Young's birthplace, provided him an early sound that he never forgot, of the wind whistling through the cracks in the cabin; "I got this start lying in my bed in the log cabin, hearing the wind blow between the criss-crossed logs." He remembers the winds in winter as "ferocious," "profound and awesome." "It wasn't as if I could turn off the wind, like somebody would turn off the radio."[1]

As Young grew older there were other sounds, mostly constant sounds: the hum of electric power lines, the sound of thousands of crickets, the drone of an electric motor. Many of these sounds became the basis for later compositions, some directly: In *The Third Dream of the High Tension Stepdown Transformer*, brass instruments, limited to four pitches, imitate the sound of high tension lines so literally it is eerie. And *The Tortoise, His Dreams and Journeys*, begun in 1964 and still ongoing, was originally inspired by the hum of a motor in his turtle's aquarium. Like Harry Partch, Young became interested in just intonation, basing an entire work, or set of works, on ratios above a single frequency. The hum, amplified, became the fundamental pitch out of which the work grew.

Nature and geography provided one force that shaped Young, the Mormon Church a second. Young was raised in a strict Mormon family in a strict Mormon community, and although his interest in other cultures and music, particularly bebop jazz and later Indian philosophy, eventually put him at odds with his religion, its influence remained with him. Young acknowledges a definite connection between the long, timeless, meditative music that he creates and the Mormon emphasis on eternity. Drones and Mormonism thus blend into one universal spirituality. And Young's opera magna, *The Well-Tuned Piano*, along with *The Tortoise, His Dreams and Journeys*, and his ever-evolving acoustical-dramatic-visual environment, the Dream House, are all still in process more than thirty years after they were originally created.[2]

In 1959 Young went to Darmstadt, where he heard David Tudor perform and encountered Karlheinz Stockhausen, who had just discovered John Cage. Stockhausen sang the praises of Cage to anyone who would listen, and Young returned to the University of California determined to bring the Cage revolution to Berkeley. His *Poem for Tables, Chairs, Benches, etc.* had the performers move furniture across the floor, the resultant sound being the piece. Young also experimented with Artaudian theater: He turned out the lights in a performance, leaving the audience to sit in total darkness while being bombarded with strange and frightening sounds; he arranged to have the lawn mowed close to the windows of a concert hall; he fried eggs on stage, and at one performance he dragged a gong on the floor while another performer banged a garbage can lid against a wall. The bewildered and angry audience at that performance reacted in a way as unpredictable, as Cageian, as the event itself: while some cursed others stood up and started singing "The Star-Spangled Banner."

After he was given a special fellowship to study in New York, which he interpreted as a one-way ticket out of town, Young connected with the most radical group in New York City, Fluxus. Here he produced a group of pieces that were unusual by any standard. They all have abstract titles, such as *Composition 1960 #1, Composition 1960 #2*, and so on. Most have nothing to do with traditional music making. Each consists of a set of written instructions telling the performer(s) to perform a certain event, such as feeding a bale of hay to a piano, or releasing butterflies in the performance space.

In their calculated absurdity Young's pieces fit right into the Fluxus milieu. They are difficult to categorize, as performance art, conceptual art, theater, or music. They are Dada in conception and Cageian in spirit. They challenge traditional notions of music as much as Cage did, the only difference being that, unlike Cage, Young did not articulate what he was doing. He let the pieces stand on their own.

Young's works, like Cage's, are essentially theater, which Young himself recognized. But they are different from Cage, at least the Cage of the 1950s. As Young himself observed, Cage's works prior to 1960 are essentially variety shows, circuses, happenings, in which a whole cluster of events, seemingly unrelated, occur simultaneously or follow each other quickly. Young's compositions demand that the performer focus on a single activity, what he later called the "theatre of the singular event." Length was often indeterminate — how long *should* a performer wait for a piano to eat a bale of hay? — but they were all similar, one activity per piece.[3]

Cage, however, was coming to that same point. In 1962, soon after Young began directing a series of events in Yoko Ono's loft, Cage premiered a new work in Japan, *o' oo"*, which he subtitled "*4' 33"* No. 2." It asked the performer to "perform a disciplined action." Unlike Young's pieces, this work allowed the performer to choose the action, although Cage did qualify what he was not supposed to do, such as play a musical composition. Nevertheless the focus on a single, disciplined action was a departure from the multivariegated events of many of his earlier works.

Within Young's 1960 pieces is one that *is* a purely aural statement, written in conventional notation and made by conventional musical instruments. *Composition 1960 #7* consists of two notes, B and F-sharp, "to be held a long time." It is pure Young: the score stipulates drone, and Young's choice of a perfect fifth has less to do with Western tradition than with acoustical properties. When performed by a number of instruments (several on each note) the clash of overtones and the pitch interactions resulting from the impossibility of maintaining an absolutely even pitch for forty minutes to two hours (roughly the time frame of typical performances), the interaction of upper partials becomes paramount. And as far as the piece itself is concerned, nothing could be minimalistically simpler. Here minimalism is reduced to its minimalistic essence.

Composition 1960 #7 also presages the direction that Young would go. Young later moved away from Fluxus, but he never abandoned its principles entirely. He continued to maintain a theatrical environment, in which he demanded complete control. He referred to the events of the time as a type of opera or musical theater, and gave a group that he formed the name "Theatre of Eternal Music." After 1960 his work combined extremely long held notes, the exploration of interacting upper partials, and theater itself.[4]

The Theatre of Eternal Music was Young's attempt at a controlled environment and a setting for constant aural and visual surprises. By 1963 Young had moved to New York City, had met and married Marian Zazeela, a visual artist who works with light displays, and by 1970 had become a disciple of the Indian musician Pandit Pran Nath. Partly through Pran Nath, partly because of his own interest in long tones, he gravitated toward just intonation and, like Partch, began to use specific intervalic ratios as the basis for his later pieces. There the similarity with Partch ends, however.

The Theatre of Eternal Music is dedicated to performances at the Dream House in New York, a sound-light environment created in Young and Zazeela's loft at 275 Church Street, in which the room itself affects the way partial combinations are perceived. They describe the Dream House as "a time installation measured by a setting of continuous frequencies in sound and light." The Dream House still opens for regular performances twice a week, on Thursdays and Saturdays from 2:00 P.M. until midnight. Young and Zazeela each present their own works, although each is designed with the other's in mind.

The Dream House consists of a large rectangular room, with most of the activity occurring in one half.[5] There speakers are mounted in cases and lights are hung from the ceiling. Sound, loud and constant, emits from the speakers, and the lights change only slowly. Change occurs primarily through the activity of the perceiver. As one moves around the room, different overtones become apparent, causing different sounds to be perceived. The same thing happens with the lights. Some of the sounds are almost painful, some more soothing and relaxing. In an almost indefinable way sound and light complement each other to create an overall effect that transcends each medium.

Young's goal was to free sound from time. If a sound has no beginning or end, then it has no duration. Nature provides examples: the waves of the ocean, the whistling of the wind, the low-pitched sound of the blood moving through the body and the higher pitch of the nervous system. Such sounds may actually begin and end, but to the observer they exist in perpetuum. Young's early pieces sought to extend sound to the point that the listener became more aware of the sound than its temporal placement. Later he sought to extend this idea even further. The Theatre of Eternal Music and its successor the Dream House is his fullest realization of this ideal. It is a sound environment, in which sounds — resonances — are set in motion, and although they vary, depending partly on where the listener is, partly on performance itself, as players enter, drop out, or change their notes, there is a constancy about the sound. Sound becomes a thing in itself, to be explored, to be noticed in new and varying ways as it proceeds; sound, pure sound, is both the topic and the essence of the event.

Yet even to speak of it as an "event" misleads, for an event implies duration. Young himself conceives many of his pieces as ongoing. In reference to his *Four Dreams of China*, he said: "I determined that individual performances of the work had no beginning or ending. Each performance is woven out of an eternal fabric of silence and sound where the first sound emerges from a long silence and after the last sound the performance does not end but merely evanesces back into silence."[6] He has brought that to reality in his most extended work, *The Tortoise*. Performances do begin and end; the motor, or the synthesizer that provides the fundamental pitch, can be turned on and off. Yet conceptually, and in this context perceptually, the iterations of the event constitute one event.

Such lack of temporality implies a consequence of even greater moment, the complete breakdown of the idea of "the piece." Young still uses traditional terminology, but the notion of environmental music carried to this extent provides no way of determining the limits and hence the boundaries of the piece. Without boundaries, can one legitimately speak of a piece? A piece may be indeterminate, such as Young's own *Composition 1960 #7*, or it may be open-ended, as jazz itself, but there are, within the conventions of musical reality, beginnings and endings. This is true even for John Cage.

When Cage put together a multimedia, multi-activity event, such as *HPSCHD*, the question arose as to what "the piece" was. When he created his indeterminate works, such as *o' oo"*, which allowed almost any event to occur, when he preached that sounds should be themselves, freed from control by the composer, the concept of "the piece" was seriously and consciously challenged. Yet for Cage there always was a score, be it no more than a set of instructions giving the performer considerable latitude (Cage never did allow complete freedom). Cage's entire work as a composer, particularly after 1950, was aimed at questioning and redefining to the Western mind just what music was, and what the relationships were between composer, participant, and listener (the latter two often blurring into one).

For the minimalists the concept of the piece became crucially important, but for practical rather than musical reasons. The place of the composer is an honored one in Western music, and most minimalists do not want to set aside that mantle. "Composer," of course, implies composition. The minimalists are concerned about their place in history, particularly in a tradition that values the composer above all other musicians.[7] But there is an even more important reason: copyright, and by extension control and royalties. Here the law drives aesthetics.

La Monte Young wants total control over what he does. When asked why he turned down a contract with Columbia, Young became visibly agitated. He jumped from his seat and began pacing around the room, saying: "I won't put out a record with *anybody* unless I have complete artistic control, from A to Z. Never. Under any circumstances. For any amount of money. That's it. Period. I won't do it." The artist Diane Wakoski described Young's style of collaboration: "There was never any question that when a musician was with La Monte, he was working with La Monte's ideas or composition. The thought that anyone . . . could ever be collaborators or co-composers in any La Monte Young project seems laughable to me. It simply wouldn't happen. . . . Everyone who knows La Monte is aware of the fact that you either play his game, or he doesn't play with you."[8]

If a piece consists of drones in an environment, if a piece is essentially improvisation, be it by an individual or an ensemble, what is the piece, and who created it? Is it the sounds that occur on each particular performance? Is the ensemble itself the creator? This question impinges on many areas of twentieth-century music, including folk, popular, jazz, where new pieces are created from chord progressions of older ones, not to mention what the improviser adds. But it becomes particularly acute in a situation such as Young's, where traditional guideposts like a recognizable melody or even rhythmic patterns are completely absent. It has also become a matter of serious contention as two performers of Young's Theatre of Eternal Music, Tony Conrad and John Cale, have claimed authorship as co-composers.

Young reacted vigorously to their claim, stating in no uncertain terms:

"*The Tortoise, His Dreams and Journeys*, both in its underlying structure and in its embodiment in the tapes recorded by The Theatre of Eternal Music, is my composition. . . . The Theatre of Eternal Music group developed around my compositions, and rehearsed and improvised with structures I established. . . . Conrad's and Cale's contributions on the level of improvisation were controlled by the underlying structure that I composed. The underlying composition is an abstract entity that could be filed in a tangible form and copyrighted as I have done." Young did go so far as to copyright his piece after the copyright law was changed in 1978 to permit submission of sound recordings rather than scores. But if the piece is ongoing and eternally incomplete, can it ever be copyrighted?[9]

These are questions for lawyers, not musical scholars; the issue has become not an aesthetic but a legal one. Philip Glass had a similar problem. In his early music he often wrote out no scores but only individual parts. Without a score, copyright was tricky. He then sent off a shorthand of the first page of his part, which he called a "lead sheet," and that satisfied the copyright office.

While at Berkeley, Young's work had a particularly strong impact on a fellow student, Terry Riley. Young and Riley had much in common: they both came from small rural western communities and they both were highly skilled jazz improvisers, Young on the saxophone and Riley on the piano.

Terry Riley's early life also parallels Harry Partch's. Riley was born in Colfax, California, a railroad town. His father worked on the railroad and moved several times during Riley's youth, remaining mostly in provincial western towns. His parents, themselves not musical, bought him a violin at a young age, but soon after he switched to piano. He grew up hearing and playing mostly popular music and jazz, but in high school he began to discover classical music. For a time he determined to become a concert pianist. In college, however, at San Francisco State University, he discovered pianists better than him, and became interested in composition. With a wife and child to support, he worked various jobs, including ragtime piano in San Francisco "saloons," and began to attend the University of California, Berkeley, where he met Young. Riley was one of the few persons who were completely overwhelmed by Young's *Trio*.

After Young left Berkeley, Riley continued to experiment. Young had converted him to the principle of stasis, but his work took a very different path. Working with a tape recorder in his garage, Riley discovered the possibilities of tape loops, and through them repetition. After graduation he went to Europe and earned a living playing piano in American army officers' clubs. Because of an opportunity to write music for a theater piece, he gained

access to the French National Radio studios. He was amazed when an engineer hooked up two tape recorders to create in essence a feedback loop: a
second machine records what the first has just played, the first then plays
back what the second has recorded, to be recorded again by the second. The
sounds get progressively denser and more complex. At this point Riley realized that his earlier experiments in his garage were quite primitive, and that
myriad patterns could be created through repetition. He first used the technique while still in Europe, with *Music for the Gifts*, which featured a performance by jazz trumpeter Chet Baker manipulated by repetitive techniques.

John F. Kennedy's assassination ended Riley's European career, because
the officers' clubs closed as a gesture of respect, and Riley and family returned to San Francisco. Riley continued to experiment with tape repetition
at the San Francisco Tape Music Center, but his big breakthrough came
through one particular live performance. An all-Riley program was given at
the Tape Music Center in November 1964. It consisted of mostly tape-loop
pieces that Riley had done, including *Music for the Gifts*, but the final piece
on the program, *In C*, was written for an ensemble of thirteen musicians accompanied by a light show. Other than the lights it had no electronics in it.
In C created a sensation and marked a turning point in minimalism. No
question it was new, different. William Duckworth later called it minimalism's "anthem." Alfred Frankenstein reviewed the concert for the *San Francisco Chronicle* under the title "Music Like None Other on Earth," predicting that it would have a profound impact on the music world. When he
reviewed the 1968 recording of *In C*, Frankenstein called it "one of the de-
finitive masterpieces of the twentieth century, probably most important
piece of music since Boulez' *Marteau sans maitre*; conceivably it is the most
important since the *Sacre*. And the reason, 'it defines a new aesthetic.'"[10]

Frankenstein's opinion was not universally shared. Alexander Fried
found *In C* "a thing of the slightest importance," and when it invaded Darmstadt, the high temple of the European and by then also the American avant-
garde, Robert Siohan considered it a "hoax" and a "practical joke," a takeoff
from John Cage, and a "thermometer of the patience of the audience." In
hindsight, while Frankenstein may have been somewhat overenthusiastic,
he was close to the mark. *In C* has become a classic, minimalism's *Le
Sacre*.[11]

In C consists of fifty-three short motivic fragments of music, and each
performer is instructed to play in order all fifty-three, but each motive may be
repeated as many times as desired. When all performers have finished motive 53 the piece is over. A piano plays a C octave quarter-note drone in the

upper register throughout, providing a steady beat as well as holding the players together.

All motives revolve around the C-major triad, although some in the middle contain F-sharps, giving a suggestion of harmonic motion. Structurally *In C* is one of the more traditional of early minimalist pieces: Not only is a beat clearly enunciated but the listener is aware of a whiff of an A-B-A structure or possibly a faint echo of sonata form: I-(V)-I, the F-sharps hinting at an actual dominant effect. Some of the patterns enhance the effect as they outline the notes of the dominant seventh chord. The title itself rings of classicism, being both a description of and a spoof on the content of the piece. It was also, in its very simplicity and title, radical, a bold departure from the prevailing academic standards of serialism, atonalism, or at the very least extreme chromaticism.

This is not to say that it is traditional, but that it gave the listener something of the past to hang on to, and thus it acted as an ideal entrée into the very different world that the minimalists were creating. After *In C*, however, Riley composed little for the rest of the 1960s and most of the 1970s. He was more interested in the experience and activity of improvisation than the creation of a piece. Through La Monte Young he also began to study with the Indian musician Pandit Pran Nath. Riley became his disciple and has devoted much of his work to keeping alive and furthering Pran Nath's musical heritage. Riley also met David Harrington of the Kronos Quartet, beginning a fruitful association that resulted in more than a dozen quartets and related pieces. Since 1980 Riley's music has become highly eclectic, remnants of minimialism remaining, improvisation often present, and an Indian influence frequently quite prominent.

One of the performers in the premiere of *In C* was a young musician from New York, Steve Reich. Reich had arrived in the Bay area to study composition with Darius Milhaud and Luciano Berio at Mills College in Oakland. He had already completed a bachelor's degree in philosophy at Cornell and done graduate work in composition at Juilliard. He found Milhaud old and tottering, more prone to reminiscing about the past than showing interest in his students' work, and he found the serial technique that Berio taught stuffy and uninspiring. Like most young composers, he felt that he *should* learn to write serial music, but, also like many, it did not connect with him. Reich began to spend more and more time in San Francisco, listening to John Coltrane among others in jazz, and writing music for a mime company. Coltrane at this time was exploring modal jazz, where he would improvise for long periods of time over a single triad.

After graduating in 1963 Reich decided to stay in San Francisco, and he began to frequent the San Francisco Tape Music Center. He also formed an improvisation group that tried to bridge jazz and Berio pitch charts. That experiment was not a success, but through it he met Terry Riley, mainly because Riley had walked out of the group's final concert. Reich, true New Yorker that he was, discovered that Riley lived on the same street he did, and banged on his door and confronted him with, "Why did you walk out of my concert?"[12] They quickly became friends.

Reich's own minimalist direction also came from tape experimentation. According to Reich, however, his breakthrough came by accident. He had recorded the sound of an African-American preacher, Brother Walter, and had extracted the phrase "It's gonna rain," from the statement "It's gonna rain after a while," in reference to the flood. Reich originally intended to set the phrase canonically, but in attempting to line the parts up on two tape recorders he noticed that one machine ran slightly faster than the other. As a consequence the two phrases gradually moved in and out of phase with each other, creating a subtle, unexpected rhythmic interaction. Instead of attempting to correct the machines or to get them to line up precisely, Reich realized that what occurred had inherent value in itself: "It was an accidental discovery, but a lot of people could have heard that same phenomenon and said, 'Line the machines up.' It impressed me that I'd hit something that was more significant than what I was trying to do in the first place. Suddenly, I got the idea for making a tape piece that would be much more of a process."[13]

Music as process and phase shifting became a Reich trademark, although it by no means marked his creative output of the time. He continued to experiment briefly with tape pieces, but after *Come Out,* a piece written specifically to support the civil rights cause, he grew restless, feeling "like a mad scientist trapped in a lab," and began to think again of live performance.[14]

Hesitant at first but encouraged by experimentation, Reich realized that phase-shift technique could be transferred to live performance. He then created a series of compositions that have become classics in the minimalist canon, beginning with *Piano Phase,* including *Violin Phase, Clapping Music,* and culminating in *Drumming.* In each the technique is similar. Two or more voices begin a pattern, and while one continues the pattern with no variation, the other shifts the pattern an incremental amount rhythmically. The parts get farther and farther apart, and then gradually come back together.

Reich is clear about his own antecedents. He attributes his development, but not his original interest, in a minimalist approach to repetitive music of two cultures, the drums of Ghana and the gamelan of Bali. Immersion in each culture resulted in two major pieces, *Drumming* and *Music for Eighteen Musicians*. Ghanaian drumming and the Balinese gamelan orchestra differ in many details but have a commonality with many types of music throughout the world, a repetitive, ritualistic process. In fact such music is common to so many cultures that it is surprising it has played so small a part in the Western art tradition. Instead the directionality that came with the emergence of tonality around the time of the Renaissance gave rise to the large narrative-dramatic structures of the eighteenth and nineteenth centuries.

Because of the ubiquity of repetitive music, one can speculate on many influences, but so far no scholar to my knowledge has suggested one that comes from nature itself: tree frogs. Anyone who has heard a forest or a jungle of tree frogs, each croaking repeatedly in a rhythm all its own, cannot miss one effect: phase shift. Phase shift is endemic to the collective ensemble of tree frogs on a warm evening. And tree frogs are common in Ghana. Did they influence Steve Reich? Chronology itself suggests otherwise, as he discovered phase shifting before his trip to Ghana, but it is hard to hear their chorus and not think of Steve Reich.

For a time Philip Glass and Steve Reich seemed like Gemini twins, although each would bristle at such an idea. They have parallel backgrounds, their paths did cross, and as youths they both displayed considerable intellectual precociousness beyond their musical talents. The parallels of course betray some very different influences and approaches to musical composition, and consequently some very different results, and although their styles each took highly different evolutionary paths, more than once they ended up in similar places.

Reich and Glass both grew up in Jewish families on the East Coast. Reich was born in New York, but because of his parents' divorce he traveled frequently to California. As a youth he studied percussion and some piano. Glass was born in Baltimore, and studied flute and then piano at an early age in the Preparatory Division of the Peabody Conservatory. Both composers went to prestigious universities at an early age, Reich to Cornell when he was sixteen, Glass to the University of Chicago when he was fifteen. Neither majored in music, both in philosophy (Glass in mathematics and philosophy). Both then went to Juilliard, where they were classmates and studied with the same composition teachers, William Bergsma and Vincent Persichetti. Following that both studied briefly with Darius Milhaud, although at different times and places. Their paths then took very different directions, although neither had heard of minimalism at that point.

While in Chicago Glass had gone through a brief serial phase, but at

Juilliard he emulated his teachers, writing in an accessible, tonal idiom. He had several pieces published and received a Ford Foundation grant to be composer-in-residence in the Pittsburgh public schools. Glass wrote *Gebrauchmusik* for school ensembles and special occasions and had more pieces published; a successful but traditional career as a composer seemed certain.

A Fulbright Fellowship to study with Nadia Boulanger in Paris followed in 1964, and Glass seemed to be on a clear path to academic stardom. The pedigree, the grants, the publications were all there. His study with Boulanger was not, however, what Glass expected. She started him all over again, with species counterpoint, a traditional compositional method of learning to combine parts polyphonically. "Species" refers to rhythmic relationships between voices, beginning with the most elemental. Expectations in her classes were high. Boulanger was teaching the basics of musicianship, but at a level that far surpassed what most students received elsewhere. Glass observed, "Her pedagogy was thorough and relentless."[15] It also helped prepare him for his next and pivotal encounter.

In his second year in Paris, Glass got a job transcribing the music of the Indian sitarist Ravi Shankar into Western notation for use in a film. The work had to be done on the spot so that French musicians could record the sound track. Struggles with barlines brought home to Glass the complex additive, cyclic, subtle nature of Indian rhythm. It was a moment of revelation that completely changed his compositional direction. Glass's "minimalism" was born of the rhythms and cyclic patterns of India.

That was not clear, however, until Glass returned to New York in early 1967 (following some travel to North Africa and India). Back in the United States he heard one of Reich's Park Place Gallery concerts and was impressed. How much Reich's music influenced what Glass next composed has been a point of bitter discord between the two composers. Glass claims that it was little, and Reich disagrees. After that encounter Glass's music took on *general* qualities similar to Reich's, although the compositional basis was different. At this time Reich was involved in phase shifting; Glass's music was based on the additive metamorphosis of repeated diatonic patterns.

Glass's *One Plus One* cries for comparison with Reich's *Clapping Music*. Both are early pieces in the new style and have simple scores consisting of nothing but tapping or clapping. Each, distilled to nothing but rhythm, illustrates its composer's basic approach. In *One Plus One* Glass instructs the performer to combine the two basic rhythmic units "in continuous, regular arithmetic progressions." The word *arithmetic* is important, as it frees the patterns from the strictures of Western meter, allowing them to combine in

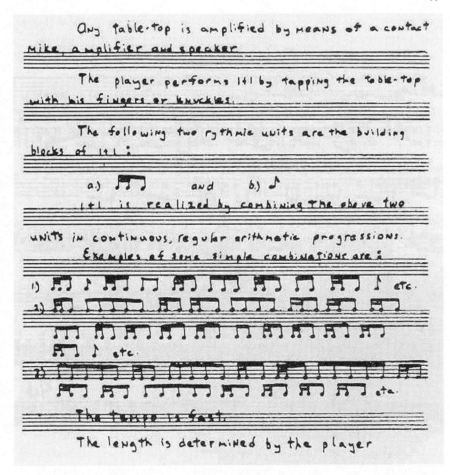

Philip Glass, *One Plus One* (© 1993 Dunvagen Music Publishers, Inc. Used by permission.)

Steve Reich, *Clapping Music*, mm. 1–3 (© 1972 Universal Edition, © renewed. All rights reserved. Used by permission of European American Music Distributors, LLC, sole U.S. and Canadian agent for Universal Edition.)

units of varying length. Glass does give examples of possible patterns but does not prescribe any particular ones, or any particular length to the piece.

Clapping Music involves two performers who are given a single basic pattern. The first player claps his pattern constantly and steadily throughout the piece. The second player, while maintaining the pattern, shifts its beginning point throughout the piece. As a consequence, in each phase shift, each part aligns differently with the other, creating a new overall combination. The piece is fundamentally cyclic, as the two parts gradually go more and more out of phase and then come back together again, ending where they had begun, in unison.

Glass and Reich faced the same practical problem: if performance was to occur, they had to make it happen. Each found the same solution, which was to form his own group. At this point they were in close contact, to the extent of sharing the same ensemble, or at least many of the same players. As their styles diverged, however, each developed his own group.

Glass's movement in a different direction than Reich went beyond their compositional bases. Glass emphasized amplified electronic sounds, particularly electronic keyboards and high volume, in his ensemble. Because of this and the prominent beat, Glass's music resembled 1960s and '70s rock, and as a consequence he developed a following among young people attuned more to popular than to classical music.

Glass's music also had a close connection to theater, although that was not obvious until his first opera, *Einstein on the Beach*, in 1976. His work with Ravi Shankar in Paris introduced him to film music, and his marriage to JoAnne Akalaitis, an actress and theater director, gave him an entrée into the theatrical world. While in Paris Glass became involved with an experimental theatrical group that later became Mabou Mines. Glass composed the music for their production of Samuel Beckett's *Play* in Paris. Although no score survives, Glass claims it was his first piece in a reductive, repetitive style.

Later, in New York, Glass was involved in further performances of the Mabou Mines company's *Play*, and he wrote music for a production of Lee Breuer's *The Red Horse Animation*. Through Akalaitis, he kept in fairly close contact with the theatrical world. When Glass met the playwright, stage designer, and theatrical director Robert Wilson after an all-night performance of Wilson's *Life and Times of Josef Stalin*, their discussion clicked for both of them.[16] And through many Thursday lunches the idea of *Einstein on the Beach* gradually emerged. Glass had already achieved considerable status in the concert world, particularly with *Music in Twelve Parts*, but *Einstein* established his reputation, inaugurated an ongoing collaboration with Wilson, and defined the direction of Glass's career. He followed *Einstein* with two other operas, *Satyagraha*, which was about Mohandas Gandhi, and *Akhnaten*, about the ancient Egyptian pharaoh — together these made up his biographical trilogy — as well as many other stage works, sound tracks for films, and recently multimedia compositions. Glass has constantly walked the line between meditative and narrative works, but drama in some form has been a fundamental constant.

Like other minimalist composers Glass was mostly ignored by the American musical establishment. Some three years after the unquestioned success of *Einstein* no large American commission had materialized, major music magazines ran few stories on him, and he was seldom played on classical-music stations. At this time the classical-music establishment tried its best to ignore minimalism. Glass himself found the situation somewhat ironic particularly compared with his earlier reception. "I had twenty published pieces and I was getting things into print as soon as I wrote them," he commented about his pre-Boulanger years, when he was "playing the game," as he put it — that is, writing in an academically accepted style.[17] What Glass didn't say was that after Paris he himself had chosen a different game: to enhance the marketability of his own ensemble, he no longer allowed his music to be published.

When Glass wasn't being ignored, commentary about him was often flippant, like that directed at the ultramoderns in the early part of the century. Irving Kolodin made reference to "Glass's tongue-in-cheek score [for *Einstein*], to hypnosis-by-repetition as practiced by Igor Stravinsky and popularized by Carl Orff (*Carmina Burana*). Here it is hypnosis-on-the-cheap, with organ (Glass), violin (Paul Zukofsky), reeds, mixing panel, and voices."[18]

Young, Glass, Reich, and Riley could be dismissed so easily because they seemed so out of sync with the late-twentieth-century musical world, where rationalism had triumphed over expression, where complexity, density, and a learned cerebralism reigned. The position of the minimalists and the serialists both can best be understood if we ask what impelled composers to adopt a position of rationalism, to renounce expression. Was it, as Paul Griffiths has suggested, a "large-scale failure of nerve"?[19]

An impulse toward rationalism may be found in the aftermath of World War II. Many cities in Europe, Germany in particular, had been virtually destroyed by the war. For anyone who has visited German cities in the past thirty years and taken in the great cathedrals, cultural monuments, or historic palaces, it is difficult to imagine just how extensive the destruction was in 1945. For much of the rest of Europe, German occupation had itself disrupted and demoralized entire populations; then, as the war ended, the full story of the Holocaust came to light. France escaped the physical destruction of Germany and Austria, but only at the price of surrender and collaboration. After the war French intellectuals not only probed their own role in the events of the war and pondered its philosophical meaning, but had to deal with the psychological burden of a new society in which much of the old order and tradition had been overthrown.

Americans had to adjust to a society totally mobilized for war, but except for the ultimate sacrifice that many paid with their lives, the nation escaped with relatively little damage. GIs returned to a country intact and poised for economic expansion. After a short, rocky period as American society readjusted to a peacetime economy, new goods of all kinds, from appliances to automobiles to entire houses began rolling out. Demand seemed insatiable. That much of the rest of the industrial world lay in chaos only provided the opportunity for one of the most sustained economic booms in modern times. The dollar ruled, both in reality and in perception, and Americans were quick to take advantage of the situation. The emerging cold war and the quickly developing nuclear standoff had a sobering effect, but if nothing else they contributed further to economic expansion, as the government poured billions into the defense industry. The potential for nuclear annihilation had if anything a greater effect in Europe, which was physically closer to the planes and later the missiles of the Soviet Union, and psychologically more troubled by events of the recent past as well as centuries of tensions and upheavals.

Yet for everyone a sense of newness hung in the air. Scientific progress — whether the efforts were grandiose, such as entirely new forms of energy, or more modest, such as more powerful tennis rackets — convinced Americans that science and technology would not only solve many problems but also make their lives better and happier. Medicine, closely related, held out much hope. Diseases could be conquered and the human life span increased dramatically, although many medical developments also created serious ethical problems and called into question traditional beliefs and values. In the arts, new media, the tape recorder, the LP, and more important television, promised to usher in an entirely new day for the artist. At the same time, photographs of the Nazi concentration camps began to appear, and their effect was profound. Susan Sontag first saw photographs of Bergen-Belsen and Dachau in 1945, and she later wrote: "Nothing I have seen — in photographs or real life — ever cut me as sharply, deeply, instantaneously. Indeed, it seems plausible to me to divide my life into two parts, before I saw those photographs (I was twelve) and after."[20] Many began to question the nature of humanity and the forces that could allow modern industrial society to make the Holocaust possible. The brutality of the Soviet gulag was still unknown, and the genocides of Cambodia, southeastern Europe, and Africa lay in the future.

By the 1960s Western culture itself was under assault. Many youths of the sixties saw the past as hopelessly outmoded, as useless. The "dawning of the Age of Aquarius" symbolized a break with the past for an entire generation. The rebelliousness inherent as each new generation struggled to assume its place expanded into a "generation gap." Historians and futurists, a new type of social scientist, spoke of history telescoping, just as they saw performances of Mozart speeding up. For the younger composer atonality seemed the wave of the future. The serialists were the rebels, fighting the traditionalists, painted at the time as romanticists who no longer realized that it was a new world. The serialists captured the high ground, and they appealed immensely to the young. Their position was enhanced by the atmosphere wrought by the cold war. The Soviet menace, bolstered by the bomb and Sputnik, seemed to threaten the very fabric of Western society. The belief that science and the universities would save Western civilization from the menace gave new prestige to academia and science. It was *the* wagon to jump on to.

Thus when the serialists, atonalists, and experimentalists relentlessly portrayed the more traditional composer as being of the past, as having had his day, as being out of touch with the new, it stung. The traditionalists may have still occupied positions of authority and commanded resources, but the age itself conspired with the new avant-garde to cast doubt and uncertainty even in their own minds. And the serialists made every effort to capture science, the ultimate authority of the time.

A binary alignment typical of most music history, between a group of young, rebellious composers, the avant-garde, and older traditional composers, seriously risks distorting the postwar situation, because no monolithic style existed at the time. On the contrary, there were three highly disparate trends after World War II. The serialists and other atonalists wrote music that was complex, highly cerebral, tightly controlled, and carefully worked out, often with involved mathematical techniques. At the same time, Cage and other aleatoric composers allowed chance to determine what happened, and the result to many seemed as much a circus of absurdity as a recognizable musical event. Then the minimalists emerged, with static and repetitive music, which used simple, diatonic materials relentlessly presented. It was more music of trance and ritual than Western dynamism. To many, minimalism was the antidote for what serialism had wrought. "It was Reich, after all, more than anyone else, who broke the stranglehold of creepy serialist music and made the new-composition world once again safe for music lovers," wrote Kyle Gann, the quintessentially downtown critic in the quintessentially downtown rag, the *Village Voice*.[21]

The classical-music world seemed to be falling apart, spinning off on its own centrifugal forces, with three directions that could not have been more divergent. Yet the most remarkable thing about these developments was not their disparity but their similarity. In the end they were three shades of the same color, each curiously representative of the immediate postwar condition. And each group of composers had the success that it did precisely because each so uncannily echoed that world, even though similarity was masked by wildly different musical means. No matter what the style, no matter how big the ego or flamboyant the personality, at some deep level, the postwar composer sought what Pierre Boulez identified as "anonymity."

Sometime in April 1949, John Cage knocked on the door of Pierre Boulez. Cage had just received a Guggenheim Foundation grant, and he had chosen to spend six months in Paris. Either Virgil Thomson or Roger Desormiere, possibly both, suggested that Cage look up Boulez, who at the time was a relatively unknown twenty-four-year-old. Thus began one of the strangest friendships in twentieth-century music. Cage was older, thirty-six, and better known, but neither of them were the icons they later became. Boulez introduced Cage to Parisian musical circles, which resulted in Olivier Messiaen arranging a performance of Cage's *Sonatas and Interludes*, with Boulez giving an introductory talk. Later Cage more than reciprocated, lobbying in the United States for Boulez's cause and helping arrange his first visit to America. When Boulez was in New York, he stayed in Cage's apartment.[22]

This friendship did not last. Later Boulez turned against Cage, much the way he had turned against his former teacher René Leibowitz. Leibowitz had been an ardent follower of Schoenberg, and when Boulez rejected Schoenberg he also rejected Leibowitz: "Leibowitz was a joke. I never forgave his dishonesty. He was serviceable at the beginning, but I began to resent him when I saw how narrow and stupid he was." Boulez was less vitriolic to Cage, but in an article that appeared in 1957, "Alea," he considered what the use of chance implied for musical composition and found it deleterious. Cage himself reacted to Boulez's hostility with a wry, almost cutting humor, but he did acknowledge that he and Boulez had a "difficult friendship."[23]

What did two such strange bedfellows see in each other in the first place, and why did they become so close, if only briefly? The answer to what brought Cage and Boulez together goes far to explain attitudes prevalent in the immediate postwar world, attitudes and aesthetic principles that affected all areas of composition.

On the surface Cage and Boulez seem completely opposite personalities: Boulez was arrogant, hostile, combative, opinionated, attacking all vestiges of the past; a man with a chip on his shoulder. Cage appeared gentle, open, charming, almost naive in his sunniness. Yet both had similar attitudes toward authority. They simply would not cotton to it. Cage was as obsessed on that point as Boulez.

Boulez's rebellious stance is the more well known, possibly because it is the more dramatic. Boulez was driven to reject many aspects of his life, violently. He could be savage when crossed, or simply when someone did not do his bidding. When he was eighteen he turned against his father, insisting on a career in music rather than engineering. Although Léon Boulez was a strong authoritarian figure, he seems to have been a good father to his children, and when faced with arguments from Pierre and his sister Jeanne, the father relented. There is no evidence of a nasty confrontation between artistically inclined son and obstinate father, or the kind of poisoned relationship that existed between Varèse and his father. Nevertheless to Boulez his father was the bourgeoisie, which he felt compelled to repudiate. He also repudiated the church. Most decisively he turned against his own mentors, as he had Leibowitz, carrying attacks on them to extremes far beyond civility or even necessity.[24]

Cage's rebellion was simple, quiet. Growing up in an atmosphere that respected intellectual and artistic freedom, Cage was less a renegade than an explorer. His rebellion took quiet forms. When he was told at Pomona College that all students were to read one particular book, Cage made a point to read every book *but* that one. Throughout his life Cage avoided situations that required him to bend to authority. He refused to take a permanent teaching position. He said again and again that he would be placed in a position of power.[25]

When Cage and Boulez met in 1949 their musical rebellions had taken on similar forms. When they discovered their apparent mutual approach to composition, their friendship was sealed. The key lay in the use of matrices, squares filled with numbers whose ordering was used to determine various parameters of the piece. The musical results for each composer were similar. It is unlikely that any audience of 1949 could hear much difference between Cage's *Music of Changes* and Boulez's *Structures*. Both are thoroughly atonal, make use of widely separated, isolated notes, spanning extremes of range, and include small clusters of seconds and sevenths, giving the music a jagged, prickly character. In both, rhythm is sufficiently irregular that the listener discerns no clear pulse or consistent motion. There is little sense of line, only of flurries of pointillistic motives, and certainly no melody in the traditional sense.

Their aesthetic goals were curiously similar — the elimination of personal expression. Through the use of matrices musical events are determined by an outside mathematical process that is independent of the desires or controlling logic of the composer. As Edward T. Cone pointed out, "In neither case (Boulez or Cage) can any musical event be linked organically with those that precede and those that follow. . . . The connections are mechanistic rather than teleological: no event has any purpose — each is there only because it has to be there."[26]

The numbers on the matrix guaranteed a mechanistic result. But how those numbers got there was profoundly different: Boulez's numbers came about through carefully thought-out mathematical formulas, Cage's by chance, through the use of coin flips as guided by the I-Ching. The numbers on the matrix determine what happens, and once they are there, does it matter how they got there? Boulez thought it did, and in the long run those differences symbolize what we understand about Cage and Boulez. And their efforts were entirely consistent with the world in which each lived. Yet the differences mask a striking similarity between what each composer sought to do that goes well beyond matrices on a page.

In France, Jean-Paul Sartre's existentialism looked out on nothingness. In his novel *Nausea* Antoine Roquentin observes, "I was just thinking that here we sit, all of us, eating and drinking to preserve our precious existence and really there is nothing, nothing, absolutely no reason for existing." Similar thinking can be found in Nathalie Sarraute's poems and Eugène Ionesco's plays. To Ionesco, "Personality doesn't exist. . . . Each character is not so much himself as another." In such a world logic, connection, causality, even words themselves, lose their meaning. The characters themselves are lost, precisely how Boulez feels his listeners should be: "I think that is exactly what a work of art should do to you; it should in the end make you feel lost, and you should know you are lost, and that is the important thing."[27]

The bleakness that led European thought to embrace the absurd was less pronounced in the United States, as the conditions that gave birth to it were not replicated. Existentialism caught on mainly on college campuses as a heady mixture for aspiring students in the humanities to emulate, but it had little resonance per se through American society. Vestiges of it, however, were everywhere in the arts, and nowhere were they more pronounced than in music. In the end, in spite of their differences, American composers were not that far from their European counterparts. And it mattered little what style their work assumed.

Boulez and Cage could be the every-European and every-American experimental composers of the postwar generation.[28] Experimental composers, whether European or American, whether they were serialists, aleatorics, or minimalists, sought to discard any vestige of personal expression, to separate as completely as possible any connection between composition and expression. They wished to suppress any trace of their personas in their pieces. Anonymity became a prime aesthetic goal. Boulez summed up this perspective by saying, "If it were necessary to find a profound motive for the work I have described, it would be the search for . . . anonymity."[29]

Serialism was the first obvious candidate for an impersonal approach — impersonality seemed built into the system. In an interview that Boulez gave to the *Washington Post* in 1971, he explained: "Our problem was to make a new musical language, seeking out what was good from the past, and rejecting what was bad. . . . What we were doing by total serialization was to annihilate the will of the composer in favor of a predetermining system." Ernst Krenek, one of the pioneers of serialism, who originally came to the United States in 1937, agreed: "One of the parameters that obviously cannot be controlled by premeditation when those so far discussed are subjected to serial ordering is the expressive, or communicative, aspect of music. . . . It so happens that serial composers are not thinking in such terms."[30]

For the most important postwar American serialist, Milton Babbitt, anonymity was not an end in itself. Science and rationality, however, were, and both Babbitt's own compositional approach, relying strongly on mathematical determinants of musical elements, and his writing about music, cloaked heavily in the language of science, have as their effect, if not intention, minimizing of personal expression. Even one of Babbitt's strongest supporters, Martin Brody, refers to Babbitt's "value-neutral, positivistic, epistemology."[31]

Later Babbitt insisted that he did not produce music mathematically, and strictly speaking he never did, but such utterances occurred in the context of a reaction in the 1990s to the pummeling serialists were taking in the press. Earlier he had said, "the twelve-tone set must absolutely determine *every* aspect of the piece" (italics in the original), and "I believe in cerebral music, and I never choose a note unless I know why I want it there." He put this into practice. The tight control of his earlier serial pieces belies a mind given to music constructed on a strictly rational, theoretical basis. After analyzing the beginning of *Three Compositions for Piano,* no. 1, Babbitt's first serial work, Paul Griffiths observed: "That eight bars of music may demonstrate so much evidence of control is some measure of Babbitt's ability to make everything in his compositions serve a constructive function, and to have a reason for everything," and, "There is something watertight about the music: every detail has an immediate answer, suggesting that every eventuality has been prepared by the composer." He argued for the use of scientific language and even the scientific method, and felt that it was incumbent on the modern composer to be able to explain his works in theoretical, scientific terms.[32]

The John Cage aesthetic has at its heart the elimination of the personal. Cage spoke frequently of renouncing control over sounds, of letting sounds be themselves, and he criticized Varèse for dealing with sound not as sound but as Varèse. Depersonalization continued with Cage's followers. Thus Michael Nyman could write of a "continuous, unbroken tradition of experimental music from Cage/Feldman/Brown/Wolff of 1950 right through to the present day [1976]," in which "composers treat sound not as material to be ordered and put into meaningful symbolic forms as a medium for human expression, but as something autonomous and impersonal."[33]

Yet even those involved in the experimental scene were aware of the affinity between the serialists and the aleatorics. Earle Brown, who worked closely with Cage in the 1950s, noticed a "similarity of poetics existing between serial and aleatoric concepts," in the "underlying acceptance of a kind of autonomy and a by-passing of subjective control." Similarly, Krenek did not fail to notice the aleatoric element in serialism: "Whatever happens at any given point is a product of the preconceived serial organization, but by the same token it is a chance occurrence because it is as such not anticipated by the mind that invented the mechanism and set it in motion." Later Kyle Gann stated this point most succinctly: "Even Cage, for all his anarchic freedom, uses the most objective musical methods possible, and if there is a difference between Cage and Babbitt, it's that Cage writes better English."[34]

Even a relatively traditional composer such as John Harbison made it clear that "I am simply not interested in the projection of personal angst," which he associated with Mahler and Viennese Expressionism. And Lukas Foss, experimenting with improvisation, claimed in his work the mantle of first anonymity. About his improvisation workshop's group compositions, which he called "anonymous compositions," Foss stated: "We were the first people, I think, in the trend for anonymity which is built into current musical expression."[35]

Minimalism itself, at least in some of its manifestations, could be equally impersonal. Minimalism has a long history of musical discovery by chance (as opposed to music created by chance), that is, the processes some minimalists used elicited unexpected and unpredictable results. Steve Reich's phase shifts were neither planned nor the realization of a theoretical concept. They were not only impersonal but, as Reich himself admitted, "accidental." He referred to his music as "more an impersonal process," and realized that even when performed by his ensemble, it was to the musicians more a letting go than an act of personal expression: "A performance for us is a situation where all the musicians, including myself, try to set aside our individual thoughts and feelings of the moment, and try to focus our minds and bodies clearly on the realization of one continuous musical process. Focusing in on the musical process makes possible that shift of attention away from he and she and you and me outwards towards *it*. By voluntarily giving up the freedom to do whatever momentarily comes to mind, we are, as a result, *free* of all that momentarily comes to mind."[36]

Although phase-shift experimentation dictated the establishment of impersonal processes that would yield surprises, and the surprises were, essentially, the goal of the composition, Reich was never willing to give up completely his own self. "Whereas he [Cage] was willing to keep his musical sensibility out of his music, I was not," he said. Reich wanted to create "music that was completely personal," using "impersonal means." He considered his efforts akin to the chaos theory concept of emergence: he knew what each part was doing but could not predict the totality. He describes one of his best-known pieces, *Drumming*, in that regard: "I know precisely what the marimbas, drums, and glockenspiels are doing, I know the notes and rhythms involved; but the number of resultant patterns set up by the relationship between them all, is more than I could spend my lifetime trying to figure out. And that's what makes the piece interesting; there's more in it than I put in. That's the joy of working with processes. If you follow your personal taste, you get your taste back. But if you follow a musical process you get your taste, plus a few surprises."[37]

In spite of all their similarities, Glass seems the polar opposite of Reich. Reich is the modernist, the experimentalist. Glass is the romantic. Whereas Reich is interested in exploring what happens when certain processes are set in motion, Glass seeks the grandiose. Originally this tendency manifested itself in sound, with an array of amplifiers, synthesizers, and mixers typical of popular music of the time. Grandiosity reached its apogee in the series of operas that are the principal works in the Glass canon. *Einstein on the Beach* is the pivotal piece, a point that Glass himself acknowledges. Although revolutionary in its studied avoidance of plot, even of dialogue, it is imposing in every way. The length, the scope, even the scenery — all are immense, deliberately outsize. And the absence of dramatic dialogue serves to call attention to the music and hence the composer. The effect can be overpowering, as the rhythmic pulse mesmerizes, and its sustainability is a credit to Glass's powers of invention. The effect is essentially a romantic one; it is the late-twentieth-century equivalent of Wagner's *gesamtkunstwerk*, a theatrical experience that overwhelms, overpowers, but seldom leaves the listener unaffected. Unlike Wagner, however, who was certain of his messianic goals to unite Germanic people through a call to their roots, Glass's work, like so much of the late twentieth century, projects a void. It is big and powerful, but at its core, it is hesitant; there is a disturbing uncertainty about its meaning.

For behind Glass's fustian sound is anonymity, the signature of the post–World War II generation. Glass's music, for all its seeming expressiveness, is at core impersonal, its essential nature underscored in the sound and timbres of the romanticism of, not the nineteenth century, but its heir, rock music.

Curiously, where personal expression did surface, it was in unusual places. La Monte Young remained a contrarian, seeing in his drones a form of personal expression. Speaking of *Trio for Strings*, which he acknowledged as "probably my most important early musical statement," Young claimed that "the concept of the expanded time structure comprised of long sustained tones and the unique tonal palette of the work came to me not by theoretical deduction but by totally inspired intuition."[38] Of course these comments were made for legal as well as financial purposes, to be able to claim a copyright, so their aesthetic veracity may be in question. Yet even though Young's static drones stand as a very personal commentary on his own early upbringing, even though as a personal style they are unique, and in their super-expanded-unrelieved constancy they seem to exist on a plane of their own, they strike most listeners as devoid of even the remotest personal expression. Young's own titles and discussions, which frequently center on dense consideration of intervalic ratios, suggest more a mathematician's approach to musical creation. It is hard to know whether they are meant as precise descriptors or a spoof in themselves.

Young and Glass ultimately found themselves on terrain not that far removed from Cage and Babbitt. For after the Second World War a desire for the impersonal, for anonymity, pervaded musical thought. Serialists, aleatoric composers, minimalists, all sought it. It was transgenerational: John Cage, born in 1912, sought it, Milton Babbitt, born in 1917, sought it, Pierre Boulez, born in 1925, sought it, Steve Reich, born in 1936, sought it. And it was a-stylistic. Composers gravitated toward it for two seemingly diametrically opposed reasons, for science or for religion. Milton Babbitt and many other serialists saw it as part of their scientific orientation; for Cage and Glass it connected with oriental religion and philosophy; for Reich it was process, a loosely scientific investigation. Yet all considered their work to varying degrees experimental. Cage made it clear that he was not only an experimenter but an inventor, a term that in modern Western culture resonates with scientific implications. And for Steve Reich the term *experiment* could easily substitute for process. The serialists hoped they would be accepted as scientists, because for them at least, as for many in the post–World War II Western world, science had become the new religion.

PART 4

The Legacy of the Mavericks

It is the fusion that is important, the fusion of music, drama, and graphic art that Wagner strove to attain. *Fantasia* is the first work that clearly indicates the possibilities.
— *New York Times*, 1940

My goals:

To create an art that breaks down boundaries between the disciplines, an art which in turn becomes a metaphor for opening up thought, perception, experience.

An art that is inclusive, rather than exclusive; that is expansive, whole, human, multidimensional.

An art that cleanses the senses, that offers insight, feeling, magic. That allows the public to perhaps see familiar things in a new, fresh way — that gives them the possibility of feeling more alive.

An art that seeks to reestablish the unity existing in music, theater, and dance — the wholeness that is found in cultures where performing arts practice is considered a spiritual discipline with healing and transformative power.

An art that reaches toward emotion we have no words for, that we barely remember — an art that affirms the world of feeling in a time and society where feelings are in danger of being eliminated.
— MEREDITH MONK, 1996

Beyond these severely definable ideas in music is the music itself, elusive to words. I call it *corporeal*, because it roots itself with other arts necessary to civilization, in a unity that is important to the whole being — mind and body. Even the visual element of seeing the instruments played is a vital one.
— HARRY PARTCH, 1957

CHAPTER 11

Looking Back

Puritanism, Geography, and the
Myth of American Individualism

B Y THE 1920s Americans had come to terms with change. The world of
the nineteenth century was but a distant memory. The village had
given way to a larger social organization, but by the time Warren
Harding was elected president in 1920 Americans had made it clear that such
structures stopped at national boundaries. Technology was to be celebrated,
not feared. The automobile, the radio, the phonograph, the telephone, elec-
tricity, had been around for years, in some cases decades, but only in the
1920s did they weave fully into the fabric of Americans' lives. The stock market was only one barometer of the nation's optimism.

The avant-garde composer felt this spirit. He celebrated the same new
that all around him were. Change, even audacious change, was possible. If
the old models did not fit, he would create new ones. The many artistic, literary, and musical societies, the magazines and the new concert series, were
a product of the same spirit that created the roaring twenties.

Yet the modernists in music faced a dilemma: how could they embrace
radical modernism and survive? Musical experimentalism had been alive
throughout the early twentieth century, but the record of success for the
more uncompromising experimentalists was dismal. Only Ornstein managed a career, and that because he was a world-class pianist. Before the 1920s
Ives, Varèse, and Ruggles found no audience for their experiments, or when
there was one, an overwhelmingly hostile reception. In the 1920s composers
tried a new and simple approach: create their own community. Its success
could not have been foreseen.

Self-organization had been a principal concept of American democracy, and had reached a heyday in the nineteenth century. From radical utopian experiments to political causes and gatherings founded on common social and artistic interests, Americans often defined their world by their associations. Musicians had done this prior to the 1920s, but for different reasons. In the early nineteenth century it fell upon the musicians themselves to organize their own public performances, be it a benefit concert or a presenting society, simply because no other performance mechanisms were in place. And the music presented, often composed by the organizers themselves, was geared more toward winning an audience than pushing the boundaries of style. The concerts, involving a potpourri of genres and even mixing amateurs and professionals, were designed to give the larger community an opportunity to hear music, not to offer a composer a forum for experimentation.

As romanticism, with its emphasis on individual creativity, led composers toward a hermeneutic self-expression, and as the notion of certain music as Art took hold, for those composers wrestling with such, the gap between public success and private accomplishment began to widen. Different composers developed various strategies to traverse this tightwire, but the issue, previously just one of many factors in the composers' compositional calculus, became an overriding consideration.

Only in the 1920s did American composers find a formula that worked, and as a consequence new and radical innovations found an acceptance hitherto unimaginable. Composers self-organized in a new way. They formed a new type of musical community. In doing so they bridged a set of dichotomies as strong as any in American musical history. They were some of the most eccentric, individualistic personalities to be found — true mavericks — yet they succeeded because they self-organized in societies so tightly knit and complete that they may be called subcultures. In this process these composers exemplified a pattern found throughout American history: a radical vision realized through communal association.

The modernist community in the 1920s was no monolith. Differences between the International Composers' Guild and the League of Composers, the two most important organizations in New York, involved issues of programming, organizational principles, and ethnic tension. But beyond the organizations two distinct schools of radical modernism began to emerge, and these would carry well into the 1960s. The division was at first continental: between East Coast and West Coast. Later the geography narrowed to Manhattan Island in New York City, as composers became identified with either downtown or uptown. But even within the confines of a single borough of a single city, the overall divide could still be found.

Members of the eastern group of the early twentieth century pursued dissonance as if their entire being depended on it. The dissonances set them apart. With it all the values most treasured by the romantics, beautiful sounds, lyrical melody, engaging harmony, and touching emotionalism, were scorned. As many writers of the time noted, the dissonances harkened back to Puritanism itself. It is no coincidence that the early leaders of the Eastern school in the 1920s, Charles Ives, Carl Ruggles, and Charles Seeger, were all New Englanders.

There are many parallels between these three, in background, outlook, personality, and even physical appearance. Yet befitting their New England origins and their places as creative artists or intellectuals, each had a unique and unusual career path, and each's creative work was individual and distinctive. They were unaware of each other until after the First World War, and they never acted as a group. But their impact on developments in the 1920s was far-reaching, and American musical history might have taken a very different path had it not been for this remarkable triumvirate, the three Charleses of New England (Ruggles was originally named Charles). At the very least, together they gave American musical modernism a decided New England dialect.

Seeger is remembered primarily as a writer and theorist. He explained musical modernism, and his treatise, *Tradition and Experiment in (The New) Music*, most of which he wrote with Ruth Crawford in 1929–31, codified and legitimized dissonance. Before that, however, his influence on modernist composers, particularly Henry Cowell and Carl Ruggles, was considerable. From 1914 to 1916 Henry Cowell, a youth of about seventeen, had studied with him at the University of California at Berkeley, and during that time he had begun to work out his own theories about dissonant counterpoint.[1]

When Seeger came east he developed a close relationship with Ruggles in spite of Ruggles's disdain for "theoretical stuff." Ruggles's work was always by trial and error, usually agonizingly slow and painful trial and error. Unlike many later twentieth-century composers, whose theoretical explanations can rival the piece itself, Ruggles realized he simply did not have the training to analyze his own works. But his results vindicated Seeger, partly because Seeger himself had a hand in his musical development. In the summer of 1921, when Ruggles was writing *Angels*, he and his wife Charlotte stayed with the Seegers at their family home in Patterson, New York. Seeger sensed that Ruggles, like Cowell, was an autodidact, and he tried to leave the young man alone to work out his pieces. But Ruggles wanted advice, and they talked. Later Ruggles acknowledged, "My style began with Seeger," and he specifically admitted, "It was 'Angels' that did it."[2]

Beyond the obvious emphasis on dissonant intervals, Ruggles sought contrary, or if that was not possible, at least static motion between lines. Such ideas, in their broad strokes, are consistent with any good counterpoint, that is, any attempt to create independent voices. It was precisely what Seeger preached. Late in life Ruggles heard Virgil Thomson describe his writing as "non differentiated secundal counterpoint." He found the phrase amusing and puzzling, but he added that he preferred Seeger's term "dissonant counterpoint."[3]

Other composers used dissonance freely and often, but none, with the possible exception of Ruth Crawford, combined dissonance and line as Ruggles did. And therein lies a stylistic paradox. For in spite of Ruggles's fascination with chordal sounds, his music is the triumph of line over harmony. And his line is, at core, romantic. But like any good New Englander with a strong romantic tinge, Ruggles did his best to hide it. Dissonance became his camouflage. The New England curmudgeon is implanted in the harmony, the dissonance representing toughness, as his good friend Ives explicitly stated many times. Ruggles himself sought a complete and uncompromising dissonance. He had to. For a dissonance that is pungent enough can — almost — hide Ruggles's soaring, breathtaking, romantic melody.

Ruggles's melody cannot be denied, however. Rather than covering it, the dissonance sits, biting, punctuating, ultimately calling attention to it. The dissonance throws the melody in sharp relief. It props up, surrounds, and ultimately enhances it by its very contrast. Ruggles's melody turns out to be Ophelia's song amidst the madness of Lear.

In that regard Ruggles diverged from Ives. Ives is the more flexible, and ultimately the greater composer: he could handle a much wider sonic palette, layer styles as well as musical events, and incorporate a much greater divergence of resources. Ives's sensitivity to text or to programmatic context is unparalleled, and no other composer has incorporated vernacular elements in such unique ways. Like Ruggles, Ives was no theorist, but he was an experimentalist, interested in exploring new and different ideas, sounds, and combinations.

Ives, Ruggles, and Seeger are the strongest adherents of a thoroughgoing and systematic dissonance. And in those dissonances one finds many echoes of Puritanism. Many contemporaries of Ives and Ruggles noticed that, and the references were invariably positive. Nicolas Slonimsky, a conductor who championed the music of the ultramoderns in the 1920s, saw the spirit of Plymouth Rock "braced against Ruggles' music to keep it from dispersing." Paul Rosenfeld, discussing Ruggles's *Men and Mountains*, equated the "harshness of certain of Ruggles' brazen sonorities" with the New England landscape, and described the piece as a Puritan sermon, in which "his acrid trumpets and trombones preach and dogmatize ministerially at imaginary congregations." To Rosenfeld, Ruggles belongs in the "ultra-religious camp of musicians"; he is "all elevation, seriousness, apocalypse." [4]

Even when Ives was still in college, John C. Griggs praised an Ives piece because "it had something of the Puritan character, a stern but outdoors strength, and something of the pioneering feeling." Lawrence Gilman, discussing Ives's Fourth Symphony, compared Ives to Jonathan Edwards and noted the composer's "irresistible veracity and strength, an uncorrupted sincerity." Clifton Joseph Furness also connected Ives's Fourth Symphony with Jonathan Edwards, in reference to the images it conjured for him: "Jonathan Edwards walked the Great White Way and talked with God!" Henry Bellamann spoke of Ives's "granitic Puritanism," a phrase Bernard Herrmann repeated some five years later. [5] Bellamann also drew a parallel between Ives and both Jonathan Edwards and Cotton Mather.

Ives himself associated dissonance with masculinity. He distinguished music that was tough, stern, manly, which he considered good, from music that was soft and effeminate, which he did not. And he saw in the Puritans positive character traits. To Ives the issue was not misogyny, for he specifically stated that many women displayed the former qualities and many men the latter: "There is only one thing they [the Puritans] were NOT — they were not effeminate — not even their ladies." [6]

The gender language had to do with the place of music in the world in which he lived. Women's accomplishments in music at this time were remarkable, although not always acknowledged. Yet the rigid separation of social and cultural life into distinct male and female spheres in the nineteenth century contributed to music's being marginalized. That so many male musicians were foreigners only reinforced the problem; they were beyond the pale of societal norm, and consequently did not disrupt the gender equation. And Ives saw this problem first-hand, in his father's attempts to succeed professionally in music.

Ives, Ruggles, and Seeger, all New Englanders, all men with an acute sense of the separate spheres, were the primary advocates of dissonance with a purpose. And for all three the purpose was the same: it made music masculine. To those musicians it rescued music from an effete romanticism.

In 1922 Carl Ruggles was asked to lecture as part of the Whitney Club Studio Talks on Modern Music. In no uncertain terms he contrasted Edward

MacDowell, whom he disparaged for his "driveling, cheap sentimentalism," with Leo Ornstein, whom he liked, as long as he remained in his dissonant period. He said of Ornstein's pieces: "There was a strength and hardness about them that augured well for his future. There are other works of that period that I like, but his later things have become mushy and soft. And show a degenerating into mannerisms."[7]

Yet other visions of dissonance appeared at this time. The most striking came from another individual on the ultramodern scene, a French émigré, Daniel Chennevière, who later took the name Dane Rudhyar. Rudhyar was deeply interested in spirituality and Eastern religious ideas, particularly theosophy. Even his treatises on dissonance have strong mystical overtones, as he connected dissonance directly with spirituality, and with the social order. It is telling that his strongest influence was on Carl Ruggles and Ruth Crawford, two composers whose own music is not only the living embodiment of Charles Seeger's theories of dissonant counterpoint, but who combined them with lines of great breadth and expressiveness. In Crawford's music Rudhyar saw spiritual qualities. Rudhyar was close to and a strong supporter of both Ruggles and Crawford, enough to arouse the enmity of Seeger, who faulted Rudhyar's terminology for its the lack of precision. Rudhyar saw this differently, however. "I wrote from a philosophical standpoint trying to understand the *life* of music," he said, "whereas Mr. Seeger writes from a technical and dogmatic point of view analyzing what to me is but the *skeleton* of music." Ruggles and Crawford unquestionably profited from both ends of the dissonant counterpoint spectrum.[8]

Dissonance receded in the 1930s as composers felt the sobering effects of events of the time as much as the rest of society. While they might long for the shocking new, the disappointments of the twenties were too much present. And there was a new economic reality, not only for themselves but for those around them. They saw the suffering that accompanied the depression, and many were moved, some to radical political action. As a new tone swept the land, it was no longer easy for composers to believe that with no compromise they could either win an audience or proceed as if it did not matter. If the people would not come to their music, then the composers must come to the people's music. Avant-garde musicians in many ways sought their folk roots. Some turned to a more conservative style, basing their symphonies and operas on American folk idioms. Others turned even more directly to folk activity, leaving behind the creation of large-scale art-music pieces entirely.

World War II changed all that, and in its aftermath came new schisms. The World War II veteran came back from a war fought in the cause of righteousness and justice to create a seemingly idyllic time (the 1950s). America had not only won the war but emerged with by far the largest and most powerful, in fact the only intact, economic engine. One of the most prosperous times in American history lay ahead. New technology burgeoned: automobiles exploded in Baroque swirls and muscle-flexing horsepower; electronics, from calculators to better phone service, and of course television, transformed almost every aspect of American culture; and even some of the worst diseases of humankind were conquered with the new antibiotics. These marvels were of course most beneficial if you were middle class and white.

For white middle-class America, it was a time of crewcuts, button-down collars, and spotless kitchens. *The Man in the Gray Flannel Suit*, the corporate man, embodied the male gender. For women there were June Cleaver and Betty Crocker. Peggy Seeger wrote "I Want to Be an Engineer," a song popularized by her brother Pete, about the obstacles faced by a girl whose parents and counselors urge her to settle down and be a wife and mother:

> When I went to school I learned to write and how to read,
> Some history, geography, and home economy.
> And typing is a skill that every girl is sure to need
> To while away the extra time until the time to breed.
> And then they had the nerve to say, "What would you like to be?"
> I says, "I'm gonna be an engineer!"
> "No, you only have to learn to be a lady —
> The duty isn't yours for to try and run the world.
> An engineer could never have a baby,
> Remember, dear, that you're a girl."

That such as song could even exist speaks volumes about that culture.

Then came the sixties: protests, long hair, LSD, Haight-Ashbury, psychedelia, free love. Bacchus routed Apollo. For the young all of history had been overthrown, and the world would never be the same. For older and more conservative Americans, the very fabric of society seemed to have broken down.

The divide affected classical music in the most basic way: the downtown-uptown cultural split. The new Lincoln Center, at Seventh Avenue and Sixty-fourth Street, epitomized uptown. It was the home of the New York Philharmonic and the Metropolitan Opera, next door to Juilliard — it was pure establishment. Leonard Bernstein and Rudolf Bing presided, and the beautiful people flocked there. Down in Greenwich Village, things were looser. Artists of all stripes and media mixed. Yoko Ono had her happenings in her loft, George Maciunas founded Fluxus, the Judson Church hosted avant-garde performances of all types, and the Club, a group of artists and some musicians, began to meet regularly at 35 East Eighth Street for weekly lectures and panel discussions. The Village had a reputation for bohemianism and shocking behavior since the turn of the century, but with the '60s the artistic stakes were raised. The most radical artists found their home downtown.

Not all downtown artists and composers lived in the Village, but the distinction was more than metaphorical. Performance venues dictated the split. When the Metropolitan Opera decided to present Philip Glass's *Einstein on the Beach* it represented a major breakthrough for minimalism and a downtown aesthetic, even though the Met itself took no risk. It was done on a normally dark night, and Glass and Wilson had to assume all financial responsibility for the performance. But a decidedly downtown composer had made that symbolic trip fifty blocks up Seventh Avenue to be embraced and blessed by the uptown establishment. And only after that event did Glass give up moving furniture and driving a taxicab to make a living.

Meanwhile, downtown artists were vying with one another over who could be the most outrageous. Bewilderment became an aesthetic goal. All norms were challenged. One conceptual artist had a friend shoot him in the arm with a .22-caliber pistol, the act itself being the artwork. In music La Monte Young's group of compositions 1960, which included feeding a bale of hay to a piano to see if it would eat it, carried the absurd to new heights.[9]

In many cases it was the absurd with a purpose, often a political one. Most downtown artists were radical, if not out-and-out anarchists. The most concentrated radical statements of the cult of the outrageous came from Fluxus, a loose-knit group led by George Maciunas. At one point Maciunas wrote:

> PURGE the world of bourgeois sickness, "intellectual," professional & commercialised culture, PURGE the world of dead art, imitation, artificial art, abstract art, illusionistic art, mathematical art, PURGE THE WORLD OF "EUROPEANISM"! . . . PROMOTE A REVOLUTIONARY FLOOD AND TIDE IN ART, Promote living art, anti-art, promote NON-ART REALITY to be grasped by all peoples.[10]

After World War II serialism became identified with the eastern establishment, even though many of the composers who were labeled serialists did not use serialism, or used it only loosely and in some cases briefly, and even though many had no New England roots. Milton Babbitt, for instance, was from Huntsville, Alabama, and Wallingford Riegger, still active in the 1950s, from Albany, Georgia. I will use "serialism" here, as the public did, to refer to composers who wrote in a dense, cerebral, highly chromatic, usually atonal style. Most either worked and lived in New York or taught at universities in the east.

The serialists followed the lead of the avant-garde composers of the 1920s who, finding the public at best skeptical, frequently hostile to their efforts, retreated and formed their own community. The difference between the two groups lay in the very different communities that they established. Although the 1920s avant-garde composers changed little the working mechanism of musical presentation, they not only took over the entire chain of events leading from composer's study to concert hall, but they went beyond that. They assumed the roles of critic, propagandist, and educator. In the completeness of their efforts they formed a relatively closed circle, into which the public was invited to jump, but only on the ultramodern's terms. They had as their model modernist literature, which did much the same thing, with its own journals and outlets for its authors.

Too many aspects of society had changed by 1950 for the model of the 1920s to be workable. One of the major differences was in the nature of patronage. Patronage in the 1920s was still individual; it was the capitalist emulation of the European aristocracy, the Gilded Age individual. Varèse's and Salzedo's International Composers' Guild was underwritten by Mrs. Harry Payne Whitney (née Gertrude Vanderbilt) and Mrs. Christian Holmes. Cecilia Bok and Elizabeth Sprague Coolidge supported dozens of other composers, including Varèse, Copland, and George Antheil. With the 1940s, nineteenth-century individual patronage had declined. The great fortunes had themselves become institutionalized. The Rockefeller Foundation, the Ford Foundation, the Mellon Foundation, and many others were created at this time. The serialists were particularly adept at securing support from these organizations, not the least because they also found an even more powerful and viable base of patronage. They discovered academia and bent it to their purposes.

The rational, scientific orientation of the serialist composer easily overcame any vestigial uneasiness other academics might have about the legitimacy of the composer in a university setting. This orientation also allowed the composer to speak the language of foundation grants, and a natural alignment soon developed among the composer, the foundations, and universities. The composer found a secure place and a power that he never before had. Through his position in academia, he could go after the riches of the foundations, while at the same time his position in academia certified him as an expert adviser to the foundations themselves. He could not only secure money but have a significant impact on how that money was distributed. Never before had the composer had so much control over his own destiny. Or, more accurately, never before had a handful of composers so much power over what was written.

To find a comparable situation we must return to the absolutist courts of seventeenth- and eighteenth-century Europe, when a composer by dint of his position as kapellmeister could determine what happened musically at a court, if he was politically astute. Thus, Jean-Baptiste Lully could become the musical dictator of the France of Louis XIV, breaking other composers who might challenge his position, because he had the active support of the king. To challenge Lully was to challenge Louis. When a composer in the 1940s and '50s secured one of the plums, a prestige appointment at a prestige East Coast school, especially a chair or a directorship, he slid into a position that not only guaranteed that he could compose whatever he wanted in comfort and security for the rest of his life — O tenure, O happy days — but that he could in essence determine the type of music others composed. It was simple; those who wrote music the "prestige chair" liked got the grants, got the opportunity to spend a year at the MacDowell Colony, or in Europe, or anywhere, with the time and support to write, or got the means to purchase electronic equipment, to experiment with the new tape recorder. Those who did not might, if they were lucky, teach four sections of music theory a semester, not nearly as good, but at least it earned a living. Composition could still occur, if the composer was not too exhausted from the classes and the piles of part-writing exercises, but then there was this other hitch. Who would perform his music and where? Who would record it? Who would publish it? Who advised the Carnegie board, the record companies, who was who on the New York scene? Who controlled those new publications springing up to explain what new music was about? O shades of Lully![11]

In all fairness most of the serial composers were relatively open about different types of music, and did not try to unilaterally impose an agenda. Some composers in positions of authority, particularly at conservatories, were oriented toward a more tonal style. And there were still enough composers, particularly older, more established ones, such as Copland and Barber, with sufficient prestige to leaven the atonalists' domination, although Copland himself flirted with serialism. Yet, whatever the reality, the *perception* existed, even among composers, that one had better write serial, or at least dense and complex music, to get any of the plums.

The atonal composers had, in full awareness, moved away from the general public. The argument was the same that the avant-garde composer of the 1920s used, with some new twists. The composer needed to be free to pursue his art, no matter where it led. If the public was with him, fine, if not, so be it. He was not anti-public, so that Milton Babbitt could say, "the notion that I'm not interested in the public is absolutely preposterous," but his job was not to cater to the public.[12]

Alignment of course with academia made that possible. And according to Mario Davidovsky, the atonal composer was much aware of the problem of community that this attitude engendered. As Davidovsky acknowledged, it forced the composer to establish his own community, just as the ultramoderns of the 1920s did. And here was the new twist, for in this case the new community need not be the autonomous, self-contained unit it was in the 1920s, because the composer found a welcome home: the community of composers who wrote radical, complex music became a subculture within the American university. Composers would break through to the general public occasionally, but their activities, including many of their performances, occurred in a university setting. Babbitt acknowledged, "The academy makes it possible for me to write the music I want to hear." New-music ensembles appeared in universities throughout the country, and recordings were usually subsidized either by the universities themselves or by those foundations that the academic composer advised.[13]

Membership in the academic community also affected what the composer wrote. There was the broader imperative: to fit in the music must be complex, challenging, intellectually rigorous. It must also be new and different. Jon Appleton, a composer active in the '60s and '70s, observed in 1979, "Innovation then becomes the most important criterion for approval by one's peers, and the result is an exponential increase in experimentation."[14]

Even though there are many divisions within the general category of what I have loosely amalgamated under the rubric of serialists, these composers are united in one thing: their belief in the supremacy of structural logic in music. In this regard it matters not whether the music is twelve-tone, serialist, freely atonal, or chromatically tonal. Rationality and structural logic become not just the vessel in which events occur, but the ur-source of the musical language itself and the determinant of how matters proceed. George Perle is known as a serialist who embraces tonality, at least in some vestigial form. He acknowledges Berg as a primary influence and has sought his own methodology within the broader framework of the twelve-tone system. One day, in listening to Stravinsky's *Rite of Spring* (while teaching music appreciation) he noticed that the opening bassoon solo begins on C and ends one-half step lower. He said: "There's a logic that gives us the potentiality for a real musical language, a language like that of Bach, Beethoven, and Schubert but different, because we have a different kind of tonal material. We have a 12-tone scale."[15] The result is a music that justifies fully its place in academia.

There was no greater spokesman for the Eastern school than Leonard Meyer, who was not a composer at all, at least professionally. Meyer was part theorist, part philosopher, and part cultural historian. In his learned style, which borrows ideas from many disciplines, Meyer is a late-twentieth-century Charles Seeger, although Meyer writes clearer prose. While he did not write about serialism per se, in two widely circulated books, *Emotion and Meaning in Music* and *Music, the Arts, and Ideas*, Meyer attempted a systematic explanation of musical value based on the idea of information. In the first book Meyer used information theory explicitly; in the second he backed away from it somewhat, but nevertheless embraced its core ideas. Even in *Music, the Arts, and Ideas* value is equated with information: "If a situation is highly organized so that the possible consequents have a high degree of probability, then if the probably occurs, the information communicated by the message (what we have been calling a musical event) is minimal. If, on the other hand, the musical situation is less predictable so that the antecedent-consequent relationship does *not* have a high degree of probability, then the information contained in the musical message will be high."[16]

Meyer essentially restates Babbitt's idea, found in his 1947 article, that the best music is the most "efficient." And by efficient Babbitt meant that which conveys the most information, that is the least cliché ridden. Meyer is very specific about clichés. By nature they are predictable, hence probable, hence "less illuminating than great poems. They are the difference between Johann Sebastian Bach and Francesco Geminiani."[17]

No type of Western music could be more efficient than twelve-tone serialism. The composer was freed, not just from the diatonic limits of an eight-tone scale, but from the harmonic patterns inevitable with tonality. All permutations were admissible, and equally probable. Tonal music of course demanded that a tonic be established and that it be reasserted in some manner at the end. Such an act by its very nature embodied cliché. In serialism the piece could be launched without tonal scaffolding, and the hierarchy of certain interval combinations, for example, 3–2–1 in the melody or 5–1 in the bass, did not limit the composer's imagination.

Even if a piece were not serial, in Meyer's scheme value equates closely with complexity. It is no wonder that the academic composers found minimalism puzzling and threatening. Minimalism did more than reject complexity. Minimalism reveled in an aesthetic based on repetition, the diametric opposite of Meyer's and Babbitt's efficiency.

Many value judgments of the second half of the twentieth century have been predicated on the premise of a musical logic, sometimes as if that logic had been established a priori. Elliott Carter has become infamous in Ives circles for his report of Ives "jacking up the dissonance," that is, adding extra dissonance to his manuscripts many years after they were originally composed.

That may well have occurred, but it seems that Carter and Ives occupied two entirely different regions on the American musical landscape. Carter underscored this with his comments about the premiere of Ives's *Concord Sonata:* "In form and aesthetic it is basically conventional, not unlike the Liszt Sonata, full of paraphernalia of the overdressy sonata school. . . . Behind all this confused texture there is a lack of logic which repeated hearings can never clarify. . . . the esthetic is naïve, often too naïve to express serious thoughts, frequently depending on quotation of well-known American tunes, with little comment, possibly charming, but certainly trivial."[18]

In this brief statement Carter capsulates much of the rhetoric and beliefs of post–World War II academics: an emphasis on logic and accepted principles of structure, dismissal of that which doesn't conform as naive and trivial, and a disdain for the vernacular. (Babbitt loved the vernacular, but he seldom brought it up until later years.) Transpose this statement 150 years, change the names to Billings and Mason, and we have played out once again a fundamental tension in American musical history, between nature and science, and less overtly between European sophistication and American naïveté. And like the early-nineteenth-century musical war between the champions of a native psalmody and the hymnodic reformers, the stakes were high: patronage that mattered most. The nineteenth-century fight was for the church's soul (and psalm-book purchases): whether western emotionally charged revivalism, or a more restrained, intellectual eastern worship would prevail; the twentieth-century clash was for a home for the composer, the university. And in both cases the battle was waged with the utmost sincerity: Mason firmly believed that in calling for a more scientific style in church music he was serving God and man by bringing man closer to God and to the proper Christian spirit. Babbitt, Carter, Sessions, equally believed in a music founded on the twentieth-century deity, science, and its home, the temple of academia.

But in these recent struggles classical music remains captive to Puritanism. Only today it is not called that. It is disguised under the term "education." Music whose appeal is not obvious, music that requires effort to grasp, serious music designed to challenge and better, that is the provenance of education. This fundamental principle even underscored the very definition of classical music itself. In one of the classic formulations, H. Wiley Hitchcock, seeking a more verbally accurate alternative to "classical" and "popular," distinguished between a "cultivated" and a "vernacular" tradition. "Cultivated" here means what most people call classical, with the clear imperative, which Hitchcock articulates, that such music be "cultivated consciously."[19]

The composer Libby Larsen speaks of the "duty to educate," a phrase that could come right out of Puritanism. It should be stressed that Larsen uses the phrase only to disagree with it, but her terminology is dead on. For many years education was seen as the savior of classical music. If the population could be educated to it, then they would come. This helped justify music departments in universities throughout the country, and courses in "music appreciation" as a staple of general education. The term itself is instructive. Composers wrote books on the subject, Aaron Copland's *Listening to Music* being only one of many.[20]

In this context in the classical-music world, complexity and difficulty are synonymous with value. Yet for all their emphasis on science, on innovation, experimentation, and the new, the outlook of serialist composers was remarkably backward-looking. This went beyond a legacy of Puritanism. Serialists had inherited and accepted wholeheartedly two romantic notions: that of the pure, abstract work of art, and that of organicism. The former provided an overarching ideal, the latter an approach, manifested in an emphasis on structure and musical logic.

The serial composer looked to the past, perhaps too strongly. For the serial composer the ghosts of Beethoven and Brahms, not coincidentally the two pillars of the German romantic tradition, were very much alive. Donald Martino, speaking of serial composers, said: "There was, and still is, the prevailing notion among us that it's pretty damn difficult to write tonal music in the 20th century and think it compares favorably with Beethoven and Brahms."[21]

The serialists' identification with the nineteenth century went beyond that, however. Martin Brody, a Babbitt apologist, in describing Babbitt's alliance with science and scientific language when discussing music, quoted an especially complex and knotty sentence of his arguing that there is "but one kind of language, one kind of method for the verbal formulation of 'concepts' and the verbal analysis of such formulations: 'scientific' language and 'scientific method.'" Brody then observed: "The flow of the argument — from concept to analysis to prediction and back to analysis and concept — rationalizes Babbitt's methodological insistence on scientific language."[22] Such flow, however, is the methodology of the old science, of linear Newtonian science, in which causality was tantamount to prediction. The new science of the twentieth century, from quantum mechanics to chaos theory to nonlinear dynamics, recognizes a less predictable but more powerful and flexible approach to addressing problems and understanding organizational relationships.

The doctrine most central to the serialists, however, the concept underlying Babbitt's use of science and his attitude toward composition, was a very nineteenth-century one: Progress. The nineteenth century spelled it with a capital P; it was the engine that reshaped not only the United States but the Western world. The twentieth-century avant-gardist put it in lower case, but like morality, it lost its importance in name only, not in fact.

Milton Babbitt may have railed about what *High Fidelity* did to his article, "The Composer as Specialist," when they placed the title "Who Cares If You Listen?" on it, but it didn't matter. The title misses the main point anyway: behind every sentence, every word, in the article is the nineteenth-century notion of Progress. Progress, disguised here as science, justifies everything the composer does: what he writes, why he writes it, why he takes the positions he does. Ernst Krenek identified serialism squarely within both progress and a linear view of evolution: "Atonality, then, appears as a state of the musical language that must be accepted as the result of evolution so long as the existence of a permanent motivating force behind the chain of historical events is acknowledged — a force which because of its one-way directedness is identified with progress."[23]

Other composers may not have spoken of the doctrine of progress by name, but the idea is fundamental to the attitudes of many who embraced atonality. Like Krenek they grounded their musical position in a long evolutionary cycle that began with advancing chromaticism in the nineteenth century, finally to culminate with the complete destruction of tonality in the twentieth. The serialists, in their view, had reached the pinnacle of the fitness landscape, and consequently Boulez and Wuorinen could dismiss anyone that did not join them on the new mountain as "useless."[24]

The avant-garde position, predicated on the twin notions of idealism and progress, resides in a thoroughgoing romanticism. The composer creates not for an audience but rather for an ideal. In such a context how the listener responds is unimportant. In another sense it is vitally important: the composer has an obligation to challenge, to be ahead of the public. He is the moral compass providing insights that the average person is neither ready for nor capable of understanding. If the audience gets it, if it likes what it hears, the composer is simply not doing his job. He has become a mere entertainer, or worse, he is no further along in his understanding than the audience itself. Of course no twentieth-century composer would use the word *moral* in this context. But one can stay ahead of the audience only if there is a line to be drawn, only if the art of music is viewed linearly. The result was a curious paradox: in a non-teleological style, stylistic teleology was all-important, and however the serialists' attitudes are framed, underpinning it all was progress.

While the East Coast composer was writhing in these final throes of the nineteenth century, new, radical ideas were coming from the West Coast:

Henry Cowell, not only his tone clusters, but later his interest in world cultures; John Cage, with new sounds and later indeterminacy; Harry Partch, and his unique instruments, tonal materials, and ideas about theater; and later La Monte Young, with strangely static drones that presaged the minimalist movement itself.

The Heliotropic Myth

The visions of these westerners give twentieth-century music a curious historical twist: the heliotropic myth in reverse. These composers all grew up in the western United States, all were active on the West Coast, particularly the Bay area, but only when they reached the east did their work come to fruition. The one exception is Harry Partch, who only visited New York briefly, and who alone received little recognition until after his death. Except for Partch all of these composers migrated to New York City, and after World War II, when downtown-uptown replaced east-west as the spatial metaphor for musical orientation, Greenwich Village became the launching pad for their assaults on eastern, uptown values.

Of the three principal composers active before World War II — Henry Cowell, Harry Partch, and John Cage — only Cowell had established himself in the twenties. And the Cowell of the 1920s is an ambivalent figure in this east-west division. He was in New York during much of the 1910s and '20s, and he was heavily influenced by Seeger, Ruggles, and Ornstein. His music seemed to be about dissonance, especially tone clusters, although the clusters themselves differed markedly from either Ives's (whom he knew nothing about in the 1910s) and Ornstein's.

Like many composers of the 1930s Cowell turned away from the dissonances, in his case tone clusters, and the radical experimentation of 1920s modernism. Unlike many eastern composers, however, he turned not to American folk roots but rather, befitting his West Coast heritage, toward a more global orientation, one that in particular looked toward Asia.

With Partch we encounter the myth of American individualism more directly and overtly than with any other composer, including Charles Ives. To virtually every commentator, whether favorably disposed toward Partch's music or not, Partch is the quintessential rugged individualist. Even a sampling of the many citations to this effect would constitute a litany worthy of the most elaborate ritualistic church. More important, however, the context in which the term appears provides real insight into the deeper meaning of the myth in American culture.

Partch is praised for his "self-reliance" and willingness to go his own way:

"He . . . followed his own musical path and created an entirely new musical world." These qualities characterize the pioneer, and writers link Partch directly to the pioneer spirit: "With his strong convictions and rugged individualism, Partch aptly conveys the stereotype of the American pioneer in the most positive sense." "Harry was a highly individualistic person, a pioneer spirit." Partch is also associated with the west in general, but it is the earlier west of self-reliance: "Harry Partch was the most important first musician of 'The West' to reclaim the art of music from the industrial revolution. . . . It was as an individual artist that he built instruments, tuned them, and wrote for them memorable musics."[25]

Partch's "salty, slangy musical language," comparable to that of Mark Twain, its "jaunty self-confidence, and harty folksiness," and its "truth," identify him as American. Other writers are less clear why Partch is American, but to many he is *the* American composer: "Harry Partch is the truest American composer yet." He is "the most American composer of all, the center and progenitor of our indigenous music culture." "Mr. Partch's music is characteristically American and could only have been written by a native." "He was a true American original."[26]

A self-reliant, autonomous, down-to-earth pioneer who spoke the language of the people, Partch exemplified the American myth. Writers associate him with Charles Ives in particular and even Carl Ruggles in this regard. "In some ways, Harry Partch belongs to that earlier, peculiarly American breed of stubborn and wonderful individualists whose best-known representatives are Ives and Ruggles."[27] Tom Johnson provides a most succinct summary, not only of Ives and Partch, but of those traits that make each appealing to the American psyche: "The two men had much in common. Ives was born in 1874, Partch not until 1901, but both were made of the same rugged individualistic stuff. Americans to the core, they thumbed their noses at just about all the conventions of their time, took completely independent routes, and left behind them large bodies of substantial works."[28]

Partch himself was much aware of the respect for rugged individualism that pervaded American society, but he also recognized the dilemma this created for the artist. "Finally, there is the tradition of rugged individualism," he said, "which we Americans put great store by, in economic fields. I'm afraid that we have not proved to be quite so courageous about rugged individualism in the creative arts."[29]

Partch sensed a problem, very real to him, as his own individualistic path, appealing as it may have been as saga, did not translate in musical circles to a career or even acceptance. Thus he saw the maverick tradition end at the edge of the musical frontier. But the problem may not have been his geography, however metaphorical. He may have mistaken fantasy, both his and America's, for reality. The idea of a pioneer, self-reliant, individualistic spirit was strong in America, but in reality does not hold up well to scrutiny. As we have seen, more often than not success came from communal action. Partch the artist may have been right about the absence of individualism in American music, but not for the reasons that he thought. American tastes in the arts just may not be that inconsistent with what American society is really all about.

In other words, with Partch, his attitudes, his music, reactions to his music, and his own response to those reactions, we confront more baldly and directly than anytime before the question of individuality and community in American beliefs and American society.

First, it should be stressed, Partch *was* the rugged individualist he is portrayed to be. But what does that mean? And what does it not mean? He did not seek obscurity, or consciously remove himself from the musical world at large. On the contrary his efforts to be recognized, to have his music performed, and to find a niche, are heroic. He simply refused to compromise. Driven by an inner creativity that seems mind-boggling, once he set his path in that room in New Orleans, he never veered from his own inner spark. From his early experiments with just intonation, and the theoretical working out it entailed, to the later stage works in which "2 ½ tons of musical instruments," later to grow to five, were often the focus, Partch maintained his vision with unerring constancy.

The instruments themselves epitomize Partch's determination. He never had a permanent home, and was forced to move literally dozens of times (not counting the years in the 1930s when he was truly homeless), sometimes several times in one year. At one point he recorded fifteen major moves in sixteen years. But he nevertheless managed to drag the instruments around and keep them in working condition, no small task in itself, as they had to be not only repaired but tuned constantly, and he regularly rebuilt them to improve them. The effort of dealing with the instruments cost Partch much physically and psychologically, particularly when they were in storage or when he was forced to move with no prospects for a place, but only once or twice late in life, as he began to weaken physically, did he even consider abandoning them.

Partch's no-compromise attitude was in part due to his vision, but also to his sheer lack of social and political skills. He was fixed, he was dedicated, and he was demanding, often to those people that wanted to help him the most. Several opportunities to affiliate with universities were lost through Partch's own difficult nature and lack of diplomacy, and many of his strongest supporters frequently found his demands exasperating and unrealistic. Had Partch a better set of social skills, his vision could have much more easily become reality.

Both Partch and Ives chose a path that would allow them to compose what they wanted, rather than what the marketplace or a patron demanded. But what values do the artistic results reflect? That is, what do their compositions tell us, not only about their own mind-set, but about the nature of their society? Here we encounter a paradox, for the two composers most lauded as particularly American for their rugged individualism wrote music that, in many and different ways, essentially celebrated community.

Partch's music is essentially communal. It is fundamentally ritual, itself a communal act, and the ensemble performance of it demands that each player enter totally into the event. There can be no standing apart and playing the notes, a typical event for many Western ensembles. The players don't each do their own thing, more or less ignoring what else is going on, as Cage often prescribes. Partch held long rehearsals and demanded that the players form a unit, a community. He held up as exemplary the final rehearsal for the recording of *Oedipus*, done in 1954, which lasted twelve hours, from 3 P.M. until 3 A.M. Everyone stayed, even though they had commitments the next day, and even though no one received any compensation.[30]

Partch's biggest pieces, *Oedipus, Revelation in the Courthouse Park, The Bewitched, Delusion of the Fury,* suggest a communal theater. Standing somewhere between Broadway theater and opera, they deal with Greek, Japanese, and even African themes, and not only the individual characters but the troupe itself, the various parts, the dancers, the musicians, have a symbolic and allegorical quality. Performances can be stylized, as when the characters assume Japanese masks in *Revelation* or makeup in *Delusion,* or the characters can seem as American as Elvis Presley, as the rock singer Dion was in *Revelation.* Yet an element of ritual pervades all of Partch's theatrical music, and this quality of ritual does much to engender a sense of community.

Partch's music became popular in the '60s, and his appeal was mostly to young people. His support at the University of Illinois came predominantly from students: his productions, of *Revelation in the Courthouse Park* and *Water! Water!* were funded by the Student Association, and performances were packed. Students themselves rallied around Partch when they discovered that he was leaving, with the local paper publishing an editorial, "Keep Partch Here."[31]

Part of the appeal was political. When dissatisfaction with the prevailing social order was festering and about to erupt among young people, Partch himself projected pure anti-establishment. It was no act; Partch's dislike of musical academia was deep-seated and overt. He advocated the complete overthrow of traditional music education. And Partch, unable to fit in, stuck out like a sore thumb. He was a cantankerous curmudgeon, who dressed and looked the part.[32]

Beyond the rebelliousness, which made identification with youth in a time of rebellion easy, Partch's embracing of the world's culture, his idealism and spiritual bent, his sardonic humor, and, in Eric Salzman's words, his "involvement with young people in a kind of communal ideal of music-making," further cemented this connection. A work such as *Revelation* was closer to a rock concert than a classical concert, or even a classical opera. In describing the music as "commonplace," Peter Yates explained: "What had begun and been dismissed by many of us, years ago, as 'corn' had become, in this ritual expression of the commonplace, the meaning of the action."[33]

Ives himself, seemingly so thoroughly New England and Puritan, is often identified with Partch as the individualistic composer par excellence. Yet Ives also celebrated community in his music. His most enduring works were either about spiritual quest or communal action. *Three Places in New England* was about three events, two communal, one personal. Other pieces, such as the holiday celebrations that Ives memorialized, or the *Yale-Princeton Football Game*, or *Hanover Square*, are about groups of people joined in a frivolous or serious bond. Even the *Concord Sonata* is as much a celebration of the spirit of the town as the individuals portrayed in the movements.

Ives did see spiritual quest as a solitary pursuit. Hence his respect for Thoreau, and the artistic depth of such works as *The Unanswered Question* and the Fourth Symphony. In the Fourth Symphony the third movement is the communal answer, posed by organized religion. That Ives found it unsatisfactory, "an expression of the reaction of life into formalism and religion," reinforces his belief that each person must find his or her own path.

Thus Ives inverted the prototypical American character, a rugged individualist who seeks spiritual solace in a communal ritual. For Ives spiritual search is very personal and individual, but secular life, one's daily here and now, is intimately bound up to community. For Ives it was the New England village, mythologized by nineteenth-century New Englanders who looked back upon a world that never existed. The New England revival, which symbolized in many ways an imagined community, became an ideal. But nevertheless it was community.

And when Ives turned to politics, it was the politics of the community, the masses, that was the locus of his beliefs. Ives drew on the Republican heritage as described by J. G. A. Pocock, which had at its heart civic responsibility. In this view of republicanism (as a political philosophy, not to be confused with the Republican party), the individual placed civic good ahead of personal gain. Not only is his song *Majority* about that, but the related essay, *The Majority*, as well. Most readers are struck by the sheer naïveté and impracticality of Ives's political solutions, for instance his belief that citizens will vote the public good above narrow interest, or will voluntarily put limits on their potential income. But if one accepts Pocock's view of republicanism, then Ives's suggestions make perfectly good sense. Ives was out of touch; this philosophy, whose historical basis at any time was questionable, had by the early twentieth century been thoroughly displaced. But it was a philosophy of community, one that recognized community as central, and like John Cage in regard to personal expression, Ives took it to its logical conclusion.[34]

Cage, like Partch and Cowell, was born in California, but geography seemed to play little role in his work. He studied with Schoenberg, who lived in Los Angeles only because world events brought him there. Schoenberg hardly represented the ethos of southern California. Most of Cage's professional life was spent in New York City, and although he first began working with dancers in the Pacific Northwest, and met Merce Cunningham there, it was only when both were in New York that their artistic collaboration blossomed. Even Cage's interest in Zen Buddhism began in New York, when he encountered D. T. Suzuki, who was lecturing at Columbia University.

Cage's seeming indifference to place mirrors his own disassociation from community. Cage called himself an anarchist, although he was not a politically active one. The body politic simply did not interest Cage the way it did Ives or Seeger. Where it did, in issues such as the environment, it was in a broadly philosophical way. Cage was no Greenpeacer. Cage himself professed to belong to no group, even shunning academic appointments because he felt it would hinder his own freedom to do precisely what he wanted. Although Cage is the spiritual father of Fluxus, he himself claimed no allegiance to the movement.[35]

Cage's music is fundamentally anticommunal. Performers do not interact on stage. Each has an assigned part, which often leaves considerable latitude for the performers to determine precisely what they will do, but usually each is expected to perform his or her part with little attention given to the others. This is partly dictated by the uncertainty about what the others will be doing, but even indeterminate music can be based on interaction among players. In a Cage piece the performers essentially coexist on stage, and Cage goes so far as to caution performers against rehearsing their parts together. Cage's collaboration with Cunningham proceeded in the same manner. Often it was less a collaboration than two simultaneous performances. Each created his own work without reference to the other, and only in the final stages did they bring them together. The result was a mini-happening, but most remarkable is that music and dance often fused very effectively. At some level Cage and Cunningham were attuned to each other's art.

Cage's anticommunalism is entirely consistent with his purpose of non-intention, a stance that almost demands some form of anarchy, but the inevitable result is a detachment from the other as well as the self. Cage's philosophy is one of tolerance, but one at odds with the interactive nature of American society.

Some aspects of minimalism are curiously close to Cage's position. Steve Reich's phase-shifting pieces parallel Cage's music in regard to the interaction of players on stage. Reich's music is completely written out, in conventional notation, and performances are relatively straightforward by modern music standards: musicians play regular instruments in a normal manner. The result itself is often a tight kaleidoscope of interlocking parts. Yet the players do not interact as much as hold their own against other parts, which may be identical except for a slight rhythmic displacement. It is a community of individuality and steadfastness, not conformance. Nothing can be more disastrous to a Reich performance than for one player to listen to and fall into line with another.

La Monte Young specifically disdained the idea of community. Young broke with Fluxus at least in part because of his unease at being a member of a community. In describing the break, Young said: "George Maciunas was very socialist and very communal, and I'm not a good group member. I am really an individual."[36]

La Monte Young sees his music as meditative and, as such, anticommunal. Marion Zazeela's lighting contributes directly to that. In an interview with Cole Gagne, Young and Zazeela stressed that with the lighting, even in a traditional theater, you feel less part of the crowd and more alone with your own thoughts. It is meditative music. Zazeela: "I think the direction of my lighting and the sculptures is towards self-reflection and a meditative atmosphere. If you actually get involved in looking at the mobiles and the lights and the shadows and thinking about the whole transfer of images that you're seeing there, it forces you to be introspective and to reflect it back on yourself."[37]

Young had experimented with lighting in a crude way while at Berkeley, although the effect seems to have been more terror than meditation. His piece *Vision* consisted of eleven sounds in thirteen minutes. Most of the sounds were unconventional, and the performers were scattered throughout the hall. The piece occurred while the audience sat in total darkness. According to Young, people in the audience laughed, giggled, and some got upset. He repeated the experiment with another piece, this time informing the audience of what was to happen. Young's purpose was partly to break the glare of the spotlight and the focus on the performer, and to develop a new composer-performer-audience relationship. But there was also a deeper purpose: "I began to realize that, if the lights are out, something very special can happen because you get into that sense of being alone with yourself (which many people can't handle)."[38]

The Edge of Chaos

As the linear universe that Isaac Newton described began to disintegrate under the probing of twentieth-century science, a new concept, the edge of chaos, appeared. The term comes from chaos theory, part of a broader constellation of ideas that go under several names: complexity theory, complex adaptive systems, nonlinear dynamics. For decades twentieth-century scientists and mathematicians had recognized three states in complex dynamic systems: fixed, periodic, and chaotic.[39] But somewhere between the fixed or periodic states and chaos was an uncharted area, where a system was poised metaphorically on the edge, or brink, not clearly falling into one or the other. About twenty years ago scientists began to concentrate on this fourth state, which they dubbed the "edge of chaos." They discovered that this was where interesting things happen. This, rather than chaos itself, is where chaos theory focuses.

As many practitioners of complexity theory have stressed, its principles apply not only to physical and biological objects but to societies and cultures as well. It also applies to history, for the edge of chaos is one of the grand themes of popular American history. For many writers this is where American history itself unfolds, this is where those defining moments of the American experience occur. Frederick Jackson Turner's frontier thesis, an idea that resonated strongly in the twentieth-century mind, is itself a striking portrayal of the edge of chaos in action. To Turner the frontier, that constantly moving line where uninhabited land gave way to settled land, defined America. Of course the land was never uninhabited, but for Turner as indeed for most nineteenth-century Americans the issue was whether Europeans had occupied it.

Important in the frontier thesis was the act of settlement itself. Along that line American character was forged. In Turner's own words:

> To the frontier the American intellect owes its striking characteristics. That coarseness and strength combined with acuteness and inquisitiveness; that practical, inventive turn of mind, quick to find expedients; that masterful

grasp of material things, lacking in the artistic but powerful to effect great ends; that restless, nervous energy; that dominant individualism, working for good and evil, and withal that buoyancy and exuberance which comes with freedom — these are traits of the frontier, or traits called out of else-where because of the existence of the frontier.[40]

The historical validity of Turner's thesis is not the issue here. What is im-portant is its mythification. Its popularity was immense, and Turner, thirty-two years old when he presented his paper, became a celebrity. From its in-ception it struck a chord in the popular imagination. For many it provided an answer to America's own uniqueness, and the early inhabitants of the fron-tier, from Daniel Boone and Davy Crockett to the cowboys of the west, were at the center of the myth.

A similar idea, that civilization was forged when it was poised between void and overrefinement, had been voiced by Emerson a half-century ear-lier, although he did not mention the frontier, and his metaphor is temporal rather than spatial. Emerson describes that moment when civilization arises but remains close to nature: "In history, the great moment is when the savage is just ceasing to be a savage. . . . Everything good in nature and the world is in that moment of transition, when the swarthy juices still flow plentifully from nature, but their astringency or acridity is got out by ethics and human-ity."[41]

Both Turner and Emerson recognized a special edge that existed in American history, the edge of chaos between nature and civilization. In their view that was where American character was formed. When civilization or individuals were in that delicate balance did they rise to their best. Their us-age corresponds precisely to the concept as found in chaos theory: "For what can the teeming molecules that hustled themselves into self-reproducing metabolisms, the cells coordinating their behaviors to form multicelled or-ganisms, the ecosystems, and even economic and political systems have in common? The wonderful possibility, to be held as a working hypothesis, bold but fragile, is that on many fronts, life evolves toward a regime that is poised between order and chaos. The evocative phrase that points to the working hypothesis is this: *life exists at the edge of chaos*."[42]

In stressing the closing of the frontier, Turner sounded a death knell for America's own self-identity. The closing of the frontier took away those very elements that had made Americans, in their own minds, superior. It took away that special relationship between man and nature that Jonathan Ed-wards, James Fenimore Cooper, Emerson, Henry David Thoreau, Walt Whitman, and many others had delineated. It necessitated either the founding of another myth or the laying in of a strain of nostalgia absent throughout much of the nineteenth century.

Nostalgia generally won out. The cowboy endured, in fiction and particularly the movies, and Americans sought new frontiers, be they in space, science, or more remote parts of the globe. The metaphor of the frontier dominated much American rhetoric, and politicians from Theodore Roosevelt to John Kennedy discovered it could be a stirring call to action.

Curiously the myth never really took hold in music. Billings and Heinrich tried; neither succeeded. Billings lived in a time of transition, when the Puritan idea of nature as desert was only beginning to loosen and the romantic view of nature grand and sublime had not yet taken hold. Billings identified closely with a raw nature, too closely for many. Heinrich, like many European immigrants, was overwhelmed with the vastness and the grandeur of the natural world about him. And Heinrich's views were shared; he rode a crest to which he was precisely contemporaneous, the glorification of nature by the Hudson River school painters and of the noble savage by both visual artists and writers.

Heinrich chose precisely the same topics that brought wealth, fame, and immortality to Thomas Cole, Albert Bierstadt, and James Fenimore Cooper. But Heinrich failed miserably. There are practical and purely artistic explanations: the difficulty of his works was often beyond what American orchestras could handle, and consequently performances were rare. When they did occur they were often unsatisfactory. But his music was performed, and at least an approximation of his music was heard. More critically, however, Heinrich, the "Beethoven of America," was, to put it bluntly, no Beethoven. His own talent was much more limited.

Billings, while untrained formally, possessed a true musical talent, yet his portrayals of nature seem lost on both his and later times. He suffered from the shifting musical ideals of the generation that followed him. In the early nineteenth century, advocates of a reform hymnody, who wished to impose a more scientific style on sacred music in particular, transformed him into a villain in the story of musical progress. His melodic gift could not be denied, but his settings were labeled crude and naive.

There is more to the problem than Heinrich's or Billings's own musical limitations, however. Music remained immune from the grand nineteenth-century myth, or at least its musical manifestations were not recognized. Simply put music was not the stuff of myth. It was too close. Music was everyday, part of life. It was at home, it was in the street, it was an activity. Federalists may have rioted in the theater when the songs of their political opponents were played, they may have, as they did from the seventeenth century, loosed themselves in an orgy of cacophonous wailing after the minister's sermon, or they may have danced themselves to exhaustion in a tavern, but no one thought of those activities as art, least of all as a mysterious combination of nature and civilization. Music may have sounded chaotic, as according to all reports performances often did, but it was not that mysterious edge of chaos. It was not, in Emerson's conception, where character was formed. It may not be coincidental that of all nineteenth-century intellectuals Emerson had little use for music.

In a discussion of Franz Schubert in 1992, the *New York Times* critic Edward Rothstein wrote, "Our cultural pantheon practically requires marginality and alienation as an entrance requirement, expanding the Romantic myths of the artist we contend we are rejecting."[43] Although he was speaking of Schubert, Rothstein voiced more generally the perception of the artist culture at the turn of the twenty-first century. Distance between the artist and the norms of society must remain, and those artists that are most successful convince us that they stand apart. When in the late nineteenth century music was finally recognized as art in America, European connection, by birth or study, was sufficient for the composer to prove an exoticness. That changed with the 1920s, as in organizing, the ultramoderns were able to implant a different view of the artist, one who goes beyond the norms of society, and who provides a decidedly unique and, most important, individual vision. That new view stayed, and became so embedded in twentieth-century American culture that its historical grounding is no longer recognized. And as American society as a whole became more industrialized and regimented, it fit that most fundamental myth of all, American individualism. Rothstein's comment essentially confirms just how deeply embedded the concept of the artist as maverick in American society is. Maverick composers are about more than a musical art—to many they are the American ideal made manifest.

CHAPTER 12

Looking Forward

"The End of the Renaissance?"[1]

W HEN I WAS A GRADUATE STUDENT, then a young professor, the music appreciation business was in its heyday. Courses like "Listening to Music," "Introduction to Music," or "Music Appreciation" proliferated on every campus, large and small, and as a graduate student I was assigned to teach several. There was no question about the purpose of this enterprise. Our job was to educate listeners to the specific point of view that music of the Western fine arts tradition was pure, abstract, and nonreferential. While most of us in the field believed that fervently, this was not, unfortunately, how most concertgoers experienced music.

For many people instrumental music served as a spur to the imagination, and visual images, even entire scenarios, were often acted out in the listener's mind. Even as sophisticated a critic as Paul Rosenfeld, an ardent supporter of radical modernism, admitted this. Hearing *Tristan und Isolde* on a phonograph conjured up for him "the perception of a dark, deep-lying region of earth, the hearth of somber flames"; on hearing the entr'acte from Musorgsky's *Khovanshchina*, Rosenfeld imagined "the colossal tonnage of mountains, the globe's entire weight, and with it the entire world's tragedy: continuous funeral marches endless as the mountains' lines; the vital progress from darkness into gray and into darkness again; the overwhelming sum of human pain and human defeat."[1] In works like Berlioz's *Symphonie fantastique* or Richard Strauss's tone poems, the vision may have been precisely targeted, a smart bomb of the aural imagination. Or it may have been more nebulous, in the inner turmoil heard in the symphonies of Beethoven.

But for much of the public, including many musically sophisticated and adept musicians, the world of sound created a world of image.

Advocates of a strictly musical approach shuddered at this type of response, considering it distinctly inferior to a more sophisticated one that involved direct confrontation with the music as it unfolded. In those music appreciation courses program music of course could be finessed: if it is good program music, it is good music without the program, so the argument ran. And part of our job was to unprogram students. In this new order musical imagination, for the listener, was to be on purely musical terms. It was a closed system: musical events implied other musical events, and the listener compared his or her purely musical imagination with that of the composer. It was also a game, although only the boldest dared utter such heresy.[2]

This entire line of thinking was explicated in detail by Leonard Meyer and later Eugene Narmour. In several books Meyer discussed how a piece generates musical expectations in the mind of the competent listener (notice the word *competent*), the unfolding of a piece being an inner dialogue between what happens and what the competent listener expects to happen. Narmour, a student of Meyer, codified this process further with an "implication-realization" model.[3]

But when Meyer confronted music of the post–World War II avant-garde, he was puzzled. It no longer conformed to his model, at least not apparently, and he was forced to conclude that Western music had undergone some sort of paradigm shift. He articulated this in a famous article titled "The End of the Renaissance?" by which he meant that teleological structures based on large-scale tonal projections, characteristic of music since the Renaissance, had run their course.[4]

Meyer was right about the end of the Renaissance, but not for the reasons he thought. The postwar paradigm shift was not about the style of a piece but about the nature of the art itself. In the past forty years the very idea of music as a separate, independent art has fundamentally eroded. And Meyer, like many others, had not recognized the implications of this. An awareness of changes in the musical landscape has grown dramatically in the past ten years, but the ominous warnings about the current state of classical music that one hears almost daily are still based on the assumption of music's autonomy. Until artists, critics, and administrators come to terms with the way our musical world has changed, further solutions will fall as flat as most previous ones have. This chapter highlights symbolically some steps in the twentieth century that have led to that change — a complete historical accounting of it would be a book, and a massive one, in itself — with special attention paid to the role of American mavericks in bringing the change about.

In the early twentieth century the radio and the record player seemed poised to revolutionize musical culture. But it turns out they were essentially extensions of the nineteenth-century aesthetic, with its emphasis on disembodied sound. In some ways they only heightened it, as they removed even the visual activity of performance itself. But we are in a different world now. Today visual images are constantly supplied for music of all sorts. With the rise of television and the growing influence of film and the Internet, the visual dimension is no longer left to the listener's imagination but has become the responsibility of the composer or the collaborator. The visual image has become the carrier of the artistic message, and music its support. Music no longer stands alone, and is not expected to. Such seems to occur only in universities and conservatories.

The end of the Renaissance was heralded not by the serialists or the free atonalists that defined an avant-garde style after World War II, those composers Meyer focused upon, but by a group of experimentalists who rejected, each in their own way, the premises upon which the very definition of art music rested. Composers that we have been following, Varèse, Cage, Partch, and others, not only sought new ways of doing things but expanded the idea of music itself to encompass dimensions that undermined seriously and fatally the closed universe the serialists had constructed.

The perspective of the postwar experimentalists was so radical that accommodation with tradition was all but impossible. They flouted the most fundamental assumptions by which the classical art proceeded, which ironically earned them the title "maverick." But because the maverick *tradition* was so strong, thanks to the early twentieth century, these later mavericks were heard; in fact because their vision seemed so beyond the bounds of acceptability the public was fascinated, and gave them the audience they might not have had otherwise.

To be fair, these changes may have occurred without this particular group of mavericks, because society itself was changing. But the maverick in this instance pointed the way, and suggested possibilities that later composers, performers, and public came to embrace. Whether driven by anger, bemusement, or experimental curiosity, the maverick laid the groundwork for the emergence of a new musical culture, the implications of which are still unclear to much of the musical world.

Yet what may be the turning point toward a new musical culture occurred outside of music, and was ushered in by someone with little knowledge of, interest in, or sensitivity to music. A critical step was taken on November 13, 1940, when Walt Disney's *Fantasia* premiered. In giving expression to his own rich visual imagination, Disney created a piece both ripe with potential and threatening in implications. In retrospect *Fantasia* is late-twentieth-century musical culture's Pandora's box, for with *Fantasia* the visual dimension could no longer be downplayed, or relegated to the listener's own fantasy. It took many years for the full implications of what *Fantasia* had loosed to become apparent, but in retrospect it was both a preview and a portent.

No question *Fantasia* was a technical tour de force. The sound in the movie house itself was a major breakthrough, for it was the first motion picture to present multitrack surround sound. In an age before the tape recorder, capturing the tracks, mixing them, and transferring them to film required pathbreaking techniques and three solid months of recording and experimentation. The film was so ahead of its time that it had to be shown as a traveling road show because only specially equipped movie houses could present it.

Fantasia itself is transitional; music and the visual entered into an uneasy balance, the aural holding its own only because its position in the minds of listeners had not yet been severely eroded. As the visual image has become more deeply embedded in our culture, the relationship has become more imbalanced, clearly tipping toward the visual. By now, practically all of us have seen a Fourth of July fireworks display choreographed to music like the one I witnessed recently in State College, Pennsylvania. An audience of two hundred thousand thrilled to the excitement of Rossini's "William Tell Overture," the principal theme of *Star Wars*, and the "Battle Hymn of the Republic," cued as they were by the visual spectacular tied so closely to the music that even offbeat syncopations of the exploding fireworks were metrically in time. I seriously doubt that the music alone would have aroused such enthusiasm.

Much of the response to *Fantasia* was predictable. Film critics hailed it, music critics were either reserved or openly hostile. Some music critics expressed dismay that Disney had somehow defiled or demeaned great masterpieces, and in doing so had distorted the nature of music. This approach is also apparent with later film critics and historians, who found Disney's ideas puerile. In his *History of the Cinema from Its Origins to 1970*, Eric Rhode wrote that Disney, who admitted "to having no ear for classical music," "adorned Beethoven's Pastoral Symphony with drawings of a coyness that seems to mock the feeling in the music," and that such a display "presses the mind back to a nursery view of things, bounded on every side by mass-produced Disney toys."[5]

B. H. Haggin was particularly outraged because Disney had "failed when he set out to be faithful to large-scale musical content and structure."

He "did not even remotely represent the substance and organic development and structural complexity of Bach's music or exert anything remotely comparable with the power of the music's formal eloquence." To Haggin the film was built on the false premise "that images are the proper effect of such music."[6] His view of things, of course, was precisely what music appreciation courses taught.

Other music critics were less disturbed by the film but nevertheless considered it troubling. In two thoughtful articles in the *New York Times* Olin Downes found that *Fantasia* raised a number of questions, particularly, what is the role of music in the film?[7] Is it the focus or is it support? While some critics, such as Franz Hoellering, were clear that "the effects achieved are nevertheless Walt Disney plus Bach or Beethoven," relegating the music to an accompanying role, Downes was not so sure. He refused to side with those who believed that each of the arts should remain separate, but he approached the film with the assumption that each maintained its uniqueness. Downes specifically addressed the question whether "each of the great arts should remain intact and lord of its own domain rather than suffer invasion and occupation by outside forces."[8]

Downes concluded that there are too many examples of crossover (not his term) in the history of music to think that it should not happen — Bach as dramatist, Schiller, poet-musician, Goethe, painter-poet, and in general opera, song, ballet. To Downes the Diaghilev ballet achieved the last great synthesis of arts, and he cited Mikhail Fokine's choreography of Nikolay Rimsky-Korsakov's *Sheherazade* as an example of "one of the great creations of that ballet." "This work," he wrote, "became a complete masterpiece, so perfect in its summation that it would be possible to believe that Rimsky-Korsakoff, long in advance, had written his music specifically for Diaghileff and his cohorts."[9]

Yet while Downes was able to recognize that two or more arts could travel together as companions, he still judged them strictly from the viewpoint of separate, independent, and unique art forms. What Downes did not consider, and what film critics did, was the possibility of dealing with an entirely new art, one that had been predicted frequently but whose realization had been at best incomplete. The word *fusion* surfaced: "It is the fusion that is important, the fusion of music, drama, and graphic art that Wagner strove to attain. *Fantasia* is the first work that clearly indicates the possibilities."[10]

Whether Disney attained the *gesamtkunstwerk* of Wagner could of course be debated. More important are the implications: whether sight, sound, and words interact in such a way that the individual elements cannot be considered alone. If the second half of the twentieth century has given birth to a new fused art form, the implications are huge: we must rethink what we mean by music, how we view it, and how we talk about it.

Did *Fantasia*, however, really herald a new age in music, or was it simply a brilliant commercial product, one man and his team's attempt to capture by animation the type of visual imaging experience common to most music listeners? Or was the music simply a vehicle for the Disney factory to introduce to the screen more characters and more adventures of already known characters? The answer lies not in the fate of *Fantasia* itself, which has become a classic in its own right, but in what has happened to the music world in general. For regardless of the merits of *Fantasia*, the direction it suggested, of a merging of aural and visual, may be the most important development in music in the late twentieth century. *Fantasia* may be less a breakthrough than a mirror.

Fantasia was not the first film to attempt some sort of symbiosis between music and visual image. The history of such efforts is not long, as the technical capacity to do so did not exist until the late 1920s.[11] Disney himself had tried something similar in a series of works that went under the rubric *Silly Symphony*, beginning in 1929. Oskar Fischinger's experiments in the 1930s ran in this direction, and he worked specifically with John Cage on at least two projects. Lem Lye attempted similar experiments at about the same time. The difference between Fischinger, Lye, and Disney was in reception. While Lye's and Fischinger's works were experimental, avant-garde, and known to only a handful of people, Disney's captured the entire nation.

In a broader sense program music of the nineteenth century may have marked the beginning of this trend. While romanticism elevated instrumental music to a position of preeminence among the arts, those romantic composers who wrote the "music of the future," Liszt, later Richard Strauss, were in their very efforts undermining what caused E. T. A. Hoffmann to put music there in the first place. Reviewing Beethoven's Fifth Symphony in 1810, Hoffmann argued for the independence of music, and that "only instrumental music, which scorns all assistance from and combination with other art, can express with purity music's peculiar nature. . . . Music is the most romantic of all the arts; one might even say that it alone is purely romantic."[12]

In 1925 Massimo Zanotti-Bianco realized how subversive program music could be, particularly when combined with modern media. He may have been the first to realize just what film could bring about. He spoke of a "surprising destiny that has lately been assigned to the 'programme,'" and further observed: "In commenting upon Strauss's 'Don Quixote,' Mr. Ernest Newman has written that only an accompanying moving picture would be its adequate interpretation. Skriabin's proposal of a flashing color-scheme already brings the screen into the concert-room. Perhaps it has come to stay. A fragmentary form of words, often supplied by critics, is but a scanty and uncertain aid toward the double effect, auditory and imaginative, at which the modern tone-poem aims. . . . Perhaps the future of programme music lies here."[13] Those music appreciation gurus may not have been so far off after all.

As the classical-music establishment debated the implications of *Fantasia*, American mavericks quickly picked up and began to explore them. The three most radical mavericks of the immediate post–World War II era, Edgard Varèse, Harry Partch, and John Cage, each in his own very different way, made the visual dimension central to their thinking. And in doing so each helped usher in fundamental changes in the American musical world.

In his extraordinary compositional silence between 1936 (when he composed *Density 21.5*) and 1954, when *Déserts* premiered, Varèse had begun to rethink his compositional goals. Most of his works of the 1920s were abstract instrumental pieces, which had at best a hint of a programmatic title. Varèse had conceived of an operatic work in 1928, *The Astronomer*, which would combine the visual, aural, dramatic, and elements of the dance into a single spectacle. It was to have a universal theme: an astronomer makes contact with a star, and the star explodes, engulfing mankind as spotlights in the theater beam directly on the audience and music overwhelms all in the space. Varèse worked with Robert Desnos and Alejo Carpentier on a libretto, but nothing came of the collaboration. He then interested Antonin Artaud, who finally produced a libretto by 1935. For whatever reasons, possibly because of Varèse's own languishing creativity at this time, the work was never completed.

Varèse attempted another major piece in 1940, *Espace*, as grand as any of his compositions. It was envisioned as a multilingual work for orchestra and an international chorus, each component singing in its own language in different parts of the world, with loudspeakers broadcasting the sound. This was to be enhanced by electrical instruments. The chorus itself was to include "laugh[ter], humming, yelling, chanting, mumbling, hammered declamation," as well as singing.[14]

Espace was never realized. Whether or not the international cooperation necessary to produce such a work was under the best of circumstances feasible, the political situation in 1940 made it impossible. Varèse returned to New York from Europe in 1940, and for several years he completed nothing. In 1947 *Etude pour Espace*, a fragment of the overall piece, was given a single performance.

Somewhere between *Espace* and his next major composition, *Déserts*,

Varèse began to envision works with a tighter aural-visual symbiosis, although the idea of such had never been alien to him. To Varèse image embodied sound. He told his wife that "once watching a display of the aurora borealis he felt an 'unbelievable exaltation — an indescribable sensation' and that as he watched those 'pulsating incandescent streamers of light' he 'not only saw but *heard* them.' As soon as he returned home he wrote down the sounds that had accompanied the movements of light."[15]

A correspondence between color and music was not unusual, for either musicians or visual artists. It was described by the seventeenth-century theorist Athanasius Kircher, and several musicians, notably Skryabin, pursued the idea.

With *Déserts* Varèse was no longer content to translate images into sounds. He wanted to serve the audience the entire package, sound and visual images together creating a single entity. This may have been adumbrated with *Espace,* in which Varèse states that the music is to coincide with "quick visual images," but where that would have gone remains uncertain.[16] With *Déserts* this goal comes to fruition, at least in conception. Varèse described the relationship between sight and sound: "Visual image and organized sound will not duplicate each other. For the most part light and sound will work in opposition in such as way as to give the maximum emotional reaction. Sometimes they will join for dramatic effect and in order to create a feeling of unity."[17]

Varèse also made clear that music was not secondary. *Déserts* is one of Varèse's few pieces with a programmatic conception, but it is not narrative. It is an extension of his lifelong interest in space, here made concrete by the geographical image of a desert. But in his conception, *Déserts* also had a symbolic and more abstract meaning: "[*Déserts*] suggests space, solitude, detachment. To me it means not only deserts of sand, sea, mountains and snow, of outer space, of deserted city streets, not only those stripped aspects of nature that suggest bareness and aloofness but also the remote inner space of the mind no telescope can reach, a world of mystery and essential loneliness. The title is personal, not intended as a description of the music." And in rejecting the narrative approach Varèse said: "There will be no action. There will be no story. There will be only images. Purely luminous phenomena."[18]

As often happened with Varèse, the first performance of *Déserts*, on December 2, 1954, at the Théâtre des Champs-Elysées, was not what he envisioned. It did cause a scandal, invoking memories of Stravinsky's *Rite of Spring* performed in the same hall fifty-one years previously, but the presentation took place in a traditional concert venue, as did a later performance in New York. It was Varèse's first use of electronic sounds, and the first piece to be broadcast in stereo in France.[19] Critics were not kind to *Déserts*, with most understandably viewing it as a strictly musical work, not the way Varèse conceived it.

As Varèse began to realize that the multimedia quality of *Déserts* could not be achieved in a concert hall, he began to pursue a film version in earnest. He later stated that he had in mind a film from the beginning. To Varèse "the idea of this project is to produce a picture new in conception in its relationship between images and sound." He told the journalist George Charbonnier that he would like to see a film made on *Déserts*. Charbonnier asked, "Do you wish that, with *Déserts*, the reverse process from the usual be done, namely that one would start from the score to construct the film?" and Varèse responded: "Yes. *Déserts* was calculated for that purpose."[20]

Varèse's interest in film dates from the 1930s, when he met Oskar Fischinger, but there is no record of any attempt at collaboration. With *Déserts* Varèse tried to contact various filmmakers, including Burgess Meredith, who had just completed *The Man in the Eiffel Tower*, and Varèse even boasted in 1949 that he and Meredith "are making a film together — *le Désert* (not documentary)." He had also discussed a film, consisting of "six hours of wordless images in conjunction with music," with Raymond Crueze, a French art dealer.[21]

And here *Fantasia* reenters the picture. Varèse tried to interest Walt Disney in *Déserts*. He wrote to Nicolas Slonimsky asking for Disney's address, and inquired whether Slonimsky knew Disney and could recommend Varèse to him. In subsequent communication with Merle Armitage, editor of *Look* magazine, it is clear that Varèse had heard of *Fantasia*, but that he was not familiar with it. Later, when he did encounter it, he was not too impressed. But in 1952 he had heard enough about what Disney had done to believe that their efforts were similar, and consequently that Disney would be interested in his own work. Possibly Varèse's connection with Leopold Stokowski, who was featured in *Fantasia*, influenced him. He put together a lengthy description, which he sent to Armitage, describing both his vision and how, technically, it might be realized. The project came to naught, and it is not clear that Disney even read the proposal.[22]

Varèse's *Déserts* begs comparison with Ives's *Universe Symphony*. Both deal with elements projected on a vast scale. Both deal with space itself. Both embody a conception beyond the realm of normal concert possibility, although Varèse saw new technology — electronic sounds and cinema — as a way of actualizing his vision. But Ives's conception is purely aural. It is an early-twentieth-century approach — it may be programmatic, but the music represents, in some ways encompasses, the visual. To Varèse the aural and the visual operate on different but essential planes, and both must be physically present. One is not a description of the other; Varèse stressed repeatedly that they were in opposition. Together they form the piece. The poor reception of the concert performances should be no surprise, for to judge it as a purely aural work misrepresents the very nature of Varèse's vision. Yet the critics cannot be faulted for that. Varèse did authorize a concert performance, and the critics could only write about what they experienced.

Varèse blended sight and sound more successfully in his *Poème électronique* of 1957. Now considered a landmark of early electronic music, the work was not designed as a composition unto itself but as the aural part of a collaboration between Varèse and the architect Charles-Edouard Jeanneret, who worked under the pseudonym Le Corbusier, with a significant contribution by the polymath architect, mathematician, and composer Iannis Xenakis.

Le Corbusier received a commission from the Philips Electrical Company, based in Holland, to design a building for the Brussels World's Fair of 1958. He envisaged essentially an electronic gesamtkunstwerk, and wrote to Philips that he planned "to create with all of you a first 'electrical show,' electronic, synchronous, in which light, images, color, space, movement, and the idea forge an astonishing whole, accessible, to be sure, to the masses."[23]

The concept for the piece was a work precisely eight minutes long that would be a combination of lights and sounds in an environment otherwise totally dark. In the letter inviting Varèse to participate in the project Le Corbusier described it vividly:

> This interior is plunged into utter darkness . . . the show will be exclusively "electric," "electronic," etc. . . . a creation of modern times, a *féerie électrique*. . . .
>
> My idea is for the music to have its place in it. Out of this darkness, illuminated by "black light," will emerge certain objects, or certain things, or ambiences of violently different colors. . . .
>
> We must create a scenario in total liaison: light, movement, image, and music.[24]

The music projected a spatial quality, created by spreading 425 speakers throughout the pavilion. Earle Brown describes how "you'd hear a sound, and it would go all the way around, like that [hand motion], and you could almost trace it in space, almost follow it with your eyes."[25]

The title *Poème électronique* more properly refers to the entire project, not just Varèse's music. Le Corbusier used it to describe the total effect, even before Varèse was approached. Unfortunately *Poème électronique* as a multimedia artwork is lost to posterity. The pavilion was torn down shortly after the

The Philips Pavilion at the World's Fair of 1958, for which Varèse wrote *Poème électronique* (Photograph courtesy of Philips Research, Royal Philips Electronics)

fair closed, and Varèse's music, for which there is no score, exists only in a three-track version from which the LP recording was made. It is all that is left of the collaboration. Thus what has become a canonical piece in the electronic-music world is only a shadow of what was originally conceived. As a totality it will never be known.[26]

An aural-visual fusion also describes the works of both Harry Partch and John Cage, although there the resemblance ends. Each approached his concept of a combined art quite differently, in intent as well as purpose and result. To Partch the unification of the arts was a conscious and specific goal. It is also endemic to Cage's work, although he never acknowledged it as such. At times he even uttered the opposite.

Cage and Partch agreed on one thing: their music was essentially theater, and through the concept of theater they achieved artistic fusion. Partch's theater was thoroughly Western: both its roots and subject matter lay in ancient Greek drama. His musical material looked back to Greek monophony and to expanded pitch resources melodically derived. In effect Partch rejected both the tonal potential and the melodic limitations imposed by post-Renaissance harmony. Most important, however, Partch's concept of corporeality, a synthesis of the sensuous and the abstract, accorded the visual a role equal to the aural. The way a performer moved was as important as the sounds produced, and Partch insisted that their movement be visibly present to the audience, an essential part of the presentation.

Corporealism, or corporeality, was much broader than the term *body* from which it is derived, but to Partch the body, its nature, its functions, and its pleasures, were very much part of his musical aesthetic. The abstract had, among other failings, forgotten the body. Partch saw mind and body as one. In probably his most succinct definition of corporeality Partch commented: "I'm sometimes pressed to explain this [the term *corporeal music*]. The best I can say is the 'corporeal' to me involves the whole body, the whole person, the whole mind."[27] According to Ben Johnston, "Corporealism was a theory that Partch lived. It is a vehement protest against what he considered the negation of the body and the bodily in society. It resulted specifically in an attack on *abstraction*. What that meant to him first of all was that music should not be separated from words of visible actions, whether theatrical, choreographic, or simply musically functional."[28]

At its simplest level this is a prescription for composition and performance: what kind of music should be written, how it should be performed, and in what type of setting. More broadly Partch's corporealism is a resurgence of the Aristotelian concept of the unity of the arts. It is another variant of an aesthetic goal that has surfaced repeatedly in the past two thousand years of Western art, the most famous advocacy of which was in Wagner's gesamtkunstwerk. It speaks of a total work of art, incorporating all the senses and modes of expression, aural, visual, verbal, and tactile.

For Partch the issue had social and ethical implications. Partch's concept of corporeality is an attack on the Cartesian dualism that has pervaded Western thought for the past three hundred years. The sensual element seems so strong in Partch's music in part because the mind-body split is simply not there. Partch's rejection of the abstract was more than a compositional decision regarding style and structure; it was a declaration of the whole of the human condition, seen in a light that Western thought had discounted if not denied for two hundred years.

The visual element came late to Partch. Earlier his focus was on an aural-verbal symbiosis. Such an approach was neither new nor unusual to Western music — song had been at the heart of Western musical culture for centuries. Partch's uniqueness lay in nuance: Partch sought to capture in music the verbal inflection of the text with far more precision than other composers did. This originally led him to go beyond the limitations of the twelve-notes-per-octave patterns of Western music. Of course many singers, especially vernacular singers, do just that. Their efforts are improvised, however, and remain open, that is, what they do is part of the performance, not the composition. Once a singer confronts Western notation, the limitations are apparent; hundreds of thousands of compositions stare out at us from the page, with twelve (or fewer) notes per octave.

Partch, however, sought to capture the inflections in the composition itself. He did have a precedent in Western music, the work of the Italian monodists at the end of the sixteenth century. Although the musical results were quite different — the monodists never could quite escape those twelve notes — Partch's ideas seem parallel. Partch owed little to Renaissance monody, however, because both went to the same source, ancient Greece. The monodists dreamed of reviving ancient Greek ideas of music, words, and drama, just as Partch did. Partch, with an ear acutely tuned to microtones and a willingness to systematize them, could shape musical lines with melodic detail unavailable to most Western composers.

Early on Partch recognized the connection between the verbal and the musical; "the verbal element is always, with me, as important as the sound element," he said, and "the verbal element was always there, from the time I was 14 and I began writing music." To Partch verbal and musical formed a unity. He conceived his music as narrative, such that word and tone were inseparable, even if the result was wordless.[29]

As his concept of corporeality developed, and as he created more of his unusual instruments, the visual dimension intensified. Regardless of when it arrived, he spoke of it as "always present in my mind as an essential factor," and made clear that it was "just as important as the other two (verbal and musical)."[30]

Partch later redefined corporeality to correspond with his own shift from voice to theater. No longer is it the single voice — monophony — but rather it is the entire act of being on stage. The physical deportment of the instrumentalist, the way the player approaches the instrument — the visual effect — all those elements that contribute to theater, encompass corporeality. Partch not only put the instruments on stage, to make them visible, but he felt that the player's movements were as important as the sounds he made. Partch took great pride in the appearance of the musicians, and their choreography followed quickly. He railed against performers who got the notes right but whose bodily movements were not consistent with the sounds. How a performer looked and moved was as important to Partch as the sounds themselves. For those who did not accede to his wishes he could be merciless:

> At *no time* are the players of my instruments to be unaware that they are on stage, *in the act.* There can be no humdrum playing of notes, in the bored belief that because they are "good" musicians their performance is ipso facto "masterly." When a player fails to take full advantage of his role in a visual or acting sense, he is muffing his part — in my terms — as thoroughly as if he bungled every note in the score. . . . there is surely some special hell reserved for the player of one of the more dramatic instruments who insists on deporting himself as though he were in tie-and-tails on a symphony orchestra's platform (such as experimental hanging by the gonads on a rebel Kithara string until he relents).[31]

Partch's instruments themselves were displayed in art galleries. In *Art in America* Mary Fuller described them as "strange and beautiful," comparing them as sculptures to the constructivists and Henry Moore.[32] And in 1966 Partch was given the Nealie Sullivan award by the San Francisco Art Institute for his contribution to the visual arts. He was the first musician to win the award.

Partch disdained the traditional concert world with an aversion that bordered on the pathological. It was too much a compromise, in spite of the visual dimension inevitably present whenever he performed. Partch stated directly: "I do not care for 'concerts.' I am concerned with music as a significantly integrated part of ritual and theater."[33] Partch considered his performances not concerts but theater. His conceptual linking of verbal and musical precluded the presentation of abstract works, no matter how well the performers moved. And once words were added, and people other than the instrumentalists were on stage, it was no longer a concert, at least in Partch's mind. For both Partch and Cage recordings were particularly problematic. When a recording of Partch's music was reviewed it often fared little better than Cage's. Thus when *Delusion of the Fury* was released by Columbia Records, David Moore, in *American Record Guide,* was not sympathetic. His review is ingenious; he leaves the impression that he is discussing the entire show, referring to visual effects, such as the tight placement of the instruments on stage, and the manner in which the musicians performed — "the

Marimba Eroica is sounded by *jumping* on the keys, if I recall aright." But he is only recalling an earlier performance of another Partch piece he once saw.

Moore judged the *Delusion* tightly against the Western canon. He applies rigorously the standards of Western art music. Even Partch's pitch resources are heard through the template of twelve-tone equal temperament: his forty-three-tone scale first is not used to create dissonance, but is instead wed to "repetitive and relatively simple harmonic progressions," and as a consequence the piece "has a marked tendency to sound like ordinary stuff played slightly out of tune."

Moore acknowledges Partch's avowed intention to create ritual, but not even ritual can hold up against the structural demands of Western art music: "Although I realize that the nature of ritual demands repetition, an hour and a quarter of harmonic sequences with little melody performed without intermission — in an idiom on instruments at which one knows not whether to laugh or to cry — seems to me to combine many of the worst aspects of the concert-hall experience which Partch claims he is trying to supplant." Moore also finds it helpful that "there are no sights to detract from the sounds. Accordingly, one can concentrate on the matter of the piece rather than on its manner."[34]

What does Moore think the "matter of the piece" is? This is no enigma. Partch's subtitle for *Delusion of the Fury* is *A Ritual of Dream and Delusion*, and Moore acknowledged that it is a "curious piece of theater," in which Partch's "subtitled description of the score as a 'ritual' is difficult to fault." But Moore is wedded to abstraction and cannot escape that framework to judge the piece as theater rather than purely aural art.

Moore was also on his own terrain. A recording by its very nature strips away all but abstract sound. It is the ideal means for the dissemination of the Western canon as developed in the nineteenth century, and any piece that wants to encompass other dimensions simply cannot. Thus Partch, Cage, Young, and others were trapped. The mechanism to reach millions of people existed, but it could present only a chimera of the real thing. And its very existence could mislead. A listener, even a sophisticated one, could easily assume that sound itself was both the ends and the means.

Unfortunately the mechanism of recording, with its promise of distribution, recognition, and income, was irresistible. Cage could not resist it, even though he tried to ignore it once the recording was made, and for Partch it was a lifeline. For several years this was Partch's principal means of support.[35]

Partch assaulted directly the world he wished to change; Cage worked elliptically. While Cage insisted that everything he did was theater, his own rhetoric dwelt little on that point. Cage presented concert situations in which the aural element, taken alone, is absurd, twenty minutes of record scratch, as one critic bemoaned.[36] Cage's absurdity had a purpose, however.

With few exceptions a Cage concert was as visual as it was aural. A Cage piece, from the earliest happenings, was a multi-sensorial event, sometimes a sumptuous challenge for the spectator, a three-ring circus, sometimes just the opposite, a moment of imposed stillness, a space for contemplation. Cage realized the importance of the visual to the concert world, and his "concerts" became theatrical events. He later said that everything he did was theater. Even in his early percussion pieces the visual dissonance between a formal concert setting, with Cage in tails and somber demeanor, and what appeared the remnants of a kitchen sale on stage had its own appeal, regardless of what was played.

Later, *how* the sounds were produced, be it by playing an instrument in unusual ways or creating them with contact microphones in unusual places, held as much fascination for the audience as the sounds themselves. The stage would be filled with unusual objects not normally found at a concert, and for most members of the audience the visual image of a stone-faced John Cage or David Tudor doing very unconcertlike acts on stage remained fixed in the memory far more vividly than the sounds themselves. Cage explained the visual significance of *Water Music*: "The *Water Music* wishes to be a piece of music, but to introduce visual elements in such a way that it can be experienced as theater. That is, it moves toward theater from music."[37]

With a Cage event, be it a solo concert or a multistage extravaganza, to break it into its component parts, the visual, the aural, the verbal, and discuss each separately becomes ludicrous.[38] Cage purposely created situations that frustrated, befuddled, and short-circuited the traditional expectations of the spectators, and the visual is essential to his success. Only through the ofttimes Dadaesque visual antics on stage can the audience's attention be maintained for Cage's message to come across.

Cage's indeterminacy takes on another twist in this situation. If the aural result was unpredictable or completely open, what was the piece? What was its locus? The obvious answer was that it lay in the instructions Cage provided and the execution of them on stage. But often the instructions were about events that were to be seen as much as heard. The sounds, uncertain if not incidental, at least no longer occupied the sacred centrality they once did. Cage's musical works in which visual activity was central were another step in the deconstruction, or more precisely the redefining, of the concert event itself. Just how important the visual element actually was in a traditional concert may be an open question, but tradition held that it was decidedly secondary. In theory at least the visual element was subordinated to

David Tudor performing John Cage's *Water Music*. The instrument in his mouth is a duck whistle. (Photograph, New York Public Library)

pure, abstract sound. Cage reordered that relationship totally. It is no wonder that when Cage acquiesced to allowing his works on records, fiasco followed.

The importance of the visual remained in Cage's collaboration with Merce Cunningham; it is by nature endemic to composition for dance, even when the music and the dance seem to coexist independently, as they often did with Cage and Cunningham. Even Cage's writings, his many books, which may be his most enduring legacy, have a strong visual component, which is as much part of the message as the words themselves. Cage's prose is somewhere between traditional narrative, the use of words as sounds, and visual art. The appearance of the page is an integral part of a Cage book, and most pages do not appear as traditional sentence-paragraph narrative. And as

norTh
Of paris, june '72:
collyBia platyphylla,
plutEus cervinus, pholiota
mutabilis and several hYpholomas.

The
dOors and windows are open.
"why Bring it back?
i'd forgottEn where it was.
You could have kept it."

he told Me
of A movie they'd seen,
a natuRe film.
he thought we would liKe it too.

The paintings
i had decided tO
Buy
wEre superfluous; nevertheless,
after several Years, i owned them.

sold Them
tO write music. now there's a third.
i must get the first two Back.
whEre
are theY?

all it is is a Melody
of mAny
coloRs:
Klangfarbenmelodie.

John Cage, page from *M* (Photograph courtesy of Wesleyan University Press)

Cage's career progressed, the traditional narrative receded into the background in favor of sound and art. When Cage read his texts aloud, the result was a musical performance. When placed in a book, the result was a work of art.

Cage wished to question our own limitations, particularly about what music was. At first his goals were modest, to ensure that noise had an equal place with pitched sounds. A broader goal was to sever the connection between music and expression, to free sounds from any meaning imposed by either the composer or the listener. In the end neither goal was out of line with

Western thought. Noise, advocated most pointedly by the early-twentieth-century futurists, had earned a solid place in Western art music well before Cage. And as we have seen, a music sans personal expression was the goal of many composers after World War II. Cage's own Zen orientation, however, caused him to go further than others in advocating the universality of music, regardless of sound or source. With Cage the distinction between a sound created as music and a sound that simply occurs seems to collapse.

Yet Cage continued to produce artworks, an apparent contradiction to his aesthetics. If the artworks are considered theatrical events, however, the contradiction becomes less pointed. Cage's most serious challenge to the art of music may have been to challenge its autonomy.

At first Varèse, Cage, and Partch were received coldly by the musical establishment. Their idea of fusion was too out of sync with the prevailing abstraction that predominated in the musical world as late as the 1980s. Significantly these composers were closer to visual artists than to other musicians. Varèse had always been close to artists. When he first arrived in the United States he roomed with the dadaist Francis Picabia, although Varèse made clear over and over that he was not a dadaist. Of course so did Picabia and Duchamp. After World War II Varèse and Cage had direct contact with the art world through the Club on Eighth Street, an organization founded by a group of twelve artists, mostly abstract, including Franz Kline, Willem de Kooning, Milton Resnick, and Alexander Calder. Varèse, John Cage, Stefan Wolpe, and Morton Feldman were the only musicians.

Varèse had known this group of artists previously. They had begun a journal, *Possibilities*, whose run consisted of one issue. That issue included the final page of Varèse's piece *Etude pour Espace*. According to L. Alcopley, Varèse did not know any of the artists before Alcopley introduced them to him, but the artists were quite interested in his work, to the extent that they formed "the main public he had." John Cage acknowledged the debt that both owed the artists—they came to their concerts when no musicians would. Cage observed that when he gave a concert, he would easily get one hundred artists but virtually no musicians in the audience.[39] But he also admitted that they came to Varèse's because they really liked his music, whereas they came to Cage's more out of a sense of obligation for a fellow radical.[40] Varèse affirmed that this affinity had an artistic basis: "At a time when only a handful of musicians understood my work, the painters and sculptors who heard my music rarely failed to respond to it. We spoke the same language in spite of the difference in the medium of expression."[41]

Yet movement toward an aural-visual symbiosis was spreading, and by the 1990s signs of it were everywhere. Popular music had become almost entirely a visual event. Videos, not audio, sold CDs. A popular artist's "act," or public persona, was carefully crafted for the right visual appeal. Costume became as important as sound, whether it was the hats of country music, the flannel shirts of grunge, or the elaborate theatrical makeup of 1970s rock. Popular music as it evolved in the late twentieth century was to be seen, not heard.

Frank Zappa had articulated that point by the 1960s. Asked about the on-stage antics of the Mothers of Invention, Zappa talked about what the kids expected: "Especially in a live concert where the main element is visual. Kids go to *see their favorite acts, not to hear them*. . . . We work on the premise that nobody really hears what we do anyway, so it doesn't make any difference if we play a place that's got ugly acoustics."[42]

The concert extravaganza replaced recordings as the focus of the star's activities. Some groups, like the Grateful Dead, went so far as to encourage bootlegs, because they knew that their financial success depended more on the tour, with all its attendant side money, than on the sale of recordings. And for most popular groups concerts themselves were elaborately staged productions with extensive theatrical effects. A concert resembled more a carnival than a traditional concert.

The crowds came to be wowed with visual fireworks, often literally. Even as traditional a singer as Chris LeDoux, a former rodeo rider who writes country songs about that world, has a concert act that has pyrotechnics at its heart. It is a sensational event, with explosions, smoke, confetti cannons, dramatic lighting, and the leaping gyrating figure of LeDoux himself, dwarfed by the spectacle that surrounds him. The music is loud and driving, very much part of the act, but at times it seems only to support the choreography, both human and mechanical. With a LeDoux show every day is the Fourth of July.

In popular music the centrality of the visual became apparent in the 1950s, more or less coincident with the arrival of television in virtually every home. Elvis Presley was transitional. His sneer and his hip movement frightened parents and middle-aged defenders of public morality, but he could sing. The sensual emotionalism of his style was fully embedded in his music, and the visual effect only enhanced what was apparent in any of his recordings. Like Frank Sinatra, Elvis Presley may have been a sex symbol, but at its heart was his voice. In the world of popular music that would soon change.

Shortly after Elvis Presley was drafted into the army and his career was put on hold, Bob Marcucci, the manager of Frankie Avalon, saw Fabian Forte and realized he had the looks, the hair, and the moves to become the next teenage sensation. The only problem was, Fabian could not sing. In this new world, however, that didn't matter. Between a major publicity campaign that emphasized his appearance and heavy doctoring of his records to disguise his lack of ability, he became a sudden, although brief, sensation.

Marcucci repeated his success a decade later, with a group assembled purely for TV, the Monkees. Yet whatever the musical limitations of Fabian or the Monkees, it was *their* voices that were heard. In the late '80s producer Frank Farren chose Rob Pilatus and Fabrice Morvan, again for their looks, and marketed them as Milli Vanilli. Their success lasted until it was discovered that someone else's voices were on their recordings and, according to some reports, Pilatus and Morvan were literally locked out of the studio during recording sessions.[43]

Throughout the sixties and seventies most popular music acts exploited the visual in different ways, from the smooth choreography of Motown to the bizarre theatricality of Kiss or Alice Cooper. In later MTV videos, elaborate staged dance routines are as important as the sounds. The concert itself, as Zappa realized, was a large communal ritual, not a place to hear a performer. As Cage predicted, music became theater. And there it has stayed.

But what about the classical-music world? Throughout the twentieth century an older fiction continued to predominate. Thanks to an indoctrination process that began as early as 1809, with E. T. A. Hoffmann's elevation of music to the greatest of the arts, because it was the purest, it came to seem unthinkable that music could be anything but an aural art.

Yet concerts themselves always had and continue to have a strong visual element. Performers have recognized, from at least the time of Liszt and Paganini, how physical presence on stage affects audience reaction, how a violinist's posture, sweep of the bow arm, and sway can communicate to an audience, how a pianist can command the stage by his bearing, and of course the dance itself is something the twentieth-century conductor has made his own art form. But such is a tacit complicity that audience and performer share. It lurks shrouded under the assumption of a pure, abstract, aural art. And unless it becomes either annoying or distracting, it is generally ignored.

But cracks in the aural bedrock on which classical culture lay were appearing everywhere. With a movement toward theater, an awareness of the potential of new media, and a breakdown of the classical-popular divide, the cracks became a chasm. Examples are so common that only a representative sampling is necessary. In the early 1970s the Kronos Quartet, specialists in contemporary music, broke with the almost sacrosanct tradition for a string quartet to dress in formal black and appeared on stage with exotic costumes and with lighting effects more suitable to a rock concert. As a consequence Kronos developed a new audience, young people who had been avoiding classical music in droves. Not unexpectedly the group was also roundly criticized by the critical establishment for its behavior.

Few events could be more solidly in the classical mainstream than Yo-Yo Ma performing the Six Cello Suites of Johann Sebastian Bach. He has recorded them twice on CD and performed the entire cycle several times, more than once at Carnegie Hall. Yet Ma has rethought these works, and his most recent release is not a CD but rather a video, in which each suite serves as essentially an aural backdrop for a visual tableau. The scenes vary: Mark Morris's dance troupe does a relatively literal interpretation of the rhythms of Suite Three; garden designer Julie Moir Messervy and Ma attempt to create an urban garden based on Suite One; Tamasaburo Bando interprets the Fifth Suite within the traditions of Kabuki dance; and the figure-skating pair Jayne Torvill and Christopher Dean skate to the Sixth Suite. Suite Two is based on etchings by Giovanni Battista Piranesi for an eighteenth-century castle, and Ma is seen performing the Sarabande in the grim virtual reality of a dungeon, surrounded by tight cells, bars, and instruments of torture. In all these scenarios the music is not just background; it is more like the catalyst for a visual scene, but the music no longer stands alone; it no longer even holds center stage.

The 1990s witnessed a new phenomenon: the formation of classical ensembles based on visual appeal. Record companies in particular recognized what had been apparent in popular music for decades: sex sells. Especially young, beautiful (preferably blond) females on CD covers. Thus we have the formation of the Australian string quartet Bond, whose own Web page describes "the four sexy, sassy, and spectacularly-gifted young women." The Web page is complete with an "image gallery" for downloading. Solo artists are similarly marketed. Violinist Lara St. John's Web site features a full-page article from the *Toronto Sun* about her titled "Sex and Violins." Dominating the page is her color photograph, eyes closed, mouth open, wearing a revealing low-cut dress, with her violin in her lap. In large letters is her comment: "I'm six feet tall. I have long blond hair. I call myself Junoesque. Curvy . . . am I supposed to hide all that?" Finally there is Linda Brava (née Lampenius), marketed as the "blond musical sensation," who posed for a provocative series of nude photographs in *Playboy*, where she was billed as the "Brahms Bombshell."[44]

Overt appeals to sexuality were not limited to young female performers. Concert managers, looking at the box-office crisis that threatened the very existence of classical music, have recently engaged in publicity tricks that verge on the bizarre. Thus David Alan Miller, when conductor of the Rochester Symphony Orchestra, appeared on stage in a black leather vest and sleeveless T-shirt designed purposely to show off his biceps, to lead a rock group, a subset of the orchestra, called the "Dogs of Desire."[45] Since then "Dogs" has become a regular part of his image.

Nowhere is the visual element more prominent than in opera. This of course is to be expected, as visual spectacle has always been an important part of opera, but today there has been a role reversal. In even the most visually sumptuous operas of the past, the audience came because of either the composer, the action, or the vocal fireworks. Song, drama, or virtuoso singer prevailed. Who remembers Verdi's stage director? Who remembers Mozart's set designer? When we speak of Mozart and Verdi, we speak of two great collaborations, between Mozart and Lorenzo Da Ponte and between Verdi and Arrigo Boito, between composer and librettist, between words and music. And in each case the composer usually gets top billing.

When the history of late-twentieth-century opera is written, Philip Glass will not be talked about apart from Robert Wilson. Peter Schaffer, Franco Zeffirelli, these are the stars. And they are designers and stage directors. In fact, *Einstein on the Beach* is sometimes referred to as Robert Wilson's opera, with music by Philip Glass. In *Einstein*, the principal portrayal of Einstein is visual. We recognize him through his visual appearance, the opera in essence being a temporal extension of the many photographs of Einstein that create his popular image. Included is the famous one of Einstein sticking out his tongue, an image duplicated prominently in the opera.

In a review of the revival of *Einstein* at the Brooklyn Academy of Music in 1985, Jack Anderson, noting that Andrew de Groat replaced Lucinda Childs as choreographer, then observed that "Mr. Wilson's basic concepts and images remained unchanged," and that while the piece "often resembled a set of paintings," nevertheless "it achieved many of its effects through movement." Anderson, to be sure, is a dance critic, but music as having an impact on the "overall effect" is virtually nonexistent. Three paragraphs later Anderson does refer to the "pulsing ostinatos of Mr. Glass's score," in reference to the sense of a train in motion. Glass's role here seems to be to supply an onomatopoeic effect. In a discussion of Glass's opera *The Voyage*, John W. Freeman wrote in *Opera News*: "Though all the singers were right on target, *The Voyage* is more to be seen than heard, a tour de force of contemporary stagecraft."[46]

More recently the composer has been all but relegated to the sidelines, as an accessory to the real event. Alex Ross called the opera *Writing to Vermeer*, by Louis Andriessen, "a conceptual theatre piece by Peter Greenaway and Saskia Boddeke, with background music by Andriessen." He went on, "*Writing to Vermeer* felt like a celebrity vehicle, and Andriessen, alas was not the famous one." As with so many contemporary opera concepts, the composers became an afterthought in the marketing of a name from the world of literature, theater, or film.[47]

The move toward theater is particularly apparent in the work of the minimalists after approximately 1980. With *Einstein on the Beach* in 1976 Philip Glass found his niche, and he is now known essentially as a theatrical composer, theater in this context metaphorically extended to include film. Glass himself considers theater where he began: "More often than not theatre was where my most innovative work began, often to be worked out and developed later in my concert music." When Glass returned to New York after his study with Nadia Boulanger, his first concert occurred at the Film-Makers Cinematheque. Glass conceived "the whole concert as a visual, as well as aural presentation." The shape of the score was part of the presentation. The pages of *Strung Out* for solo violin were attached to two sides of a wall, the violinist walking around the wall as she played. *Music in the Form of a Square* for two flutes was set up in a large square, one player walking around the inside of the square, the other the outside in the opposite direction. The piece was over when they met.[48]

The sculptural quality of these works was no accident. Glass at the time worked as an assistant to the sculptor Richard Serra. And as it did for many downtown musicians, support and encouragement came from many in theater and the visual arts.

Whereas Glass has defined himself as essentially a theatrical composer, Steve Reich remained much closer to the classical-music ideal, and his reception has been different. Reich himself stated: "Music must be listened to as pure sound-event, and act without any dramatic structure." Not surprisingly Reich has fared much better than Glass in the world of classical music and classical-music criticism. To some critics Reich has become the most important figure in minimalism. As Robert T. Jones observed in 1983, Reich's music is for the concert stage.[49] It was thus no coincidence that at the New International Young Composers Concert Series in 1979, sponsored by the Reich Music Foundation, most of the pieces consisted of "pure music, as opposed to pieces in verbal, theatrical, or conceptual frameworks."[50]

Richard Taruskin placed Reich at the apex of the classical hierarchy: "Mr. Reich can go permanently astray now and never lose the distinction of having given classical music back first its youth and finally its soul in the waning years of the 20th century. It is something for which the musicians of the 21st century will remember him and be grateful. We can be grateful already."[51]

Philip Glass has not fared as well. Critics have wondered if Glass has become victim to his own aesthetic. When does the repetition itself become mere affectation? When does it stop being archetypal and become banal? Did Glass fall into the same trap that John Cage did, at some point concentrating on being the person that success and the media made him out to be? Did he lose the underlying premises of his works?[52]

Beyond the criticism lies a recognition and a fear: that Glass indeed has abandoned those premises on which critics work, that Glass's theatrical works may be beyond their grasp, floating in a synthetic world as free as his own spaceship. Reich, on the other hand, has won the hearts of critics, for he has remained within the Renaissance tradition; he has held steadfast to the notion of a purely musical work of art, whatever its style.

Not entirely so! Even though Reich seems much closer to the classical mainstream than Glass or Young, he too has moved toward a theatrical environment. Like Young, Reich is married to a visual artist, and, like Young and Zazeela, Reich and his wife, Beryl Korot, collaborate. Their most extensive collaboration was *The Cave*, which premiered in 1993. It is based on the Cave of Machpelah, in Hebron, the legendary burial place of Old Testament patriarchs. Reich and Korot explored the cave through interviews with Jews, Muslims, and Christians, all of whom attach symbolic importance to the place. In the work itself multiple video images are projected and coordinated with Reich's music written for thirteen instruments and with text, which consists partly of biblical quotation and partly of comments from interviewees.

Controversy has swirled around the piece since its inception. In particular, what is it? Reich insists that it is not an opera, at least in conventional terms. He separates himself from Glass: "I am not like Glass a theater composer; I don't carry the theater around inside me." Reich's work is not traditional theater, in the sense of plot, development, narrative, dialogue, buildup, and dénouement, but then neither is *Einstein. The Cave*, however, is a theatrical experience, much as Cage's music is, much as 1970s rock is. It is a situation in which the attendees (audience is too limited a term here) find themselves in an environment in which visual images, setting, and music contribute equally. Music becomes part of the totality, more than background, but no longer a thing unto itself.

Even in some of Reich's more abstract pieces, some of the most traditionally oriented critics have recognized how important the visual dimension is to one of his concerts. Reich's *Music for Eighteen Musicians* is in title, style, and concept a piece of pure abstract music. Yet when it was performed on September 21 and 23, 2000, Paul Griffiths, known for his alignment with the uptown avant-garde, went out of his way to comment on the enhancement that seeing the performance brings.[53] Griffiths began another article

Performance of Steve Reich's *The Cave* (Photograph by Andrew Pothecary)

about Reich, "Steve Reich: Music That Must Be Seen to Be Loved," with the observations:

> Steve Reich writes action music, music that is keyed into the physical actions it exerts in performance and that is always busy and active in how it moves through time. Radio listeners to his concert at Merkin Hall on Thursday night, broadcast live on WNYC-FM, will have missed how, for instance, the drumsticks started to flicker over a line of bongos as the players moved

rhythmically out of phase with one another in the first part of "Drumming," or how Mark Stewart's fingers, poised over his electric-blue electric guitar, picked out the main line in "Electric Counterpoint." Works for musicians playing against recorded images of themselves — like "Electric Counterpoint" or, coming at the end of this program, "Different Trains" for string quartet — show a particular loss when there is nothing to distinguish the visible performers from the invisible.[54]

Often forgotten is the strong theatrical or visual component of some of the earliest and most traditional classics of minimalism. La Monte Young's pieces take place at the Theatre of Eternal Music, in place since 1962, and his sounds work closely with Marian Zazeela's lights. Even the space itself becomes part of the production, as its acoustical properties are part of the compositional equation. And the first performance of Riley's *In C* was not strictly an aural event: "The lights went down, two projectors filled the room with coloured lights and abstract patterns, and the fourteen musicians plunged into the raucous and thrilling opening of *In C*."[55] *In C* premiered in November 1964, after Riley had returned from Europe, and after he had visited Young in New York and had witnessed the Theatre of Eternal Music. He must have seen Zazeela's lights, and almost certainly discussed them with Young and Zazeela.

Minimalism by its very style lends itself to a visual symbiosis. Western music's special quality came from its structural potential, embedded in its sense of drive and directionality. That is precisely the element lacking in minimalism. Minimalism has been called surface music, a pejorative term for those oriented toward deep structure. Minimalism's sheer repetitiveness buries any sense of a clear teleological structure and instead creates a quality of ritual, at times hypnotic, at other times suggestive. In such situations the mooring that in the past held the listener's imagination in check, a complex hierarchical web of musical interactions and interrelationships, is absent, and the listener's imagination is freed to take flights of fancy, unfettered by the structural demands that characterized most Western music. And once the formal underpinning has been removed, there are no shackles on music's associative potential, its suggestiveness, whether in the listener's or the composer's imagination.

The popularity of minimalism in the 1970s and '80s raises the question of the relationship between composer and audience. As is well known, somewhere around 1950 the connection between contemporary composer and audience seemed to come apart completely. This tendency began with the avant-garde of the 1920s, and even earlier with Leo Ornstein, whose performances drew audiences but often only to be amused by the apparent absurdity of what he did. Ornstein himself reacted by moving to a more accessible, more "expressive" (his term) style. Some composers in the twenties wanted to turn their back on the general public, but by and large that attitude did not prevail until after World War II, when Milton Babbitt gave it its paradigmatic voice. Even then it was less a desire than a way of accepting what had become a nasty reality: the public for advanced serialism was extremely small. The eastern-establishment composers took solace in their music's own complexity, which provided them a simple explanation for the problem: most listeners could not understand what they were doing.

Yet by and large they missed the point, as did Leonard Meyer when he spoke of the "end of the Renaissance." The issue had little to do with the "serial wars," the fight between composers writing atonal music and those writing more audience-friendly music. Driving a wedge further between the two was the beginning of a more fundamental change, in the place of music itself in the culture. As the visual element gained prominence, the romantic notion of music as a pure, abstract, disembodied, aural art began to disintegrate.

Thus we come to the answer to the serial wars discussed in Chapter 7. They were fought on specious premises from the first, for *in the end style made little difference. Whether a piece was serial, freely atonal, or tonal, was moot.* No matter how complex a composer's music was, or conversely how hard he tried to make it accessible, he was fighting a losing battle. The neo-romantics garnered a much larger audience than the serialists ever did, and so-called postmodernists punched up their music with an eclectic blend of past and present, classical and popular, but in the past fifty years no composer of essentially abstract art music has had a major impact on American culture.[56] The reason: Americans are just not listening. The very premise on which such a composer worked, the creation of a purely aural artwork, a "unified, closed totality," has fundamentally eroded.[57]

Cage saw it early. Thus his success. Even the minimalists, ostensibly the most successful group of composers in the last half-century, have moved into theater. Frank Zappa not only perceived the rock concert as such, but even conceived his compositions visually. He saw them as "sound sculptures": "Once the music comes off the paper and goes into the air, what you're doing is literally making a sound sculpture . . . the duration of the piece occupies a space of time — that's your canvas."[58]

Roland Barthes is close to the mark when he speaks of the disintegration of the individual arts. He considered the visual to be "music's silent partner," and he envisioned the creation of new objects and a new language, "when the solidarity of the old disciplines break down . . . in the interests of a new object and a new language." He saw this particularly in Fluxus: "Music's silent partner has always been the visual; what emerges in Fluxus is symbiosis of this coexistence."[59]

A Fluxus performance may involve sounds, but they are usually incidental to the theatrical nature of the event. They are a result of what the score prescribes, but not the purpose of the score itself. Here we might distinguish between scores that represent sound and those that are performative — that instruct the performer to do certain things. A traditional score is hieratic, a graphic representation, with precise coordinates, of a sound event. The score to Bach's Sonata in D minor for Solo Violin tells the violinist what notes to sound, in what rhythm, and with what articulation. A hieratic score is in essence a visual representation of the sound. Thus a pianist with no experience playing the violin could re-create the performance in her head.

Performative or theatrical scores describe an action, in which the sound is either unclear or incidental. It may tell the performer to "draw a straight line," or to "feed a bale of hay to a piano." Thus Young's *Composition 1960 #7*, which contains the notes B and F-sharp in standard notation, differs from those. It is hieratic in that it is sound-specified, at least in terms of pitch, and loosely speaking in terms of rhythm. The instruction "a long time" does not indicate an exact time, but it is different from a term such as *andante* or *allegro* only by degree.

In some instances the lines between the arts have been so blurred that even the most basic terminology, such as composer, becomes problematic. This has given rise to an entire new genre called performance art. As with any new classification, terminology can be nebulous. Many performance artists, such as Chris Burden or Vito Acconci, belong more closely to the world of the visual arts, as for them sound is only incidental to their conceptualizations. Some performance artists, however, center their work squarely in sound. This created immense problems for the musical world, which in the late twentieth century struggled with the very definition of the musical art.

No one, except possibly John Cage, has exposed the insularity of the musical world in the late twentieth century more than Meredith Monk. Unlike Cage, however, she did not set out specifically to challenge what we mean by music, although like Cage a specific musical philosophy crystallized over the years. She began by simply letting her creativity take her where it would, and it took her and her audiences to extraordinary places. As an artist Monk cannot be confined to a single discipline, and since the 1960s she has produced a body of work that obscures the line between the various arts so thoroughly that any attempt at classification seems at best moot.

Meredith Monk's oeuvre only underscores how isolated the field of music was in the late twentieth century. She has received immense recognition: a MacArthur Fellowship, two Guggenheims, a Brandeis Creative Arts Award, three Obies (including an award for Sustained Achievement), two Villager Awards, a Bessie for Sustained Creative Achievement, the 1986 National Music Theatre Award, sixteen ASCAP Awards for Musical Composition, the 1992 Dance Magazine Award, honorary Doctor of Arts degrees from Bard College, the University of the Arts, and the Juilliard School. But she does not appear in the 1980 edition of *The New Grove Dictionary of Music and Musicians*, although she is in the 2000 edition and she does make it into *The New Grove Dictionary of American Music*. She is not in Eliott Schwartz and Daniel Godfrey, *Music Since 1945*, or in Bryan R. Simms, *Music of the Twentieth Century*, and is given one sentence in Paul Griffiths, *Modern Music and After*, where she is labeled a minimalist because of her "minimalism of voices." Even before the 1980 *New Grove* she had created *Juice*, *Key*, *Education of the Girlchild*, *Vessel*, *Our Lady of Late*, *Quarry*, *Dolmen Music*, and many other works.

Does Monk belong to the history of twentieth-century music? Is she a composer? That such a question could even be asked says much about the state of music today. Monk herself is not equivocal: "I call myself a composer." She believes that music is at the heart of her creative work: "Even if I'm working with musical theater or with images, I think of that as a kind of musical composition. I'm always thinking in musical terms, even with images."[60]

The public did not always see it that way. To many her journey to composition was a roundabout one, even if her musical centeredness was always there. Earlier in her career dance seemed a more consuming interest, and when her first pieces began to appear in the 1960s, Monk was known primarily as a dancer and choreographer. Even then, however, she resisted that label and was troubled when others identified her as such. But from the beginning she could not be confined to a single discipline. Her early works, such as *Sixteen Millimeter Earrings*, or *Juice*, occupied that area somewhere between dance and theater, buttressed by imaginative use of slides and film.

Monk had grown up with music. On her mother's side her great-grandfather was a cantor in Moscow, her grandfather a violinist and a baritone at the court of Nicholas I. When he came to the United States he opened a conservatory in Harlem. Her grandmother was a concert pianist, and her mother a classically trained singer who appeared in commercials on radio. Monk herself claims that she sang before she talked, and that she read music before she read words. She later studied voice and piano, but her most influential childhood experience may have been Dalcroze Eurhythmics, a system that teaches children to experience rhythm through body movements. It is part dance training and part musical training, and can lead to perception of complex patterning, as when the foot moves to three beats while the arm moves to four.[61]

Monk grew up in New York City and Connecticut (she was born in New York, not Peru, as some accounts state), and attended Sarah Lawrence College, where she majored in combined performing arts. She continued to study voice and appeared in opera workshops. She partly earned her way through Sarah Lawrence by singing folk music with her guitar — the early sixties was the height of the folk-music craze — and appeared briefly in a rock band called Inner Ear.

Monk also stood out at Sarah Lawrence as a choreographer and dancer, and when she went to New York soon after graduation in 1964, the performing arts were in a state of turbulence. John Cage and Merce Cunningham staged events, often with a visual setting added by Robert Rauschenberg or Jasper Johns, and happenings were at their peak. Fluxus was active, and conceptual art, with its performance element, was challenging the meaning of art as fundamentally as Cage attempted to do in music.

In this environment Monk did not seem out of place. She associated with the Judson Dance Theater, an avant-garde ensemble, and emerged as a public persona from the dance world, for through dance critics she was introduced to the New York public, even though some early pieces such as *Blueprint/Overload* had original music by her. But it was apparent even then that Monk could not be confined to the world of dance, and reviewers stretched to determine what she did. In a caption beneath one picture of Monk was the comment, "She admits her work is beyond the stretchable definition of 'dance,'" and one reviewer, hearing that her mother, who appeared in *Juice*, did not understand what she was doing, said Monk's work had "baffled other than her mother."

By the time of *Juice* in 1969, however, dance critics threw up their hands and had to conclude, "Monk's latest works are not dances."[62] Monk herself called *Juice* a "theater cantata." Most of her pieces were theatrical, and many involved multimedia. Monk even created films, notably, *Sixteen Millimeter Earrings* and *Quarry*.

Monk was evolving artistically. The voice, the aural, began to assume a more central role in Monk's thinking. Monk herself describes the change as sudden: "After I graduated, I came to New York and wasn't singing that much; I was working with text and movement. One day, I started vocalizing, and I guess I had a kind of 'Eureka!' flash, the idea that the voice could have the kind of range that movement has — that there could be a vocabulary for voice as individual as movement."[63]

She calls it a revelation; it is her artistic epiphany. Monk dated it to late 1965, and while the public may have continued to associate her with the dance world, her own work began to assume two directions. She refers to her creative work as a tree with two branches: one the concert tradition, the other the theatrical tradition. For several years her large-scale theatrical, performance-piece settings gained the most attention. In 1970 she released her first solo vocal album, *Key*, and began to give solo recitals, sometimes accompanied by only herself at the piano or, in one case, by herself playing wine glasses.

Key, accompanied by an electronic organ, jew's harp, and mridangam, is textless. Each song is given a descriptive title: "Porch," "Understreet," "Vision," "What Does It Mean," "Change," but there is little clue beyond that what the songs mean. Interspersed between the songs are three verbal monologues, created and performed by members of her company. They are "dreams which evoke visual images in the mind of the listener." They provide little information about the meaning of the other songs, however, beyond suggesting images that may carry over in the listener's mind. Broadly speaking Monk's songs are programmatic vocal pieces. Monk herself has stated that she wants her music to spark the listener's imagination; she likes to put together pieces that suggest emotions, human interaction, but that allow the listener to fill in specifics about what it means.[64]

Key is to Monk more than a collection of songs, however. In style, content, and the use of extended vocal techniques, it does not easily fall within the classical tradition. She referred to it as "invisible theater," each song introducing a character, emotion, or landscape, all of it remaining unspecified. *Key*, as many of Monk's works, yanks the ground out from under the listener on first hearing. The traditional landmarks — text, a defined vocal quality, what we call singing, at times even pitch — are gone, and we are in a strange, foreign landscape, engulfed by ur-rhythms and odd vocal utterances that suggest a primordial world of raw emotion. Monk herself states that is her goal: "I was trying for a visceral, kinetic song form that had the abstract qualities of a painting or a dance. . . . each song became a world in itself with its own timbre, texture, and impulse. I was trying for a primordial musical utterance which would uncover shards of memory and feelings that we don't have words for."[65]

To put a Monk piece in a standard frame, be it that of the musical analyst or simply the listener's musical expectations, not only invites aesthetic disaster but misrepresents her art. Monk must be met on her own terms, even though they may seem outside the realm of what the average listener thinks of as music.

This is not to suggest a Cageian challenge to the meaning of music. Many of her concerns are those that occupy every composer: manipulation of figures, explorations of new sounds, and form. Monk's interest in form is so great that she considers herself a classicist. She takes great care in working out the structure of a piece, and has found that changing one note can necessitate rethinking the entire work. She will develop an idea, then take it into rehearsal and have the performers experiment with it, possibly even improvise on it, then go back and work on it some more. Her creative process is a combination of solitary inspiration and group dynamics.[66]

Key and *Our Lady of Late* are purely vocal works, with minimal accompaniment: *Our Lady of Late* is accompanied only by a wine glass. It opens with an instrumental percussion introduction tapped on the glass. Then, running her fingers on the rim, Monk maintains a constant slightly sharp F-sharp drone. Monk plays her voice against the F-sharp, at times joining it so carefully in color one can hardly distinguish which is which, at times creating pulsating dissonances with it, and at times using it as a launching pad for a dazzling display of extended vocal techniques. But the effect is never virtuosity in itself. Like most of her pieces, the utterances are textless, but her voice takes on innumerable shades of color and emotion. It can show anger, happiness, fear, and sorrow. Growth from *Key* to *Our Lady of Late* is noticeable. The voice of *Our Lady of Late* is much more flexible, the vocal palette richer, the colors deeper and more varied. Monk in fact compares her style of composing to painting, where she takes a canvas, lays down a background, then puts layers on top of that. In spite of her dance background she believes that as a creator she is closer to a painter than to a choreographer, although her manner of working with ensembles resembles that of a choreographer.[67]

By the mid-1970s, her process of vocal discovery was more or less complete, although as late as 1994 Monk said, "I sense that I am at the threshold of finding out what my new voice might be." Music was the core from which an entire work, even those that contained theatrical elements or movement, emanated. In later years theatrical works assumed a less prominent role, although the exceptions, such as *Atlas*, because of their sheer magnitude, stand out. According to Monk the reason for her artistic shift was partly practical and partly artistic. Large theatrical pieces and films became more difficult to fund, and, "Starting around 1970 I began to distrust the theater a little bit. All that hiding behind the fourth wall — and I began to think of music concerts as more *honest*." Recently she spoke of being a bit uncomfortable with the prevalence of illusion that characterizes theater. Monk has always sought a direct, human expression. Nevertheless, she does have at least one film project in mind.[68]

In 1978 Monk formed her own vocal ensemble, which has remained in existence. In 1971 she began to title her larger theatrical works operas, including *Vessel: An Operatic Epic* (1971), *Quarry, an Opera* (1976), *Recent Ruins: An Opera* (1979), and in 1991 she was commissioned to do her first formal opera, *Atlas: An Opera in Three Parts*, for the Houston Grand Opera Association.

Her later works became even more tightly fused, even more difficult to categorize, and for observers and critics, even more stupefying. Newspapers were faced with a dilemma, who should review a Monk work. At times the problem became expensive; when *The Games* was done at the Brooklyn Academy of Music in 1984, the *New York Times* sent not one but three critics to review her, a music critic, a theater critic, and a drama critic. Not even Disney or John Cage could command that kind of interest.

The critics could not even agree on what *The Games* was. John Rockwell, a music critic, called it "an evening of musical theater," Jack Anderson, a dance critic, labeled it a theater piece, but one "in which all components were so adroitly joined that one never thought of wondering who was responsible for any given sequence." Mel Gussow, a theater critic, termed it a "metamedia performance piece." There was almost universal agreement on one aspect of Monk's work, however: she had fused the different arts together so well that breaking them into their different components seemed almost beside the point. Rockwell spoke of the "categorical chaos" that greeted the mere announcement of a new Monk piece, and John Perrault, when he reviewed *Blueprint* (1) and *Overload/Blueprint* (2), admitted that her work "defies categories."[69]

In 1987 Bernard Holland, in reviewing a Monk concert, clearly didn't quite know what to make of it all. He offered the following apologia, a statement that undoubtedly resonates for many of his generation: "[Describing himself] He has passed through the front door of middle age; he greeted the advent of Elvis Presley in the 1950s, then vanished to foreign lands for most of the Roaring Sixties. He must take as an act of faith the cultural frame in which Miss Monk's art is set, with its resonances of barriers broken, chances taken, new languages created. He was not there to experience it himself." Holland then went on to observe that when the different parts are taken separately they are not much but they all add up to something greater than the parts.[70]

Monk is well aware of what she is doing: breaking down the boundaries between the different arts. At times she has attempted to transform music into dance, literally. More often she has sought to fuse together the arts so thoroughly that the individual ones are no longer extractable. "My work is like a colored liquid; it keeps changing. . . . Most people think only of the containers, the names, the certain times, the repeatability, the objecthood. In theater process mixture — category-lessness — is not understood." More to the point, in 1984 she told John Rockwell: "For me, there's no separation [between the arts]. I simply don't think of the different arts as different. I just think of me doing my work. It's all part of one form." In "Mission Statement, 1983, Revised 1996," she stated as her goals, "to create an art that breaks down boundaries between the disciplines, . . . an art that seeks to reestablish the unity existing in music theater and dance, the wholeness that is found in cultures where performing arts practice is considered a spiritual discipline with healing and transformative powers."[71]

This does not mean that in every piece the elements will be in perfect balance. *Dolmen Music* is as close as any Monk to a pure musical event. The players sit on stage in a semicircle and sing, accompanied only by Robert Een's cello. But even within that constricted setting the players interact with one another, in dialogue and counterpoint. The human element, something vital to Monk's creativity, is there, obvious, in the body language and facial expressions of the performers. And they give big clues to the textless utterances.

In other works the defining element is the space in which the events occur, a sort of theatrical setting, only the setting is not the theater but the environment itself. Often pieces have multiple settings. *Vessel*, which Monk calls an operatic epic, unfolds in three places: Part One in Monk's own loft; Part Two in The Performing Garage, and Part Three in a parking lot and an adjacent church. As in many Monk pieces, she creates a fantasy world, which in this case stands in marked tension to the stark industrial reality about her. At the same time this was no piece about twentieth-century mechanization, industrial decay, or urban blight. In a sense of course it was, but the actual topic was Joan of Arc.

Theatrically Monk adds a narrative layer to the happenings.[72] This both transforms and limits the nature of the piece. Narrativity demands a linearity that is typically not present in a happening. Monk's is not a pure linearity; scenes unfold to present a cumulative narrative, but individual scenes themselves are often static. Even more important, narrativity demands focus on the single event. While each scene may be static, at any one time there is one scene, not the multi-ring circus of the happening.

Monk's narrativity is also inherently musical, a reflection of her own orientation. Hers is traditional music, the music of the Renaissance, the music that Cage and the minimalists sought to escape. Even more traditional is Monk's favored medium, the voice, although the result is anything but tradi-

Meredith Monk on stage (Photograph by Massimo Agus)

tional. In stripping the voice of its common role, support of words, to present pure sounds, her music resides in the interstices between pure sound and articulated language. Unencumbered by discourse, context, or intellectual overlay, the sounds retain a razor-sharp emotional directness. Possibly for that reason her music has a mythic dimension that recalls a time when language itself was just emerging in the human species.

The very primal qualities that Monk sought, however, create their own limits. In stripping away externals such as text, in reducing accompaniment to a minimum, and in presenting only her voice, Monk spectacularly attained her desired results, to present directly and powerfully the most fundamental primordial emotions. But this only goes so far, and soon the effect becomes repetitive. Stripping all down to such essentials leaves little room for variety at the deepest artistic level. From *Key* to *Our Lady of Late* to *Volcano Songs*, we do hear a growth, but it is primarily her growth as a singer, as her voice becomes more flexible, subtle, and capable of greater effects. Compositionally we bump into limits imposed by her goal.

Monk's most powerful pieces, however, transcend this limitation through another element, counterpoint. But the term must be extended beyond its normal usage. When Monk calls herself a contrapuntist, she means it in a multimedia sense.[73] On the surface, *Turtle Dreams (Waltz)* is essentially a concert piece, for four singers. But it was conceived with costumes, some abstract narrative, and a minimal choreography for the singers, which consists mostly of a shuffling motion that gradually comes to resemble a ballroom box step. At one point a female performer in a white dress slowly boxes across the stage with an invisible partner. And occasionally the other members of the ensemble suddenly, briefly break out of their basic step, as if they were momentarily possessed. Monk refers to the visual action in *Turtle Dreams* specifically as a counterpoint to the aural.

Monk's early piece *Raw Recital* provides an important clue to her idea of counterpoint. *Raw Recital* began as any other recital; she sang vocal works by Bach and Purcell, among others, to piano accompaniment. Then, while the accompanist played the piano parts again, Monk danced. The pianist did not attempt to add the vocal line, but stayed with the original accompaniment; Monk's dancing was intended to represent the line she had just sung. Sound and movement become as one.[74]

For a musician used to staying strictly with the musical medium as traditionally conceived, the implications of Monk's actions challenge the very meaning of the term *contrapuntal*. For a dancer the leap is not as great, for bodily movement often receives its impulse from musical movement. Dance terminology itself is strikingly similar to musical terminology: choreographers, for instance, speak of movement, phrases, repetition, and intensification.

Even within the musical genre, however, Monk's greatest strength is as a contrapuntist. Monk sometimes does write traditional counterpoint, as the imitation at the beginning of "There Are Three Heavens and Hell," or the intricate interaction of parts in *Dolmen Music*. Layering is important, as voices often interact over an ostinato background, which itself can consist of several strata or be as simple as the drone of a wine glass. But when Monk's great variety of vocal sounds becomes the material of contrapuntal elaboration the result is both emotionally powerful and musically arresting. Monk's counterpoint is an artistic equivalent of the scientific concept of emergence. Neither traditional counterpoint nor extended vocal techniques can explain the overall effect of the two as Monk combines them.

Monk's theatrical pieces embody the same contrapuntal qualities, only here more elements come into play. In many cases space is as important as movement or sound, and the interaction between performers is more pointed as they assume more defined characters. The images that often accompany a Monk theatrical work, including film, add another contrapuntal layer to the mix. Precisely because of their contrapuntal character, however, they present an integrated whole that defies reduction to their component elements.

Monk sees herself squarely within the American maverick tradition: "I remember years ago when people were trying to identify my style of music, and I always say I feel like I come from this maverick tradition of Henry Cowell, Charles Ives, Harry Partch, and I remember being on this panel for grant applications one time, and it was this kind of multicultural thing, and I said, 'What about us in the American maverick tradition?'" Henry Cowell was a particularly strong influence through recordings of his that she discovered at Sarah Lawrence.[75]

Yet if Meredith Monk is to be compared with any composer, it would be Harry Partch. Both create in their characters and themes archetypes, and in doing so have sought to capture a primal, ritualistic, theatrical experience in their work that looks back to a much earlier time. Both believe in a directness of emotional communication through their music, unencumbered by theories and philosophies of the past several hundred years. Both use musical materials that go far beyond the twelve notes of the tempered scale. Both created their own unique musical instruments, Partch literally building his as a carpenter, Monk through discovery and experimentation with her own voice. And most important, both believe in a complete fusion of the aural and the visual.

Monk's approach to the contrapuntal element also parallels Partch's. With both Monk and Partch the measure of a piece lies in the interactions that ensue, sometimes between different instrumental lines, but more often going beyond the aural. To Partch each instrument has its own character, which is reflected in the music. Thus we have Partch's admonition that the performer not just re-create sounds but enter fully into the corporeality of his or her part, which includes body movement, almost a type of choreography dictated by the instrument itself. Corporeality and artistic fusion go hand in hand with Partch.

Although Monk is aware of Harry Partch, she knows him, as most musicians do, for his forty-three-tone scales. In other words she doesn't know him. Partch considered this aspect of his music incidental, claiming "that precious 43 is the one-half truth of the one-fourth factor." For two of America's most important mavericks, separated by two generations and a continent, bringing to their work such different raw materials and developing such different themes, to arrive at such similar places speaks strongly to the power of those forces of change that have embroiled and disturbed the musical world.

The work of Monk, Partch, Cage, and other artists points to a revolution in music as profound as any that has happened in the past four hundred years, one that goes beyond style to the very purpose and nature of music. No longer is music seen as a thing-in-itself, an abstract entity to be considered purely in terms of its own internal relations. No longer is it a spur to visual conjuring of a magical world whose populating is left to the listener's imagination. Music is now perceived as part of a broader art, one that fuses the aural and the visual and sometimes the verbal so completely that we can no longer speak of each in isolation. Music: the term itself needs to be revisited. The internal actions and workings of the aural remain relevant, but to speak of art, high or low, to consider the significance and meaning of a piece — that is, to ask artistic and aesthetic questions — a new perspective is needed, one that goes beyond the aural, and I suspect that with it must come a new vocabulary.

We don't have to give up what we have. I still love to play my cello, and revel in the pure sound that is produced. Those abstract compositions that were created in the past several hundred years remain enduring monuments to the human spirit. But there are other ways, and historians, performers, or simply listeners need to recognize that. Most performers and listeners already have, but historians have been slower. Although many have acknowledged the new landscape, most history and criticism remains insular, an affair purely of sound. Critics especially have the task of coming to terms with an art world that looks very different from what prevailed as little as fifty years ago. Musical criticism, at its most serious, will need to become a cooperative endeavor, as musicians reach out across disciplines to embrace the other arts, and in many cases to learn. New vocabularies, new ways of hearing, and seeing, and new experiences await. American mavericks have pointed the way; artists — we can often no longer speak of composers — have discovered it, and the public itself, in its embrace of an aural-visual-verbal fusion, has endorsed it.

Bach, Beethoven, Brahms, will not disappear. They will be there, but *how* is the question that awaits the new century. Technology undoubtedly will play a major part. It can not only alter the landscape but create new ones, such as Piranesi's castle in which Yo-Yo Ma plays Bach. Concerts will continue to move toward theater, opening even further possibilities. The historian can only look at what happened and, if sufficiently reckless, venture a guess about the future. It is up to the artist to determine what will happen.

NOTES

CHAPTER 1: We, the Rebels

1. This anecdote is discussed in Chapter 7.

CHAPTER 2: William Billings

1. Quoted in Broyles, *"Music of the Highest Class,"* 34.

2. Billings, *New-England Psalm-Singer*, i, 32.

3. A bequest of one shilling suggests that Billings's father was estranged from the rest of his family. Such a bequest was a common way of discouraging heirs from challenging a will. McKay and Crawford, *William Billings of Boston*, 32.

4. McKay and Crawford, *William Billings of Boston*, 36.

5. Quoted in Nathan, *William Billings, Data and Documents*, 14. Few documents about Billings exist, and Nathan has assembled virtually all extant ones.

6. Nathan, *William Billings, Data and Documents*, 17.

7. McKay and Crawford, *William Billings of Boston*, 41.

8. McKay and Crawford, *William Billings of Boston*, 107.

9. *Columbian Magazine*, April 1788, quoted in Nathan, *William Billings, Data and Documents*, 13. The other American genius the article discussed was the poet Robert Bolling. "William Billings," *The Musical Reporter* (Boston), July 1841. Quoted in Nathan, *William Billings, Data and Documents*, 31.

10. *Columbian Magazine*, April 1788, reprinted in Nathan, *William Billings, Data and Documents*, 13.

11. Billings made a number of changes in the *Singing Master's Assistant* version. He removed many octave doublings in *New-England Psalm-Singer*, most in the bass line. Their removal may have been practical. The lower octaves might be difficult to sing, although they are not *that* low. Given the haphazard, amateur nature of his singing groups, however, he may have had a problem. Yet the changes in the *Singing Master's Assistant* version create a more interesting and sophisticated sonority. The existence of two versions suggests that to Billings line was more important than harmony. Some changes were probably done for melodic reasons; the soprano, mm. 9–10, and the alto, mm. 9–11, both have more interesting lines in *Singing Master's Assistant*. The melody has only one small change, at m. 13, but it makes a big difference. The *Singing Master's Assistant* version, with a dotted quarter and an eighth note, has a more dynamic quality than the original with two quarter notes. As this particular high F is the climactic note of the melody its slight prolongation coupled with the additional rhythmic impetus of the dotted rhythm is crucial to the overall shape of the tune.

In both versions Billings uses complete triads throughout, unusual for eighteenth-century tunebooks in general. The only open sound, in the fourth beat of m. 14, occurs only because of arpeggiation in the bass. Even though the sound is full, however, the settings are not free from harmonic faults according to common practice standards. Most are parallel fifths and octaves, a common error that every student of music theory quickly learns to avoid. There are four sets of parallels in both versions, and in only one instance do the *Singing Master's Assistant* changes correct one. Even in that case, however, m. 10, the elimination of one set of parallel octaves creates another, which makes it difficult to say that Billings made the change specifically to correct harmonic difficulties.

12. Louis C. Elson, in *The National Music of America*, has a relatively balanced but typical nineteenth-century account of Billings. He found much fault with Billings's untutored style, and he had no use whatsoever for the fuging tunes, which "might make Bach's bones rattle" (72), but he recognizes that Billings wrote a lot of other music, and found much strength in his other music. Elson calls Billings a "musical Paul Bunyan" (68). He also recognizes the importance of Billings's patriotic music. And while Billings may have been "uncouth in expression and utterly untrained in the school of music which he undertook to compose," Elson does conclude that Billings was "the right man in the right place" (75).

13. The text was written by Reverend Mather Byles, who, as we will see later, was himself a maverick. It was originally called "New-England Hymn."

14. The *Boston Magazine*, November 1783, does not identify Billings as editor. "On the Seduction of Young Women" appeared in the *Boston Magazine*, November 1783, 18. It is signed simply "Truelove."

15. The allegory was published as *The Porcupine, Alias the Hedge-Hog: or, Fox Turned Preacher*, by L.S. Living in Fox-Island.

16. Billings, *Fox Turned Preacher*, 4.

17. The fox argues that he could not participate in singing because the "Psalms were so filled with Hebrewisms, and often mentioning Jerusalem, Tyre and Sidon, and other places up the Straits, which were now in possession of the Turks, who are all unbelievers, that for his part he thought the bare mentioning of them bordered upon infidelity; and besides, King David make frequent mention of *Babylon*, that great whore, first gets people drunk, and then commits fornication with them" (10).

18. As is the case in virtually all of Billings's writing outside the tunebooks, his role in *The American Bloody Register* is not entirely clear. He is listed as a "transcriber." His role was likely more than simply transcription, however. The pamphlet came out very soon after Billings was involved with the *Boston Magazine*, and it is so consistent with other articles associated with him that Billings probably was the instigator of it.

19. In the early eighteenth century, publishers in London began to collect broadsides together and publish them in books. Two of the most popular were: *A Compleat History of the Lives and Robberies of the most Notorious Highway-men, Foot-pads, Shop-lifters, and Cheats of both sexes, in and about London and Westminster, and all parts of Great Britain, for above an Hundred Years past, continued to the present time. Adorn'd with the Effigies, and other material Transactions of the most remarkable Offenders, The Fifth Edition adorn'd with Cuts,* by Captain Alexander Smith (London, 1719), and *A General and True History of the Lives and Actions of the most Famous Highwaymen, Murderers, Street-Robbers, etc. To which is added a genuine Account of the Voyages and Plundres of the most Noted Pirates, Interspersed with Several Remarkable Tryals of the most Notorious Malefactors, at the Sessions-House in the Old Baily, London, engraved on copper-plates,* by Capt.

Charles Johnson (London, 1734). For a discussion of this literature see Shepard, *The History of Street Literature*, 100.

20. "The Life of Sawney Beane," *Boston Magazine* 1 (October 1783), 23–25. It is apparent in the articles that the magazine was addressed to ladies, e.g. "Fable," "Receipt for making a Good Lady," "Unexpected Surprise," "On the Seduction of Young Women," which is more a word of warning to young women than a tale that would titillate men. This makes the inclusion of Sawney Beane even more remarkable.

21. The phrase "morality play of westerward expansion" comes from Nash, *Wilderness and the American Mind*, 24.

22. Nash, *Wilderness and the American Mind*, 28–29; Heimert, "Puritanism, the Wilderness, and the Frontier," 169–74; Carroll, *Puritanism and the Wilderness*, 136–37.

23. Information about Billings's associates is taken from McKay and Crawford, *William Billings of Boston*, 65–67.

24. Gould, *Church Music in America*, 46.

25. Oliver's comment is quoted in McKay and Crawford, *William Billings of Boston*, 67.

26. Eaton, *The Famous Mather Byles*, 164, 169–70. Eaton gives no further information about the source of Eliot's letter to Belknap.

27. Byles entitled the poem "New-England Hymn." And even though Byles's Tory leanings later became apparent, they were not in 1770. "New-England Hymn" is a celebration of liberty in New England, a sentiment that no doubt attracted Billings to the poem.

28. Eaton, *The Famous Mather Byles*, 109. The entire poem is fourteen stanzas.

29. Bentley, *The Diary of William Bentley*, II, 350–51. The entire obituary is quoted in McKay and Crawford, *William Billings of Boston*, 186; Gould, *Church Music in America*, 46, comments on Billings's voice; Eliot's letter is quoted partially in McKay and Crawford, *William Billings of Boston*, 87 and 127.

30. Pierce, unpublished "Memoirs," quoted in Nathan, *William Billings, Data and Documents*, 46; McKay and Crawford, *William Billings of Boston*, 207. Pierce's reference to Billings's "screams" requires explanation. Pierce undoubtedly meant it as critical, but only in the context of a style change that occurred in the early nineteenth century (Pierce was writing in 1839). Billings's music was keyed to a different type of choral singing than prevalent today. A harsher, more strident, more nasal sound was actually desired in the eighteenth century. This sound as well as the harmony came under heavy attack from the scientific reformers of the early nineteenth century, who sought to bring church music into line with standard European practice. The two were intimately tied; the open harmonic intervals of the older style gave the more nasal sounds a special resonance. Take the eighteenth-century sound away and the harmony becomes "cloying," and so on, as the reformers argued. It is ironic but understandable that in this day of historical awareness in performance few choirs are willing to risk imitating eighteenth-century sounds when performing Billings's pieces.

CHAPTER 3: The Log Cabin Composer

1. James B. Finley, quoted in Weisberger, *They Gathered at the River*, 33–34.

2. Quoted in Broyles, *"Music of the Highest Class,"* 76.

3. An extended discussion of Mason's and Dwight's contributions can be found in Broyles, *"Music of the Highest Class."*

4. Sonneck's statement is quoted in Upton, *Anthony Philip Heinrich*, xi.

5. There is no mention of Heinrich, for instance in W. L. Hubbard, ed., *History of American Music*, William S. Matthews, *A Hundred Years of Music in America*, or Frederic Louis Ritter, *Music in America*.

6. We do not know what type, because it was crushed and destroyed in an accident on a ship to London in 1826 (Upton, *Anthony Philip Heinrich*). Upton's biography, based on the scrapbooks, is the only extended treatment of Heinrich.

7. Direct conversion from 1800 Austrian florins to 2001 U.S. dollars is almost impossible to do with any accuracy. Beethoven's agreement in 1808 for an annual stipend in Vienna from Viennese aristocrats to keep him from moving provided for 4000 florins, considered the equivalent of a good court appointment and enough to live on comfortably. This suggests that a florin would be worth at least ten dollars, probably more, in today's currency.

8. The comment is from Ludlow, *Dramatic Life As I Found It*, 55.

9. Members of Drake's family consisted of Samuel Drake, Jr., who was also a violinist, Alexander Drake, his wife, Francis Ann Denny, Julia Drake, and James G. Drake, the only offspring of Samuel, Sr., who tried to pursue a career outside the theater. He was a gifted singer and guitarist, and while young did participate in Drake productions in that context (Hill, *The Theatre in Early Kentucky*, 130–35).

10. Heinrich described his sojourn in the wilderness in a London newspaper, in a letter to Albert Gallatin, the American minister at London, quoted in Upton, *Anthony Philip Heinrich*, 97.

11. It was not until the 1840s, when European violinists such as Ole Bull and Henri Vieuxtemps toured the United States, that the violin itself was recognized throughout American culture as something other than a fiddle (Broyles, "Music of the Highest Class," 295).

12. Review of "Be silent now ye merry strains," "Fantasia vocale," "The Twin Brothers," and "The Twin Sisters," *Quarterly Musical Magazine and Review* 10 (1828), 528–29.

13. Comment that Heinrich wrote on the manuscript to his song "How Sleep the Brave," quoted in Upton, *Anthony Philip Heinrich*, 40.

14. Review of *The Dawning of Music in Kentucky*, in *Euterpeiad* 2 (April 13, 1822); all italics in the original. The entire article is quoted in Upton, *Anthony Philip Heinrich*, 66–67.

15. Boston *Daily Advertiser*, May 29, 1823, quoted in Upton, *Anthony Philip Heinrich*, 70.

16. Scrapbook, 1060. The newspaper is not identified.

17. Wolfe, *Early American Music Engraving and Printing*, 241.

18. Heinrich's account: "Once when I was vegetating in my Bardstown log house, upon roots, milk and bread, quite solitary, I was not a little frightened after midnight whist playing on the violin a dead march in honor of my poor departed wife, when a negro, prowling about, burst suddenly upon the shattered door of my hut, which was blocked up with large sticks of wood. He soon pacified my agitation by his harmonious request that I would go on playing, as he had been attracted solely by the sweet sounds. I began again the dirge which pleased him amazingly; so much so that he requested it again, handing me at the same time a fippenny bit. True fact. I, of course, returned him the bit and gratified him with the tune. This adventure with the negro, at dead of night, in the lonely forest, seemed to me rather poetical. I liked the good ear, taste and generosity of the sable visitor exceedingly." According to Upton, this account was reported in the Boston *Courier*, 1846, and the New York *Tribune*, May 5, 1846. Upton, *Anthony Philip Heinrich*, 40.

19. The Boston *Gazette* reprinted an article, "The Western Minstrel," identified only as a "London paper." The *Gazette* article is in the Scrapbook, p. 424, and quoted in Upton, *Anthony Philip Heinrich*, 95. "The Remarkable Story of A. P. Heinrich" is in the Scrapbook, p. 15, and quoted in Upton, 97.

20. Both Moore's letter and the Canzonets are quoted in Upton, *Anthony Philip Heinrich*, 101–3.

21. *Quarterly Musical Magazine and Review*, 528–29.

22. *Quarterly Musical Magazine and Review*, 529.

23. Howard, *Our American Music*, 227.

24. *The Musical World and New York Musical Times*, April 30, 1853, quoted in Upton, *Anthony Philip Heinrich*, 222.

25. I use the term American Indian here rather than Native Americans, because Heinrich's Indians were not real (although he did specifically refer to famous Native Americans of the time), but romanticized creatures of his and others' imaginations.

26. Thomas Grey, "Orchestral Music," 470. On October 6, 1830, Mendelssohn sent a sketch of the opening twelve measures to his family, presumably inspired by his visit to the Isle of Hebrides.

27. *The Criterion* 30 (May 24, 1858), 58, quoted in Maust, "The Symphonies of Anthony Philip Heinrich Based on American Themes," 185.

28. Heinrich, *The Western Minstrel*, Preface.

29. Maximilian's *Travels in the Interior of North America* is reprinted in Goldthwaite, *Early Western Travels*; Maust, "The Symphonies of Anthony Philip Heinrich," 175–76.

30. "Theatrical," *New York Evening Post*, no. 6153, March 19, 1822.

31. Novak, *Nature and Culture*, 189.

32. Mussik, *Skizzen aus dem Leben des sich in Amerika*, 18–20, quoted in English in Upton, *Anthony Philip Heinrich*, 143.

33. Hewitt, *Shadows on the Wall*.

34. Novak, *Nature and Culture*, 18.

35. These reviews are found in the Heinrich Scrapbook, p. 878, and are quoted in full in Upton, *Anthony Philip Heinrich*, 187–88.

36. Upton, *Anthony Philip Heinrich*, 192–93.

37. *The Musical World and New York Musical Times*, April 30, 1853, 273–74.

38. The article was written by Julie de Marguerittes, a singer-writer active in New York at this time. It is in the Scrapbook, p. 1112, and quoted in Upton, *Anthony Philip Heinrich*, 224.

CHAPTER 4: Precursors

1. Martens, *Leo Ornstein*, 16.

2. Van Vechten, *Music and Bad Manners*, 170.

3. Draft of letter to Walter Goldstein, 1921, apparently never sent: "Ain't never heard nor seen any of the music — not even a god damn note — of Schoenberg-Scriabin — Or Ornstein — Just because I swear and use cuss-words, aint no sign my name is Murphy" (Ives Papers 29/13), quoted in Swafford, *Charles Ives*, 319. Ives is defending against Gordon's claim that the *Concord Sonata* resembled the "Schoenberg-Scriabin-Ornstein idiom." Although there is no record of Ornstein and Ives meeting, Ives's statement strains credulity: Ornstein was too prominent for Ives to have been unaware of him. Ornstein's Bandbox concerts in 1915 created a sensation and were reported in the New

York newspapers. In 1916, G.F.H. commented, "So much has been written about Leo Ornstein. . . . Surely no pianist of recent years has aroused more discussion" (G.F.H., *Musical America* 27, no. 9 [January 1, 1916], 18), and in 1917 J.O.I. referred to him as "the intransigent pianist, who has set the entire musical world by the ears and who is probably the most discussed figure on the concert stage at the present time" (J.O.I., *Baltimore Evening Sun*, February 10, 1917, reprinted in *Musical Courier*, 74, no. 1 [March 15, 1917], 7). Literally dozens of articles about Ornstein appeared in the New York newspapers, and we know that Ives regularly read newspapers. There are clippings files in the West Redding House, and Ives composed many pieces based on contemporary events (see Vivian Perlis, comp., "Charles Ives Papers," Yale University Music Library Archival Collection, mss. 14, p. 194). Two examples of pieces based on contemporary events are "General Slocum," based on an explosion of a ferryboat, and "The Indians." For a discussion of Ives's reliance on newspaper articles in regard to the latter see Von Glahn, "Charles Ives, Cowboys and Indians," 292–94. Of course Ives may have read about Ornstein without actually hearing his music. Ives may have been unaware of Schoenberg in the 1910s, but much circumstantial evidence points to a knowledge of Skryabin's music. Ives apparently drafted his letter in a fit of pique, and his decision not to send it may have reflected his own realization on cooling down that what he had written was not entirely the case.

4. Exact dates are not clear.

5. Rosenfeld, "Ornstein," 84.

6. Edvard Grieg, *Butterfly*, Op. 43, No. 1, Ede Poldini, *Marche Mignonne* (Columbia A 1445), and Frédéric Chopin, *Impromptu*, Op. 29, *Etude in G-flat*, Op. 10, No. 5 (Columbia A 1473). They were issued in February and March 1914, and recorded May 10, 1913.

7. Kramer, "Leo Ornstein, Pianist," 23.

8. Vivian Perlis, Interview, Yale Oral History Project in American Music, December 8, 1972, Waban, Massachusetts, quoted in Perlis, "The Futurist Music of Leo Ornstein," 737.

9. Deems Taylor, "Mainly About Music," *New York World*, October 1, 1922, in "The New York Scrapbooks"; Martens, *Leo Ornstein*, 57.

10. In that sense Ornstein differs from Henry Cowell, who independently came upon tone clusters at virtually the same time. To Cowell dissonance clusters were also color, but the clusters were essentially the sound spectrum between two outer pitches. He was more interested in the overall, cumulative, and often programmatic effects of a series of similar clusters, and frequently combined them with diatonic lines, as in the "Tides of Manuanmen," one of his first experiments in that direction. To Cowell clusters create a splash of sound, to Ornstein a very specific harmonic combination.

11. Martens, *Leo Ornstein*, 24–25.

12. R.C., "Futurist Music. Wild Outbreak at Steinway Hall," London *Daily Mail*, March 2, 1914; "A 'Futurist' Recital. Mr. Ornstein's 'Impressions,'" London *Daily Telegraph*, March 28, 1914, 7. Martens, *Leo Ornstein*, 26, lists the Ornstein pieces for the second recital.

13. Martens, *Leo Ornstein*, 26; C.N., "Music in London. Leo Ornstein. Some Frank Impressions," *The Musical Standard* (London), April 18, 1914, 374.

14. James Huneker, "The Seven Arts," *Puck*, April 17, 1915, 11; "Montreal Likes Ornstein's Futurism," *Montreal Star*, February 14, 1916, reprinted in *Musical Courier* 72, no. 8 (February 24, 1916), 29; Eric De Lamarter, "Pianists Three and Their Gentle Ways," *Chicago Tribune*, March 26, 1916; J.L.H., "A Critic Abroad," *Musical America* 23, no. 9 (January 1, 1916), 18; Trachtenberg, ed., *Memoirs of Waldo Frank*, 65.

15. "The Music of a Day," *New York Times*, November 26, 1916.

16. Quoted in Severo M. Ornstein, liner notes, *Leo Ornstein, Sonata for Cello and Piano, 3 Preludes* LP, Orion ORS 76211.

17. "Ornstein Interviewed," *Musical Courier* 88 (January 31, 1924), 62; Terrance J. O'Grady, "A Conversation with Leo Ornstein." *Perspectives of New Music* 23 (Fall–Winter 1984), 127; both quoted in Metzer, "The Ascendancy of Musical Modernism in New York City," 122.

18. Leo Ornstein, interviewed by the author, Green Bay, Wisconsin, June 26, 1998.

19. The Piano Concerto was a reworking of the Sonata for Two Pianos of 1921. According to Severo Ornstein, Ornstein stated that the concerto represented an extensive rewriting, although its extent cannot be determined because the two-piano version has not survived.

20. Shameless plug: A biography of Leo Ornstein is currently being written by Michael Broyles and Denise Von Glahn, to be published by Indiana University Press.

21. Rosenfeld, "Leo Ornstein," 267–80.

22. Philip Sunderland, Interview, in Perlis, *Charles Ives Remembered*, 16. Sunderland was ninety-seven years old at the time he talked to Perlis.

23. Ives, *Memos*, 115–16.

24. Swafford, *Charles Ives*, 159–60, quotes some of the reviews.

25. For a discussion of the projected opera, see Cooney, "Reconciliations," 100–106.

26. For a revision of how close Ives was to the heat generated by the Armstrong investigation and how its aftermath affected his career, see Broyles, "Charles Ives and the American Democratic Tradition," 135–42.

27. Broyles, "Charles Ives and the American Democratic Tradition," 158.

28. Swafford, *Charles Ives*, 180.

29. New York violinist and conductor Edgar Stowell described "The 'St.-Gaudens' in Boston Common," the first piece in Ives's set *Three Places in New England*, as "awful." Max Smith, an old friend and music critic for the *New York Press*, called the *Concord Sonata* both "awful" and "horrible." Swafford, *Charles Ives*, 219–20. A description of the encounter with Milcke appears in Swafford, *Charles Ives*, 220–21, and Ives, *Memos*, 70.

30. Swafford, *Charles Ives*, 236; David Woolridge, *From the Steeples and Mountains*, 150–51, claims to have talked with a retired timpanist who played Ives's Third Symphony in Munich in 1910 under Mahler.

31. Ives, *Memos*, 59.

32. Swafford, *Charles Ives*, 198. Inflation calculators are taken from the Bureau of Labor Statistics, www.lib.umich.edu/govdocs/historiccpi.html, and the University of Michigan Documents Center, www.lib.umich.edu/govdocs/steccpi.html.

33. A precise inventory of his compositions by 1920 is difficult because it is not clear when he wrote some. This is especially true of songs, a number of which he composed between 1920 and 1926. Most of his instrumental music was composed by this time, although many pieces did not take final form until later.

34. The letters are contained in the Charles Ives Papers. They are summarized in Swafford, *Charles Ives*, 319–20. Bellamann's article, "Concord," *Double Dealer*, October, 21, is in the Ives Papers, Box 27, Folder 8. Furness's article "Mysticism in Modern Music" appeared in *Threefold Commonwealth* in 1926. A copy is in the Ives Papers, Box 56, Folder 1.

35. Lawrence Gilman, "Music," *New York Herald-Tribune*, January 21, 1939.

CHAPTER 5: "Prologue to the Annual Tragedy"

1. For example Edgard Varèse's founding of the New Symphony Orchestra in 1918, which is discussed later in this chapter.

2. In what is still the most detailed study of American musical organizations of the 1920s, Metzer, "The Ascendancy of Musical Modernism in New York City," 156–62, surveyed the various groups organized in the United States to support composers, starting with the Manuscript Society, and including the Modern Music Society, the New Music Society of America, the Franco-American Musical Society, later renamed the Pro Musica Society, and the American Music Guild. Metzer sees the work of new-music groups of the 1920s as building on earlier ones: "The new music groups of the 1920s expanded upon the initial efforts of the Modern Music Society." Furthermore, although Metzer recognizes the different foci of the various organizations — some were dedicated to radical modernism, others more conservative — and although Metzer acknowledges that some had greater influence than others, his own language, which explicitly includes all shades of new groups, acts to smooth the continuum, discounting the differences in approach and motivation that characterized the ultramodern societies almost as much as their musical choices. In fact, Metzer, in citing precedents, not only connects the new organizations of the 1920s with recent European effects, such as the Verein für Musikalische, founded by Arnold Schoenberg in Vienna, and Les Six, a joint effort of six composers in Paris, but draws a line of connection going back to the medieval music guilds.

Oja, *Making Music Modern*, the most important study of art music in New York in the 1920s, also smooths many of the sharp edges dividing organizations, compositional schools, and attitudes of the time. Oja discusses many differences between various organizations but does tend to blur distinctions between the ICG and the League of Composers, on one hand, and more conservative organizations, such as the Pro Musica Society and the American Music Guild, on the other. Oja does acknowledge the more conservative outlook of the latter but, in stressing the international flavor of all of these organizations, concentrates more on the similarities than the differences between them (178–79).

Oja and Metzer both show exemplary scholarship, but they found what they sought, and they were not examining evidence that might separate individual years. Beyond Oja and Metzer, few writers have examined the overall musical climate in which these organizations flourished. Most writers are composer-centric, discussing individual composers and what they wrote, with only a passing mention of musical organizations or reception.

3. Ornstein himself described his Violin Sonata, Op. 31, this way, as we saw in Chapter 4.

4. Quoted in Mattis, "Edgard Varèse and the Visual Arts," 98.

5. Stieglitz's lack of nostalgia is unusual, for the trait pervaded American culture in general; it is a principal theme, for instance, in Ives's music. See Feder, *Charles Ives*, in which Ives's nostalgia is a principal topic throughout the book. For broader discussions of the impact of nostalgia on American attitudes, see Wiebe, *The Search for Order*, and Lears, *No Place of Grace*.

6. Francis Picabia, letter to Alfred Stieglitz, Barcelona, January 22, 1917, quoted and translated in Mattis, "Edgard Varèse and the Visual Arts," 98.

7. Naumann, *Making Mischief*, 189, 193, 222–23; both Picabia and the painter Albert Gleizes asserted that the war had made artistic creation impossible in Europe ("French Artists Spur on an American Art," *New York Tribune*, October 24, 1915).

8. Copland and Perlis, *Copland, 1900 Through 1942*, 42–43.

9. The most extensive list of Harmony and Charles Ives's reading is in a small diary, dated 1919, in the Charles Ives Papers, MSS 14, Box 45, Folder 8.

10. Ware, *Greenwich Village*, 235–67. Ware does discuss the Village in the earlier years. For Ives's attitude toward nudity in painting, Ives diary entry, June 26 [1914], Charles Ives Papers, Box 45, Folder 12.

11. Thomas Vincent Cator, letter to *Musical America* 21, no. 9 (January 2, 1915), 24–25, letter dated December 17, 1914; Buchanan, "Ornstein and Modern Music," 174.

12. Finck, "The Place of Music in American Life," 490, 511.

13. Charles Ives, letter to Walter Goldstein, Ives Papers, Box 29, Folder 13, quoted in Swafford, *Charles Ives*, 319.

14. Lott, "'New Music for New Ears,'" 267.

15. The next chapter discusses Varèse's career in more detail.

16. Paul Rosenfeld, letter to Sherwood Anderson, June 24 (1920), Newberry Library, Anderson Collection, An, Box 20, Folder 31.

17. Rosenfeld to Anderson, January 1 [1921].

18. Leibowitz, ed., *Musical Impressions*, xix; Mellquist and Wiese, *Paul Rosenfeld, Voyager in the Arts*, xx.

19. Rosenfeld, "Leo Ornstein," 267.

20. Paul Rosenfeld, "Musical Chronicle," 657, reprinted with slight modification as "All-American Night" in Rosenfeld, *Musical Chronicle*, 259–60.

21. Copland and Perlis, *Copland, 1900 Through 1942*, 101.

22. Rosenfeld, "Leo Ornstein," 233.

23. Copland and Perlis, *Copland, 1900 Through 1942*, 102, 110–12, 117.

24. Rosenfeld's other books were *By Way of Art*, *Men Seen*, and *Port of New York: Essays on Fourteen American Moderns*, as well as a novel, *Boy in the Sun*.

25. Rosenfeld, *Hour with American Music*, 133–34; Paul Rosenfeld, letter to Sherwood Anderson, November 29 (n.y.), Newberry Anderson Collection, Folder 31.

26. Rosenfeld, *Musical Chronicle*, 3–10. The piece was written in August 1921 and originally published without the title in his "Musical Chronicle" column in *The Dial* 71 (1921), 487–91.

27. Deems Taylor, "Mainly About Music," *New York World*, October 1, 1922, in "The New York Scrapbooks."

28. Sternberg, "Against Modern'ism,'" 6.

29. W. J. Henderson, "Obstinate Conductors Play Music Progressives Do Not Like Hoping to Make Them Like It," *New York Herald*, February 13, 1921, in "The New York Scrapbooks." Mahler died in 1911 and Skryabin in 1915. Mahler's music is decidedly romantic, and Skryabin's is mostly romantic, although in his later works he began to move beyond romantic harmonies and tone colors.

30. Technology is the wild card in the consideration of developments of the 1920s. I believe that its ramifications are vast, and that I have only scratched the surface in that regard. This topic awaits further research.

31. "In words and music, the negro side expresses something which underlies a great deal of America — our independence, our carelessness, our frankness, and gaiety. In each of these the negro is more intense than we are, and we surpass him when we combine a more varied and more intelligent life with his instinctive qualities." Seldes, *The Seven Lively Arts*, 145–46.

32. Charles Ives, handwritten drafts for the essay "Emasculating America," Charles Ives Papers, Box 25, Folder 7; Sousa quoted in McLuhan, *Understanding Media*, 275–76.

CHAPTER 6: The Community of the Ultramoderns

1. Historians and sociologists have suggested many definitions of community, but most follow the broad lines suggested here. For a summary of the different definitions see Bender, *Community and Social Change in America*, 3–11.

2. Ives's last visit to Danbury occurred in 1939. When he saw how it had changed he put his head in his hand and cried, "I'm going back. You can't recall the past." Feder, *Charles Ives*, 346.

3. Gann, *American Music in the Twentieth Century*, 27.

4. L. Varèse, *Varèse: A Looking-Glass Diary*, 33.

5. Schuller, "Conversation with Varèse," 32.

6. Russolo, *The Art of Noise*, 6.

7. Mattis, "Varèse and the Visual Arts," 101.

8. Mattis, "Varèse and the Visual Arts," 116. Mattis translates the last sentence, "L'Amérique qui doit s'organiser est forcée à un grand effort financier," as "America that must organize itself is compelled to make a great financial effort."

9. "Berlioz Compositions Heard in Oratorio and Concert," *New York Tribune*, April 2, 1917; "Sing Requiem Mass for the War's Dead," *New York Times*, April 2, 1917.

10. Mattis, "Varèse and the Visual Arts," 117.

11. Mattis, "Varèse and the Visual Arts," 127.

12. Mattis, "Varèse and the Visual Arts," 147, 131; L. Varèse, *Varèse: A Looking-Glass Diary*, 132.

13. Ouellette, *Edgard Varèse*, 53; Lott, ""New Music for New Ears,'" 267.

14. Edgard Varèse, "A League of Art, A Free Interchange to Make the Nations Acquainted," *New York Times*, March 23, 1919, quoted in Mattis, "Varèse and the Visual Arts," 120.

15. In addition to his alleged Harvard connection Ruggles also claimed to have studied boat design at MIT with a Professor Frisbee. No Frisbee taught boat design at MIT, and Ruggles never enrolled there. A John Frisbee taught free evening classes at the Hawes School in South Boston, and they included art and naval architecture. Ruggles probably attended these and from them developed enough skill to work for a time as a draftsman. Many of his later press releases contained similar shaded claims. Ziffrin, *Carl Ruggles*, 23–57 and *passim* relates many instances of this.

16. Terman, *The Intelligence of School Children*, 246.

17. Charles Seeger, "Henry Cowell," 288; Mead, "The Amazing Mr. Cowell," 65.

18. Seeger, "Henry Cowell," 323.

19. "Walter Damrosch's 4,000th Concert — Conductor Discusses Modern Music," *New York Times*, March 22, 1925.

20. Ziffrin, *Carl Ruggles*, 64.

21. Rita Mead, *Henry Cowell's New Music*, 23.

22. The 1920s was the most productive time in Varèse's life. For a while he composed roughly one major instrumental work a year: *Amériques* (1917–21), *Hyperprism* (1922–23), *Octandre* (1923), *Intégrales* (1924–25), *Arcana* (1925–27). He had enough momentum to write *Ionisation* (1929–31), which closed this fertile chapter. After that Varèse returned briefly to France and practically went silent for nearly two decades.

23. Pescatello, *Charles Seeger*, 6.

24. Pescatello, *Charles Seeger*, 42–43.

25. "Toward the Establishment of the Study of Musicology in America," unpublished paper, in the Seeger Collection, Library of Congress, quoted partially in Pescatello,

Charles Seeger, 55–56. The "virus of musicology" comment is from Henry Cowell, "Charles Seeger," in *American Composers on American Music,* 122–23.

26. Years later Seeger said, "I jolly well was fired by the Acting President of UC, Gayley." Charles Seeger, letter to Richard Reuss, June 18, 1977, quoted in Pescatello, *Charles Seeger,* 78.

27. Carl Ruggles, lecture in series: "The Whitney Club Studio Talks on Modern Music, March 31, 1922." Handwritten notes for lecture, in Carl Ruggles Papers, Box 18, Folder 18, p. 6.

28. It is divided into two parts, I, "Treatise on Musical Composition," and II, "Manual of Dissonant Counterpoint," and finally appeared in a collection of Seeger's writings: Seeger, *Studies in Musicology II,* 49–228.

29. *Musical America* 34, no. 13 (July 23, 1921), 1, 6; a reproduction of the leaflet is in L. Varèse, *Varèse: A Looking-Glass Diary,* 151–52.

30. Lott, "'New Music for New Ears,'" 282.

31. Edgard Varèse, "The Music of Tomorrow," *London Evening News,* June 14, 1924; Reis, *Composers, Conductors, and Critics,* 3.

32. Metzer, "The Ascendancy of Musical Modernism in New York City," 219, discusses the audiences for ICG concerts.

33. Lawrence Gilman, "New Works at the Season's First International Guild Concert," *New York Herald-Tribune,* December 8, 1924.

34. Minna Lederman, quoted in Olin Downes, "The League of Composers, Accomplishments of Ten Years Devoted to Production of Contemporaneous Works," *New York Times,* November 6, 1932.

35. Rosenfeld, *By Way of Art,* 14.

36. "Modern Music Guilds and Their Messages," *Christian Science Monitor,* May 15, 1926.

37. Cowell, "Batons Are Scepters," 374.

38. Lott, "'New Music for New Ears,'" 269.

39. Oja, "Women Patrons," 245.

40. Oja, "Women Patrons," 245.

41. Reis, "Contemporary Music and the Man on the Street," 27.

42. L. Varèse, *Varèse: A Looking-Glass Diary,* 165, 188; Claire R. Reis, unpublished transcript of a recorded interview with Vivian Perlis, January 1976–January 1977, Oral History Project, American Music, Yale University, pp. 64–65.

43. L. Varèse, *Varèse: A Looking-Glass Diary,* 190–91.

44. L. Varèse, *Varèse: A Looking-Glass Diary,* 191; Perlis, Reis transcript, 65.

45. Dane Rudhyar, letter to Carl Ruggles, February 7, 1977, quoted in Archabal, "Carl Ruggles," 45. For a discussion of Rudhyar and his overall influence see Oja, *Making Music Modern,* 97–111.

46. Mattis, "Varèse and the Visual Arts," 175–76. The league symposium was announced in *The League of Composers Review* 1, no. 1 (February 1924), back of title page.

47. Mattis, "Varèse and the Visual Arts," 176; Ziffrin, *Carl Ruggles,* 136, 195, 253.

48. Reis, Perlis Interview; Oja, "Women Patrons," 259; Leibowitz, ed. *Musical Impressions,* 135–36; Rosenfeld, *By Way of Art,* 14.

49. For a discussion of the Jewish issue in Rosenfeld's criticism, see Oja, *Making Music Modern,* 307–8; Paul Rosenfeld, letter to Sherwood Anderson, October 31, 1926, Anderson Collection, An, Box 20, Folder 33; Owens, *Carlos Salzedo,* 6.

50. Ouellette, *Varèse,* 68–69; Metzer, "Ascendancy of Musical Modernism in New York City," 196; Varèse to Ruggles, July 18, 1926, Carl Ruggles Papers, Box 5, Folder 114.

51. For more on the role of women's clubs see Whitesitt, "'The Most Potent Force' in American Music," and Whitesitt, "The Role of Women Impresarios in American Concert Life," 159–80.

52. Ticknor, "The Steel-Engraving Lady and the Gibson Girl," 106.

53. Mattis, "Varèse and the Visual Arts," 150, 152. For a discussion of Whitney's activities see Tarbell, "Gertrude Vanderbilt Whitney as Patron," 10–22.

54. After Varèse resigned, the orchestra continued under the direction of Arthur Bodansky, then Willem Mengelberg, with more traditional repertoire. The New York Philharmonic absorbed it in 1921 (Metzer, "The Ascendency of Musical Modernism," 44).

55. Reis, *Composers, Conductors, and Critics,* 10.

56. Edgard Varèse, "Manifesto," leaflet distributed by Varèse and Carlos Salzedo. *Musical America* printed it July 23, 1921.

57. According to Lott, "'New Music for New Ears,'" this "was one example of the Guild functioning outside the realm of the musical establishment in its early years" (282).

58. Edgard Varèse, "The Music of Tomorrow," *The Evening News* (London), June 14, 1924, reprinted in *The Musical Standard,* July 12, 1924, 14.

59. Lederman, *The Life and Death of a Small Magazine,* 8.

60. Lederman, *The Life and Death of a Small Magazine,* 4.

61. The term itself appears in Seeger, "On the Moods of a Music Logic," 228; Seeger's overall concern with this problem is apparent in many articles collected in Seeger, *Studies in Musicology, 1935–1975.* "On the Moods of a Music Logic" is reprinted there, pp. 64–101.

62. See Oja, *Making Music Modern,* 198, for a further discussion of these lectures.

63. In the case of some particularly long and complex pieces, select movements were published, such as the second movement of Charles Ives's Fourth Symphony. Ives himself provided anonymous financial support (known only to Cowell) to the journal for many years.

64. Lederman, *The Life and Death of a Small Magazine,* 8.

65. Reis, *Composers, Conductors, and Critics,* 7. Ezra Pound is the most well known American writer associated with Fascism. Mattis, "Varèse and the Visual Arts," 175–76, has a discussion of Varèse's attitudes toward Hitler.

66. Edwards, *Flawed Words and Stubborn Sounds,* 32–33.

67. Copland and Perlis, *Copland, 1900 Through 1942,* 110.

68. Copland was generous toward Thomson, even though they were never close. Thomson and Sessions held mutual feelings of distrust (Tommasini, *Virgil Thomson,* 191). Thomson was never associated with either the ICG or the league, and he wrote of the league's "letting me know I was not part of their power-group" (Thomson, *Virgil Thomson,* 138).

69. "Composers Assail Critics at Yaddo," *New York Times,* May 2, 1932.

70. Olga Samaroff's review in the *New York Evening Post* was titled "Expected Riots Peter Out at George Antheil Concert — Sensation Fails to Materialize" (April 11, 1927), quoted in Oja, *Making Music Modern,* 93. Oja discusses other similar reactions to the concert.

71. F. D. Perkins, "The Case of the Hiss and the Three Outbursts of 1922–23," *New York Tribune,* April 15, 1923.

72. Edgard Varèse, letter to Carl Ruggles, n.d. (letter in Louise Varèse's hand), Ruggles Collection, Box 5, Folder 114.

73. W. J. Henderson, "Work by Edgard Varèse Nearly Causes a Riot at Concert," *New York Herald*, March 11, 1923.

74. "The Music of the Day," *New York Times*, November 26, 1918; Olin Downes, "International Composers' Guild Concert," *New York Times*, January 14, 1924.

75. Trachtenberg, ed., *Memoirs of Waldo Frank*, 65.

76. Anderson, "Leo Ornstein," 14.

77. "Review of First ICG Concert," *Musical Courier*, c. December 1922, Ruggles Collection, Box 10, Folder 1.

78. Louise Varèse, interviewed by R. Allen Lott, in Lott, "'New Music for New Ears,'" 276; Mead, *Henry Cowell's New Music*, 455; Reis, *Composers, Conductors, and Critics*, 3; Deems Taylor, "At the Vanderbilt," *New York World*, January 14, 1924; Lawrence Gilman, "The International Composers' Guild," *New York Tribune*, January 14, 1924; see also Lott, "'New Music for New Ears,'" 276–77.

79. Edgard Varèse, "The Music of Tomorrow," *London Evening News*, June 14, 1924, quoted in Metzer, "Ascendency of Musical Modernism," 218; Reis, *Composers, Conductors, and Critics*, 7.

80. The Cambrian Explosion occurred around 550 million years ago when, according to evolutionary biologist Stuart Kauffman, after billions of years of single-cell organisms, "All hell broke loose," and "a burst of evolutionary creativity generated almost all the major phyla" on earth (Kauffman, *At Home in the Universe*, 13).

81. Cowell, ed., *American Composers on American Music*. The phrase "the last banquet" is a metaphorical extension of Roger Shattuck's "The Last Banquet," in *The Banquet Years*, 353–60. Shattuck uses the term to describe an actual banquet that served as the end of an era in French culture.

82. Cowell, ed., *American Composers on American Music*, iv–v. On pp. 3–10 he defines his eight categories: (1) "Americans who have developed indigenous materials or are specially interested in expressing some phase of the American spirit"; (2) "Foreign-born composers who have made America their home and developed indigenous tendencies"; (3) "Americans who are in many respects original but are influenced by modern Teutonic music"; (4) "Americans who also are often somewhat original but who follow either modern French or 'neoclassical' tendencies"; (5) "Americans who do not attempt to develop original ideas or material but who take those which they already find in America and adapt them to a European style"; (6) "Americans who work along conservative lines and make no attempt to write anything departing from general types of European music"; (7) "Foreign-born Americans who continue to compose in European fashion"; (8) "young composers who give promise of developing originally and becoming independently American."

83. Cowell, ed., *American Composers on American Music*, 4.

CHAPTER 7: New Directions

1. Griffiths, *Modern Music and After*, 4; Peyser, *Boulez*, 19.

2. Boulez, "Schoenberg Is Dead," *The Score*, reprinted in Boulez, *Stocktakings from an Apprenticeship*; the quotations are from *Stocktakings*, 211, 213.

3. Morgan, *Twentieth-Century Music*, 341–42.

4. New York did not necessarily have the first symphony orchestra in the country, but the New York Philharmonic, founded in 1842, is the oldest major orchestra currently in existence.

5. Pierre Boulez, letter to John Cage, June 1950, in Nattiez, ed., *The Boulez-Cage Correspondence*, 63.

6. Of the many articles written about Boulez at the time, see Stephen E. Rubin, "Boulez at the Philharmonic: The Iceberg Conducteth," *New York Times*, March 25, 1973, and Harold C. Schonberg, "Summing Up the Boulez Era," *New York Times*, May 15, 1977.

7. Duckworth, *Talking Music*, 78.

8. Mead, *An Introduction to the Music of Milton Babbitt*, 305.

9. Bruno, "Two American Twelve-Tone Composers," 22, 170.

10. Anthony Tommasini, "Finding More Life in a 'Dead' Musical Idiom," *New York Times*, October 6, 1996.

11. Babbitt, quoted in Ewen, *Composers Since 1900*, 22. Heinrich Schenker (1865–1935) was a German theorist who developed new ways of examining tonal music, particularly the standard concert literature. His influence in music theory is comparable to that of his contemporary Einstein in physics.

12. Bernstein, *The Unanswered Question*, 421–22; Gann, *American Music in the Twentieth Century*, 218–19.

13. Donal Henahan, "And So We Bid Farewell to Atonality," *New York Times*, January 6, 1991; Eric Salzman, "Recordings: Stockhausen Explained," *New York Times*, February 25, 1962; Harold C. Schonberg, "Future of the Symphony," *New York Times*, October 24, 1965; Harold C. Schonberg, "The New Age Is Coming," *New York Times*, January 14, 1968. All these are quoted in Straus, "The Myth of Serial Tyranny," 331.

14. K. Robert Schwarz, "In Contemporary Music, a House Still Divided," *New York Times*, August 3, 1997.

15. Straus, "The Myth of Serial Tyranny," 301–44.

16. Shreffler, "The Myth of Empirical Historiography," 30–39.

17. In 1996, a lengthy discussion of the question of the impact that serialists had on American music occurred on the Internet list of the American Musicological Society. A number of composers, some of whom had studied with Babbitt and others, wrote in support of Straus's research, and some expressed concern that audiences were no more in favor of non-serial atonal music than serial compositions. The latter, I believe, is an inadvertent acknowledgment of the problem, an example of the distance that existed between composer and audience. Expecting a typical audience to distinguish stylistically between Davidovsky, Carter, Martino, and Babbitt, for instance, suggests that indeed many composers were out of touch with audiences.

18. David Wright, "A Friendship Formed During a Changing of the Guard," *New York Times*, November 15, 1998.

19. Babbitt, "Who Cares If You Listen?" 38–40, 126–27.

20. Babbitt, "Who Cares If You Listen?" 38.

21. Babbitt, "Who Cares If You Listen?" 126.

22. "An Interview with Barney Childs, 1962," in *Contemporary Composers on Contemporary Music*, ed. Schwartz and Childs, 369.

23. Bell, "*I* Care If You Listen."

24. "The *New York Times* Looks Back: Sputnik," www.nytimes.com/partners/aol/special/sputnik/ (accessed March 14, 2001); Sosna, "The NEH and American Cultural Nationalism."

25. All of the social science disciplines had older roots, but the computer in each revolutionized research, particularly in making possible more sophisticated statistical models. For a discussion of this aspect of Babbitt's writing see Brody, "'Music for the Masses,'" 163–64.

26. Babbitt, "The Unlikely Survival of Serious Music," in *Words About Music*, ed. Dembski and Straus, 164.

27. Schwarz, "In Contemporary Music, a House Still Divided."

28. Bruce Trinkley, interviewed by the author, February 3, 1999.

29. Schwarz, "In Contemporary Music, a House Still Divided."

30. Straus, "The Myth of Serial Tyranny," 309.

31. Anthony Tommasini, "When Bernstein Saw the Future," *New York Times*, July 22, 1988, online edition.

32. Gann, *American Music in the Twentieth Century*, 229.

33. Gann, *American Music in the Twentieth Century*, 221.

34. Gann, *American Music in the Twentieth Century*, 220.

35. Robert Starer, interviewed by the author, July 14, 1999.

36. Schwarz, "In Contemporary Music, a House Still Divided."

37. Anthony Tommasini, "Ned Rorem, Getting Through the Music," *New York Times*, Tuesday, January 21, 1998, online edition.

38. Schwarz, "In Contemporary Music, a House Still Divided."

39. Schwarz, "In Contemporary Music, a House Still Divided."

40. Tawa, *American Composers and Their Public*, 171.

41. Wayne Alpern, e-mail message posted to the Society for Music Theory List, April 23, 2000.

42. Schwarz, "In Contemporary Music, a House Still Divided."

CHAPTER 8: Postwar Experimentalism

1. Revill, *The Roaring Silence*, 47–49.

2. Erik Satie, "Memories of an Amnesiac" (fragments), quoted in Mattis, "Varèse and the Visual Arts," 124. Varèse's comment is from the same page in Mattis.

3. Pritchett, *Music of John Cage*, 12.

4. Revill, *The Roaring Silence*, 51.

5. Salzman, "Review of Records," 261.

6. Revill, *The Roaring Silence*, 76.

7. Pence James, "People Call It Noise — But He Calls It Music," *Chicago Daily News*, March 19, 1942, reprinted in Kostelanetz, ed., *John Cage*, 61–62.

8. Cecil Smith, *Chicago Daily Tribune*, March 2, 1942, quoted in Revill, *The Roaring Silence*, 76.

9. James, "People Call It Noise," 62.

10. Pritchett, *The Music of John Cage*, 89.

11. Revill, *The Roaring Silence*, 167.

12. Revill, *The Roaring Silence*, 166.

13. Schonberg, "The Far-Out Pianist," 49.

14. Cage, "A Composer's Confessions," 6–15, quoted in Pritchett, *The Music of John Cage*, 59. It was published only after Cage's death. In 1982 he stated that the lecture was not published, "nor will it be." Kostelanetz, *Conversing with Cage*, 66,

15. Fleming and Duckworth, ed., *John Cage at Seventy-five*, 21.

16. In November 1996, Irwin Kremen, to whom the score was given, clarified in an e-mail in the John Cage list, "Silence," the nature of the original score. "Silence-digest," Saturday, November 9, 1996, Vol. 1, No. 138.

17. Larry Solomon, "Silence-digest," Tuesday, January 14, 1997, Vol. 1, No. 149.

18. Cowell, "Current Chronicle," 123–24.

19. Cowell, "Current Chronicle," 126.

20. Revill, *The Roaring Silence*, 161; Kostelanetz, "Conversation with John Cage," in Kostelanetz, ed., *John Cage*, 27. The interview occurred in the summer of 1966.

21. Cage, *Silence*, 12.

22. Kostelanetz, "Conversation with John Cage," 22–23.

23. Kostelanetz, "Conversation with John Cage," 27.

24. The Cage quotation is taken from Nyman, "Music," 192; Sims, *Music of the Twentieth Century*, 307–11, 416–17, divides his discussion between Cage's theatrical pieces and his other works.

25. Salzman, "Imaginary Landscaper," quoted in Kostelanetz, *Writings About Cage*, 1.

26. Exact dates are not clear. The first public license was issued to KQL, September 13, 1921, but it may have never gone on the air. KJC, generally considered the first commercial station, received a license on April 10, 1922, but had been informally broadcasting sporadically since September 10, 1920, as 6ADZ. Web site, "A Chronology of AM Radio Broadcasting, Part 1: 1900–1922," http://members.aol.com/jeff560/chrono1.html, accessed May 25, 2001.

27. Kostelanetz, *Conversing with Cage*, 2–3.

28. Kostelanetz, *Conversing with Cage*, 4.

29. Kostelanetz, *Conversing with Cage*, 4–5; interview with Lou Harrison, in Duckworth, *Talking Music*, 104.

30. Revill, *The Roaring Silence*, 77–78; Tomkins, "Profiles," 80.

31. John Cage, interview with William Duckworth, in Fleming and Duckworth, ed., *John Cage at Seventy-five*, 27.

32. The article originally appeared in *The Score and I.M.A. Magazine*, June 1955, reprinted as "Experimental Music: Doctrine," in Cage, *Silence*, 14.

33. Cage, "Experimental Music: Doctrine," 17.

34. Kostelanetz, "Conversation with John Cage," 27.

35. Kostelanetz, "Conversation with John Cage," 28.

36. Nyman, *Experimental Music*, 194.

37. Harrison, "The New York Music Scene," 24.

38. Kostelanetz, *Conversing with Cage*, 120; Revill, *The Roaring Silence*, 206.

39. Each of the reviews was written on October 13, 1952. The excerpts are quoted in "The Concert Hall," 20–21.

40. Bagar, quoted in "The Concert Hall," 20.

41. A typical review was the tongue-in-cheek commentary by Sabin, "Quarter Century of John Cage," 16–17, which begins by quoting Emily Dickinson, "Much madness is divinest sense"; Revill, *The Roaring Silence*, 191–92; audience reaction can be heard on the LP recording of the concert.

42. Cage, *The Twenty-Five-Year Retrospective Concert of the Music of John Cage* (1959).

43. Cage said: "In recent years my musical ideas have continued to move away from the object (a composition having a well-defined relationship of parts) into process (nonstructured activities, indeterminate in character)." Quoted in Borden, "The New Dialectic," 47.

44. Daniel, "Loops and Reels," 63.

45. "The Twenty-Five-Year Retrospective Concert of the Music of John Cage," 955.

46. Heinrich Stroebel, quoted in Stuckenschmidt, "Modern Music Festival at Doneueschingen," 18; Weissman, "Current Chronicle: Italy," 247.

47. Daniel, "Loops and Reels," 63; Kostelanetz, *John Cage (Ex)plain(ed)*, 35.

48. Schonberg, "The Far-Out Pianist"; Borden, "The New Dialectic," 47.

CHAPTER 9: The Maverick Core

1. Cott, "The Forgotten Visionary," 32.

2. For a person of so much peregrination he kept an amazing amount of material, in the form of his own writings and ruminations, photographs, and clippings. These have been assembled and reproduced in Blackburn, ed., *Harry Partch*. Along with Gilmore, *Harry Partch: A Biography*, they provide surprisingly full and rounded picture of Partch.

3. Partch as a symbol of American individualism is discussed further in Chapter 11, but as one example of a writer who has perpetuated the myth, in March 1972, shortly before Partch's death, Eric Salzman published an article in *Stereo Review*, about *Delusion of the Fury*, "A Visit with Harry Partch." The article articulates many of the principal themes of the Partch myth that has so resonated with American culture. He views Partch's hobo years not as a result of economic desperation but as an early-day Jack Kerouac's years "on the road." He praises Partch's vision and idealism, which remained ever clear. And he lauds Partch's instrument building as an example of "Yankee ingenuity" (94).

4. Gilmore, *Harry Partch*, 17–19. Much of the following narrative about Partch's life is indebted to this book.

5. Gilmore, *Harry Partch*, 44.

6. Reprinted in facsimile in Blackburn, ed., *Harry Partch*, 8.

7. Partch, *Genesis of a Music*, x.

8. In Blackburn, ed., *Harry Partch*, 9.

9. Sablosky, "Forty-three to the Octave"; Blackburn, ed., *Harry Partch*, 254, 283. Partch also reacted vehemently when John Cage attempted to symbolically stress the number 43 in editing a statement of Partch's, as recounted later in this chapter.

10. "Speech New Route to Music, *Oakland Tribune*, November 12, 1931; Redfern Mason, "Music Gamut of Speech Is Noted Down," *San Francisco Examiner*, November 29, 1931; Paul S. Nathan, "Music Composer Invents New System," *Oakland Post-Enquirer*, March 1, 1932; R.D.S., *Oakland Tribune*, March 1, 1932; Alexander Fried, "Declamation Music Given by Originator," *San Francisco Chronicle*, February 10, 1932. These clippings were collected by Partch in "Gems from my Scrapbook, 1931," and "Gems from my Scrapbook, 1932," and are reproduced in Blackburn, ed., *Harry Partch*, 13–15.

11. "So far as I can see, it (creation of quarter-tones) would simply provide material for a 24-tone row. And I feel that this is one thing the world can easily do without." Partch, "Barbs and Broadsides," 15.

12. Harry Partch's description, quoted in Gilmore, *Harry Partch*, 113.

13. The person who invited Partch to Chicago is never named; Partch wrote: "In the summer of 1941, quite casually, I met a man, a divinity student, who became interested in my work and described it to a friend in Chicago. The friend wrote to me almost immediately, invited me to Chicago if I could get there on my own, and ended his letter: 'May God's richest blessings be upon you.'" Partch, *Genesis of a Music*, 323–24.

14. Gilmore, *Harry Partch*, 137–38.

15. Partch, *Genesis of a Music*, 321–22.

16. Partch, *Genesis of a Music*, 321.

17. Partch, *Genesis of a Music*, 323.

18. Partch, *Genesis of a Music*, 323.

19. Paul Bowles, "Harry Partch Given Program of His Own Works," *New York Herald-Tribune*, April 23, 1944; H., "New York Concerts," 19; "'Speech Music' Is Novelty," 17.

20. For comments about the 1920s and '40s see Olin Downes, "American Music Heard at Museum," *New York Times*, May 24, 1941; Harrison, "Season's End," 235–36.

21. Brandt quoted in Gilmore, *Harry Partch*, 150. Brandt also observed, "but in 1944 things were so stone age they would have said the same things about Charles Ives"; "'Speech Music' Is Novelty"; Henry Simon, in *P.M.* magazine, April 24, 1944, quoted in Blackburn, ed., *Harry Partch*, 76; R.L., *New York Times*, April 23, 1944, quoted in Blackburn, ed., *Harry Partch*, 76.

22. Blackburn, ed., *Harry Partch*, 480; Olin Downes, "Hollowness of Much Music Reflects World of Today," *New York Times*, June 1, 1941; Luening, *The Autobiography of Otto Luening*, 443–44.

23. John Lardner, *New Yorker*, May 27, 1944, 22, reproduced in Blackburn, ed., *Harry Partch*, 75.

24. Blackburn, ed., *Harry Partch*, 87.

25. The essay is reproduced in Partch's typescript in Blackburn, ed., *Harry Partch*, 84–86; this comment is from p. 85.

26. Blackburn, ed., *Harry Partch*, 86.

27. Harry Partch, "Some Old and New Thoughts After and Before the Bewitched," typescript reproduced in part in Blackburn, ed., *Harry Partch*, 218–28. The earlier part is in Harry Partch, *Bitter Music*, 231–38. This quote is from Blackburn, ed., *Harry Partch*, 218.

28. Harry Partch, letter to Peter Yates, April 15, 1955, quoted in Gilmore, *Harry Partch*, 227.

29. Gilmore, *Harry Partch*, 243, 245.

30. Gilmore, *Harry Partch*, 249–50; Blackburn, ed., *Harry Partch*, 253.

31. Gilmore, *Harry Partch*, 254.

32. Partch, postcard to Peter Yates, June 6, 1961, quoted in Blackburn, ed., *Harry Partch*, 302.

33. John Chalmers, interviewed by Thomas McGeary, 1984, tape at the "Harry Partch Oral History Project," University of Illinois, cited in Gilmore, *Harry Partch*, 345–46.

34. Harry Partch, letter to Lou Harrison, August 18, 1966, quoted in Blackburn, ed., *Harry Partch*, 399.

35. Harry Partch, letter to Peter Reed, December 8, 1954, reproduced in Blackburn, ed., *Harry Partch*, 213, 214.

36. Harry Partch, "On G-String Formality," typescript, Madison, Wisconsin, 1946, reproduced in Blackburn, ed., *Harry Partch*, 84–87.

37. Partch, *Genesis of a Music*, 8.

38. Partch, *Genesis of a Music*, 71.

39. Chapter 12 contains a more detailed discussion of Partch's ideas of corporealism and the visual dimension.

40. Most of these comments were made in various letters that Partch wrote to friends. They may be found in Blackburn, ed., *Harry Partch*, 145, 279, 391, 435.

41. This correspondence is reproduced in Blackburn, ed., *Harry Partch*, 403–4.

42. Blackburn, ed., *Harry Partch*, 435; Bowen, "Harry Partch's Music Between the Keys," 53.

43. This story is told in Walley, *No Commercial Potential*, 26–27, and in Ruhlmann, "Frank Zappa: The Present Day Composer," 11–12.

44. Zappa, *The Real Frank Zappa Book*, 31. Russo, *Cosmik Debris*, 8, has a reproduction of the *Look* magazine article and the Varèse cover.

45. Zappa, interview by Martin Perlich.

46. Russo, *Cosmik Debris*, 13, reproduces some of the newspaper clippings about Zappa's art career.

47. Sheff, "Interview with Frank Zappa," 62.

48. Russo, *Cosmik Debris*, 24, reproduces the front page of the Ontario-Upland (California) *Daily Report*, which describes the bust.

49. Shelton, "Son of Suzy Creamcheese," 11–12.

50. Hansen, "We're Only in It for the Money," 16.

51. Hopkins, "The Rolling Stone Interview: Frank Zappa," 11.

52. Manville, "Does This Mother Know Best?" 56–57.

53. Walley, *No Commercial Potential*, 104.

54. A performance of this at the Royal Albert Hall on June 6, 1969, is included in Zappa's album *You Can't Do That on Stage Anymore*, vol. 5. While the visual is obviously missing, one can get an idea of the absurdity of the stage activity from the audio track.

55. Shelton, "Son of Suzy Creamcheese," 11.

56. "Frank Zappa, American Composer," online documentary, at www.zappa.com.

57. Zappa, *The Real Frank Zappa Book*, 169.

58. "If I'm not rehearsing I spend about 16, 18 hours a day down here [in the workroom] . . . if I'm not here, I usually do about 10, 14 hours in the studio, seven days a week." Zappa, *Frank Zappa: In His Own Words*, 66.

59. Felton, "What Zappa Did to Zubin Mehta," 18.

60. Felton, "What Zappa Did to Zubin Mehta," 18.

61. Walley, *No Commercial Potential*, 103.

62. Walley, *No Commercial Potential*, 105, 103–4, 211.

63. For a discussion of the issue of juxtaposition in twentieth-century modernism, see Shattuck, *The Banquet Years*, 325–52.

64. "DB Music Workshop: Frank Zappa's 'Little House,'" 32.

65. "DB Music Workshop," 32.

66. Zappa, *The Mothers—Fillmore East, June 1971*.

67. Watson, *Frank Zappa*, 134; Walley, *No Commercial Potential*, 195, 87.

68. Josef Woodard, "Zappa: The License to Be a Maniac," *Musician*, 1986, reprinted in *Society Pages*, no. 33, December 1986, 18, quoted in Watson, *Frank Zappa*, 421–22.

69. Russo, *Cosmik Debris*, 101.

CHAPTER 10: Minimalism and Strange Bedfellows

1. Schwarz, *Minimalists*, 16.

2. Duckworth, *Talking Music*, 215. At least one critic noticed the eternal quality in Young's music also: John Perreault described a Young-Zazeela concert as "like hearing a small piece of eternity." "La Monte Young's Tracery: The Voice of the Tortoise," *Village Voice*, February 22, 1968, 27.

3. Schwarz, *Minimalists*, 31–32.

4. Duckworth, *Talking Music*, 236.

5. The room is sort of divided by inner areas marked "Staff Only."

6. Young, "Notes on The Theatre of Eternal Music and The Tortoise, His Dreams and Journeys."

7. There is considerable irony in this aspect of the Western tradition. For although composers garner more respect, and more lines in the histories, composition is not what pays. In the classical world today performers and conductors fare much better than composers. The reason is discussed in Chapter 12.

8. The Young quotation is from Strickland, *American Composers*, 60; Wakoski's comment is from Young, "Notes on The Theatre of Eternal Music," 20.

9. Young, "Notes on The Theatre of Eternal Music," 14–15, 25.

10. Alfred Frankenstein, "Music Like None Other on Earth," *San Francisco Chronicle*, November 8, 1964; Frankenstein, "'Veritably a Dilly,'" 104.

11. Fried, "Samuel Starts in C," 12; Siohan, "Humor and Sarcasm at Darmstadt," 8.

12. Strickland, *Minimalism: Origins*, 185–86.

13. Duckworth, *Talking Music*, 297.

14. Strickland, *American Composers*, 192.

15. Glass, *Music by Philip Glass*, 15.

16. Given the collaborative, experimental way Wilson works, it is difficult to place him into a traditional theatrical category.

17. Jones, "Musician of the Month," MA 4.

18. Kolodin, "For the Record," 37.

19. Griffiths, *Modern Music and After*, 51.

20. Sontag, *On Photography*, 20.

21. Kyle Gann, "Reich On," *Village Voice* 41 (February 27, 1996), 47.

22. Nattiez, ed., *The Boulez-Cage Correspondence*, 5–7.

23. Boulez, *Stocktakings from an Apprenticeship*, 211, 213; Boulez, "Alea," 839–57, reprinted in English in Boulez, *Stocktakings*, 26–38; Nattiez, ed., *The Boulez-Cage Correspondence*, 20–24, discusses Cage's reaction; Kostelanetz, *Conversing with Cage*, 121.

24. Peyser, *Boulez*, 24–25.

25. Kostelanetz, *John Cage (Ex)plain(ed)*, 4.

26. Cone, "Analysis Today," 176.

27. Sypher, *Loss of the Self in Modern Literature and Art*, 87–88, 99; Boulez, "The Composer and Creativity," 121.

28. The terms "experimental music" and the "experimental tradition" have become common designations for the most radical composers from Ives to "Cage and beyond" (Nyman, *Experimental Music: Cage and Beyond*), composers generally associated with the avant-garde or ultramodern school before World War II, and downtown after World War II. I am using "experimental music" here not to designate a historical grouping but rather to designate composers who approached their craft in the spirit of scientific investigation.

29. Boulez, "Sonata, que me veux-tu?" 154.

30. Boulez, quoted in Copland, *The New Music, 1900–1960*, 173; Krenek, "Extents and Limits of Serial Techniques," 93.

31. Brody, "'Music for the Masses,'" 165.

32. Bruno, "Two American Twelve-Tone Composers," 22, 170; Duckworth, *Talking Music*, 82; Griffiths, *Modern Music and After*, 62–63; Brody, "'Music for the Masses,'" 165–66.

33. Cage, *Silence*, 84; Nyman, "Hearing/Seeing," 235.

34. Brown, "The Notation and Performance of New Music," 181; Krenek, "Extents and Limits of Serial Techniques," 93; Kyle Gann, "Minimalism vs Serialism: Let X = X," *Village Voice*, February 24, 1997, 76.

35. Gagne and Caras, *Soundpieces*, 198.

36. Wasserman, "An Interview with Composer Steve Reich," 46.

37. In Wasserman, "An Interview with Composer Steve Reich," 48.

38. Young, "Notes on The Theatre of Eternal Music," 2. Between September 23, 2000, and June 23, 2001, Young presented at the Dream House the following piece: *The Base 9:7:4 Symmetry in Prime Time When Centered above and below The Lowest Term Primes in The Range 288 to 224 with The Addition of 279 and 261 in Which The Half of The Symmetric Division Mapped above and Including 288 Consists of The Powers of 2 Multiplied by The Primes within The Ranges of 144 to 128, 72 to 64 and 36 to 32 Which Are Symmetrical to Those Primes in Lowest Terms in The Half of The Symmetric Division Mapped below and Including 224 within The Ranges 126 to 112, 63 to 56 and 31.5 to 28 with The Addition of 119.*

CHAPTER 11: Looking Back

1. Seeger's treatise in *Studies in Musicology II*, 17–267; see Chapter 6 for further discussion of Cowell's early life and his work with Seeger.

2. Ziffrin, *Carl Ruggles*, 70–71.

3. Ziffrin, *Carl Ruggles*, 251.

4. Slonimsky, "Composers of New England," 26–27; Rosenfeld, *An Hour with American Music*, 104.

5. The Griggs comment was related by Ives in *Memos*, 38; Lawrence Gilman, "Music," *New York Herald-Tribune*, January 31, 1927; Henry Bellamann, program notes for Pro-Musica, Inc., Concert, January 29, 1927, Town Hall, New York City. Herrmann, "Charles Ives," 99–100.

6. Charles Ives, letter to William Lyon Phelps, January 6, 1937, in Charles Ives Papers, Box 31, Folder 6.

7. Ruggles, notes for the Whitney Club Studio Talks on Modern Music, March 31, 1922, in the Carl Ruggles Papers, Box 18, Folder 18.

8. For a discussion of Rudhyar's ideas and influence see Oja, *Making Music Modern*, 97–126; Rudhyar's comment appears on p. 115. For a discussion of the relationship between Rudhyar and Crawford see Tick, *Ruth Crawford Seeger*, 48–50.

9. Chris Burden, "Shoot," Performance Piece, F-Space, Santa Ana, November 19, 1971.

10. Quoted in Smith, "Developing a Fluxable Forum," 3–4.

11. Philip Glass's position is typical of many non-atonal composers. He applied for grants for eleven years from the Guggenheim, Rockefeller, Mellon, and Koussevitzky foundations, and did not get money from any. "None of the new-music foundations would support my music. . . . List them. All the new-music people — zip!" Duckworth, *Talking Music*, 336.

12. Duckworth, *Talking Music*, 87.

13. Davidovsky, cited in Appleton, "Electronic Music," 104; Babbitt, in Duckworth, *Talking Music*, 89. The largest of the performance grants was for the Louisville Symphony project, which was funded by a major grant from the Rockefeller Foundation.

14. Appleton, "Electronic Music," 104.

15. Griffiths, "George Perle."

16. Meyer, *Music, the Arts, and Ideas*, 27.

17. Meyer, *Music, the Arts, and Ideas*, 27 (quoting Norbert Wiener), 25–26.

18. Carter, "The Case of Mr. Ives," 175–76.

19. Hitchcock, *Music in the United States*, 43.

20. Larsen, "The Revolution in Sound in America Since 1948"; Copland, *What to Listen for in Music*.

21. Schwarz, "In Contemporary Music, a House Still Divided."

22. Brody, "'Music for the Masses,'" 163.

23. Krenek, "Tradition in Perspective," 32.

24. *Fitness landscape* is a term from complexity theory and evolutionary biology used to describe metaphorical terrain that agents must negotiate to succeed.

25. Bauman, "Review: 17 *Lyrics of Po*, etc.," 176; Hackbarth, "Tonality in *Daphne of the Dunes*," 57; Danlee Mitchell, quoted in Dery, "Bang a Gong," 53; Lou Harrison, in Doty, "From the Editor," 2.

26. Anderson, "New Works," 77; Dery, "Bang a Gong," 49; Kyle Gann, "The Peerless Partch," *Village Voice*, February 18, 1992, 20; Anderson, "New Works," 77; Bauman, "Review: 17 *Lyrics of Po*, etc.," 176.

27. Brozen, "Debuts and Reappearances," MA, 17.

28. Tom Johnson, "New Music," *High Fidelity/Musical America* 25 (November 1975), MA, 12–13.

29. Harry Partch, lecture to Broadcast Music, Inc. (BMI), San Francisco, June 20, 1963, in Blackburn, ed., *Harry Partch*, 317.

30. Blackburn, ed., *Harry Partch*, 406.

31. "Keep Partch Here," editorial in the *Champaign-Urbana Spectator*, April 24, 1961.

32. Partch's most well known comments about musical education are in "On G-String Formality," an essay written while he was at the University of Wisconsin, Madison, in 1946. It is reproduced in Blackburn, ed., *Harry Partch*, 84–87.

33. Salzman, "A Visit with Harry Partch," 94; Yates, "Revelation in Illinois," 29, quoted in Blackburn, ed., *Harry Partch*, 302–6.

34. Broyles, "Charles Ives and the American Democratic Tradition," 118–60.

35. Snyder, "An Interview with John Cage," 15.

36. Duckworth, *Talking Music*, 238.

37. Gagne, *Soundpieces 2*, 484.

38. Gagne, *Soundpieces 2*, 485.

39. A system, be it a collection of molecules, an array of blinking lights, an ecology, or a culture, could quickly settle into a fixed point and come to a halt, as a ball does in a concave bowl; it could settle into a periodic repetitive state, as the fluctuation of predator and prey population in an environment does, or it could be without discernible pattern, in a chaotic, unpredictable state, such as traffic in New York City. Traffic in New York City may not be totally chaotic, however, as certain cyclic patterns, such as rush hours, occur.

40. In Conlin, "Immigrants and the West in American Consciousness," 188–89.

41. Conlin, "Immigrants and the West in American Consciousness," 188.

42. Kauffman, *At Home in the Universe*, 26; emphasis added.

43. Edward Rothstein, "Was Schubert Gay? A Testy Debate," *New York Times*, February 4, 1992.

CHAPTER 12: Looking Forward

1. Rosenfeld, *Discoveries of a Music Critic,* 5–6.

2. Yet while this came across loud and clear and was drilled even more powerfully into aspiring musicians, how many students in a one-semester introduction to what classical music was about came out of the class actually thinking in such terms? I now wonder, in disparaging "nonessential" imaging in the listening process, how many students we actually turned off of classical music.

3. Meyer, *Music, the Arts, and Ideas*; Meyer, *Emotion and Meaning in Music*; Narmour, *The Analysis and Cognition of Basic Melodic Structures.*

4. Meyer, "The End of the Renaissance?" originally in *Hudson Review,* reprinted in Meyer, *Music, the Arts, and Ideas,* 68–84.

5. Rhode, *History of the Cinema,* 273.

6. Haggin, "Films," 514.

7. Olin Downes, "'Fantasia' Discussed from the Musical Standpoint—Sound Reproduction Called Unprecedented," *New York Times,* November 14, 1940; Olin Downes, "Disney's Experiment: Second Thoughts on 'Fantasia' and Its Visualization of Music," *New York Times,* November 17, 1940.

8. Downes, "Disney's Experiment."

9. Downes, "Disney's Experiment."

10. "Mr. Disney and 'Fantasia,'" *New York Times,* November 15, 1940.

11. Theoretically this could be done, as Charlie Chaplin did in *The Circus,* where he specified in detail what an orchestra in the movie-house was to play during each scene. Until talking pictures were invented in the 1920s, however, the possibility of putting the entire product onto the film, and consequently achieving a tight integration that could be shown anywhere, did not exist.

12. Hoffmann, "Review of Beethoven's Fifth Symphony," 151.

13. Zanotti-Bianco, "Edgard Varèse and the Geometry of Sound," 35, quoted in Mattis, "Edgard Varèse and the Visual Arts," 159. Mattis, 160–62, notes other writers who echoed similar thoughts.

14. Norman, "Edgard Varèse: Ionization-Espace," 259–60, quoted in Mattis, "Edgard Varèse and the Visual Arts," 181.

15. Louise Varèse, *Varèse,* 100–101.

16. Mattis, "Edgard Varèse and the Visual Arts," 182.

17. Abraham Skulsky, "Varèse Set to Launch Electronic Music Age," *New York Herald-Tribune,* January 24, 1954.

18. Varèse, "My Titles," unpublished notes, quoted in Mattis, "Edgard Varèse and the Visual Arts," 192.

19. Mattis, "Edgard Varèse and the Visual Arts," 190.

20. Mattis, "Edgard Varèse and the Visual Arts," 195–96.

21. Mattis, "Edgard Varèse and the Visual Arts," 193.

22. Mattis, "Edgard Varèse and the Visual Arts," 195–96.

23. Mattis, "Edgard Varèse and the Visual Arts," 228.

24. Mattis, "Edgard Varèse and the Visual Arts," 246.

25. Earle Brown interview, March 1990, in Mattis, "Edgard Varèse and the Visual Arts," 228.

26. To Jonathan Bernard's credit, he did not even try to analyze *Poème électronique* in his book, *The Music of Edgard Varèse,* admitting that "without exact notation, no meaningful analysis is possible" (243). Yet the problem is bigger than the absence of a

score; even had Bernard a score, to discuss *Poème électronique* as a thing-in-itself would be comparable to analyzing a film with only a copy of the dialogue.

27. Partch, "Barbs and Broadsides," 9.

28. Johnston, "The Corporealism of Harry Partch," 85–86.

29. Jacobi, "The Strange Realm of Harry Partch," 14.

30. Harry Partch, letter to William Wilder, July 21, 1957, quoted in Blackburn, ed., *Harry Partch*, 496.

31. Partch, "Manual on the Maintenance and Repair of — and the Musical and Attitudinal techniques for — Some Putative Musical Instruments," written January to August 1963, reproduced in Blackburn, ed., *Harry Partch*, 321.

32. Fuller, "Harry Partch, Musician-Sculptor," 47.

33. Harry Partch, letter to Charles Moritz, editor, *Current Biography*, July 5, 1963, in Blackburn, ed., *Harry Partch*, 318.

34. Moore, "Delusion of the Fury," 544–46.

35. Partch frequently felt the need to apologize for his recordings, as in the following letter to William Wilder, a seventeen-year-old fan who had written to Partch: "The visual element of my concepts, which is always present in my mind as an essential factor, must be abandoned along with the idea of phonograph records, and if you could *see* I am sure that such nonsense would fall into place. There was a kind of spontaneous demand for records among the people who *saw* the performance of Oedipus at Mills College in 1952. Having seen, the memory of the visual aspect was recalled whenever they played the records. . . . But one who has never seen my instruments nor any theater performance with them has nothing to recall, and in the present circumstances I am quite helpless to change this, at the same time being very grateful that anyone in this situation has the intuition to buy my records." Letter dated July 21, 1957, quoted in Blackburn, *Harry Partch*, 496.

36. Partch agreed with such an assessment. In reference to Cage, Partch stated, static is static, whether created by drinking carrot juice or scratching a feather on a stylus. Letter to Peter Garland, February 28, 1972, reproduced in Blackburn, ed., *Harry Partch*, 435.

37. Kostelanetz, *Conversing with Cage*, 107.

38. Some Cage pieces, particularly the late time-bracket pieces, are purely aural. But the overwhelming bulk of the Cage canon, and those works that established his reputation, almost invariably have an important visual element.

39. Mattis, "Edgard Varèse and the Visual Arts," 217.

40. Mattis, "Edgard Varèse and the Visual Arts," 211.

41. "Edgard Varèse on Music and Art," 187–88.

42. Kant, "Frank Zappa: The Mother of Us All," 14.

43. *The Guinness Encyclopedia of Popular Music*, 3:1698.

44. www.bond-music.com/contentsindex.htm; www.eroicatrio.com/html/photos.html; www.larastjohn.com/reviews/articles/torontosun.html; Peter Dobrin, "How Far Will Industry Push to Market Classical Music," *New York Times*, June 6, 2000.

45. Audrey Choi, "Modern Maestros Conduct Themselves in Offbeat Fashions," *Wall Street Journal*, January 1, 1996.

46. Jack Anderson, "How Avant-Garde Works Resemble Romantic Classics," *New York Times*, January 6, 1985; Freeman, "In Review: New York City," 37.

47. Ross, "White Noise," 83.

48. Glass, *Music by Philip Glass*, 19–20.

49. Mertens, *American Minimal Music*, 88; Richard Taruskin, "A Sturdy Bridge to the 21st Century," *New York Times*, August 24, 1997 (online version); Jones, "An Outburst of Minimalism," MA 26–27.

50. Tom Johnson, "How They Do It in London and California," *Village Voice*, February 5, 1979, 63.

51. Taruskin, "A Sturdy Bridge to the 21st Century."

52. Carl, "The Politics of Definition in New Music," 112; Adlington, "Through a Glass Darkly," 164–65.

53. Griffiths, "A Composer May Age, but the Compositions Are Ever Young."

54. Paul Griffiths, "Steve Reich: Music That Must Be Seen to Be Loved," *New York Times*, January 11, 1999, online version.

55. Schwarz, *Minimalists*, 43.

56. Some composers have done well, such as Arvo Pärt or the early minimalists, and there are aficionados for many styles, but except for a handful of works, few pieces have gained wide acceptance. Curiously those that have garnered a larger audience have written primarily repetitive or meditative music, music which challenges the tenets of the Western canon of the past 250 years.

57. "Unified, closed totality," is from a program note by Milton Babbitt to his composition *Dual*, quoted by Rockwell, *All-American Composition in the Late Twentieth Century*, 28.

58. Schneckloth, "Frank Zappa, Garni Du Jour, Lizard King, Poetry and Slime," 45.

59. Shaw-Miller, "'Concerts of Everyday Living,'" 17.

60. Duckworth, *Talking Music*, 346. She made a similar statement in a personal interview with the author, New York City, November 30, 2000.

61. Meredith Monk, interview with the author, New York City, November 30, 2000; Bear, "Meredith Monk: Invocation/Evocation," 80–81.

62. Deborah Jowitt, "How Do You Hear a Dancer?" *New York Times*, September 12, 1971.

63. Jon Pareles, "Meredith Monk, Two Decades Later," *New York Times*, May 17, 1985.

64. Meredith Monk, liner notes, CD booklet, *Key*; Monk, interview with the author.

65. Monk, liner notes in *Key*.

66. Monk, interview with the author.

67. Monk, interview with the author. *Our Lady of Late* was originally written to accompany a dance by William Dunas, in 1972. In 1973 she performed it in a concert version.

68. Monk, "Ages of the Avant-Garde," 191; John Rockwell, "Meredith Monk Opens the Next Wave," *New York Times*, October 7, 1984.

69. Rockwell, "Meredith Monk Opens the Next Wave"; Jack Anderson, "'The Games'—Serious Science Fiction on Stage," *New York Times*, October 21, 1984; Mel Gussow, "Theater: Next Wave Festival Opens," *New York Times*, October 11, 1984; Perrault, "Monk's Mix," 23.

70. Bernard Holland, "Stage: Meredith Monk's Mélange," *New York Times*, November 22, 1987.

71. Monk, "Journal Entry, January, 1970," 30; Rockwell, "Meredith Monk Opens the Next Wave"; Monk, "Mission Statement, 1983, revised, 1996," 17.

72. Berger, "A Metaphoric Theater," 44.

73. Monk, interview with the author.

74. Jack Anderson, "Monk's Inimitable Images," *New York Times*, February 18, 1979.

75. Monk, interview with the author.

BIBLIOGRAPHY

Adlington, Robert. "Through a Glass Darkly." *Musical Times* 135 (March 1994): 164–65.

Albanese, Catherine. "Davy Crockett and the Wild Man; Or, The Metaphysics of the *Longue Durée*." In *Davy Crockett: The Man, The Legend, The Legacy, 1786–1986*, ed. Michael A. Lofaro, 80–101. Knoxville: University of Tennessee Press, 1985.

Anderson, Margaret C. "Leo Ornstein." *Little Review* 3, no. 3 (May 1916): 13–15.

Anderson, Owen. "New Works: International Music Congress." *Music Journal* 26, no. 8 (1968): 77.

Appelby, Joyce. *Telling the Truth About History.* New York: W. W. Norton, 1994.

Appleton, Jon H. "Electronic Music: Questions of Style and Compositional Technique." *Musical Quarterly* 65, no. 1 (1979): 103–10.

Archabal, Nina Marcheti. "Carl Ruggles: An Ultramodern Composer as Painter." Ph.D. diss., University of Minnesota, 1979.

Babbitt, Milton. "Who Cares If You Listen?" *High Fidelity* (February 1958): 38–40, 126–27.

———. *Words About Music: The Madison Lectures*, ed. Stephen Dembski and Joseph N. Straus. Madison: University of Wisconsin Press, 1987.

Bauman, Carl. "Review: *17 Lyrics of Po*, etc." *American Record Guide* 59, no. 5 (1996): 176–79.

Bear, Liza. "Meredith Monk: Invocation/Evocation, A Dialogue with Liza Bear." In *Meredith Monk*, ed. Deborah Jowitt, 78–93. Baltimore: Johns Hopkins University Press, 1997.

Bell, Douglas. "*I* Care If You Listen." Essay on Web page [www.musdoc.com/classical/Care.html]. Accessed June 20, 2001.

Belmont, I. J. *The Modern Dilemma in Art: The Reflections of a Color-Music Painter.* New York: Harbinger House, 1944.

Bender, Thomas. *Community and Social Change in America.* New Brunswick, N.J.: Rutgers University Press, 1978.

Bentley, William. *The Diary of William Bentley, D.D., Pastor of East Church, Salem, Massachusetts.* 4 vols. Salem, Mass.: Essex Institute, 1905–14.

Berger, Mark. "A Metaphoric Theater." In *Meredith Monk*, ed. Deborah Jowitt, 44–48. Baltimore: Johns Hopkins University Press, 1997.

Bernard, Jonathan. *The Music of Edgard Varèse.* New Haven: Yale University Press, 1987.

Bernstein, Leonard. *The Unanswered Questions: Six Talks at Harvard.* Cambridge: Harvard University Press, 1976.

"Be Silent now ye merry Strains, Fantasia vocale, The Twin Brothers, The Twin Sisters." All composed by A. P. Heinrich, London. *Quarterly Musical Magazine and Review* (London) 10 (1828): 528–29.

Billings, William. *The American Bloody Register.* Boston: E. Russel, 1784.

———. *The Continental Harmony.* Boston: Isaiah Thomas and Ebenezer T. Andrews, 1794.

———. *Music in Miniature.* Boston: B. Johnson, 1779.

———. *The New-England Psalm-Singer.* Boston: Edes and Gill, 1770.

———. *The Porcupine, Alias the Hedge-Hog: Or, Fox Turned Preacher, by L.S. Living in Fox-Island.* Boston: Benjamin Edes & Sons, 1784.

———. *The Psalm-Singer's Amusement.* Boston: by the author, 1781.

———. *The Singing Master's Assistant.* Boston: Draper and Folsom, 1778.

———. *Suffolk Harmony.* Boston: J. Norman, 1786.

Blackburn, Philip, ed. *Harry Partch.* St. Paul, Minn.: American Composers Forum, 1997.

Borden, Lizzie. "The New Dialectic." *Artforum* 12 (March 1974): 47.

Boulez, Pierre. "Alea." *La Nouvelle revue française* 59 (November 1957): 839–57.

———. "The Composer and Creativity." *Journal of the Arnold Schoenberg Institute* 11, no. 2 (1988): 108–22.

———. "Schoenberg Is Dead." *Score* 6 (February 1952): 18–22.

———. "Sonata, que me veux-tu?" In *Orientations: Collected Writings of Pierre Boulez,* ed. Jean-Jacques Nattiez, tr. Martin Cooper, 143–54. Cambridge: Harvard University Press, 1968.

———. *Stocktakings from an Apprenticeship.* Collected by Paul Thévenin, tr. Robert Piencikowski. Oxford: Clarendon Press, 1991.

Bowen, J. David. "Harry Partch's Music Between the Keys." *Stereo Review* 6 (February 1961): 50–53.

Brody, Martin. "'Music for the Masses': Milton Babbitt's Cold War Music Theory." *Musical Quarterly* 77, no. 2 (1993): 161–92.

Brown, Earle. "The Notation and Performance of New Music." *Musical Quarterly* 72, no. 2 (1986): 176–82.

Broyles, Michael. "Charles Ives and the American Democratic Tradition." In *Charles Ives and His World,* ed. J. Peter Burkholder, 118–60. Princeton, N.J.: Princeton University Press, 1996.

———. *"Music of the Highest Class": Elitism and Populism in Antebellum Boston.* New Haven: Yale University Press, 1992.

Brozen, Michael. "Debuts and Reappearances." *High Fidelity/Musical America* 18 (December 1968): MA17.

Bruno, Anthony. "Two American Twelve-Tone Composers: Milton Babbitt and Ben Weber Represent Opposing Views." *Musical America* 71, no. 3 (1951): 22, 170.

Buchanan, Charles L. "Ornstein and Modern Music." *Musical Quarterly* 4, no. 2 (1918): 174.

Bunyan, John. *Pilgrim's Progress*. London: Nathaniel Ponder, 1678.

Cage, John. "A Composer's Confessions." *Musicworks* 52 (Spring 1992): 6–15.

———. "Experimental Music." *Score and I.M.A. Magazine* (June 1955): 65–68.

———. *Silence*. Cambridge, Mass.: MIT Press, 1966.

———. *The Twenty-Five-Year Retrospective Concert of the Music of John Cage*, LP recording. New York: George Avakanian, 1959. No LP number.

Carl, Robert. "The Politics of Definition in New Music." *College Music Symposium* 29 (1989): 101–14.

Carl Ruggles Papers. Yale University Music Library Archival Collection (New Haven).

Carroll, Peter N. *Puritanism and the Wilderness: The Intellectual Significance of the New England Frontier, 1629–1700*. New York: Columbia University Press, 1969.

Carter, Elliott. "The Case of Mr. Ives." *Modern Music* 16 (March–April 1939): 172–76.

Cator, Thomas Vincent. Letter to *Musical America* 21, no. 9 (January 2, 1915): 24–25.

Charles Ives Papers. Compiled by Vivian Perlis. Yale University Music Library Archival Collection MSS 14, Catalogue (New Haven, 1983).

Chevalier, Leila. "The Battle of the Music-Makers: Between the Ultra-Modernists and Reactionaries Rages War to the Death." *Arts and Decoration* 17 (October 1922): 405, 454, 456.

"A Chronology of AM Radio Broadcasting, Part 1: 1900–1922." Web page [http://members.aol.com/jeff560/chrono1.html]. Accessed May 25, 2001.

C.N. "Music in London. Leo Ornstein. Some Frank Impressions." *Musical Standard* (London) (April 18, 1914): 374.

"The Concert Hall." *Bulletin of the American Composers Alliance* 2, no. 4 (1952): 20–21.

Cone, Edward T. "Analysis Today." *Musical Quarterly* 46, no. 2 (1960): 172–88.

Conlin, Joseph R. "Immigrants and the West in American Consciousness." In *High Brow Meets Low Brow: American Culture as an Intellectual Concern*, ed. Rob Kroes, 187–208. Amsterdam: Free University Press, 1988.

Cooney, Denise Von Glahn. "Reconciliations: Time, Space, and the American Place in the Music of Charles Ives." Ph.D. diss., University of Washington, 1995.

Copland, Aaron. *The New Music, 1900–1960*. New York: W. W. Norton, 1968.

———. *What to Listen for in Music*. New York: McGraw-Hill, 1939.

Copland, Aaron, and Vivian Perlis. *Copland, 1900 Through 1942*. New York: St. Martin's Press/Marek, 1984.

Cott, Jonathan. "The Forgotten Visionary." *Rolling Stone* 158 (April 11, 1974): 32–38.

Cowan, George A., David Pines, and David Meltzer, eds. *Complexity: Metaphors, Models, and Reality*. Santa Fe Institute Studies in the Science of Complexity, *Proceedings*, vol. 19. Reading, Mass.: Addison-Wesley, 1994.

Cowell, Henry, ed. *American Composers on American Music: A Symposium*. Stanford, Calif.: Stanford University Press, 1933.

——. "Batons Are Scepters." *New Freeman* 1, no. 1b (July 2, 1930): 374.

——. "Current Chronicle, New York." *Musical Quarterly* 38, no. 1 (1952): 123–36.

Crawford, Richard. *The American Musical Landscape.* Berkeley: University of California Press, 1993.

Daniel, Oliver. "Loops and Reels." *Saturday Review* 52 (April 12, 1969): 63.

"DB Music Workshop: Frank Zappa's 'Little House.'" *Downbeat* 36, no. 22 (October 30, 1969): 30, 32–33.

Dery, Mark. "Bang a Gong." *Keyboard* 16, no. 6 (1990): 49–54, 59.

Doty, David B. "From the Editor: Harry Partch and the Just Intonation Network." *1/1* 8, no. 4 (1994): 2, 17.

Duckworth, William. *Talking Music: Conversations with John Cage, Philip Glass, Laurie Anderson, and Five Generations of American Experimental Composers.* New York: Schirmer, 1995.

Dyke, Chuck. Review of *The Origins of Order: Self-Organization and Selection in Evolution,* by Stuart Kauffman, *Complexity: Life at the Edge of Chaos,* by Roger Lewin, and *Complexity: The Emerging Science at the Edge of Order and Chaos,* by M. Mitchell Waldrop. *Configurations* 2, no. 3 (1994): 576–78.

Eaton, Arthur Wentworth Hamilton. *The Famous Mather Byles: The Noted Boston Tory Preacher, Poet, and Wit.* Boston: W. A. Butterfield, 1914.

"Edgard Varèse on Music and Art: A Conversation Between Varèse and Alcopley." *Leonardo* 1, no. 2 (1968): 187–95.

Edwards, Allen. *Flawed Words and Stubborn Sounds: A Conversation with Elliott Carter.* New York: W. W. Norton, 1972.

Elson, Louis C. *The National Music of America.* Boston: L. C. Page, 1900.

Ewen, David. *Composers Since 1900: A Biographical and Critical Guide.* New York: H. W. Wilson, 1969.

"Father Heinrich's Valedictory Concert." *Musical World and New York Musical Times* (April 30, 1853): 273–74.

Feder, Stuart. *Charles Ives: "My Father's Song."* New Haven: Yale University Press, 1992.

Federoff, Nina V. Conversation with author, March 1994, State College, Pennsylvania.

Felton, David. "What Zappa Did to Zubin Mehta." *Rolling Stone* no. 62 (July 9, 1970): 18.

Ferris, Jean. *America's Musical Landscape.* Madison, Wis.: Brown and Benchmark, 1990.

Fétis, F. J. *Biographie universelle des musiciens et bibliographie générale de la musique.* Paris: H. Fournier, 1835–44.

Finck, Henry T. "The Place of Music in American Life." *Etude* 22 (1904): 490, 511.

Fleming, Richard, and William Duckworth, eds. *John Cage at Seventy-five.* Lewisburg, Pa.: Bucknell University Press, 1989.

Frankenstein, Alfred. "'Veritably a Dilly': The Disc Debut of Composer Terry Riley—In C." *High Fidelity/Musical America* 19 (February 1969): 104.

Freeman, John W. "In Review: New York City." *Opera News* 57 (June 2, 1993): 37.

Fried, Alexander. "Samuel Starts in C." *American Musical Digest* 1, no. 3 (1969): 12–13.

Fuller, Mary. "Harry Partch, Musician-Sculptor." *Art in America* 52, no. 6 (1964): 47.

Gagne, Cole. *Soundpieces 2: Interviews with American Composers.* Metuchen, N.J.: Scarecrow Press, 1993.

Gagne, Cole, and Tracy Caras. *Soundpieces: Interviews with American Composers.* Metuchen, N.J.: Scarecrow Press, 1982.

Gann, Kyle. *American Music in the Twentieth Century.* New York: Schirmer, 1997.

G.F.H. *Musical America* 27, no. 9 (January 1, 1916): 18.

Gilmore, Bob. *Harry Partch: A Biography.* New Haven: Yale University Press, 1998.

Glahn, Denise Von. "Charles Ives, Cowboys and Indians: The Other Side of Pioneering." *American Music* 19, no. 3 (2001): 291–314.

Glass, Philip. *Music by Philip Glass.* Edited by Robert T. Jones. New York: Harper and Row, 1987.

Gleick, James. *Chaos: Making a New Science.* New York: Viking, 1987.

Goehring, Edmund J., ed. "Approaches to the Discipline." *Current Musicology* 53 (Fall 1992).

Goldthwaite, Reuben. *Early Western Travels, 1748–1846.* Cleveland: Arthur H. Clark, 1906.

Gould, Nathaniel. *Church Music in America.* Boston: A. N. Johnson, 1853.

Grey, Thomas. "Orchestral Music." In *The Mendelssohn Companion,* ed. Douglas Seaton, 395–533. London: Greenwood Press, 2001.

Griffiths, Paul. "A Composer May Age, but the Compositions Are Ever Young." *New York Times* (September 26, 2000). Article on Web page [www.nytimes.com/2000/09/26/arts/26REIC.html].

———. "George Perle: A Serialist Who Adheres to Tonality." *New York Times* (December 28, 1999). Article on Web page [www.nytimes.com].

———. *Modern Music and After: Directions Since 1945.* Oxford: Oxford University Press, 1995.

The Guinness Encyclopedia of Popular Music. Vol. 3, ed. Colin Larkin. Chester, Conn.: New England Publishing Association, 1992.

H. "New York Concerts." *Musical America* 64, no. 8 (April 1944): 19.

Hackbarth, Glenn. "Tonality in *Daphne of the Dunes.*" *Percussive Notes (Research Edition)* 21, no. 6 (1983): 65–71.

Haggin, B. H. "Films." *Nation* 151, no. 21 (November 23, 1940): 513–14.

Hansen, Barret. "We're Only in It for the Money." *Rolling Stone* 1, no. 8 (April 6, 1968): 16.

Harré, Rom. *Varieties of Realism: A Rationale for the Natural Sciences.* Oxford: Blackwell, 1986.

Harrison, Jay. "The New York Music Scene." *Musical America* 84, no. 3 (1964): 24.

Harrison, Lou. "Season's End, May 1944." *Modern Music* (May–June 1944): 233–37.

Hartz, Louis. *The Liberal Tradition in America: An Interpretation of American Political Thought Since the Revolution.* New York: Harcourt Brace, 1955.

Hastings, Thomas. *Dissertation on Musical Taste.* Albany, N.Y.: Websters and Skinners, 1822.

Heimert, Alan. "Puritanism, the Wilderness, and the Frontier." In *Puritanism and the American Experience*, ed. Michael McGiffert, 163–77. Reading, Mass.: Addison-Wesley, 1969.

Heinrich, Anthony. *The Western Minstrel*. Philadelphia: Bacon & Co., 1820.

Hempel, Carl. "The Function of General Laws in History," *Journal of Philosophy* 39 (1942): 35–48.

Herrmann, Bernard. "Charles Ives." *Trend, A Quarterly of the Seven Arts* (September–October–November 1932): 99–101.

Hewitt, John Hill. *Shadows on the Wall*. Baltimore: Trumbull Brothers, 1877.

Hill, West T., Jr. *The Theatre in Early Kentucky, 1790–1820*. Lexington: University Press of Kentucky, 1971.

Hitchcock, H. Wiley. *Music in the United States: A Historical Introduction*. Englewood Cliffs, N.J.: Prentice-Hall, 1974.

Hoffman, E. T. A. "Review of Beethoven's Fifth Symphony." Translated by F. John Adams. In *Beethoven, Symphony No. 5 in C minor*, ed. Elliot Forbes, 151. New York: W. W. Norton, 1971.

Holland, John. *Emergence: From Chaos to Order*. Reading, Mass.: Helix Books, Addison-Wesley, 1998.

Hopkins, Jerry. "The Rolling Stone Interview: Frank Zappa." *Rolling Stone* 2, no. 3 (1968): 11–14.

Howard, John Tasker. *Our American Music: A Comprehensive History from 1620 to the Present*, 4th ed. New York: Thomas Y. Crowell, 1965.

Hubbard, W. L., ed. *History of American Music*. Toledo: Irving Square, 1867; revised, 1908.

Huneker, James. "The Seven Arts." *Puck* (April 17, 1915): 11.

Ives, Charles. *Memos*. Edited by John Kirkpatrick. New York: W. W. Norton, 1972.

Jacobi, Peter. "The Strange Realm of Harry Partch." *Music Magazine* 164 (July 1962): 14–16.

J.L.H. "A Critic Abroad." *Musical America* 23, no. 9 (January 1, 1916): 18.

———. "New Music." *High Fidelity/Musical America* 25 (November 1975): MA12–MA13.

Johnson, Steven. *Emergence: The Connected Lives of Ants, Brains, Cities, and Software*. New York: Simon and Schuster, 2001.

Johnston, Ben, "The Corporealism of Harry Partch." *Perspectives of New Music* 13, no. 2 (1975): 85–97.

J.O.I. *Musical Courier* 74, no. 1 (March 15, 1917): 7.

Jones, Robert T. "Musician of the Month: Philip Glass." *High Fidelity/Musical America* 29 (April 1979): MA4.

———. "An Outburst of Minimalism." *High Fidelity/Musical America* 33 (February 1983): MA26–MA27.

Jowitt, Deborah, ed. *Meredith Monk*. Baltimore: Johns Hopkins University Press, 1997.

Judkin, Jeremy. *Music in Medieval Europe*. New York: Prentice-Hall, 1989.

Kammen, Michael G. *American Culture, American Tastes: Social Change and the Twentieth Century*. New York: Alfred A. Knopf, 1999.

Kant, Larry. "Frank Zappa: The Mother of Us All." *Downbeat* 36, no. 22 (October 30, 1969): 14–15.

Kauffman, Stuart. *At Home in the Universe: The Search for the Laws of Self-Organization and Complexity.* New York: Oxford University Press, 1995.

———. *The Origins of Order: Self-Organization and Selection in Evolution.* New York: Oxford University Press, 1993.

Kolodin, Irving. "For the Record." *Saturday Review* 6 (July 7, 1979): 37.

Kostelanetz, Richard. *Conversing with Cage.* New York: Limelight Editions, 1994.

———. *John Cage (Ex)plain(ed).* New York: Schirmer, 1996.

———. *Writings About Cage.* Ann Arbor: University of Michigan Press, 1991.

———, ed. *John Cage.* Documentary Monographs in Modern Art, ed. Paul Cummings. New York: Praeger, 1970.

Kramer, A. W. "Leo Ornstein, Pianist: A Study." *Musical America* (July 8, 1911): 23.

Krenek, Ernst. "Extents and Limits of Serial Techniques." In *Problems of Modern Music*, ed. Paul H. Lang, 72–94. New York: W. W. Norton, 1960.

———. "Tradition in Perspective." *Perspectives of New Music* 1 (Fall 1962): 27–38.

Larsen, Libby. "The Revolution in Sound in America Since 1948." Lecture given at the National Conference of the Sonneck Society of America, Kansas City, Mo., February 21, 1998.

Lears, T. J. Jackson. *No Place of Grace: Antimodernism and the Transformation of American Culture, 1880–1920.* New York: Pantheon, 1981.

Lederman, Minna. *The Life and Death of a Small Magazine (Modern Music, 1924–1946).* ISAM Monographs, 18. New York: Institute for Studies in American Music, 1983.

Leibowitz, Herbert A., ed. *Musical Impressions: Selections from Paul Rosenfeld's Criticism.* New York: Hill and Wang, 1969.

Lewin, Roger. *Complexity: Life at the Edge of Chaos.* New York: Macmillan, 1992.

"The Life of Sawney Beane." *Boston Magazine* (October 1783): 23–25.

Lochhead, Judy. "Hearing Chaos." *American Music* 19, no. 2 (2001): 210–46.

Lott, R. Allen. "'New Music for New Ears': The International Composers' Guild." *Journal of the American Musicological Society* 36, no. 2 (1983): 266–87.

Ludlow, Noah M. *Dramatic Life as I Found It: A Record of Personal Experience; With an Account of the Rise and Progress of the Drama in the West and South, With Anecdotes and Biographical Sketches of the Principal Actors and Actresses Who Have at Times Appeared upon the Stage in the Mississippi Valley.* St Louis: G. I. Jones, 1880.

Luening, Otto. *The Autobiography of Otto Luening.* New York: Scribners, 1980.

McIntosh, John. *The Origin of the North American Indians.* New York: Nafis and Cornish, 1843.

McKay, David P., and Richard Crawford. *William Billings of Boston.* Princeton, N.J.: Princeton University Press, 1975.

McLuhan, Marshall. *Understanding Media: The Extensions of Man.* New York: McGraw-Hill, 1965.

Manville, W. H. "Does This Mother Know Best?" *Saturday Evening Post* 241, no. 1 (January 13, 1968): 56–57.

Martens, Frederick H. *Leo Ornstein: The Man, His Ideas, His Work.* New York: Breit-kopf and Hartel, 1918.

Matthews, William S. *A Hundred Years of Music in America.* Chicago: G. L. Howe, 1889.

Mattis, Olivia. "Edgard Varèse and the Visual Arts." Ph.D. diss., Stanford University, 1992.

Maust, Wilber Richard. "The Symphonies of Anthony Philip Heinrich Based on American Themes." Ph.D. diss., Indiana University, 1973.

Maximilian, Prince of Wied. *Travels in the Interior of North America, 1832–1834.* London, 1843.

Mead, Andrew. *An Introduction to the Music of Milton Babbitt.* Princeton, N.J.: Princeton University Press, 1994.

Mead, Rita H. "The Amazing Mr. Cowell." *American Music* 1, no. 2 (1983): 63–89.

———. *Henry Cowell's New Music, 1925–1936: The Society, the Music Editions, and the Recordings.* Ann Arbor, Mich.: UMI Research Press, 1981.

Mellquist, Jerome, and Lucie Wiese. *Paul Rosenfeld, Voyager in the Arts.* New York: Creative Age Press, 1948.

Mertens, Wim. *American Minimal Music.* Translated by J. Hautekiet. London: Kahn and Averill, 1983.

Metzer, David Joel. "The Ascendancy of Musical Modernism in New York City, 1915–1929." Ph.D. diss., Yale University, 1993.

Meyer, Leonard B. *Emotion and Meaning in Music.* Chicago: University of Chicago Press, 1956.

———. "The End of the Renaissance?" *Hudson Review* 6, no. 2 (1963): 169–86.

———. *Music, the Arts, and Ideas: Patterns and Predictions in Twentieth-Century Culture.* Chicago: University of Chicago Press, 1967.

Mink, Louis O. *Historical Understanding,* ed. Brian Fay, Eugene O. Golob, and Richard T. Vann. Ithaca, N.Y.: Cornell University Press, 1987.

"Modern Music Guilds and Their Messages." *Christian Science Monitor* (May 15, 1926): 16.

Monk, Meredith. "Ages of the Avant-Garde." In *Meredith Monk,* ed. Deborah Jowitt, 187–91. Baltimore: Johns Hopkins University Press, 1997.

———. Interview by author, November 30, 2000, New York.

———. "Journal Entry, January, 1970." In *Meredith Monk,* ed. Deborah Jowitt, 30. Baltimore: Johns Hopkins University Press, 1997.

———. Liner notes in *Key.* Lovely Music, Ltd. LCD 1051. CD.

———. "Mission Statement, 1983, revised, 1996." In *Meredith Monk,* ed. Deborah Jowitt, 17. Baltimore: Johns Hopkins University Press, 1997.

Moore, David W. "Delusion of the Fury, a Ritual of Dream and Delusion." *American Record Guide* 38 (July 1972): 544–46.

Morgan, Robert P. *Twentieth-Century Music.* New York: W. W. Norton, 1991.

Mussik, F. A. *Skizzen aus dem Leben des sich in Amerika befinden deutschen Tondichters Anton Philipp Heinrich, nach authentischen Quellen bearbeitet.* Prague, n.p., 1843.

Narmour, Eugene. *The Analysis and Cognition of Basic Melodic Structures: The Implication-Realization Model.* Chicago: University of Chicago Press, 1990.

Nash, Roderick. *Wilderness and the American Mind.* 3d ed. New Haven: Yale University Press, 1982.

Nathan, Hans. *William Billings, Data and Documents.* Detroit, Mich.: Information Coordinators, 1976.

Nattiez, Jean-Jacques, ed. *The Boulez-Cage Correspondence.* Translated by Robert Samuels. Cambridge: Cambridge University Press, 1993.

Naumann, Francis M., with Beth Venn. *Making Mischief: Dada Invades New York.* New York: Whitney Museum of American Art, 1996.

"The New York Scrapbooks." Microfilm of reviews of concerts in New York City, at the New York Public Library, *ZAN–*M28, reel 25.

Norman, Dorothy. "Edgard Varèse: Ionization-Espace." *Twice a Year* 7 (1941): 259–60.

Novak, Barbara. *Nature and Culture: American Landscape and Painting, 1825–1875.* New York: Oxford University Press, 1995.

Nyman, Michael. *Experimental Music: Cage and Beyond.* New York: Schirmer, 1974.

———. "Hearing/Seeing." *Studio International* 192 (November–December 1976): 233–43.

———. "Music." *Studio International* 192 (September–October 1976): 192–94.

Oja, Carol. *Making Music Modern: New York in the 1920s.* New York: Oxford University Press, 2000.

———. "Women Patrons and Crusaders for Modernist Music: New York in the 1920s." In *Cultivating Music in America: Women Patrons and Activists Since 1860,* ed. Ralph P. Locke and Cyrilla Barr, 237–61. Berkeley: University of California Press, 1997.

Ornstein, Severo M. Liner notes in *Leo Ornstein, Sonata for Cello and Piano, 3 Preludes.* Orion ORS 76211. LP.

Ouellette, Fernand. *Edgard Varèse.* Translated by Derek Coltman. New York: Orion, 1968.

Overman, E. S. "The New Science of Management: Chaos and Quantum Theory and Method." *Journal of Public Administration Research and Theory* 6, no. 1 (1996): 487–99.

Owens, Dewey. *Carlos Salzedo: From Aeolian to Thunder, a Biography.* 2d ed. Chicago: Lyon and Healy, 1993.

Parker, John Rowe. "The Dawning of Music in Kentucky." *Euterpeiad* 2 (April 13, 1822).

Partch, Harry. "Barbs and Broadsides." Transcribed by Danlee Mitchell and Jonathan Glasier. *Percussive Notes* 18, no. 3 (1981): 7–15.

———. *Bitter Music: Collected Journals, Essays, Introductions, and Librettos.* Edited by Thomas McGeary. Urbana: University of Illinois Press, 1991.

———. *Genesis of a Music: An Account of a Creative Work, Its Roots and Its Fulfillments,* 2d ed. New York: Da Capo, 1974.

Perlis, Vivian. *Charles Ives Remembered: An Oral History.* New Haven: Yale University Press, 1974.

――. "The Futurist Music of Leo Ornstein." *Notes* 31, no. 4 (June 1975): 735–50.

Perrault, John. "Monk's Mix." In *Meredith Monk,* ed. Deborah Jowitt, 23–25. Baltimore: Johns Hopkins University Press, 1997.

Pescatello, Ann M. *Charles Seeger: A Life in Music.* Pittsburgh: University of Pittsburgh Press, 1992.

Peyser, Joan. *Boulez.* New York: Schirmer, 1976.

Prigogine, Ilya. *The End of Certainty: Time, Chaos, and the New Laws of Nature.* New York: Free Press, 1997.

Pritchett, James. *The Music of John Cage.* Cambridge: Cambridge University Press, 1993.

Reis, Claire. *Composers, Conductors, and Critics.* New York: Oxford University Press, 1955.

――. "Contemporary Music and the Man on the Street." *Eolian Review* 2, no. 2 (1923): 24–27.

――. Interview by Vivian Perlis, January 1976–January 1977. Oral History Project, American Music. Yale University, New Haven.

Revill, Peter. *The Roaring Silence, John Cage: A Life.* New York: Arcade, 1991.

Rhode, Eric. *History of the Cinema from Its Origins to 1970.* New York: Hill and Wang, 1976.

Ritter, Frederic Louis. *Music in America.* New York: B. Franklin, 1890.

Rockwell, John. *All-American Composition in the Late Twentieth Century.* New York: Alfred A. Knopf, 1983.

Rosen, Charles. *The Classical Style: Haydn, Mozart, and Beethoven.* New York: W. W. Norton, 1972.

Rosenfeld, Paul. *Boy in the Sun.* New York: Macaulay, 1929.

――. *By Way of Art.* New York: Coward-McCann, 1928.

――. *By Way of Art: Criticisms of Music, Literature, Painting, Sculpture, and the Dance.* Freeport, N.Y.: Books for Libraries Press, 1967. Reprint of 1928 edition.

――. *Discoveries of a Music Critic.* New York: Harcourt, Brace, 1936.

――. *An Hour with American Music.* Philadelphia: J. B. Lippincott, 1929.

――. "Leo Ornstein." In *Musical Portraits: Interpretations of Twenty Modern Composers,* 267–80. New York: Harcourt, Brace, 1920.

――. *Men Seen.* New York: Dial, 1925.

――. *Modern Tendencies in Music.* Caxton Music Series, 28. New York: Caxton Institute, 1927.

――. "Musical Chronicle." *Dial* 72 (June 1922): 657.

――. *Musical Chronicle (1917–1923).* New York: Harcourt, Brace, 1923.

――. "Ornstein." *New Republic* 7 (May 27, 1916): 84.

――. *Port of New York: Essays on Fourteen American Moderns.* New York: Harcourt, Brace, 1924.

Ross, Alex. "White Noise." *New Yorker* (July 31, 2000): 83.

Ruhlmann, William. "Frank Zappa: The Present Day Composer." In *The Frank*

Zappa Companion: Four Decades of Commentary, ed. Richard Kostelanetz, 5–43. New York: Schirmer, 1997.

Russo, Gregg. *Cosmik Debris: The Collected History and Improvisations of Frank Zappa*. Floral Park, N.Y.: Crossfire, 1998.

Russolo, Luigi. *The Art of Noise*. Translated by Robert Filliou. New York: Something Else, 1967.

Sabin, Robert. "Quarter Century of John Cage." *Musical America* 78, no. 7 (June 1958): 16–17.

Sablosky, Irving. "Forty-Three to the Octave." *New York Times*, July 21, 1957.

Salzman, Eric. "Imaginary Landscaper." *Keynote* (September 1982).

———. "Review of Records." *Musical Quarterly* 64, no. 2 (April 1978): 261–63.

———. "A Visit with Harry Partch." *Stereo Review* 28, no. 3 (1972): 94.

Schilling, Gustav. *Encyclopädie der gesammten musikalischen Wissenschaften, oder universal Lexicon der Tonkunst*. Stuttgart, n.p., 1836.

Schneckloth, Tim. "Frank Zappa, Garni Du Jour, Lizard King, Poetry and Slime." *Downbeat* 45, no. 10 (May 18, 1978): 15–17, 44–46.

Schonberg, Harold C. "The Far-Out Pianist." *Harper's* 220 (June 1960): 49–54.

Schuller, Gunther. "Conversation with Varèse." *Perspectives of New Music* (Spring–Summer 1965): 32–37.

Schwartz, Elliott, and Barney Childs, eds. *Contemporary Composers on Contemporary Music*. New York: Da Capo, 1998.

Schwarz, K. Robert. *Minimalists*. London: Phaidon, 1996.

Seaton, Douglass. *Ideas and Styles in the Western Musical Tradition*. Mountain View, Calif.: Mayfield, 1991.

Seeger, Charles. "Henry Cowell." *American Magazine of Art* 33 (May 1940): 322–27.

———. "On the Moods of a Music Logic." *Journal of the American Musicological Society* 13 (1960): 224–61.

———. *Studies in Musicology, 1935–1975*. Berkeley: University of California Press, 1977.

———. *Studies in Musicology II: 1929–1979*, ed. Ann M. Pescatello. Berkeley: University of California Press, 1994.

Seldes, Gilbert. *The Seven Lively Arts*. 2d ed. New York: A. S. Barnes, 1957.

Shattuck, Roger. *The Banquet Years: The Origins of the Avant-Garde in France, 1885 to World War I*. Garden City, N.Y.: Anchor Books, Doubleday, 1961.

Shaw-Miller, Simon. "'Concerts of Everyday Living': Cage, Fluxus, and Barthes, Interdisciplinarity and Inter-Media Events." *Art History* 19, no. 1 (1996): 1–25.

Sheff, David. "Interview with Frank Zappa." *Playboy* 40, no. 4 (1993): 55–72.

Shelton, Robert. "Son of Suzy Creamcheese." *New York Times*, December 25, 1966.

Shepard, Leslie. *The History of Street Literature: The Story of Broadside Ballads, Chapbooks, Proclamations, News-Sheets, Election Bills, Tracts, Pamphlets, Cocks, Catchpennies, and Other Ephemera*. Detroit, Mich.: Singing Tree, 1973.

Sherwood Anderson Papers. Newberry Library: Anderson Collection (Chicago).

Shreffler, Anne C. "The Myth of Empirical Historiography: A Response to Joseph N. Straus." *Musical Quarterly* 84, no. 1 (2000): 30–39.

Sims, Bryan R. *Music of the Twentieth Century: Style and Structure.* New York: Schirmer, 1996.

Singal, Joseph. "Beyond Consensus: Richard Hofstadter and American Historiography." *American Historical Review* 89 (October 1984): 976–1004.

Siohan, Robert. "Humor and Sarcasm at Darmstadt." *American Musical Digest* 1, no. 2 (1969): 8–9.

Slonimsky, Nicolas. "Composers of New England." *Modern Music* 7 (February–March 1930): 24–27.

Smith, Owen. "Developing a Fluxable Forum: Early Performance and Publishing." In *The Fluxus Reader,* ed. Ken Friedman, 3–21. West Sussex: Academy Editions, 1998.

Snyder, Ellsworth. "An Interview with John Cage: John Cage Discusses Fluxus." *Art and Design* 8, nos. 1–2 (January–February 1993): 15–19.

Sontag, Susan. *On Photography.* New York: Farrar, Straus and Giroux, 1977.

Sosna, Morton. "The NEH and American Cultural Nationalism." Unpublished paper delivered at the Annual Meeting of the Organization of American Historians, Washington, D.C., March 1990.

"'Speech Music' Is Novelty." *Musical Courier* 129, no. 9 (May 5, 1944): 17.

Starer, Robert. Interview by author, July 14, 1999, Woodstock, N.Y.

Sternberg, Constantin von. "Against Modern'ism.'" *Musical Quarterly* 7, no. 1 (1921): 6.

Straus, Joseph. "The Myth of Serial Tyranny." *Musical Quarterly* 83, no. 3 (Fall 1999): 301–43.

Strickland, Edward. *American Composers: Dialogues on Contemporary Music.* Bloomington: Indiana University Press, 1991.

———. *Minimalism: Origins.* Bloomington: Indiana University Press, 1993.

Stuckenschmidt, H. H. "Modern Music Festival at Doneueschingen Shows Vivid Contrast." *Musical America* 74 (December 15, 1954): 18.

Swafford, Jan. *Charles Ives: A Life with Music.* New York: W. W. Norton, 1996.

Sypher, Wylie. *Loss of the Self in Modern Literature and Art.* New York: Random House, 1962.

Tan'sur, William. *The Royal Melody Compleat.* London: R. Brown, for James Hodges, 1755.

Tarbell, Roberta K. "Gertrude Vanderbilt Whitney as Patron." In *The Figurative Tradition and the Whitney Museum of Art: Paintings and Sculpture from the Permanent Collection,* ed. Patricia Hills and Roberta K. Tarbell, 10–22. New York: Whitney Museum of Art, 1980.

Tawa, Nicholas. *American Composers and Their Public: A Critical Look.* Metuchen, N.J.: Scarecrow, 1995.

Terman, Lewis M. *The Intelligence of School Children.* Boston: Houghton Mifflin, 1919.

Thomson, Virgil. *Virgil Thomson.* New York: Alfred A. Knopf, 1966.

Tick, Judith. *Ruth Crawford Seeger: A Composer's Search for American Music.* London: Oxford University Press, 1997.

Ticknor, Caroline. "The Steel-Engraving Lady and the Gibson Girl." *Atlantic Monthly* 88 (July 1901): 105–8.

Tomkins, Calvin. "Profiles: Figure in an Imaginary Landscape." *New Yorker* 40 (November 28, 1964): 80.

Tommasini, Anthony. *Virgil Thomson: Composer on the Aisle.* New York: W. W. Norton, 1997.

Trachtenberg, Alan, ed. *Memoirs of Waldo Frank.* Amherst: University of Massachusetts Press, 1973.

Treitler, Leo. *Music and the Historical Imagination.* Cambridge: Harvard University Press, 1989.

Trinkley, Bruce. Interview by author, February 3, 1999, State College, Pa.

"The Twenty-Five-Year Retrospective Concert of the Music of John Cage." *American Record Guide* 26 (August 1960): 955.

"Two American Twelve-Tone Composers." *Musical America* 71, no. 3 (1951): 22, 170.

Upton, William Treat. *Anthony Philip Heinrich, a Nineteenth-Century Composer in America.* New York: Columbia University Press, 1939.

Van Vechten, Carl. *Music and Bad Manners.* New York: Alfred A. Knopf, 1916.

Varèse, Edgard. "A League of Art: A Free Interchange to Make the Nations Acquainted." *New York Times,* March 23, 1919.

———. "The Music of Tomorrow." *Musical Standard* (July 12, 1924): 14.

Varèse, Louise. *Varèse: A Looking-Glass Diary.* New York: W. W. Norton, 1972.

Von Glahn, Denise. "Charles Ives, Cowboys and Indians: The Other Side of Pioneering." *American Music* 19, no. 3 (2001): 291–314.

Walley, David. *No Commercial Potential: The Saga of Frank Zappa.* New York: Da Capo, 1996.

Ware, Caroline F. *Greenwich Village, 1920–1930.* Berkeley: University of California Press, 1963.

Wasserman, Emily. "An Interview with Composer Steve Reich." *Artforum International* 10, no. 9 (1972): 45–48.

Watson, Ben. *Frank Zappa: The Negative Dialectics of Poodle Play.* New York: St. Martin's Griffin, 1996.

Weisberger, Bernard A. *They Gathered at the River: The Story of the Great Revivalists and Their Impact upon Religion in America.* Boston: Little, Brown, 1958.

Weissman, John S. "Current Chronicle: Italy." *Musical Quarterly* 49, no. 2 (1963): 240–47.

Whitesitt, Linda. "'The Most Potent Force' in American Music: The Role of Women's Music Clubs in American Concert Life." In *The Musical Woman,* ed. Judith Long Zaimont, vol. 3, 663–81. Westport, Conn.: Greenwood, 1991.

———. "The Role of Women Impresarios in American Concert Life, 1871–1933." *American Music* 7, no. 2 (Summer 1989): 159–80.

Wiebe, Robert H.. *The Search for Order, 1877–1920.* New York: Hill and Wang, 1967.

Wolfe, Richard J. *Early American Music Engraving and Printing.* Urbana: University of Illinois Press, 1980.

Woolridge, David. *From the Steeples and Mountains, a Study of Charles Ives.* New York: Alfred A. Knopf, 1974.

Wright, David. "A Friendship Formed During a Changing of the Guard." *New York Times,* November 15, 1998.

Yates, Peter. "Revelation in Illinois." *Arts and Architecture* (August 1961): 4–6, 28–29.

Young, La Monte. "Notes on The Theatre of Eternal Music and The Tortoise, His Dreams and Journeys." Statement on Web page [www.virtulink.com/mela/ LMY.htm]. Accessed May 30, 2001.

Zanotti-Bianco, Massimo. "Edgard Varèse and the Geometry of Sound." *Arts* 7 (1925): 35.

Zappa, Frank. *Frank Zappa: In His Own Words.* London: Omnibus Press, 1993.

——. Interview by Martin Perlich, 1972. Web page, St. Alphonzo's Pancake Home-page for Zappa Fans [www.science.uva.nl/robbert/zappa/].

——. *The Mothers — Fillmore East, June 1971.* Ryko RCD 10512. CD.

——. *You Can't Do That on Stage Anymore.* Vol. 5. Ryko RCD 10569/70. CD.

Zappa, Frank, and Peter Occhiogrosso. *The Real Frank Zappa Book.* New York: Simon and Schuster, 1989.

"Frank Zappa, American Composer." Online documentary on Web page [www. zappa.com].

Ziffrin, Marilyn. *Carl Ruggles: Composer, Painter, and Storyteller.* Urbana: University of Illinois Press, 1992.

INDEX